COMPUTATIONAL MODELS OF
NATURAL LANGUAGE PROCESSING

Fundamental Studies
in Computer Science

VOLUME 9

NORTH-HOLLAND
AMSTERDAM · NEW YORK · OXFORD

Computational Models of Natural Language Processing

Edited by

BRUNO G. BARA
Università di Milano, Italy

and

GIOVANNI GUIDA
Politecnico di Milano, Italy

1984

NORTH-HOLLAND
AMSTERDAM · NEW YORK · OXFORD

ISBN: 0 444 87598 0

Publishers:
ELSEVIER SCIENCE PUBLISHERS B.V. (NORTH-HOLLAND)
P.O. Box 1991
1000 BZ Amsterdam
The Netherlands

Sole distributors for the U.S.A. and Canada:
ELSEVIER SCIENCE PUBLISHING COMPANY, INC.
52 Vanderbilt Avenue
New York, N.Y. 10017
U.S.A.

Library of Congress Cataloging in Publication Data

Main entry under title:

Computational models of natural language processing.

   (Fundamental studies in computer science ; v. 9)
   Includes index.
   1. Linguistics--Data processing--Addresses, essays,
lectures. I. Bara, Bruno G., 1949-   . II. Guida,
Giovanni, 1951-   . III. Series.
P98.C6123 1984   410'.28'54   84-13689
ISBN 0-444-87598-0

PRINTED IN THE NETHERLANDS

To our wives
Marcella and Antonia

PREFACE

This book is the result of a work started about two years ago, with the aim of assembling a collection of papers which could contribute to a unitary understanding of the multidisciplinary area of Natural Language Processing. A unifying point of view of the different paradigms of artificial intelligence, linguistics, and cognitive science may be identified, in our opinion, in the fundamental issue of developing computational models of language competence. We claim that progress in the design of high-performance natural language systems greatly depends on the advances in the study of theoretical models of language comprehension and production. The main concern of the volume is therefore the illustration of models for natural language processing, and the discussion of their role in the development of computational studies of language.

The volume contains 14 papers, including an introductory paper by the editors. All papers are original, unpublished contributions, and present significant research results, often supported by experimental activity. The volume is intended for scholars acquainted with natural language research, but not necessarily specialists in all the disciplines included in the area of natural language processing.
A brief presentation of the content of each paper follows.

In the introductory paper (Competence and performance in the design of natural language systems) Bruno G. Bara and Giovanni Guida divide the models used in the study of natural language processing into three classes: cognitive, pragmatic, and linguistic. They sketch a brief history of computational linguistics, using paradigmatic examples to discuss the roles of competence and performance in the design and evaluation of natural language systems.

Gabriella Airenti, Bruno G. Bara, and Marco Colombetti analyze in their paper (Planning and understanding speech acts by interpersonal games) communication as a mean for an agent to gain co-operation for the execution of a plan which requires many agents to be successful. Therefore, starting from the intentions of a first agent, a pragmatic model is developed to explain how it is possible to obtain that a second agent intends to perform the role that the first agent assigned to him in the original action plan. Games are introduced as mutually shared knowledge structures, used for planning and understanding speech acts. Examples of different kinds of games are discussed in detail, accounting for failure and failure recovery in communication.

The paper of Amedeo Cappelli, Giacomo Ferrari, Lorenzo Moretti, and Irina Prodanof (A framework for integrating syntax and semantics) deals with the problem of integration of syntactic and semantic processing in the parsing of natural language. Assuming that both syntax and semantics have relevant specific roles in language comprehension, the authors present a hypothesis of integration, which consists in defining a general processor which can manipulate representations of different levels, through the activation of complex functions. This model is supported by several linguistic motivations, and it appears intuitively close to the human process of understanding.

Cristiano Castelfranchi, Domenico Parisi, and Oliviero Stock describe in their contribution (Knowledge representation and natural language: Extending the expressive power of proposition nodes) a knowledge representation schema focused on proposition nodes in semantic nets. A number of developments and improvements to the classical approach of Schubert (1976) is proposed, with the aim of fully exploiting the expressive power of complex proposition nodes in representing in a subtle and detailed way the meaning of natural language utterances.

Garrison W. Cottrell and Steven L. Small present in their paper (Viewing parsing as word sense discrimination: A connectionist approach) the first results that connectionism is obtaining in the study of natural language. This fairly new research paradigm utilizes a parallel architecture, significantly different from the sequential computation model of a usual computer and closer to that of a human brain. The kernel of this approach is represented by an active semantic network scheme, which entails a large number of interconnected computing units that communicate through weighted levels of excitation and inhibition.

Danilo Fum, Giovanni Guida, and Carlo Tasso present in their paper (A propositional language for text representation) a representation language which is proved to support a detailed and transparent formalization of the meaning of a natural language text. Several aspects of meaning representation, including quantification, reference, and time, are discussed in detail. A sketch for the implementation of a parser, able to generate a propositional representation from a natural language input text, is also described.

The paper by Eva Hajičová and Petr Sgall (From topic and focus of a sentence to linking in a text) analyzes the role of the topic-focus articulation in determining the structure of a text. A connection is established between topic-focus articulation and coreference. This kind of linking in a text is based on an account of the degree of salience of the elements belonging to a common knowledge base, shared by the speaker and the hearer.

The paper by Eduard H. Hovy and Roger C. Schank (Language generation by computer) is focused on the problem of language production. The research paradigm is the well known conceptual dependency theory, based on semantic primitives. A major point in this contribution is represented by the very refined process of language generation, which takes explicitly into account social, psychological, and pragmatic aspects of conversation to produce text tailored to the various types of hearers.

Jiang Xinsong, Li Yingtan, and Chen Yu present in their contribution

(Understanding the Chinese language) a comprehensive survey of Chinese language processing. The paper discloses to Western researchers several of the peculiarities of Chinese language, and discusses the basic issues of the problem of Chinese processing by computer. The major research projects presently ongoing in China and the results so far achieved are presented as well.

The paper by Philip N. Johnson-Laird (Semantic primitives or meaning postulates: Mental models or propositional representations?) faces the problem of the deep structure of language. The procedural semantics paradigm he proposes, allows the meaning of words to be decomposed into more primitive notions: namely, mental models. The introduction of mental models resolves the controversy over whether semantic primitives are equivalent to sets of meaning postulates, and the controversy over whether images are equivalent to sets of propositions.

The paper by Wendy G. Lehnert (Narrative complexity based on summarization algorithms) deals with the information processing requirements involved in the memory representation of narrative structures. The author introduces the notion of algorithmically equivalent plot unit graphs, which characterize narratives that can be processed by the same summarization retrieval algorithm. The notion of algorithmic equivalence creates a partition - weaker than that produced by the usual relation of isomorphism - of the set of plot unit graphs into classes. Three of these classes, which appear to produce reasonable summaries for a majority of the narratives, are discussed in detail.

Kathleen R. McKeown presents in her paper (Using focus to constrain language generation) a mechanism for text generation, which utilizes the focus of attention to guide the ability to make reasoned choices both from a large number of possible things to say, and from a large number of expressive possibilities. A computational model of focus of attention is developed, and a procedure is proposed to select words and syntactic structures that best express the system's intent, thus ensuring that the resulting text is coherent.

Alexandre S. Narin'yani discusses in his paper (Towards an integral model of language competence) a comprehensive model of language competence which includes in an integrated scheme syntax, semantics, and pragmatics. This general paradigm comprehends a hierarchy of models at different levels: physical world, social environment, verbal interaction, speech acts, coherent text, sentences. The model of speech interaction, anaphora as a part of the coherent text model, and a fragment of the sentence model are considered and discussed in detail.

Brian Phillips presents in his paper (An object-oriented parser) an analyzer of natural language expressions devoted to deal in an effective way with structural ambiguity. The focus of his contribution is on how syntactic analysis and semantic interpretation can co-operate to resolve ambiguities as soon as possible, in order to prevent an explosive growth of alternatives. A left-corner parsing algorithm with a reachability matrix for top-down filtering of rule selection is adopted. The parser is governed by a breadth-first control paradigm, which includes a delay mechanism used to queue constituents until all alternative analyses of a phrase have been completed.

Bruno G. Bara
Giovanni Guida

CONTENTS

Computational Models of Natural Language Processing
B.G. Bara and G. Guida (eds.)
© Elsevier Science Publishers B.V. (North-Holland), 1984

COMPETENCE AND PERFORMANCE

IN THE DESIGN OF NATURAL LANGUAGE SYSTEMS

Bruno G. Bara*, Giovanni Guida°

***Unità di Ricerca di Intelligenza Artificiale**
Università di Milano
Milano, Italy

° Progetto di Intelligenza Artificiale
Politecnico di Milano
Milano, Italy

A taxonomy of models for natural language processing is presented. The basic tenets of the three classes obtained - cognitive, pragmatic, and linguistic - are discussed. Competence models are claimed to be fundamental for the development of computational study of language: this issue is supported by a brief history of NLP. The relationship between competence and performance is analyzed.

1. MOTIVATION

Natural Language Processing (NLP) is an important research area for several reasons. First of all it has practical utility in several application domains, including man-machine interfaces, intelligent access to data bases, easy use by non-specialists of complex software systems, computer assisted instruction, machine translation. The impact of NLP on industrial applications is rapidly growing, pushed by availability of small, fast, powerful, cheap processors, optimized for symbolic computation. Practical effects of natural language systems are expected to be remarkable in the next few years.
Second, NLP is a focal topic in several disciplines, namely philosophy, psychology, linguistics, and computer science. The study of language competence in humans and machines deserves, moreover, a specific attention in artificial intelligence and cognitive science, as it is one of the most subtle and revealing manifestations of the activity of human mind. As Rosenschein (1983) asserts, NLP represents today a crucible for computational theories of cognition.

Our concern in this paper is NLP from the point of view of basic models for language comprehension and production. We will be involved neither with applied NLP, nor with highly specialized issues concerning the more technical aspects of the disciplines of the area. Our interest is on computational models, and it is motivated by their relevance for the advancement of scientific understanding of natural language. The computational paradigm offers, in fact, a solid set of tools for scientific rigor in these complex studies, and it represents a common background on which a constructive co-operation of several disciplines is possible.

2. A TAXONOMY OF MODELS FOR NATURAL LANGUAGE PROCESSING

NLP involves several kinds of models. The models introduced below represent three different points of view from which it is possible to study NLP. The types of models we identify are:

<u>Cognitive</u> - Cognitive models are aimed at the study of human mental processes, and at their implementation on a computer. The term 'cognitive' has to be intended here in a broad sense, i.e. including emotions, affects, motivations, etc., in addition to its basic meaning which refers to perception, reasoning, and problem solving. Cognitive model treat language as a medium for expressing mental states, considered as the source and destination of speech acts. In fact, cognitive modeling is concerned with what (structures and processes) is behind linguistic communication: where utterances first originate and where they are finally interpreted. Some authors (e.g. Johnson-Laird, 1983) focus on these basic mental units, their structure, and their management procedures, while the actual translation of mental states into linguistic utterances is left outside the model itself. Other authors (see Bresnan, 1982), on the contrary, try to directly connect the basic mental units with the linguistic apparatus, in order to give a cognitive explanation of the surface structure of language as well.

<u>Pragmatic</u> - Pragmatic models study language as a medium for interpersonal communication, i.e. for transferring information from a speaker to a hearer in order to affect his mental processes and behaviour. Austin (1962) divides speech acts in locutionary (the language), illocutionary (how language is used), and perlocutionary (for what language is used). The distinction has been generally accepted in computational pragmatics: see, for example, Cohen and Perrault (1979) for the simulation of direct speech acts, and Perrault and Allen (1980) for simulation of indirect speech acts. Pragmatics initially neglected the surface structure of language; in fact Searle (1969) claims the pragmatic equivalence between sentences like "Do you reach the salt?" and "Please pass me the salt!". Complex models are required to account for the fact, obvious for linguists and cognitive scientists, that surface structure plays a crucial role in planning and executing an effective utterance. To obtain the same performative effect from different partners in different contexts, different surface strategies are generally needed: in some case an order is appropriate, in other cases a graceful request is more convincing (Airenti, Bara, and Colombetti, 1983).

<u>Linguistic</u> - Linguistic models have been the first and basic results of the computational study of language, and they are still playing a leading role in NLP. They aim at analyzing the structure of language and at justifying the relationships between structure and meaning. The work of Woods (1970, 1981) during its evolution from ATN to KL-ONE, is an excellent example of the classical linguistic tradition.

It has to be noted that the distinction we draw among models is not a clear cut one. The three kinds of models are partially overlapping: each of them focuses on a specific aspect, but, at the same time, it also involves part of the other models. A partial exception is linguistics, which, in principle, can proceed independently from the others. In fact, it is possible to study language per se, without bothering neither of the deep mental structures which justify it (beliefs, desires, wants, etc.), nor of the goals it is expected to pursue (to inform, convince, induce, etc.). A basic requirement, however, even for merely linguistic models, is that they guarantee suitable, compatible interfaces with the results of cognitive and pragmatic research.

The taxonomy proposed reflects the three main facets of language: the conscious and unconscious mechanisms to which we can ultimately reconduct it; the interpersonal reasons for which language is used; and the effective production, handling, and understanding of utterances.

We have not considered in our taxonomy other interesting models, like the psycholinguistic and neuropsychological ones, as they basically deal with (human) behaviour, i.e. linguistic utterances and their, possibly pathological, modifications. The reason is that they are mainly involved with performance, and, as we shall explain below, this is a major limitation for their theoretical relevance. Nevertheless, these studies are obviously useful as constraints for competence models and for the evaluation and testing of artificial systems. Think, for instance, to the problem of graceful degradation. As the connectionistic approach argues (see Cottrell and Small, 1984), a simulation system should be able to reduce its performance smoothly, exactly like a brain-damaged person may loose some linguistic abilities (consider, e.g., Broca's aphasics, who perform better as hearers than they do as speakers - Zurif and Blumstein, 1978). Humans are not all-or-nothing systems, and this is a type of constraint very few artificial systems can meet.

The three types of models above sketched do not coincide with any classical distinction of the NLP area into disciplines. For instance, linguistic models may originate in non-linguistic fields, such as, for example, computer science.
Among all the disciplines belonging to the NLP area artificial intelligence plays a unifying role, as it offers a common paradigm shared by several researchers, even if students with heterogeneous backgrounds - from philosophy of language to man-machine systems. Artificial intelligence supports, in fact, a sound computational approach which is used to interlink philosophy, psychology, and linguistics around a unitary goal: providing a formal description of the processes underlying language competence and of the objects involved in these processes. Artificial intelligence also offers a rich bag of tools for this kind of rigorous research.

3. COMPETENCE AND PERFORMANCE DEFINED

The classes of models identified in section 2 mostly rely on competence criteria. In NLP <u>competence</u> may be defined as the set of capabilities put into a system: i.e. designed and implemented. In addition, it requires the visibility of the procedures and models utilized; on the contrary, their similarity to human mechanisms is not necessary. <u>Performance</u> may be defined as the set of capabilities shown by a system during operation: i.e. its behaviour in real situations.
When Chomsky (1957) originally discussed the term competence, he was almost exclusively concerned with the syntactic aspects of language - the tacit knowledge of language. But now, the concept of competence tends to cover each component of language: not only syntax, but also semantics and pragmatics.

The history of NLP shows an increasing attention to competence models in the development of the computational studies of language. At the beginning of modern computational linguistics, in the early sixties, explicit models of competence are poor, and they are only scarsely utilized to design running systems. The experimental work and the engagements of artificial intelligence pushed research to propose richer models in order to improve performance. Since then, the importance of competence has constantly been growing: applicative progress has always been connected to progress in the adequacy of models. No system performs well without reason!

A closer look at the history of NLP and an analysis of present trends can reinforce this statement. We can identify three major phases in the development of the concept of modeling in NLP:

1st stage: <u>Mimicking</u>
Programs like BASEBALL (Green, Wolf, Chomsky, and Laughery, 1962) and ELIZA (Weizenbaum, 1966) use simple search algorithms to connect input and output. Input sentences must belong to a very limited class of linguistic possibilities, and the answers given by the program are predetermined. The appeal of these types of systems relies on the natural appearance of the sentences they can accept and generate. The similarity of human procedures of comprehension and production is purely a fact of brilliant mimicking of the surface structures of the input/output sentences. Performance is here very high in appropriately restricted domains, but more extended and objective testing reduces it to zero.

2nd stage: <u>Internal representation of knowledge</u>
Systems like Semantic Memory (Quillian, 1968) begin to explore the problem of knowledge representation. The input sentence is analyzed and translated into an internal form, independent from the original English-like structure. Successive evolution of this generation of programs (e.g. SIR, by Raphael, 1968) enriches the data base with inference algorithms, which enable the system not only to represent the meaning of a sentence, but also to perform simple deductions on it. Even if one is far from the complex inferences usually drawn in a natural dialogue, still these systems can capture some of the meaning of an utterance.

3rd stage: <u>Models of language</u>
Systems like LUNAR (Woods, 1973) and SHRDLU (Winograd, 1972) for the first time tackle the problem of processing both syntax and semantics, i.e. of accounting both for the surface structure and for the deep meaning of linguistic utterances. In limited domains, programs of this class are able to parse an input sentence, to understand some of its meaning, to relate it to the data base, and to reason about it. The design of systems integrating syntax and semantics has attracted the attention of researchers in a continuum till nowadays. The explicit goal of this effort is to reach a deeper comprehension of language through the construction of sound models of competence which, in turn, can lead to an improvement in performance.

4. IS COMPETENCE NECESSARY TO PERFORMANCE?

So far, we have discussed a taxonomy of the models involved in NLP, their intrinsic computational nature, and how they rely on competence. We focus now on the role the study of models is having and will have in the next future both on research at the level of individual projects, and on the overall advancement of the discipline.

We can identify an abstract life-cycle in the design and implementation of a system for natural language processing. At the beginning, the user expresses his needs and defines the capabilities he expects from the system. This specification can be given through the definition (e.g. by means of significant examples) of the set of natural language utterances the system should be able to process. Taking the user's specifications into account, the designer devises the models that will supply the system with the appropriate competence, and implements them into a running mechanism. During operation, the system will show its capabilities. System performance has now to be tested in order to verify whether it meets user's requirements.

A first kind of evaluation (<u>surface evaluation</u>) is appropriate for this task: directly comparing input/output system performance with user's requirements (see Guida and Mauri, 1984). Evaluating performance is clearly crucial to test how much a system fulfills the needs of the user, but it is not enough to know why the system performs as it actually does. A second kind of evaluation (<u>deep evaluation</u>) is needed: relating performance to competence, and then adequating models to meet given performance requirements.

The role of competence models is crucial for making this kind of life-cycle a productive process: only when the results can be related to the models on which they rely, experimental activity is really useful to the progress of scientific research.

An impediment to the development of the NLP research is the lack of a real knowledge transfer among different projects. This includes several aspects:

- the deficiency of formal tools for system evaluation (both surface, i.e. merely input/output, and deep, i.e. concerning competence models);

- the difficulty (or often even impossibility) to compare one system with another;

- the practical and theoretical difficulties in integrating results obtained by different scholars into new projects (each research project usually utilizes only a very limited amount of the experience gained by other groups - mostly at a merely philosophical level).

A major reason for this situation can be recognized, first, in the absence of a common formalism for describing systems at different levels of abstraction: performance, internal structure, knowledge representation, algorithms, etc., and, second, in the low level of abstraction of current descriptions of the implemented systems and of the models on which they rely.

Overcoming isolation would greatly contribute to the progress in this area, which is now lacking accumulation. A desirable implosion effect could push very rapidly NLP towards more ambitious achievements. Competence models can play a basic role in the integration of the several research efforts currently carried on in the area of NLP: they represent in fact the adequate level of abstraction at which achievements of different projects can be compared and integrated.

A fundamental mechanism can be recognized as an accelerator in the progress in natural language research:

- designing computational models;

- implementing systems;

- evaluating surface performance;

- relating performance to competence in such a way as to gain a deep understanding of the system behaviour and collecting useful experience for improving competence models;

- comparing results obtained by different projects at a sufficiently abstract level, and integrating them in the design of new systems.

Competence is the only factor which can provide a good degree of confidence in the expected performance of natural language systems in broad domains, beyond what is directly visible and testable. Performance can in fact be measured by mere input/output experiments, but a concrete reliability of the system behaviour can only be guaranteed by detailed knowledge and evaluation of its internal operation.

REFERENCES

Airenti G., Bara B.G., and Colombetti M. 1983. Planning perlocutive acts. Proc. 8th International Joint Conference on Artificial Intelligence, Karlsruhe, FRG, 78-80.

Austin J.L. 1962. How to Do Things with Words. Oxford University Press, New York, NY.

Bresnan J. (Ed.) 1982. The Mental Representation of Grammatical Relations. The MIT Press, Cambridge, MA.

Chomsky N. 1957. Syntactic Structures. Mouton, The Hague, NL.

Cohen P.R. and Perrault C.R. 1979. Elements of a plan based theory of speech acts. Cognitive Science, 3(3).

Cottrell G.W. and Small S.L. 1984. Viewing parsing as word sense discrimination: A connectionist approach. This volume.

Green B.F. Jr., Wolf A.K., Chomsky N., and Laughery K. 1962. BASEBALL: An automatic question answerer. In E.A. Feigenbaum, J. Feldman (Eds.), Computers and Thought. McGraw Hill, New York, NY.

Guida G. and Mauri G. 1984. A formal basis for performance evaluation of natural language understanding systems. American Journal of Computational Linguistics, 10(1).

Johnson-Laird P.N. 1983. Mental Models. Harvard University Press, Cambridge, MA.

Perrault C.R. and Allen J.F. 1980. A plan based analysis of indirect speech acts. American Journal of Computational Linguistics, 6(3-4).

Quillian M.R. 1968. Semantic memory. In M. Minsky (Ed.), Semantic Information Processing. The MIT Press, Cambridge, MA.

Raphael B. 1968. SIR: A computer program for semantic information retrieval. In M. Minsky (Ed.), Semantic Information Processing. The MIT Press, Cambridge, MA.

Rosenschein S. 1983. Natural language processing: Crucible for computational theories of cognition. Proc. 8th International Joint Conference on Artificial Intelligence, Karlsruhe, FRG, 1180-1186.

Searle J. 1969. Speech Acts. Cambridge University Press, Cambridge, UK.

Weizenbaum J. 1966. ELIZA: A computer program for the study of natural language communication between man and machine. Communications of the ACM, 9.

Winograd T. 1972. Understanding Natural Language. Academic Press, New York, NY.

Woods W.A. 1970. Transition network grammars for natural language analysis. Communications of the ACM, 13(10).

Woods W.A. 1973. Progress in natural language understanding: An application to lunar geology. Proc. AFIPS Conference 42, 1973 National Computer Conference, AFIPS Press, Montvale, NJ.

Woods W.A. 1981. Procedural semantics as a theory of meaning. In A. Joshi, B.L. Webber, I. Sag (Eds.), Elements of Discourse Understanding.Cambridge University Press, Cambridge, MA.

Zurif E.B. and Blumstein S.E. 1978. Language and the brain. In M. Halle, J. Bresnan, G.A. Miller (Eds.), Linguistic Theory and Psychological Reality. The MIT Press, Cambridge, MA.

ACKNOWLEDGMENTS

We wish to thank Gabriella Airenti, Marco Colombetti and Philip N. Johnson-Laird for reading and commenting a draft of this paper.

Computational Models of Natural Language Processing
B.G. Bara and G. Guida (eds.)
© Elsevier Science Publishers B.V. (North-Holland), 1984

PLANNING AND UNDERSTANDING SPEECH ACTS
BY INTERPERSONAL GAMES

Gabriella Airenti*, Bruno G. Bara*, Marco Colombetti°

*Unità di Ricerca di Intelligenza Artificiale
Università di Milano
Milano, Italy

° Progetto di Intelligenza Artificiale
Politecnico di Milano
Milano, Italy

In this paper we present a model for planning a speech act
in order to have somebody perform an action, and for
recovering from possible failures. The model accounts for
the competence aspects of the process involved in planning
and understanding two paradigmatic perlocutionary speech
acts: inducing and convincing.
Our tenets are:
- an actor is able to simulate the mental processes of his
partners, both when planning and when understanding;
- any action can be reconducted to a standing intention
which represents its ultimate motivation;
- all communicative interactions are governed by knowledge
structures (games) shared among the actors;
- communication about the world is always accompanied by
communication about the respective roles of the partners,
which is necessary to account for the ability of performing
perlocutionary acts.
A detailed example is analyzed, possible failure are
identified and failure recovering strategies are discussed.

1. INTRODUCTION

Human action is mostly interpersonal, and thus reveals the ability of actors to
cooperate in a synchronized way. As actions are performed on the basis of a
previously built plan, it follows that an actor can build and execute
interpersonal plans. Such plans contain both actions to be performed by the
planner himself and actions to be performed by other actors (partners). For
instance, a person may intend to drink a martini assigning to a friend the task
of mixing it. To achieve this goal the planner has to induce the partner to
perform his role in the plan. A plan can be interpersonal also because it
contains actions which are expected to cause an effect on the mental state of a
partner. An example is the action of informing a friend that Stella is married to

---

Acknowledgments - This research has been supported by a grant of the Consiglio
Nazionale delle Ricerche (C.N.R.), under contract CT.83.02177.04.

cause him to believe that she has a husband.

In the following we shall argue that action should be defined as intentional. A consequence of this is that to induce a partner to perform his role in an interpersonal plan requires that the planner causes an appropriate intention in his partner. Therefore, actions for causing an effect on the mental state of a partner are necessarily part of any interpersonal plan. This leaves us with the problem of explaining how actors may deal with the intentions of partners.

The usual way for a planner to gain the cooperation of a partner is through communication. Nevertheless the desired action can be obtained from the partner in a noncommunicative way: for example spilling the martini on a friend's jacket to induce him to take it off and check whether he is concealing a gun. In this paper we shall restrict to the case implying communication. To deal with communication within the context of action, we assume the standpoint of speech act theory. Therefore we shall consider any communicative transaction as an intentional action. In fact we generalize the concept of speech act to include in it both verbal and nonverbal communicative acts.

Communicative acts have to be planned like all other actions. Therefore a fundamental component of interpersonal planning is devoted to plan communicative transactions in order to induce the partner to cooperate. Moreover, to achieve a felicitous outcome of the interaction, the partner has to understand the planner's communicative acts. An interesting situation to be analyzed is when for any reason the outcome of the interaction is not felicitous. For instance if a passer-by asks to a shopkeeper for information without receiving an answer, he may wonder about the reasons of his failure, in order to plan a second attempt.

The previous considerations suggest that any theory of human interpersonal action should account for:

- knowledge structures and their manipulation procedures involved in human interactions, and in particular in planning and understanding communicative acts;
- strategies for recovering from failure.

Aim of our work is to build a theory of the cognitive processes underlying interpersonal action. In this paper we present the kernel of such a theory showing its adequacy in satisfying the proposed criteria. In particular, we introduce a model of interactions between two actors, involving planning and understanding a single communicative act.

From speech act theory we mutuate the concept of speech act and the notions of illocution and perlocution (Austin, 1962). In particular we have been influenced by Searle's reflections on indirect speech acts (1979) and the intentionality of action (1983). As regards the AI tools we have been using, we refer to the formalization and implementation of speech acts realized by Cohen and Perrault (1979), Perrault and Allen (1980), Allen (1983). Finally, standard AI techniques for plan formation have guided the development of our model of interpersonal planning.

2. INTERPERSONAL ACTION AND COMMUNICATION

Following Searle (1983) we define action as intentional behavior, i.e. a behavior which is performed by the actor on the basis of its mental representation. Any theory of intentional action has to commit to a hypothesis about the generation of intentions. A few considerations will be helpful in order to make sound assumptions on this matter.

A first consideration is that, under given conditions, an intention may be derived by another one. For instance, the intention of drinking a glass of water (or of eating an orange) may derive from the intention of relieving one's thirst. However not all intentions derive from preexisting ones. In fact, in order to avoid infinite regression, we must presuppose mental processes able to generate basic intentions. A most evident case concerns intentions which stem from basic needs. For instance the intention of relieving thirst originates from the recognition of an internal state of biological need. In other cases intentions can descend from needs which are not simply biological. For instance, the intention of enjoying the company of a friend may be related to an affective need.

 Consider another example: a physician, when requested by a patient, has the intention to treat him; such an intention descends from the standing intention of acting as a professional physician. We shall argue in Section 4 that the intention of treating a patient derives from the standing intention of being a professional physician at each occurrence of a patient's request. On the contrary the standing intention need not be derived each time the appropriate situation occurs. In fact standing intentions are long -term intentions that, once derived, remain active and are used in a way similar to basic intentions.

We now turn to the problem of causing a partner's intention. As already pointed out, this problem is crucial in interpersonal planning. Given the three kinds of intentions we have assumed (basic, derived, standing), causing an intention in a partner cannot be regarded as a straightforward transmission of the intention by the planner. Thus, the only possible strategy for the planner is to cause the derivation of the desired intention from basic or standing intentions of the partner. To accomplish this goal the planner has to trigger an opportune process. As an example let us consider a farmer who intends to keep a thief away from his granary. The farmer could accomplish this goal by threatening the thief with his rifle. The farmer plans his action, relying on the basic intention of the thief to preserve his life, and assuming that from such an intention the intention to run away would be derived.

But, consider a different example. If John goes to a bakery and asks for some bread, the baker expects a highly stereotyped interaction to take place between him and John, in which he will receive a certain amount of money in change of the requested bread. The felicitous transaction between John and the baker is made possible by their shared knowledge of the rules usually followed in a shop. In the example John derives the intention of paying from his standing intention of being an honest person. The baker derives the intention to serve the customer from his intention of acting as a professional baker; moreover both actors use the same knowledge to simulate the respective partner in the process of deriving intentions. This generates John's expectation to be served and the baker's expectation to be paid.

We believe that most human interactions rely on knowledge structures, which we call games, shared by the actors and describing their respective roles (see Airenti, Bara, and Colombetti, 1983). Games can be shared by two subjects (like in the case of husband and wife) or by a group (e.g. the rules of behavior of the employees in a company), or by almost everybody (e.g. social rules of politeness like to thank a passer-by who answers a question about a street).

As suggested by the example presented above, games are used to derive non standing intentions from standing ones: different games can lead to different standing intentions.

3. BASIC HYPOTHESES

In this section we make explicit the hypotheses on which we base our model.

The simulation hypothesis. The ability of people to act relies on their capacity to model the external world in order to plan and recognize actions and events. When dealing with the physical world, an actor represents it in terms of physical states and causal relations. When an actor interacts with human partners, he has to model them also in terms of mental states, in particular of beliefs and intentions. Even very simple interactive behavior may involve the use of complex models of the partners. The complexity of the models depends on what the actors intend to obtain in a given situation. In some cases, a very simple model of the partner is enough; when a subject has to deal with failure recovery, or wants to plan a deceit, or even to discover a deceit, models of increasing complexity are required (Taylor and Whitehill, 1981).

The simulation hypothesis suggests that the limit of the complexity one may reach in interacting with others is determined by his ability to simulate the partners.

On the basis of the previous considerations, we adopt a model of the planner which embeds a model of the partner (see Fig. 1). Therefore, we claim that the planner is able to make a functionally adequate simulation of the partner; i.e., a simulation of motivations, intentions, beliefs, etc. In Figure 2 we symbolize with an arrow the fact that the actual partner corresponds to the representation the planner has of him; this is a case of successful simulation.

When the simulation of the partner fails, the possible causes are:
- an error in the attribution of the content of the mental states (e.g., the intention the planner attributes to the partner is uncorrect);
- the choice of an inadequate level of complexity in the simulation (e.g., the planner does not simulate that the partner has a deeper, maybe deceitful, intention).

In turn, the partner is able, when recognizing the planner's plan, to make a simulation of the planner.A consequence of the reciprocal simulation is that the models of the planner and of the partner allow for several levels of nested beliefs. In each inference only finitely nested beliefs are exploited. However, such beliefs may be derived from an actor's assumption that a piece of knowledge is shared with a partner. In the literature shared knowledge is represented by mutual beliefs (Bruce and Newman, 1978) that are equivalent to infinitely nested beliefs (Fig. 3).

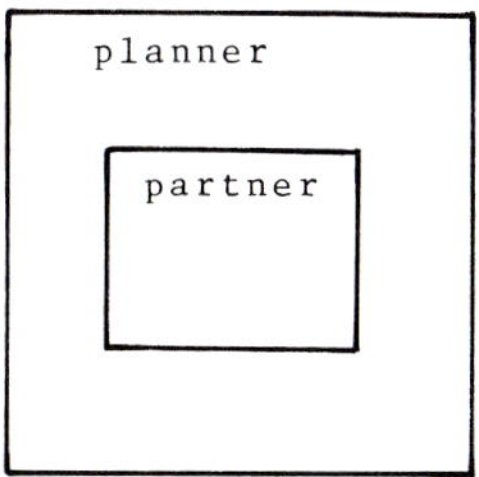

Fig. **1.** Model of the planner embedding a model of the partner

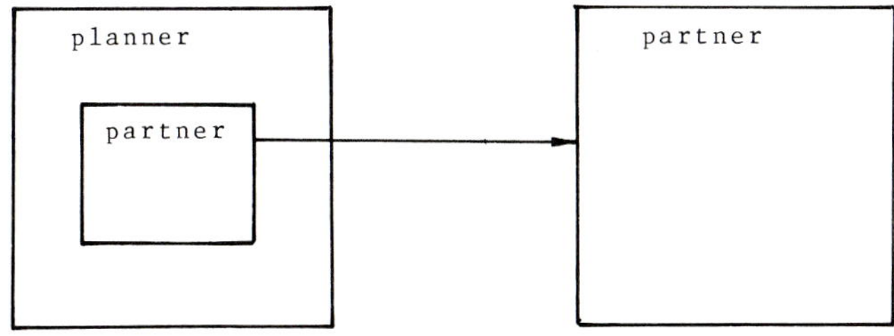

Fig. **2.** Models of the planner and of the partner

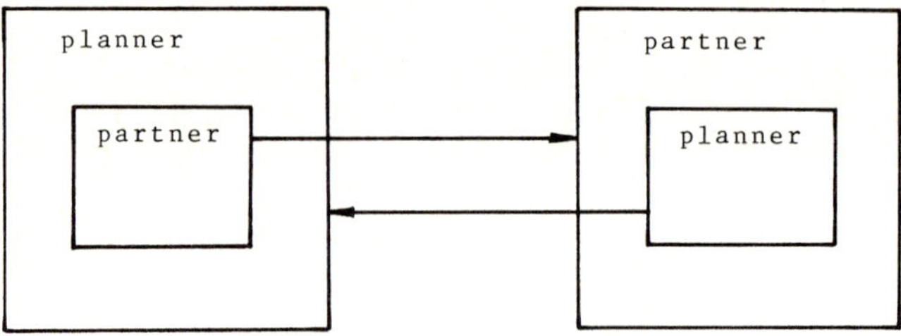

Fig. **3.** Nested models of the planner and of the partner

While this general hypothesis governs the whole planning process, each of the following hypotheses corresponds to a specific inference rule used in building the plan. In the figures we use a slot-filler formalism to express both actions and states (world states and mental states). For example, the formula:

        INDUCE [x,y]
        action CURE [y,x]

represents x's action of inducing y to cure him. Actors and objects (when existing) are put in square brackets; other parameters are specified as fillers of slots, which are given explicatory names. Similarly, the formula:

        WANTS [y]
        action CURE [y,x]

expresses y's mental state of intending to cure x.

The effect hypothesis. Bringing about a fact can always be viewed as the effect of an action.

The intentional action hypothesis. As we have already stated in Section 2, we define action as intentional behavior. More precisely, we assume that the necessary and sufficient conditions for the realization of an action are the ability and the intention of the actor to perform that action. The corresponding rule is depicted in Figure 4.

The motivation hypothesis. Humans possess standing intentions which represent the motivational aspect of action. While the standing intentions of a subject may change over a reasonably long period of time, we assume that they remain stable during a single interaction. The corresponding rule is depicted in Figure 5, where we assume that a standing intention is represented by a theme. A theme (see Wilensky, 1983) is a structure containing an if-part and a then-part: when the if-part is detected by the subject who has the theme, the then-part is generated.

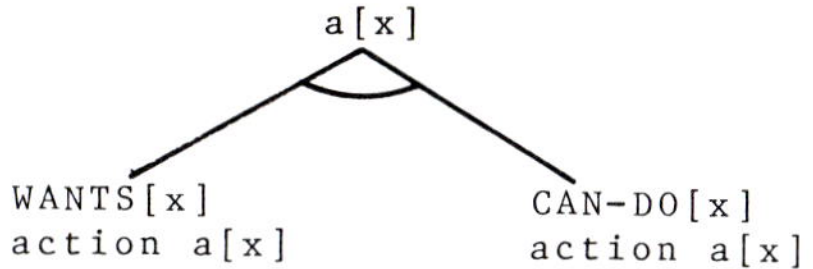

Fig. **4.** The intentional action rule

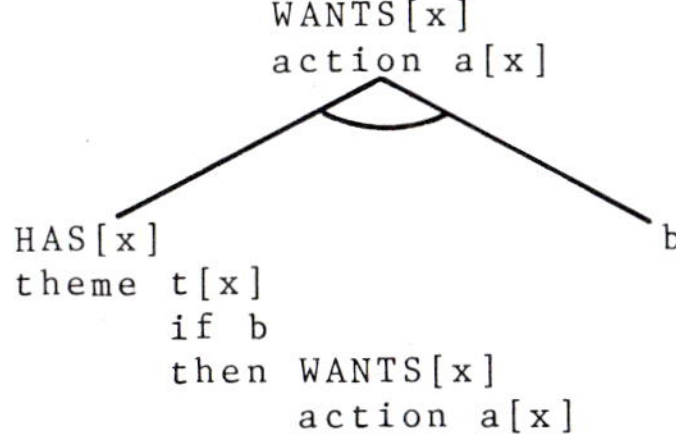

Fig. **5.** The motivation rule

We introduce next some hypotheses about human interactions. We assume that humans possess knowledge structures representing stereotyped interactions among actors (<u>games</u>). In this paper we shall deal with socially determined games, which we call contracts; the general structure of a contract includes at least two actors (the client and the contractor), its conditions of validity, and a list of actions to be performed by the two actors.

The relevant hypotheses about the use of contracts are:

<u>The role playing hypothesis.</u> The intention of an actor to play his role in the contract, together with his assumption that the contract binds him to a specific action, implies the actor's intention to perform that action (see Fig.6 for the corresponding inference rule).

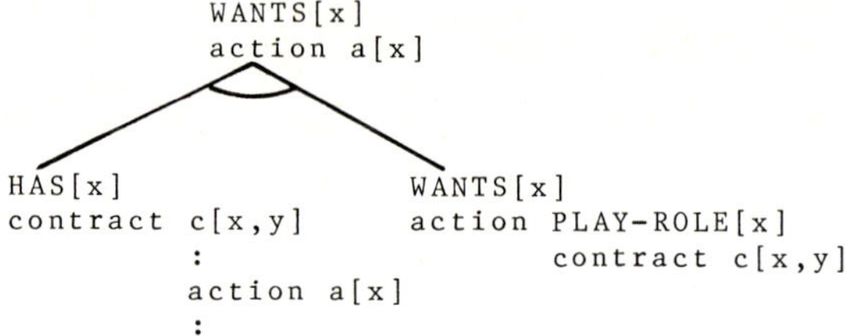

Fig. **6.** The role playing rule

<u>The role declaration hypothesis</u>. The client's intention to communicate to the contractor his intention that the contractor perform a specific action, together with the client's assumption that the contract binds the contractor to that action and with the client's belief that the contract is valid, implies the client's intention to communicate to the contractor his intention to play his role in the contract (see Fig. 7 for the corresponding inference rule).

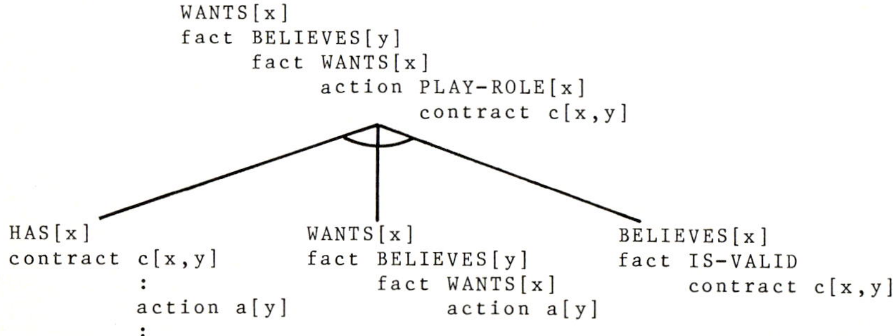

Fig. **7.** The role declaration rule

The remaining hypotheses concern some assumptions that an actor makes about the world and the others, in relation with the acquisition of new beliefs.

The sincerity hypothesis. An actor's intention that somebody else believe a fact, together with the actor's sincerity, implies that the actor believes that fact. The corresponding inference rule is given in Figure 8.

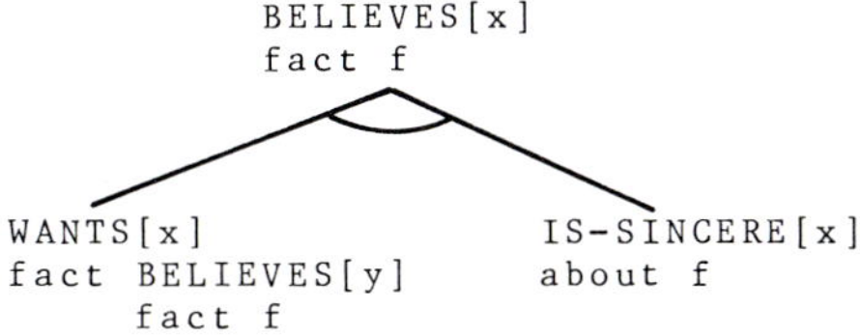

Fig. **8.** The sincerity rule

The informant hypothesis. An actor's belief in a fact, together with his being well informed about that fact, implies the truth of the fact. We give in Figure 9 the corresponding inference rule.

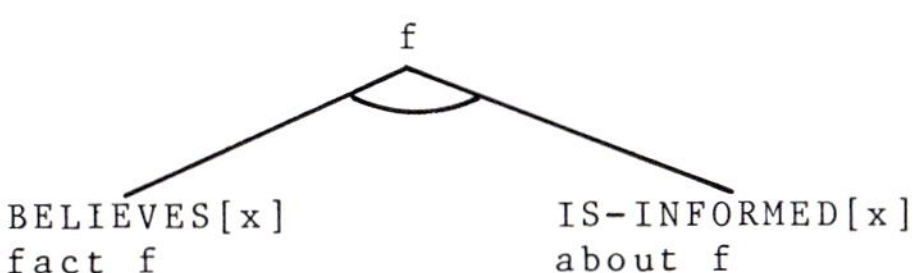

Fig. **9.** The informant rule

In the following section we analyze how an actor brings about intentions and beliefs in a partner. According to our effect hypothesis, we postulate two kinds of actions: CAUSE-TO-WANT and CAUSE-TO-BELIEVE. Such actions may be realized through either communicative or noncommunicative strategies. Our interest here is only in the communicative aspect.

We consider CAUSE-TO-WANT to be communicative if it is performed through an illocutionary act. In this case the action of causing an intention can be viewed as a perlocutionary act and we call it an INDUCE action. Analogously we single out the perlocutionary act of causing a belief and we name it a CONVINCE action.

In the following we analyze an actor A forming a plan in order to induce a partner P to perform a specific action. We schematize the interaction between A and P as follows:

i)   A performs an illocutionary act of requesting that P performs a specific action;

ii) a process of inducing is triggered by the illocutionary effect and generates the perlocutionary effect that P wants to perform the requested action. The main point here is that the process of inducing actuates the transition from A's want to P's wants;

iii) this transition is realized by A through an action of convincing P about A's intention of playing his role in the interaction.

4. AN EXAMPLE : ARTHUR GOES TO THE DOCTOR

Story (1) :

(1) Pamela is in her medical office. Arthur comes in and tells here he has a recurrent headache. She examines him and gives him an appropriate prescription. The patient asks for the bill and pays.

We present a formalization of this story, following the rules given in the previous section. Let Arthur be actor A and Pamela, the doctor, be partner P. The present section is devoted to the analysis of the inference process which leads actor A to plan an action of request in order to induce P to cure him.

The global inference process is represented as a tree having a root, a number of intermediate AND nodes, and leaves. The root is the original planner's goal; an intermediate node is logically implied by its immediate successors according to a specific inference rule; a leaf represents an unconditioned assumption made by the planner.

The inference process is analyzed at four levels of detail. At each level, we detail an action which has been left unanalyzed at the previous level. The actions that deserve further analysis are enclosed in a rectangular box.

The slot-filler formalism is also used to describe the contract (Fig. 12) and the theme (Fig. 13). In the inference tree, the predicate HAS is used to express the fact that a subject has knowledge of a contract or is motivated by a theme.
We shall describe only the knowledge structures and the mental processes of actor A. Consistently with the simulation hypothesis, in our model the partner is considered as represented by A. The model is described below, following the schemes in Figures 10-15. All inferences are based on inference rules which are justified by the assumptions made in the previous section.

Figure 10. By the rule of intentional action, the action of curing somebody is derived from the ability and the intention of the doctor, P, to perform that action. Therefore, A has to plan an INDUCE perlocutionary act to make P cure him. As regards the ability preconditions of P's action (CAN-DO), we assume that A takes them for granted.

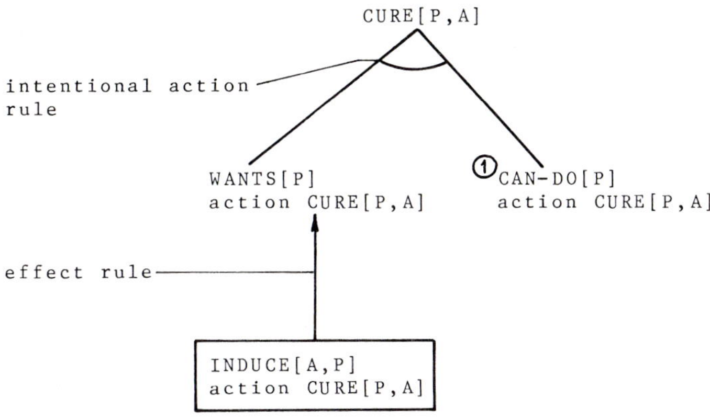

Fig. 10. The plan for being cured: first level of detail

<u>Figure 11</u>. The first inference is based on the role playing rule. On the basis of such a rule, P's want to cure A is derived from P's want to play his role in the DOCTOR contract, together with P's assumption that the DOCTOR contract binds him to cure the client. The DOCTOR contract is described in Figure 12.

The second inference is based on the motivation rule. On the basis of such a rule, P's want to play his role in the DOCTOR contract is derived from four beliefs of the contractor P, together with the PROFESSION theme (described in Fig. 13). The contents of the beliefs are: the validity of the contract (i.e. the satisfaction of its validity conditions), the satisfaction of the CAN-DO and WANT preconditions for A's PLAY-ROLE action, and the satisfaction of the CAN-DO preconditions for P's PLAY-ROLE action. As regards the four beliefs which correspond to the activation conditions of the theme, three are given for granted and one is derived by the next inference.

The third inference assumes P's belief about A's intention to play his role to be the effect of a CONVINCE perlocutionary act performed by A. Consistently with our goal of describing a communicative interaction, we assume that the CONVINCE action is realized by an illocutionary act of INFORM. In Figure 14 we enlarge the CONVINCE perlocutionary act.

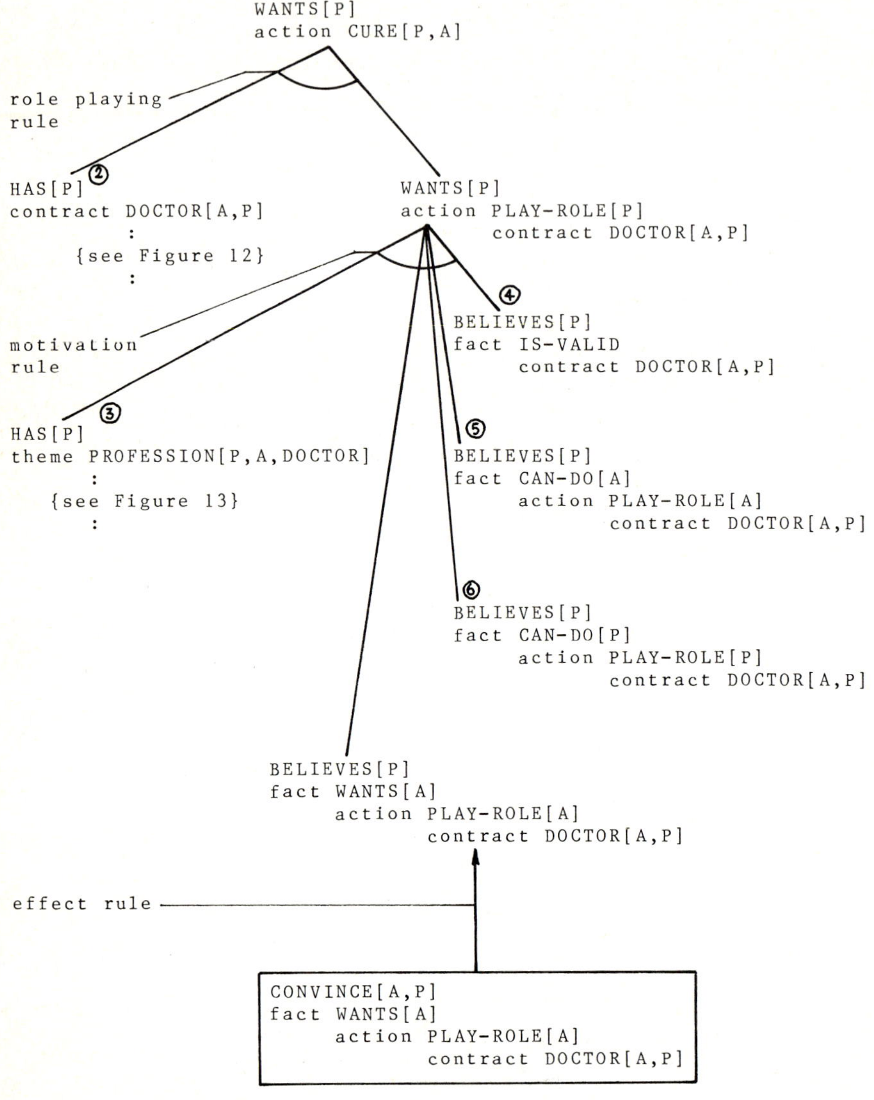

Fig. 11. The plan for being cured: second level of detail

```
contract  DOCTOR[x,y]
          client x
          contractor y

validity conditions

          HAS-PROFESSION[y]     and     IS-ON-SERVICE[y]
          prof PHYSICIAN

action    CURE[y,x]

action    BILL[y,x]
          amount a

action    PAY[x,y]
          amount a

endcontract
```

Fig. **12.** The DOCTOR contract

```
theme PROFESSION[y,x,c]
      subject y
      client x
      contract c

if    WANTS[x]                    and    IS-VALID
      action PLAY-ROLE[x]                contract c[x,y]
             contract c[x,y]

      and    CAN-DO[x]                   and    CAN-DO[y]
             action PLAY-ROLE[x]                action PLAY-ROLE[y]
                    contract c[x,y]                     contract c[x,y]

then  WANTS[y]
      action PLAY-ROLE[y]
             contract c[x,y]

endtheme
```

Fig. **13.** The PROFESSION theme

Figure 14. The effect of the CONVINCE action is derived by the informant rule from P's belief that A believes that A intends to play his role in the DOCTOR contract, together with P's belief that A is informed about his own intention of playing his role. This fact can be taken for granted here on the basis of the assumption that any subject is informed about his own intentions.

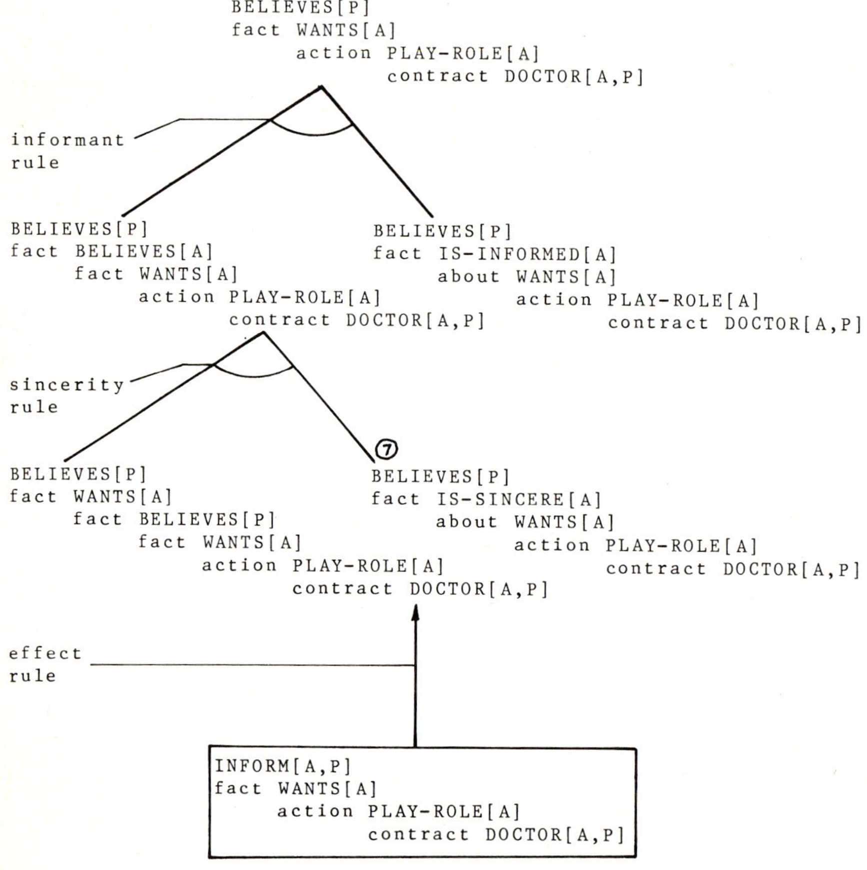

Fig. 14. The plan for being cured: third level of detail

The former belief is derived by the sincerity rule from P's belief that A wants that P recognizes A's want to play his role in the contract, together with P's belief that A is sincere about such an intention. We assume that sincerity is taken for granted in this kind of interactions. The first belief to which the sincerity rule is applied, corresponds to the effect of A's illocutionary act of informing P about his want to play his role. In Figure 15 we enlarge the INFORM illocutionary act.

Figure 15. The action of informing is reduced, via the role declaration rule, to three conditions: P's recognition of A's want that P recognizes A's want that P cures him; P's belief that A believes the DOCTOR contract to be valid; P's belief that A assumes the contract to bind P to the action of curing clients. The first condition is the effect of a REQUEST illocutionary act performed by A. We shall not discuss the REQUEST action here, as it has been thoroughly analyzed in the literature (Cohen and Perrault, 1979; Perrault and Allen, 1980; Allen, 1983).

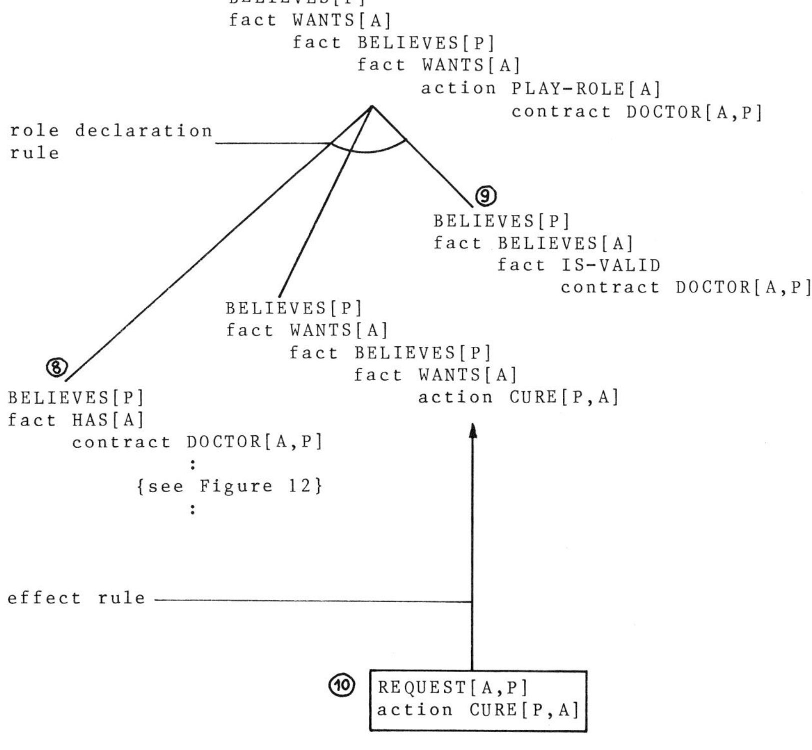

Fig. 15. The plan for being cured: fourth level of detail

5. ERROR DETECTION AND FAILURE RECOVERY

One of the qualifying points for a theory of planning is the possibility of accounting for any type of failure which may in principle occur during the execution of the plan and for the failure recovery capabilities of actors. This requires the identification of the failure points in the plan and the attribution of a specific cause to the failure. The interest for failure is justified by the fact that a powerful way to test a competence theory of planning, such as the one presented here, is to verify whether it accounts for all possible execution failures.

In this section we analyze all the failures which our model accounts for. These should exhaust the possibilities of failure in the execution of an act of inducing within an interaction regulated by a preexisting contract. The model describes the failures at the given level of abstraction. For instance the fact that a sphygmomanometer is broken is not explicitly considered in the model, but has to be reconducted to the CAN-DO preconditions of the action of curing.

In our model, a failure occurs when the client's attempt to induce the contractor to perform an action is not followed by the performance of that action. This means that at least one of the inferences described in the previous section has not been drawn by the contractor. This event cannot be attributed to a deficiency of the inference rules, since they are based on general competence assumptions. Therefore, possible failures are determined by the fact that at least one antecedent of an inference does not hold. This corresponds to considering each leaf of the inference tree described in Figures 10-15 as a possible failure point. The only exception is with the informant rule: we do not admit the possibility for a subject not to be informed about his own intentions. The failure points correspond to the facts the planner has taken for granted during the process of plan formation. The grounds on which the planner takes some facts for granted are not considered in our model, as this is a knowledge representation problem. In any plan formation task, the planner has to take for granted some facts which are impossible or uneconomical to check: for instance, while starting a car, one normally assumes that the engine is in order. This problem has been addressed by Wilensky (1983), who refers to the facts taken for granted by a planner as implicit preconditions.

Our choice has been to identify the main inference path which leads from the illocutionary act of requesting to the perlocutionary act of inducing, and to consider that all side assumptions are given for granted. As regards facts which are not taken for granted but are reduced by an inference rule, we do not admit the possibility of a failure. In fact each inference rule describes a piece of competence which we assume to be possessed by all humans.

Reasons for possible failures (see circled numbers in Figures 10,11,14,15) are therefore:

(1), Fig. 10. The contractor cannot perform his action because a precondition does not hold (e.g. a broken sphygmomanometer);

(2), Fig. 11. There is a discrepancy between the client's and the contractor's representations of the contract, in that the contractor's representation does not contain the action that the client wants the contractor to perform. This kind of failure is likely to occur with fairly complex contracts; for instance, the client could think that the DOCTOR contract also contains the contractor's action to supply drugs, while this may not be true in the contractor's representation of the contract where the doctor only prescribes them.

(3), Fig. 11.   The contractor does not possess the PROFESSION theme in the form supposed by the client (e.g. a careless doctor who gives the patient hurried advice, without visiting him).

(4), Fig. 11.   In the contractor's opinion the contract is not valid (e.g. the patient does not keep an appointment and arrives too late).

(5), Fig. 11.   The contractor does not believe that the client can play his role (e.g. the doctor thinks that the client has not enough money for the requested treatment).

(6), Fig. 11.   The contractor believes he cannot play his role (e.g. the doctor thinks he is not an expert of the disease suffered by the client).

(7), Fig. 14.   The contractor does not believe that the client is sincere in manifesting the intention to play his role (e.g. the doctor thinks that a young client obliged by his parents to come is disguising his symptoms).

(8), Fig. 15.   The contractor thinks that there is a discrepancy between his own representation of the contract and the client's representation. In fact the contractor thinks that the client's request has not been made as part of a mutually known contract DOCTOR. For example if the client is European, an American doctor may think he is not prepared to pay, believing there is a National Health Service covering the expenses.

(9), Fig. 15.   The contractor has no reason to assume that the client believes the contract to be valid (e.g. a request of a remedy made during a social dinner).

(10),Fig. 15.   The contractor does not understand the client's request (e.g. the client is a foreigner, or the old doctor is deaf, etc.).

As previously stated, our model represents the formation of a plan for a perlocutionary act as a cognitive process of the actor. Therefore, the analysis of failures we have presented can in principle be performed by the actor himself, in order to identify the reason of a failure and to plan a recovery strategy.

After the identification of a failure, the planner can resort to two lines of recovery: changing his plan in order to comply with the world (<u>replanning</u>), or changing the world in order to mantain his plan (<u>side planning</u>). In our model these strategies are viable at each of the failure points we have identified. As regards planning, the aim is to limit the extension of modifications, keeping them as local as possible. As regards side planning, the problem is that some of the conditions responsible for failure may not be realistically modifiable by the planner.

In our model, the types of conditions which may cause a failure are: ability preconditions of an action, beliefs, motivations, and knowledge of contracts. We now examine each of them.

Recovery for an ability precondition:

- replanning. Since the action cannot be executed, the actor has to surrogate it with another one. The new action may be of the same type but with different parameters (for instance in (1), Fig.10, the client could go to another doctor), or of a different type (for instance, the client could decide to call a friend known to suffer of the same desease and ask him for advice).

- side planning. The actor must build a plan in order to achieve the ability precondition which failed (e.g. in (1), Fig.10: try to help the doctor to repair the broken part of the sphygmomanometer).

Recovery for a belief condition:

- replanning. The actor must alter the original plan in order to make a specific belief unnecessary. The replanning strategy is not general, but depends on the role of that belief in the plan. For instance, in (5), Fig. 11, the belief is part of the activating conditions of the PROFESSION theme. In order to bypass that belief, it is necessary to invoke another theme. Thus, if the physician thinks that the client cannot pay the bill, the client might threaten, or blandish, or implore him. In each of these cases, a theme different from PROFESSION would be invoked. Note that the use of a different theme does not usually allow the actor to apply the DOCTOR contract. Therefore more extensive replanning is needed on the basis of a different kind of game.

- side planning. The actor must plan a CAUSE-TO-BELIEVE action either by an act of convincing or by noncommunicative means. In the previous example, the client might convince the physician that he is able to pay the bill. At least in one case, however, the action of convincing is particularly difficult: in (7), Fig. 14, where the contractor does not believe that the client is sincere about his intentions, we can expect that the client's action of convincing him about his sincerity will be critical, as it requires in turn a sincerity condition.

Recovery for knowledge and motivation:

- replanning. Failures (2) and (3), Fig. 11, depend on the use of general mental structures (a contract and a theme) by the contractor. In these cases, to replan means to form a new plan which does not depend on such structures. For example, as regards (3), the same strategies applied in case (5), (threaten, blandish, implore, etc.), can be tried.

- side planning. In order to form a side plan here, the contract case must be distinguished from the theme case. In the contract case the client must convince the contractor that his own representation of a contract is the correct one. For instance in (2), Fig. 11, the client should convince the doctor that the DOCTOR contract binds him to give the prescribed drugs. In the theme case, the client must motivate the contractor to act as a real professional. The possibility to actuate such a strategy seems however highly problematic, as an actor might modify the motivational structure of another subject only through a long-term interaction.

6. TWO LEVELS OF COMMUNICATION

In this section we analyze the chain of inferences previously presented to figure out the main theoretical issues.

Figure 16 is a recapitulatory scheme of all the speech acts involved in the transaction analyzed. The planner, in order to obtain the perlocutionary effect to have the partner induced to perform an action, has to induce him to play his role in the game which assignes to him the desired action. Such a result can be achieved if the partner has an adequate motivation which, as we have already seen, requires that he is convinced that the planner in turn intends to play his role in the game. Therefore, the planner has to convince the partner about his own intention, and this amounts to performing a different perlocutionary act.

In order to convince his partner, the planner must perform the illocutionary act of informing him about his intention to play his role. The action of convincing is successful if the partner understands the illocutionary act and if he assumes that the planner is sincere. The main assumption here is that the illocutionary act of informing the partner about one's intention to play, is realized through the illocutionary act of requesting the desired action within the validity context of the game.

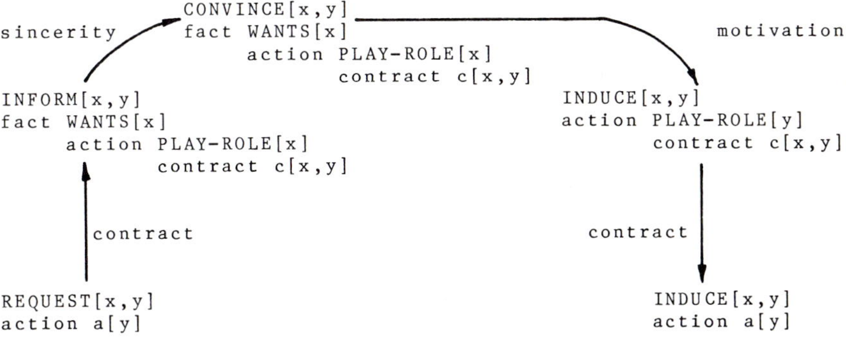

Fig. **16.** The global structure of an INDUCE perlocutionary act

The same inferences used to model the planner can also be viewed as a model of the partner. Perrault and Allen (1980) and Wilensky (1983) argue that planning and understanding are symmetrical processes that exploit the same knowledge. This standpoint is consistent with our simulation hypothesis (Section 3), which assumes that the planner simulates the understanding process of the partner while planning his speech acts. The simulation is successful when the partner, starting from the recognition of the illocutionary speech act, goes through the same inference steps made by the planner, though in the reverse order. When this is not the case, the simulation proves unsuccessful, and the perlocutionary speech act is unfelicitous, leading to one of the failures analyzed in Section 5.

The main theoretical implications of the model we have presented are discussed below.

The request of an actor, intended to induce a partner to perform an action, is always paralleled by communication about the respective roles, in order to meet the partner's motivation to cooperate.

Consider the following story (2):

(2) The boss and his secretary are sitting in their office with the window open;

    (2.a) The boss says it is cold and his secretary stands up and closes the window;

    (2.b) the secretary says it is cold and the boss replies she can close the window.

In story (2) the same statement assumes two different meanings depending on the respective roles of speaker and hearer. We can explain case (2.a) considering the statement of the boss as a request that the secretary close the window. In case (2.b) the statement of the secretary can be interpreted as a request of permission to close the window. Both cases admit alternative explanations according to different intentions of the actors. In (2.a) the boss could have no intention of indirectly requesting the cooperation of his secretary. In this case, her response could be interpreted either as a misunderstanding or as an intentional redefinition. In case (2.b) the statement of the secretary could be an indirect request that the boss close the window. Also the answer of the boss can be viewed either as an actual misunderstanding or as an intentional redefinition.

In story (1), Section 4, Arthur, while requesting Pamela to treat his headaches, is proposing himself as a client and asking her to play the role of the doctor.

Let us follow our character in a different story (3):

(3) Pamela goes to a party. Having known she is a doctor, Arthur offers her a glass of wine and tells her he has a recurrent headache;

    (3.a) Pamela discusses with him of the disease and advises him about the best treatment.
    Arthur warmly thanks her.

 (3.b) Pamela replies giving him the phone number of her office.
    Arthur coldly thanks her.

 (3.c) Pamela smiling discusses the symptoms.
    Arthur thanks her and they go on chatting up for the rest of the
    evening.

In story (3) Arthur proposes to the partner to play her usual professional role, but in an inadequate setting. Response (3.a) can be viewed either as the playing of a politeness game, quite appropriate in the party context, or as the extension of the doctor game beyond the usual setting.

Response (3.b) can be attributed to a refusal of the doctor to meet the request on the basis of the wrong context.

In case (3.c) Arthur's request is interpreted by Pamela not as the first move of the doctor game, but as a pretext for starting a social game.

As it appears from the example above, communicating about the respective roles requires that the request is interpreted with respect to a game, within its validity context.

Besides, the analysis of the examples shows that communicative exchanges are based on the roles played by the actors in the interaction. In fact, roles are determinant for playing a communicative act, for understanding it, and for planning the response. Games are the knowledge structures which codify such roles in a specified context and are used for the functions just mentioned (see Section 2).

Moreover, in order to explain why the partner accepts the role proposed by the planner or rather makes a new proposal, we must take into account the motivations of the partner. Different kinds of games are played on the basis of different motivations. For instance the motivations which underlie professional practice are different from those involved in friendship. For our purpose, a motivation can be regarded as a mental structure which generates an intention under given conditions. For example, the motivation of preserving one's life generates the intention to run away from a dangerous situation.

The critical feature of motivations for playing a game is that they always contain, among their conditions of activation, the fact that the planner is proposing himself as a player of the game. For instance, if one asks for a coffee in a coffee shop, he is proposing himself as a client and thus activates the waiter's motivation to do his job.

Finally, an action of inducing may be performed through the same request, via different game-motivation pairs. For instance in (3) the doctor could interpret Arthur's request as a seductive approach and either accept or refuse the interaction on that basis. To be able to give an adequate answer, the partner has to solve the ambiguity possibly contained in the first move of the planner. The suitable strategy for the partner is to understand which is the standing intention that the actor is trying to activate in the partner himself. Ambiguity may be used consciously by the planner to allow the partner to accept or re-define the game with some freedom, and avoiding an explicit discussion or refusal of the game proposed.

7. DISCUSSION

In this paper we have presented a model for planning a speech act in order to have somebody perform an action, and for recovering from possible failures.

Aim of the model is to account for the competence aspects of the process involved in planning and understanding two paradigmatic perlocutionary acts: inducing and convincing.

The tenets of our work are the following:
- the actor both when planning and when understanding is able to simulate the mental processes of his partner;
- any action can be reconducted to a standing intention which represents its ultimate motivation;
- all communicative interactions are governed by knowledge structures - games - shared among the actors. Each action may be interpreted as a move in the game;
- communication about the world is always accompanied by communication about the respective roles of the partners. Communication about roles is necessary to account for the ability of performing perlocutionary acts.

Our model is not intended to provide a step-by-step simulation of the performance of actors engaged in communicative exchanges. In particular we do not commit to the hypothesis that the whole process described is carried on each time a speech act is produced or interpreted. For instance, the planner may have in his general knowledge the information that a request may be used to induce somebody to perform a desired action. This would allow the planner to shortcut most of the inference process presented before. Similar considerations are advanced by Bach and Harnish (1979) in their discussion of the psychological reality of speech acts.

Moreover, humans are often able to recover from failures, thus revealing the ability to recognize the causes of their failures. This means that humans, when required, can produce inferences which are at least as rich as the ones we have described.

A further point to discuss is the relation between deceit and the sincerity hypothesis we introduced in Section 3. To plan a deceit, the planner has to be able to simulate the fact that the partner relies on the sincerity hypothesis, without actually being himself bound to be sincere. To discover a deceit, the partner must be able to reconstruct the inference chain of the deceitful planner, exploiting a further level of nested beliefs. The model presented should allow for the treatment of deceitful interactions, because the planner's intention to play his role occurs only within the partner's representation of the planner. Therefore, our model is compatible with the situation in which the planner does not actually intend to play his role.

REFERENCES

Airenti G., Bara B.G., Colombetti M. 1983. Planning perlocutionary acts, Proceedings 8th IJCAI, Karlsruhe, DFR.

Allen J.F. 1983. Recognizing intentions from natural language utterances. In: Brady M., Berwick R.C., eds., Computational models of discourse, M.I.T. Press, Cambridge, Mass.

Austin J.L. 1962. How to do things with words. Oxford University Press, London, U.K.

Bach K., Harnish R.M. 1979. Linguistic communication and speech acts, M.I.T. Press, Cambridge, Mass.

Bruce B.C., Newman D. 1978. Interacting plans. Cognitive Science, 2.

Cohen P.R., Perrault C.R. 1979. Elements of a plan based theory of speech acts, Cognitive Science, 3.3.

Perrault C.R., Allen J.F. 1980. A plan based analysis of indirect speech acts, American Journal of Computational Linguistics, 6,3-4.

Searle J.R. 1979. A taxonomy of illocutionary acts.In: Expression and meaning, Cambridge University Press, Cambridge, UK.

Searle J.R. 1983. Intentionality, Cambridge University Press, Cambridge, UK.

Taylor G.B., Whitehill S.B. 1981. A belief representation for understanding deception, Proceedings 7th IJCAI, Vancouver, B.C.

Wilensky R. 1983. Planning and understanding, Addison-Wesley, Reading, Mass.

Computational Models of Natural Language Processing
B.G. Bara and G. Guida (eds.)
© Elsevier Science Publishers B.V. (North-Holland), 1984

A FRAMEWORK FOR INTEGRATING SYNTAX AND SEMANTICS

Amedeo Cappelli, Giacomo Ferrari, Lorenzo Moretti, Irina Prodanof

Istituto di Linguistica Computazionale
Consiglio Nazionale delle Ricerche
Pisa, Italy

This article outlines a computational model within which syntactic and semantic processing are integrated. Linguistic theory has seen a continuous increase in the relevance of the lexicon and lexical semantics has recently been incorporated into syntactic rules. On the computational side, different control structures have been designed, making it possible for the syntactic and semantic component to interact. However, compared with syntactic processors, semantic ones are still far from being able to account for human processing. The proposed hypothesis consists in distinguishing a processor 'toutcourt' and some symbolic representations of different levels. This hypothesis would seem to be supported by i) some linguistic phenomena whose processing actually involves different levels of information in a single process, and ii) the difficulty in drawing a definite boundary between semantic interpretation and semantic information needed for processing. With the above purpose in mind, a set of general processing actions and their application to functional grammar are described, together with a language for manipulating knowledge structures. Finally, a hypothesis of how such a language might be integrated into the general processor is discussed.

1. INTRODUCTION

One of the crucial problems of Computational Linguistics, as well as of theoretical linguistics, is the development of a model of interaction between syntax and semantics, that is both intuitively natural and adequate from the point of view of explicative power.

The approaches to this problem fall into two categories: those that make a clear separation between the two components from the point of view of processing and representation and those that mix everything together in a kind of semantic or cognitive processing.

This latter view, which in general consists in denying the relevance of syntax, has not substantially contributed to the clarification of the problem.

Systems like LIFER (Hendrix et al., 1978) or PLANES (Waltz et al., 1976) use a 'semantic grammar' (Burton, 1976) to convert surface strings directly into semantic interpretations without passing through a syntactic representation. However, the strict dependency of the categories used in grammar on the domain of application is in itself the negation of the principle of generalization, which should characterize any theoretical result. Moreover, semantic grammar has always been used as an engineering device and has not made any contribution to linguistic theory.

An assumption of theoretical relevance underlies the theories of Schank (1972),

Schank & Abelson (1977) especially that of 'conceptual dependency'. One of his major claims consists in denying the utility of a syntactic approach, thus suggesting the non autonomy of a syntactic component in the process of understanding. Many systems have been implemented based on this view, in which fragments of semantic and distributional information are associated with lexical entries, and a global representation, in terms of a conceptual dependency network, is progressively built up by merging them (Riesbeck, 1976; Lehnert, 1978). However, during processing, syntactic classifications are used and the structure building activity as well as the opening and closing of constituents takes place in accordance with certain well established syntactic notions. This seems to show that it is impossible to process natural language without a deeper insight into the role of syntax and the way it works.

In fact, positions which draw neat boundaries between syntax and semantics have made an important contribution to the study of these components taken in isolation. On the other hand psychology and neurolinguistics give rich evidence in favour of a syntactic information processing, while no explicit evidence is found against it.

The approach presented in this article will assume the existence and the relevance of both syntax and semantics. The relationship between them will be investigated and discussed in detail from the point of view of processing as well as representation. A hypothesis of integration will be presented, which consists in defining a general processor which activates complex functions to manipulate representations of different levels. The structure of the processor as well as the functions which map directly linguistic units on to knowledge structures will be described. Some problems arising from the higher degree of complexity of this model will be also discussed.

2. FUNCTIONS OF A SEMANTIC COMPONENT

2.1 Lexicon and Linguistic Theory

Lexical restrictions have been and are invoked to prevent misanalyses of a sentence or to constrain the alternative choices in a process of syntactic analysis. Subcategorizations and selection restriction features have conveniently performed this job. They have been used to check the well-formedness of structures and, on the computational side, all the parsers for natural language include some devices for the treatment of such features (Woods, 1973; Petrick, 1972; Robinson, 1975).

Whether such features belong to semantics or to some other linguistic level is a questionable matter but they have generally been intended as carrying some semantic information.

More recently, linguistic theory has seen a continuous increase in the importance of the lexicon in the process of sentence structuring.

Lexical Functional Grammar (Kaplan & Bresnan, 1981) and Generalized Phrase Structure Grammar (Gazdar, 1982) make the relationships between phrases explicit by means of rules which are associated with lexical items and have a clear connection with what is referred to by Gazdar as "real semantics".
The verb 'hand' is defined in Lexical Functional Grammar by the two forms

        'HAND <($\uparrow$ SUBJ)($\uparrow$ OBJ)($\uparrow$ TO OBJ)>'
        'HAND <($\uparrow$ SUBJ)($\uparrow$ OBJ2)($\uparrow$ OBJ)>'

These are clearly stated to be semantic forms and "there are very strong compatibility requirements between (a semantic form) and the f-structure in

which it appears".
The representations of the same verb are given by Gazdar in Montague's intentional logic notation (Montague, 1974) associated with Jackendoff's $\overline{X}$ notation (Jackendoff, 1977):

$$\langle [\overline{v} \ V \ \overline{\overline{N}} \ \overline{\overline{P}}], \ V' \ (\overline{\overline{P}}'') \ (\overline{\overline{N}}'') \rangle$$
$$\langle [\overline{v} \ V \ \overline{\overline{N}} \ \overline{\overline{N}}], \ V' \ (\overline{\overline{N}}'') \ (\overline{\overline{N}}'') \rangle$$

Although "intentional logic is invoked ...purely as an expository device" and it "can be eliminated in favor of defining the real semantics", in both these grammatical theories some lexical semantics is embedded in the theoretical frame and somehow affects the structuring of a sentence. In this way the lexicon plays a more active role in the process of comprehension than it did in the previous models.

2.2 Computational models of semantic interpretation

All the computational models of Natural Language Understanding embody a semantic interpreter, i.e. an algorithm that maps a syntactic representation of a sentence on to a representation of its meaning. Two entities are involved in semantic intepetation: the semantic representation and the process of interpretation itself.

In almost all the computational systems, languages strongly related to formal logic are used to represent the meaning of the syntactic construction of the sentence. This is certainly the most generalizable aspect of representation, as logic is accepted as an abstract formalism through which mechanisms of reasoning can be described. This abstractness should guarantee domain independency and generality. The application domain provides appropriate descriptions of objects and operations which words and clauses are related to in order to be interpreted.

In Woods' (1973) MRL (Meaning Representation Language), a general logic schema of representation for sentences is

$$(FOR \ \langle quant \rangle \ X \ / \langle class \rangle : (p \ X) \ ; \ (q \ X))$$

and the sentence

(1) The man I see is mortal

is mapped onto the form

$$(FOR \ THE \ X \ / \ MAN : (SEE \ I \ X) \ ; \ (MORTAL \ X))$$

which is to be paraphrased as 'for the object X in the class MAN, such that it is true that I see X, it is also true that X is mortal'.

From the sentence

(2) Print all the samples which contain silicon

the following analogous logic expression is extracted

$$(FOR \ EVERY \ X1 \ / \ (SEQ \ SAMPLES): (CONTAIN \ X1 \ /OVERALL \ SILICON);$$
$$(PRINTOUT \ X1))$$

in which the words SAMPLES and SILICON are directly related to the structure of a database and PRINTOUT is actually a command.

The algorithms may intepret syntactic trees by different strategies. Early Qestion Answering systems, such as LUNAR (Woods et al., 1972) or REQUEST (Plath, 1976), prefer to apply a general interpretation algorithm once a syntactic tree has been completed. Other systems, such as SHRDLU (Winograd, 1970) or, more recently, PSI-KLONE (Bobrow & Webber, 1980) interpret subtrees by transmitting them to the semantic module. Transmit actions occur as soon as a syntactic structure fragment has grown to a significant point.

In both systems, semantic interpretation is called by the grammar and returns values to it.

In SHRDLU interpretation is made by a collection of different programs ('specialists') which actually build parts of the representation, which are then merged.

In PSI-KLONE, instead, phrases are inserted in an already existing network and at the end a semantic description in the formal-stylized subset of English called JARGON is generated.

Although the primary function of the semantic module in these systems is to provide information for semantic interpretation, the screening out of semantically non validated syntactic trees is an obvious consequence. This fact has been exploited in recent systems to control syntactic analysis and increase the efficiency by constraining non-determinism. In one case specialized procedures associated with any type of node are triggered as soon as a syntactic node is filled (Lesmo & Torasso, 1983).

The PARNAX system (Comino et al., 1983), instead, separates the deterministic semantic interpretation algorithm from the non-deterministic validation algorithm which runs semantic rules in parallel with the syntactic analysis. Parallelism has been generally used in other systems to handle efficiently multiple knowledge sources which cooperate in the finding of the good analysis of an utterance (Reddy et al., 1973; Reddy et al., 1977).

This tendency to make syntax and semantics dialogue between each other has given rise to a set of interesting control structures.

The most widely used consists in suspending the syntactic process and waiting for some value returned by semantics as the result either of specialized procedures associated with some linguistic element (Winograd, 1970; Lesmo & Torasso, 1983) or of the call for a general semantic interpretation routine (Bobrow & Webber, 1980). Suspension points and actions to be taken depending upon the value returned are specified in the grammar. In PARNAX, instead, the interaction between syntactic and semantic parallel processes and the selection of the validated analysis is based on a general criterion of association between the results of the two processes, which is embedded in the control structure.

Semantic interpretation algorithms are in general well grounded from the formal point of view of computation, but little psychological verification or theoretical work has been devoted to the investigation of their analogies with human understanding processes. Thus no attempt has been made to prove that some specific algorithm or piece of algorithm adequately accounts for the process of human understanding. On the contrary a rich literature is devoted to providing syntactic processing with plausible psychological foundations.

3. SOME REQUIREMENTS FOR PROCESSING NATURAL LANGUAGE

3.1 General features of Natural Language Processing systems

From the above 'historical' considerations some features may be pointed out which are common to many systems and can be considered as well established facts in Computational Linguistics theory.

The core mechanism of any Natural Language Processing system is an algorithm that analyses sentences in accordance with a grammar, i.e. associates with each input sentence a structure in a representation language. Such a process is performed on the basis of certain strategies which, in some cases, have been compared with the human strategies of sentence comprehension (Bever, 1970). General constraints that certain grammatical theories impose on the movement of constituents, such as 'subjacency' (Chomsky, 1977) or 'nearly nestedness' (Kaplan & Bresnan, 1981) turn out to be constraints on the scope of processing in certain contexts (Marcus, 1980).

This is an approximation of the notion of 'processor' developed and discussed, more than others, by Kaplan (1972, 1978). The grammars handled by these algorithms are in general strictly syntactic. Nevertheless, as we have seen, an interaction with the semantic and/or pragmatic level has often been invoked, especially for an efficient treatment of certain phenomena which defy the ability of ordinary syntactic processing.

It has already been observed about the semantic level, that many requirements have been dictated, some approaches to a description have been given and some formalisms have been tried, whereas few explicative algorithms have been devised. That amounts to saying that the notion of the semantic processor has not been theoretically evolved to the same level of refinement as that of the syntactic processor.

3.2 Two questions on relating syntax and semantics

The fact that semantic interpretation is performed by an autonomous component regardless of the way the control structure calls for it is a state-of-art matter in computer science. This architecture of semantic interpretation has been shown to be insufficient to cover a well developed notion of 'semantic processing' for Natural Language. This inadequacy possibly stems from a real difficulty in defining semantic interpretation independently from the syntactic processor. A good motivation for this seems to be the peculiar character of ambiguity in Natural Language, which in many cases is not precisely localized within the syntactic or semantic level.

Thus, the problem of the relationship between the use of semantics during syntactic processing and the algorithm of interpretation could be summarized in the following two questions:

- Is it possible that psychological evidence in favour of a "syntactic information processor" is, instead, in favour of an "information processor" 'toutcourt', called "syntactic" just because it handles distributional phenomena? An affirmative answer is possible if it could be shown that those syntactic processing difficulties for which an intervention of semantics is invoked cannot really find a solution by passing information from one level to the other, but by actually defining special processes to handle complex information.

- When we talk of semantic constraints, which type of semantic information are

we referring to? What is the relationship between the description of a word
(construction, phenomenon) at the level of our knowledge of a given reality
and of its linguistic use? A hypothesis of unicity of such a description
should   unify the two functions of both providing a representation of the
meaning and constraining the process of analysis. The focus of attention
should thus concentrate on the process of deducing the information relevant to
the process from a knowledge component, rather than on the process of handling
rigidly predefined sets of features in rules of well-formedness.

4. SOME CRUCIAL PHENOMENA

A certain number of linguistic phenomena show how semantic interpretation,
semantic constraints and syntactic process are intertwined, and give a hint to
answer to the first question asked above (3.2).

4.1 PP-placement

A significant example is PP-placement, a serious problem in parsing efficiency,
but also a challenge to find out what information at which level can provide the
solution.

A prepositional phrase (PP) is made up of a preposition followed by a noun
group. It can function both as an adjunct to a clause and as a qualifier of a
noun group which it is attached to. In this latter use it can be recursively
embedded in a PP as a modifier of its noun group component. Such a nesting can
be of considerable depth as in

(3) the appearance of the man under the tree with a broken branch near the edge
     of the road to the town with a market (Winograd, 1983)

However, as the structure representing these sequences of PP's is not purely
right branching for all sequences, a high degree of structural ambiguity is met
by parsers. The quoted example has 429 parsings. The decision about which noun
group in a structure a PP is to be attached to has been referred to as the
problem of PP-placement (Woods, 1973).
An obvious remedy is to incorporate in the parser some semantic processing in
order to determine the scope of a PP and eliminate some interpretations before
outputting them. In one of our previous experiments we tried to use some
features associated with the noun embedded in the PP and a sort of case frame
associated with prepositions and verbs. The arguments of a verb (strict
subcategorization) were selected, to which functional labels determined by the
same verb were assigned. The remaining PP's were assigned less restricted
labels, determined by their prepositions (Cappelli et al., 1980, 1983).

The descriptive apparatus is a heavy one (features, case frame, functional
labels), but the solution is not a direct answer to the problem of PP-placement.

In fact, the algorithm identifies those PP's that can be directly related to the
verb and gives a priority to these relationships. Thus, what it actually does is
hypothetically reduce the number of cases in which a decision is to be taken,
but not activate a decision procedure.

A direct connection of the syntactic structures to a semantic network has been
made in the RUS system (Bobrow, 1978), in which phrases are attached, by
cascading (Woods, 1980), to concepts of a KL-ONE network. Restrictions
expressed in the network return either a success or a failure of the currently
proposed placement in the structure.

Another attempt to treat the verbal case frame (Cappelli et al., 1981) consists in associating with each verb procedures which give a cognitive interpretation of cases. They are functions that map syntactic schemata on to a cognitive structure, thus directly linking arguments to a hierarchy of superconcepts. Handling such a network is equivalent to the computation of complex functions which evaluates elements of different levels and of different depths of description.

The most interesting point of this approach consists in directly relating a syntactic structure to a cognitive one. For instance, assigning the label INSTRUMENT to a PP means explaining it at a deeper level, but it has appeared that such a label is often induced from a cognitive structure idiosyncratically related to lexical items.

4.2 Binding

A group of linguistic phenomena exhibit comparable features in their treatment, even though they have different linguistic motivations. It has already been shown that trace binding in Equi-NP deletion, Wh-movement, NP movement, gapping, antecedent/(pro)nominal binding, lexical anaphor and VP deletion "fall together in the functional domain of parsing" (Berwick & Weinberg, 1983). This demonstration has been given for one linguistic theory and for a deterministic parser. Nevertheless the possibility of treating some of the quoted phenomena, often referred to by other names, had already been discussed also in the framework of an ATN parser (Cappelli et al., 1983; Kwasny & Sondheimer, 1981). Ellipsis and relative clauses have been added to this list (Prodanof & Ferrari, 1983).

All these phenomena are characterized by the need for an operation of linking of a given symbol (e, trace, pronoun) to an antecedent. They can be divided into two categories; those constructions for which the linking of the surface symbol to its antecedent can be generatively predicted and those in which the symbol indicates the necessity for a linking but this must be executed by a variously constrained search procedure. To the first class belong those constructions for which syntactic rules are in themselves sufficient for parsing. This is the case, for instance, of Equi-NP deletion, where the deleted NP is in the matrix in a syntactic function determined by its main (STRANS) verb.

To the second class belong those phenomena, such as subject ellipsis or pronoun binding, in which the antecedent may be placed unboundedly backward.

In the sentences

(4) A credette di x udire un rumore
    A thought to x hear a noise
(5) A persuase B a x fuggire
    A persuaded B to x run away
(6) A ordino' a   B di x sedere
    A ordered (to) B to x sit down

the choice of the NP to be linked to x is unambiguously determined by the syntactic idiosyncrasies of the main verbs (credette, persuase, ordino').

On the contrary, in

(7) Giovanni disse a sua moglie che molti dei suoi colleghi pensavano che
    John said to his wife that many of his collegues thought that   (he)
    sarebbe stato licenziato.
    would have been fired.

an unbounded number of embedded sentences with different subjects may lie between the ellipsis and its filler. The choice of the filler can be made by using morphological restrictions imposed by the participle. 'Sarebbe stato licenziato' being masculine (fem. 'licenziata') excludes 'sua moglie' from the possible candidates, limiting the choice to either 'someone else' or 'Giovanni'.

The same argument is true for pronoun binding in pairs like

(8a) Giovanni chiese a Maria di accompagnarla
     John   asked   Mary to accompany her
(8b) Giovanni chiese a Maria di accompagnarlo
     John   asked   Mary to accompany him

in which the morphological features of the pronoun constrain the linking.

Relative pronouns also need to be linked to an antecedent and in addition, they determine the boundary of a higher clause, although their position in the string does not necessarily coincide with such a boundary.

In fact, while in

(9) il cane # che   morde
    the dog   which bites

'che' coincides with the left boundary of the relative clause, in

(10) il cane # della fedelta'   del quale nessuno dubita
     the dog   about the faithfulness of which nobody is in doubt

such a boundary is moved three words backward. The identification of the antecedent must be performed first, since in general the boundary is inserted immediately after it.

From an abstract viewpoint all these cases can be processed in two steps. The first one consists in recognizing the necessity for a linking action from the occurrence of a pro-forma (pronoun, relative pronoun) or a violation of well-formedness (gapping: Cappelli et al., 1981). The second one is a process that searches for a referent also taking into account conditions whose evaluation can take place regardless of the type of the constraints.

In the examples introduced above, we have discussed only syntactic and morphological constraints but they do not exhaust the entire set of possibilities. It is, in fact, a commonplace that, for instance, pronoun binding and resolution of ellipsis are, to some extent, affected also by semantics or pragmatics (Marcus, 1980). However, a computational hypothesis which commits the solution of a phenomenon to the next module does not provide the instrument to explain it exhaustively, since the pieces of information involved are not integrated in a process. The fact that all the above phenomena can be and have partially been unified on a functional ground seems to prove that it is actually possible to propose a single process into which different representations can be embedded and evaluated.

5. AMBIGUITY OF SEMANTIC DESCRIPTION

As has already been shown, the semantic representation of a sentence has its own syntax, in general provided by either logic or, more recently, some other (knowledge) representation language. We have also observed that the 'real' meaning of the variables involved, i.e. the nominal expressions, is ultimately determined by their attachment to precise objects in a precise data or knowledge base. Anyway the idiosyncrasies of nominal words, be they expressed either as lexical features or in any other way, are mostly used to bear constraints and eliminate syntactic ambiguity. Lexical items are, therefore, described in two ways: as cognitive units, or real world objects, and as linguistic units bearing indications about how they behave linguistically in a sentence.

However, there is an ambiguity between the two types of descriptions.

Traditional lexical features, such as Human, Abstract, Physical Object etc., are used as linguistic descriptions, but they may be found as nodes in a network representing objects. In fact, one often finds them inserted in the examples of semantic networks (Hendrix, 1978; Bobrow & Webber, 1980).

They may also be found in a pure semantic rule, such as the following, taken from Woods (1978).

```
(S:CONTAIN
     (S.NP  (MEM 1 SAMPLE))
     (S.V (OR (EQU 1 HAVE)
              (EQU 1 CONTAIN)))
     (S.OBJ (MEM 1 (ELEMENT OXIDE ISOTOPE)))
  --->  (QUOTE (CONTAIN (# 1 1) (#3 1))))
```

The check for MEMbership of nodes of the category SAMPLE is clearly referred to the actual occurrence of the noun in node 1 in the data base of samples. Nevertheless it acts also as a linguistic condition exactly equivalent to the subsequent (EQU 1 HAVE) or to the condition (MEM 1 WHQ) in the following rule

```
(D:WHQ-PL
     (NP.DET (AND (MEM 1 WHQ) (EQU 2 PL)))
     ---> (QUANT (FOR EVERY X / (# 0 NRULES) :
             (# 0 RRULES) ; (PRINTOUT X))))
```

Such categories could easily be used as restrictions during the process.

Although two different semantic descriptions are often used for lexical items, redundancy and overlapping sometimes occur. This is an argument in favour of integrating them into a single cognitive description to which both tasks are committed.

6. AN EXPERIMENTAL GENERALIZED PROCESSOR

6.1 General assumptions

A first step towards a better understanding of how the two levels might interact consists in designing a parser which is able to manipulate a wide range of representation formalisms. In fact, if we assume that a single processor is to carry on the analysis at all levels, we have to enable it to process complex combinations of even non-homogeneous symbols.
The structure resulting from the analysis of the string need not be a mere parse tree nor need it be directly dependent upon the parsing algorithm and the grammar. Incoming information is, therefore, to be stored into a space of memory by explicit structure specifying actions, rather than into prestructured chunks of memory such as (parse) tree fragments or registers.

Since opening, closure and attachment of phrases/clauses are not necessarily dependent upon syntactically predictable structures, a rich set of functions that access the memory space in an explicit way is also necessary. For example, in the sentences

(11) Ho visto   il parco della casa
      I have seen the park of the house
(12) Ho visto   il parco di notte
      I have seen the park by night

the process of recognition should proceed in the same way both for (11) and (12)
by opening a structure at 'il' and a second structure at 'di'.   In (12), only
when 'notte' is met, the early closure of 'il parco' can be decided. However if
a strategy of late closure had been chosen, it should be desirable not to
backtrack, but   simply to   manipulate the   hypothesized structure.   This
manipulation affects symbols of a different nature integrated into a symbolic
system which must be represented in highly structured data types.

Many computational linguistics arguments are also in favour of such requirements
for a generalized parser (Prodanof & Ferrari, 1982).

6.2 Memory accessing actions

EXAM-LC (EXtendend Access and Manipulation of the Left Context) is a small set
of abstract operations on a space of memory containing the current hypothesis
about the analysis of the whole parsed segment of the input. We will refer to
such a structured space as Current Global Hypothesis (CGH).

The abstractly defined actions are described below.

An opening and a closing action will respectively start and end the storing of
the information related to a phrase/clause in a current subspace subsequently
merged with the global space. The way of storing depends upon the representation
of the output and the corresponding actions are designed in accordance with it.

A retrieving action will have two participants, a symbol that triggers the
action (trigger) and the information to be retrieved (the target of the action).
After the identification of a trigger (a gap to be filled, a verb which requires
the subject-verb agreement test), the action may be reduced to a single general
algorithm of three steps,

i) extraction of constraints which must guide the search for the target,
ii) scanning of the CGH under the specified conditions, and
iii) retrieving of the required information.

On this functional ground, the same description fits more or less all the cases
discussed under 4.2.

The action of searching back may be constrained by several types of
restrictions, including

i) morphological features, i.e. the gender and number of the pronoun, as in
example (8), or those required for agreement by the syntactic environment (e.g.
the verb), as in (7)
ii) syntactic idiosyncrasies of some lexical item such as the STRANS verbs that
determine which of their arguments is to be the subject of the complement, as
shown in (4,5,6,),
iii) semantic features or cognitive descriptions that may be introduced into the
process, and
iv) syntactic determination of the scope of the search, such as 'subjacency'.

Retrieving of the antecedent may actually correspond to two different operations
depending upon whether the antecedent to be bound linearly precedes or follows
the symbol it is to be bound to.   In fact, in many common sentences the

antecedent linearly follows its dependent, as in

(13) Quando   si arrabbia, Giovanni diventa rosso
     When (he) gets angry, John   becomes red
(14) Se lo vedi,   saluta   Giovanni da parte mia
     If (you) see him, say hallo to John   on my behalf

In these cases, the binding should take place in two steps: the flagging of the
need for a forward binding and the moving of the pointer from the antecedent,
once detected, to the flag.

Many of the retrieving actions will end up with a binding or, more generally,
with a moving action. This can be realized in at least two ways, by actually
copying the retrieved constituent into the trigger subspace or simply by moving
a pointer from one to the other.

A reconfiguration action is necessary in order to modify an already (partially)
built structure, as new incoming information indicates the need for such a
change. The types of modifications to be performed depend on the representation
of the output.

A good and perhaps generally valid example is the relative clause. Relative
pronouns need to be bound to an antecedent and, besides, are the surface signal
of an embedding. No special processing difficulty is proposed by sentence (9),
where the relative pronoun occurs exactly where the embedding begins. In this
case a scope restriction can limit the search for an antecedent to the
immediately preceding Noun Phrase (NP). But in (10), where the phenomenon called
pied-piping occurs, the relative clause boundary is set three words before the
relative pronoun.

In this case an action which structurally modifies the left context can be
proposed. It should embed the component(s) being processed in a relative clause
as the relative pronoun is met.

A final type of access to the left context is the relabelling of a processed
constituent, already used for passive transformation.

6.3 An experimental implementation

An experimental realization of the above discussed ideas has been implemented in
the frame of the ATN parsing algorithm (Prodanof & Ferrari, 1983).

A functional representation à la Kay (1979) is used. A detailed explanation of
this formalism is not necessary to the understanding of this article. It is
enough to know that its basic unit is the attribute-value pair, where an
attribute is a symbol (label) and a value is a symbol or another functional
description. In the sentence

(15) He killed her

a possible pair is SUBJ=he, or SUBJ=HEAD=he together with SUBJ=CAT=PRON etc. Any
sequence of symbols is a path leading to a value; thus the value of SUBJ=HEAD is
'he'.

The functions that access the data structure are instances of those introduced
in 6.2, specifically designed to treat this type of representation.   The term
'constituent' will be used to identify the set of paths starting from the same
label (radix).

The basic features of the ATN parser used in our previous experiments (Cappelli et al., 1980), i.e. the network formalism and the parsing algorithm, are kept, while the data structure and the whole set of actions and forms have been modified. Also the use of the push-down mechanism has been modified to some extent.

The data structure is a list which is mainly accessed by using a typical stack policy. It represents a unique memory space not split into registers. The state saving mechanism necessary for the treatment of non-determinism is provided by ND-LISP (Montangero et al., 1976), an extension of MAGMA-LISP (Asirelli et al., 1975), the dialect of LISP in which the system is written. At any point non-determinism is called, the previous context, in particular the data, is saved and only the new values are set in the current context.
This list contains at any point of the process the Current Global Hypothesis (CGH), i.e. the entire left context literally represented in terms of attribute-value pairs.
The following is a list in Backus notation of the functions which access the CGH.

Actions

```
    a. <storing actions>::=
       ADD pair location |
       ASSIGN label path
       <location>::= NIL | <form>
       <label>::= any label
       <pair>::= label value
       <value>::= * | <form>

    b. <list manipulation>::=
       PUSH |
       POP |
       INSERT data item
       <data>::= any data
       <item>::= <form>
```


Forms

```
       FIND path test level dtype |
       FINDVAL path test level dtype|
       LOCATE path test level dtype
       <path>::= <label+>
       <test>::= T | any test
       <level>::= T | CL
       <dtype>::= T | ND | L
```


The basic storing action is ADD which is used to store any incoming piece of structure. The string

(16) il cane
     the dog

recognized by the network in Figure 1,

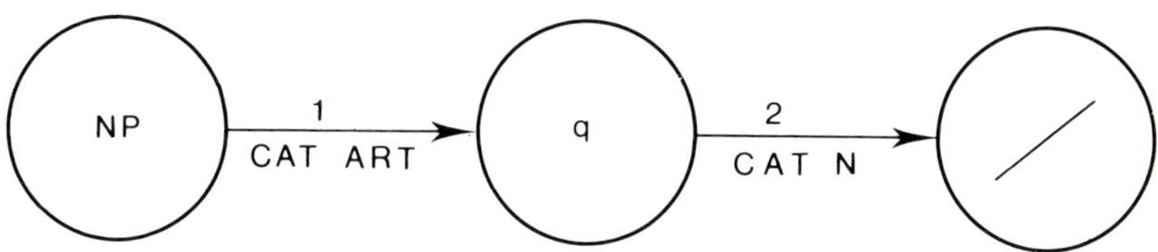

Figure 1 - A Transition Network for recognizing simple NP's.

is stored by the following actions

```
(ADD (DET *))
(ADD (HEAD *))
```

If location is NIL, the current constituent is meant, otherwise the form LOCATE specifies the path leading to the radix to which the new pair is to be ADDed.

Relabelling of a constituent is done by the action ASSIGN. In the sentences

(17a) Il cane mangia
      the dog eats
(17b) Il cane e' mangiato
      the dog is eaten

the NP 'il cane' will be first labelled FOCUS or FIRSTNP. Then, after having recognized the verb, the action

```
(ASSIGN SUBJ (LOCATE FOCUS T CL T))  or
(ASSIGN OBJ (LOCATE FOCUS T CL T))
```

will properly classify the Noun Phrase as

```
SUBJ or OBJ = FOCUS = DET = IL
                    =HEAD = N = CANE
```

Extraction of information is done by the forms FIND, which returns a pair, and FINDVAL, which returns only the value of a pair. LOCATE works exactly in the same way, but returns a pointer to a given radix. All three functions can work in different modes. They can either search only the current level (CL) or through the entire list (T). In this latter case the current level is excluded and, if no further options are specified, the lower (the nearest to the top) occurrence is returned. Another option (dtype) returns all the occurrences either appended in a list (L) or one by one, non-deterministically (ND). A third option evaluates conditions in order to select the component identified by the specified path.

In sentence (7) the antecedent retrieving is performed by the form

```
(FINDVAL (SUBJ) (AND (EQ (FINDVAL (SUBJ NUM) T T ND)
                         (FINDVAL (HEAD NUM)T CL T))
                     (EQ (FINDVAL (SUBJ GEN) T T ND)
                         (FINDVAL (HEAD GEN) T CL T))) T ND)
```

which searches for a subject through all the levels non deterministically. Such an NP must agree in number and gender with the current level head, i.e. the verb. An 'anaphoric' facility is implemented to avoid repeating an embedded form with the same argument as the embedding one. Thus the actual form looks slightly different. If this expression is embedded in the function

```
(ADD SUBJ ________)
```

the correct subject(s) is (are) copied in the complement. We do not intend to suggest that the correct mechanism of trace/antecedent binding is the copying of the antecedent in the trace position. A slightly modified version of this function might produce the insertion of the antecedent path.

The last three actions, PUSH, POP, and INSERT, manipulate the items in the list. PUSH adds a new (empty) item in front of the list. The elements of the constituent being analysed (phrases or sentences) are ADDed in this top item, which has been therefore referred to as current level. POP removes the current top-item and embeds it into the new top-item, possibly assigning a label to the corresponding constituent. Finally INSERT inserts an item, corresponding to a new level, somewhere back between 'item' and the front part of the list, and fills it with 'data'.

List manipulation takes place independently of the starting or the ending of the process expressed in a subnet. Thus a constituent can be POPed after the completion of its recognition procedure, when its function is clarified as well.

The arc recognizing an object, for ex., can be expressed as follows

```
(START NP T
       (COND (FIND (SUBJ) T CL T)
       (POP OBJ))
       (TO qi))
```

which means that if there is already a subject, the current constituent must be POPped with the label OBJ.

The use of the INSERT function is primarily motivated by the treatment of certain relative clauses. Relative pronouns are surface signals that trigger the embedding into a relative clause of the currently processed constituent(s).

In sentence (10) such an embedding takes place immediately after 'cane', thus producing

```
(il cane (RELCL (della fedelta' (del quale)) nessuno dubita))
```

The general rule may be formulated as follows: 'a new level labelled RELATIVECLAUSE is to be inserted immediately after the antecedent of the relative pronoun'. Analysis of (10) will therefore proceed as follows:

- when the relative pronoun 'quale' is encountered, an appropriate application of the FIND form returns the lower head which agrees in number and gender with the determiner ('de-l') of 'quale', i.e. 'cane'. This is the antecedent.

- the function

                    (INSERT RELCL (LOCATE...as for FIND))

inserts a new item with label RELCL.

- on the same arc the function (POP DI-ARG) embeds 'del quale' in 'della fedelta'' and a second POP embeds (della fedelta' (del quale)) into the recently inserted relative clause constituent.

- the recognition of a relative clause is continued by a (START S....) arc. The control is finally then returned to the NP process with the complex NP 'il cane...'as the current constituent.

7. OPERATIONS ON KNOWLEDGE

If the process of understanding is seen as a direct mapping on to a knowledge base, attention needs to be focused on those cognitive operations which store and manipulate knowledge. In particular it is necessary to individuate:

i)   the formalism to represent knowledge objects in a knowledge structure which
     simulates a sort of long-term memory (LTM);
ii) the actions, triggered by linguistic facts, which manipulate objects.

7.1 A formalism for representing knowledge

The representation formalism that has been adopted for this experimental step is the one offered by SI-Nets. This formalism is realized by a Knowledge Language, KL-Magma which is a version of KL-ONE implemented in MAGMA-Lisp (Asirelli et al., 1975). It is similar to the one described in Brachman (1979), Brachman et al. (1978); it also takes into account the versions given in Porta & Vinchesi (1982) and Cappelli & Moretti (1983b). As in KL-ONE, KL-Magma formal objects are Concepts, Roles and Structural Descriptions (see Figure 2).

Concepts are descriptional structures providing an intensional representation of the domain to be modelled. Concepts are divided into Generic, for prototypes, and Individual, for individuals.

Roles are descriptional structures representing parts of Concepts, i.e. properties of prototypes and individuals.

Structural Descriptions are sets of relationships between Roles which give a wholistic structure to Concepts.

Objects are connected with one another via Cables and Wires, thus realizing Structured Inheritance.

KL-Magma is a language isomorphic to SI-Nets formal objects, since it contains functions for creating and manipulating single objects within the network. The problem then arises to establish a correspondence between the objects and the operations of an SI-Net and those used by natural language.

For this purpose, a new language, KL-Conc, has been designed which manipulates the LTM (Cappelli, Moretti & Vinchesi, 1983; Cappelli & Moretti, 1983a). The functions of this language try to simulate the conceptual operations underlying the communicative use of natural language realizing, in this sense, the interpretative aspect of many linguistic elements such as articles, adjectives, PPs, relative clauses etc. In other words, we have reduced the conceptual aspect of many linguistic units to a set of functions of a KL, which can be manipulated by the processor. So, in the processor there exist a set of

A. Cappelli et al.

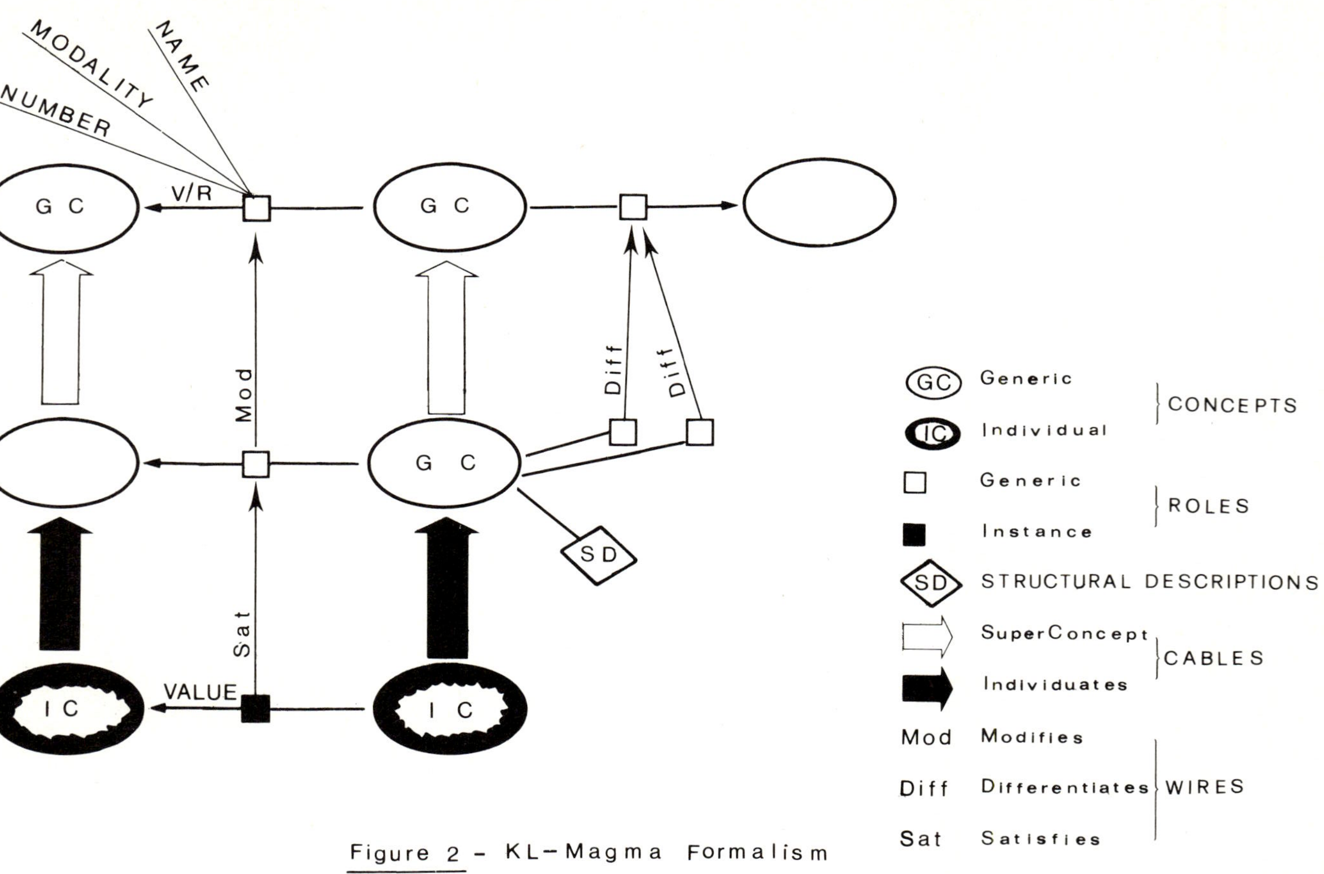

Figure 2 – KL–Magma Formalism

functions directly affecting the knowledge stored in the LTM. The consequence
is that within the processor it is possible to handle, at the same time,
different classes of symbolic systems.

7.2 Knowledge manipulating functions

The most relevant functions of KL-Conc are described hereafter. Their semantics
is given in terms of operations on SI-Nets.

As far as generic knowledge is concerned, the function:

$$< GEN\ arbitrary\_name >$$

returns the generic concept named by arbitrary_name. If the concept does not
exist in the LTM a new generic concept is created. The new concept is then
returned. This function works both as a predicate and as a creating function.
The function

$$< NEWIND\ arbitrary\_name >$$

creates a new individual concept and establishes it as an individuator of the
generic concept named by arbitrary_name; if the generic concept does not exist
in the LTM it is created.

The function

$$< JUSTONE\ arbitrary\_name >$$

verifies whether there exists a unique individual either named by arbitrary_name
or returned by tests or combinations of tests expressed in KL-Conc syntax. It is
used to verify if the object is unique as to its name, or as to one of its
properties etc.

This function has a complex behaviour, since, intuitively, it must verify the
uniqueness of an object and must return: i) the individual if unique; ii) the
list of individuals if more than one satisfies the conditions given by the
assertions; iii) NIL if no individual exists satisfying the conditions. The
three answers have different meanings, since they imply different operations to
be triggered on the memory spaces or, at any rate, they have different effects
on the behaviour of functions where JUSTONE can be nested.

The function:

$$< TEST\_CONFIGURATION\_OF\_PROPERTIES\ arbitrary\_name1\ arbitrary\_name2 >$$

verifies whether arbitrary_name2 exists in the horizontal chain of roles
starting from arbitrary_name1 (see Figure 3). It returns the chain itself;
otherwise it returns NIL.

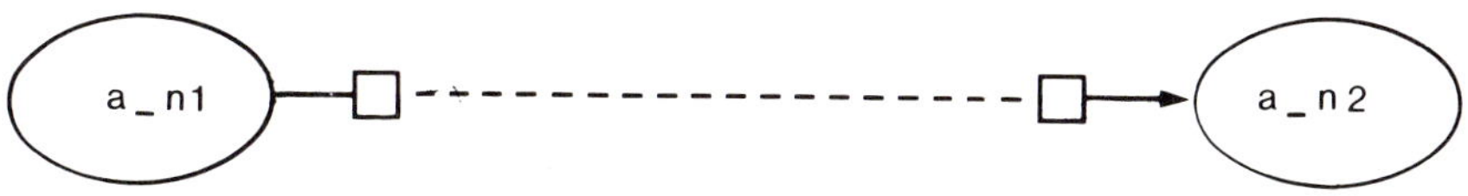

Figure 3 - Network structures manipulated by T_C_of_P function

The function:

```
<ADD_CONFIGURATION_OF_PROPERTIES arbitrary_name1 arbitrary_name2 >
```

adds a role to a concept. The distinction between generic and instance roles need not be explicitly stated in the function. Taking natural language as the reference point, the distinction between prototypes and individuals is peculiar only to certain linguistic elements; in the case of operations on properties, no distinction is made; the conceptual operations governing the operations on properties control the correct application of the adding or testing properties. Consequently, the function ADD_CONFIGURATION_OF_PROPERTIES is designed in order to make it possible to trigger the correct procedures depending on the type of objects which it is applied to.

When applied to individual concepts, this creates a new instance role establishing it as a satisfier of a higher generic role of the generic concept ancestor of the individual concept. If a possible generic role does not exist it is created without inserting any restriction on the potential value of the generic role, since it could be a more general concept than the generic concept ancestor of the value of the newly created instance role. The structures created by this function are shown in Figure 4 by dotted lines.

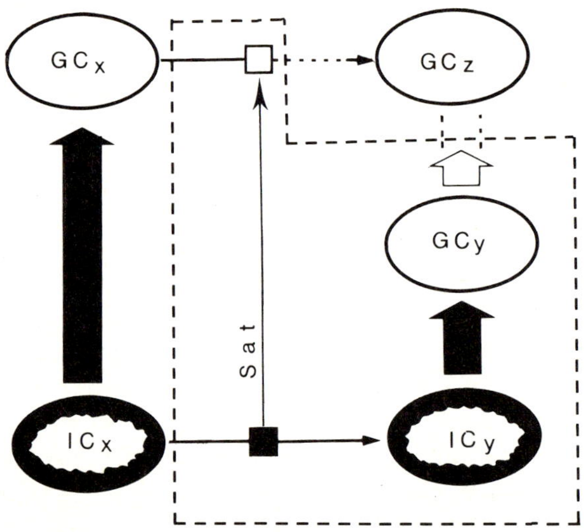

Figure 4 - Network structures created by A_C_of_P function

When applied to generic concepts, the function adds a new generic role, trying to link it with a higher generic role. If no generic role is found, a higher generic role is created without providing it with any information other than the one inferred from the structure of the newly created subrole.

KL-Conc is a compact way of handling SI-Nets since it manipulates coherent pieces of network instead of single syntactic objects such as, for instance, single roles or role values. Thus, the complex structures that each KL-Conc function manipulates are closer to the ones used by natural language. In fact, performing a single operation in natural language means contemporaneously testing, creating, and modifying global pieces of knowledge instead of affecting single atomic objects.

8. THE HYPOTHESIS OF INTEGRATION

We have already stated (see above 7.1) that KL-Conc functions try to simulate conceptual operations underlying the communicative use of natural language. KL-Conc functions enable the user to individuate or to create objects, to test properties of objects etc. represented in a data base of knowledge (LTM). These conceptual operations are assumed to be analogous to those used by human beings to communicate facts in a given situation. In a model of comprehension they act as the basic cognitive operations by which a message in natural language is understood.

These functions are integrated into a processor of the type described above (see 6.) as cognitive generalized actions for storing and manipulating fragments of structured knowledge. In this way the processing is also charged with part of the interpretation and manipulation of the representation of the world, in terms of the storing and retrieving of the information which is necessary for the completion of the analysis.

The actions of knowledge manipulation are distributed along the analysis path and are triggered as soon as cognitively relevant linguistic units occur, without waiting for syntactic structures to be completed. Thus, for instance, the appearance of an adjective can often activate an adding or testing of properties independently of the completion of the constituent in which it appears. The processor acts as a control structure which establishes the sequence of cognitive operations in accordance with the surface distribution of linguistic units and of purely syntactic facts such as the opening, closing, and embedding of constituents.

This model would appear to be intuitively analogous to the human process of understanding.

The following sentences may now be considered:

(18a) Il bambino rosso
      the child red   (= the red-haired child)
(18b) Il bambino che e' rosso
      the child who is red (= red-haired)
(18c) Il bambino con i capelli rossi
      the child with the hair red
(18d) Il bambino con i capelli di colore rosso
      the child with the hair of colour red

All of them correspond to the knowledge structure shown in Figure 5.

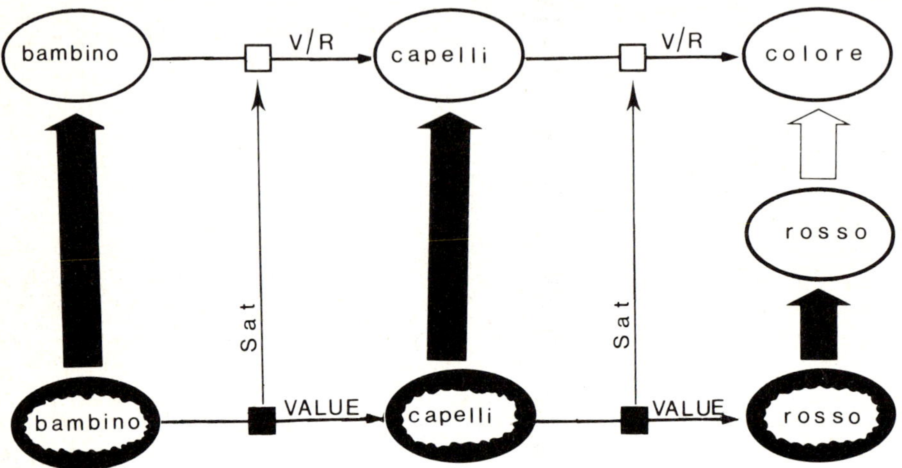

Figure 5 - The knowledge structure for sentences 18a-d

They assert a configuration of properties of a specific child; each sentence uses different surface structures thus specifying different details of this conceptual structure.

The indication of the operations for the building or handling of such knowledge structures as those in Figure 5 is mostly entrusted to specific lexical items occurring in the string.

The article identifies the status of a knowledge object X. In particular 'il' may activate both the function (GENERIC X) when referring to an abstract prototype, as in the sentence:

(19) Il tavolo e' un mobile
     The table is a piece of furniture

and the function (JUSTONE X) when referring to an individual object, as in the sentences 18a-d.

This distinction between generic and individual knowledge is completely covered by the structure of SI-Nets formalism. This creates a new type of ambiguity in the analysis of sentences whose solution depends on the checking of complex parsing situations. A complex parsing situation consists of the syntactic literal context of the processor and the specific knowledge structure of the objects involved in the process. It can be suitably represented by the CGH.

The processor should, therefore, have a mechanism for storing possible conceptual functions and explicit strategies for selecting the appropriate functions on the basis of the evaluation of complex parsing situations.

In this view KL-Conc functions are triggered in the presence of given conditions arising from complex situations in the memory of the processor. For example, in

Italian an adjective can trigger an operation on properties of some concept if
it morphologically agrees with the noun which identifies that concept.   The
specific operation is then determined by the type of operation previously
initiated. Thus, if a function for creating a new object has been instantiated,
no test for existing properties can be activated, but the mentioned adjective
will be intended as adding a property. In this way every operation activation
follows some sort of local plan, to be added to the complex parsing situation.

Let us now analyze the sentences 18a-d in detail in order to clarify their
structure from a conceptual viewpoint and to describe some tools of the
processor which make it possible to access and to handle such structures.
Sentence 18a expresses only a part of the conceptual structure of Figure 5.
This is more exactly shown in Figure 6.

Figure 6 - The knowledge structure of sentence 18a

The dotted line between 'bambino' and 'rosso' shows that a part of the
conceptual structure has been omitted in the surface string, since the use of
the adjective generally hides part of a reasoning process, whose complete
structure is represented in Figure 5.   SI-Nets formalism makes it possible to
represent declaratively the fact that the noun-adjective pair indicates two
extreme points of a complex conceptual representation. It is therefore possible
to design appropriate functions which manipulate these representations. In
particular these cases are treated by the two KL-Conc functions:

ADD_CONFIGURATION_OF_PROPERTIES

TEST_CONFIGURATION_OF_PROPERTIES

which, respectively, add properties to an object, marking or reconstructing the
appropriate structure, or test properties of objects starting from two points of
a chain.

Also sentence 18b, containing a relative clause, covers a part of the network of
Figure 5 and can be analysed by an analogous sequence of functions. The division
of relative clauses into explicative and restrictive is conveniently expressed
in terms of ADD_ and TEST_ C_of_P respectively. The syntactic processing of the
relative pronoun specifies the parameters of the KL-Conc functions in that it
solves the ambiguity between subject and object of the relative clause.

Prepositional phrases show a sort of analogy with adjectives. They indicate
intermediate points of the chain identified by the noun-adjective couple. Like
the adjective, they can be conceptually described by the two KL-Conc functions
ADD_CONFIGURATION_OF_PROPERTIES and TEST_CONFIGURATION_OF_PROPERTIES. Sentences
18c and 18d specify, by surface means, intermediate parts of the conceptual
structure shown in Figure 5. For instance 18c can be translated into a sequence
of KL-Conc functions, each of which operates on a domain defined by the previous
one:

(JUSTONE bambino) (T_C_of_P capelli) (T_C_of_P rosso))

9.CONCLUSIONS

In the previous paragraph a very naif model has been sketched in which some actions are activated by lexical items in their syntactic (distributional) positions and selected on the basis of conditions imposed by the global analysis situation. These actions operate directly on knowledge, building and manipulating knowledge structures.

The direct mapping from strings on to knowledge in a frame in which top-down syntactic parsing is used to predict the assembling of typically bottom-up interpreting functions turns out to be the more suitable and psychologically more likely model of understanding.

However the domain on which such a model can operate is obviously restricted to descriptions and assertions, which can be encoded into a knowledge structure in a direct way. Comprehension of other types of texts, such as for instance stories or dialogues, requires a more complex frame within which also the model of the communicative situation is to be represented.

Also some technical aspects of processing have not been touched and require deeper investigation. In particular it is still unclear how the knowledge manipulating functions, which are strongly connected with the meaning of lexical items, are embedded in complex parsing processes with many embedded levels of recursion.

Finally, the relationship between parsing non-determinism, ambiguity of competing knowledge structures for a given input and the selective power of complex analysis situations must still be experimentally investigated.

REFERENCES

Asirelli, P., Lami, C., Montangero, C., Pacini, G., Simi, M., & Turini, F., MAGMA-Lisp Reference Manual (N.T. C75-13). Pisa: IEI-CNR, 1975.

Berwick, R.C., & Weinberg, A.S., Syntactic Constraints and Efficient Parsability. In Proceedings of the 21st Annual Meeting of the Association for Computational Linguistics. Menlo Park, CA., 1980.

Bever, T.G., The Cognitive Basis for Linguistic Structures. In J.R. Hayes (Ed.), Cognition and the Development of Language. New York, 1970.

Bobrow, R.J., The RUS System. (BBN Report 3878), Cambridge, Mass.: Bolt, Beranek and Newman, Inc., 1978.

Bobrow, R.J., & Webber, B.L., PSI-KLONE: Parsing and Semantic Interpretation in the BBN Natural Language Understanding System. In Proceedings of the CSCSI/CSEIO Annual Conference, 1980.

Bobrow, R.J., & Webber, B.L., Knowledge Representation for Syntactic/Semantic Processing. In Proceedings of the First Annual National Conference on Artificial Intelligence. Los Altos, Ca.: Kaufmann, 1980.

Brachman, R.J., Ciccarelli, E., Greenfeld, N., & Yonke, M., KLONE Reference Manual. (BBN Report 3848). Cambridge, Mass.: Bolt, Beranek and Newmann Inc., 1978.

Brachman, R.J., On the Epistemological Status of Semantic Networks. In N. Findler, (Ed.), Associative Networks: Representation and Use of Knowledge by Computers. New York: Academic Press, 1979.

Burton, R.R., Semantic Grammar: An Engineering Technique for Constructing Natural Language Understanding Systems. (BBN Report 3453). Cambridge, Mass.: Bolt, Beranek and Newman, Inc., 1976.

Cappelli, A., Ferrari, G., Moretti, L., Prodanof, I., & Stock, O., Automatic Analysis of Italian. In Proceedings of the AISB80. Amsterdam, 1980.

Cappelli, A., Ferrari, G., Moretti, L., Prodanof, I., & Stock, O., Il Trattamento di Alcuni Fenomeni Anaforici Mediante un ATN. In Atti del Seminario Sull'Anafora. Firenze, 1981.

Cappelli, A., Ferrari, G., Moretti, L., & Prodanof, I., Towards an Integrated Model of Sentence Comprehension. In A. Cappelli (Ed.), Research in Natural Language Processing in Italy. Pisa: Giardini, 1981.

Cappelli, A., Ferrari, G., Moretti, L., Prodanof, I., & Stock, O., Costruzione, Sperimentazione ed Estensione di un ATN come Modello di Analisi del Linguaggio Naturale. Ricerche di Psicologia, 1983, 25, 159-184.

Cappelli, A., & Moretti, L., An Approach to Natural Language in the SI-Nets Paradigm. In Proceedings of the First Conference of The European Chapter of the Association for Computational Linguistics. Menlo Park, Ca., 1983a.

Cappelli, A., & Moretti, L., Aspetti della Rappresentazione della Conoscenza in Linguistica Computazionale. Pisa: Pacini, 1983b.

Cappelli, A., Moretti, L., & Vinchesi, C., KL-CONC: A Language for Interacting with SI-Nets. In Proceedings of the Eighth International Joint Conference on Artificial Intelligence. Los Altos, Ca.: Kaufmann, 1983.

Chomsky, N., ON Wh-movement. In P. Culicover, T. Wasow & A. Akmajan (Eds.), Formal Syntax. New York: Academic Press, 1977.

Comino, R., Gemello, R., Guida, G., Rullent, C., Sisto, L., & Somalvico, M., Understanding Natural Language through Parallel Processing of Syntactic and Semantic Knowledge: an Application to Data Base Query. In Proceedings of the Eighth International Joint Conference on Artificial Intelligence. Los Altos, Ca.: Kaufmann, 1983.

Gazdar, G., Phrase Structure Grammar. In P. Jacobson & G. Pullum (Eds.), The Nature of Syntactic Representation. Dordrecht: D. Reidel, 1982.

Hendrix, G.G., Encoding Knowledge in Partitioned Networks. (TN 164). Menlo Park, CA.: SRI, 1978.

Hendrix, G.G., Sacerdoti, E.D., Sagalowicz, D., & Slocum, J., Developing a Natural Language Interface to Complex Data. ACM Transaction on Data Base Systems, 1978, 3, 105-147.

Jackendoff, R., X Syntax: a Study of Phrase Structure. Cambridge, Mass.: MIT Press, 1977.

Kaplan, R.M., Augmented Transition Networks as Psychological Models of Sentence Comprehension, Artificial Intelligence, 1972, 3, 77-100.

Kaplan, R.M., Computational Resources and Linguistic Theory. In TINLAP-2. University of Illinois, 1978.

Kaplan, R.M., & Bresnan, J., Lexical Functional Grammar: a Formal System for Grammatical Representation. In J. Bresnan, (Ed.), The Mental Representation of Grammatical Relations. Cambridge, Mass.: MIT Press, 1981.

Kay, M., Functional Grammar. In Proceedings of the fifth annual meeting of the Berkeley Linguistics Society. Berkeley, 1979.

Kwasny, S.C., & Sondheimer, N.K., Relaxation Techniques for Parsing Grammatical Ill-formed Input in Natural Language Understanding Systems. American Journal of Computational Linguistics, 1981, 7, 99-108.

Lehnert, W.G., The Process of Question Answering. Hillsdale, New Jersey: Lawrence Erlbaum, 1978.

Lesmo, L., & Torasso, P., A Flexible Natural Language Parser Based on Two-Level Representation of Syntax. In Proceedings of the First Conference of The European Chapter of the Association for Computational Linguistics. Menlo Park, CA., 1983.

Marcus, M.P., A Theory of Syntactic Recognition for Natural Language. Cambridge, Mass.: MIT Press, 1980.

Montague, R., The Proper Treatment of Quantification in Ordinary English. In R.H. Thomason, Formal Philosophy. New Haven: Yale University Press, 1974.

Montangero, C., Pacini, G., & Turini, F., ND-LISP Reference Manual. (T.N. C76-3). Pisa: IEI-CNR, 1976.

Petrick, S.R., Transformational Analysis. (IBM RC 3870). Yorktown Heights, New York: IBM Research Center, 1972.

Plath, W.J., REQUEST: A Natural Language Question Answering System. IBM Journal of Research and Development, 1976, 4.

Porta, O., & Vinchesi, C., Un Sistema per la Rappresentazione della Conoscenza: Aspetti Concettuali e di Implementazione. Unpublished Thesis, Pisa: Istituto di Scienze dell'Informazione, 1981.

Reddy, R.D., Erman, L.D., Fennel, R.D., & Neely, R.B., The Hearsay Speech System: An Example of the Recognition Process. In Proceedings of the 3rd International Joint Conference on Artificial Intelligence. Los Altos, Ca.: Kaufmann, 1973.

Reddy, R.D., & CMU Speech Group, Speech understanding system: Summary of results of the five-year research effort at CMU. (Technical Report). Pittsburg, Penns.: Carnegie-Mellon University, 1977.

Riesbeck, C.K., & Schank, R.C., Comprehension by Computer: Expectation-based Analysis of Sentence in Context. (Research Report 78). New Haven: Yale University, 1976.

Robinson, J.J., Performance Grammars. In R. Reddy, (Ed.), Speech Recognition. New York: Academic Press, 1975.

Robinson, J.J., DIAGRAM: a Grammar for Dialogues. (TN 205). Menlo Park, Ca.: SRI, 1980.

Schank, R.C., Conceptual dependency: a Theory of Natural Language Understanding. Cognitive Psychology, 1972, 3, 552-631.

Schank, R.C., & Abelson, R.P., Scripts, Plans, Goals and Understanding. Hillsdale, N.Y.: Lawrence Erlbaum, 1977.

Waltz, D.L., Finin, T., Green, F., Conrad, F., Goodman, B. & Hadden, G., The PLANES System: Natural Language Access to a Large Data Base. (Report T-34). Urbana: University of Illinois, 1976.

Winograd, T., Procedures as a Representation for Data in a Computer Program for Understanding Natural Language.(T.N. AI TR-1). Cambridge, Mas.: MIT, 1970.

Winograd, T., Language as a Cognitive Process - Syntax. Readings, Mass.: Addison-Wesley Publishing Company, 1983.

Woods, W.A., Kaplan, R.M., & Nash-Webber, B., The Lunar Sciences Natural Language Information System. (Final Report 2378). Cambridge, Mas.: Bolt, Beranek and Newman Inc., 1972.

Woods, W.A., An Experimental Parsing System for Transition Network Grammars. In R. Rustin, (Ed.), Natural Language Processing. New York: Algorithmic Press, 1973.

Woods, W.A., Semantics and Quantification in Natural Language Question Answering. In M.C. Yovits, (Ed.), Advances in Computers. New York: Academic Press, 1978.

Woods, W.A., Cascaded ATN Grammars. American Journal of Computational Linguistics, 1980, 6, 1-12.

Computational Models of Natural Language Processing
B.G. Bara and G. Guida (eds.)
© Elsevier Science Publishers B.V. (North-Holland), 1984

KNOWLEDGE REPRESENTATION AND NATURAL LANGUAGE:
EXTENDING THE EXPRESSIVE POWER OF PROPOSITION NODES

Cristiano Castelfranchi, Domenico Parisi, Oliviero Stock

Reparto Processi Cognitivi e Intelligenza Artificiale
Istituto di Psicologia, C.N.R.
Roma, Italy

A knowledge representation scheme for natural language
processing is described which focusses on proposition
nodes and their role in a number of representation tasks.
Proposition nodes are distinguished from predicate nodes.
They play a role in representing linguistic structures
and the status of propositions in the mind. Propositional
nodes can also be made of parts and such complex propositional nodes can be used to represent various aspects of
semantic memory and beliefs about other minds' beliefs.

1. INTRODUCTION

The aim of this paper is to demonstrate the great expressive power that
"proposition nodes", if appropriately used, can have for knowledge representation
and natural language understanding. It is not our intention to describe a detailed
formalism for knowledge representation but only to illustrate a line of research
that eventually should produce a good formalism. Therefore, questions of
correctness of the representation scheme as a whole (and of completeness,
soundness, consistency, etc.) will be left aside and the emphasis will be on how
to take into account linguistic and psychological evidence within a basic semantic
network formalism.

The present work focusses on the problem of proposition nodes in semantic networks
but it is part of a more general project aimed at defining a knowledge
representation for natural language processing. We are not interested in knowledge
representation systems that are based on a priori philosophical or epistemological
considerations, or adopt formal logical solutions which appear to us to be
artifactual even if efficient. We want to develop a system for representing
knowledge which is justified by linguistic facts, i.e. a system that can represent
in a subtle and detailed way the meanings of words, sentences, and texts and can
be operated upon by the procedures which are necessary for language comprehension
and production, inference, question answering, and conversation. We believe that
such a representation can have a usefulness beyond natural language processing;
for example, it could be of interest for a knowledge base that must interface
with natural language.

In the paper we take Schubert (1976) as our main reference for two reasons. First,
this is one of the most important works specifically dedicated to proposition
nodes. What we propose is a number of developments and changes with respect to
Schubert's treatment. Secondly, aside from Schubert's use of logical quantifiers,

his approach is one of the most congenial to the knowledge representation scheme that we have in mind for representing the meanings of sentences and texts. (For a representation of some natural language quantifiers, see Castelfranchi and Parisi, 1981). Another approach which is very consonant to ours is Shapiro's (1979), but he is not specifically interested in complex proposition nodes, which is the theme of the present paper.

According to Schubert (1976), in the tradition of semantic networks "propositions consist of subgraphs with links to a predicative concept and to a suitable number of conceptual arguments for the predicate. Explicit proposition nodes are sometimes introduced as points of attachment for these links, and as units on which proposition operators (e.g. "know that") can operate. Arguments of n-ary predicates may be distinguished by the use of link labels, distinct linkage types, or binary decomposition of predicates".

Schubert himself proposes that in addition to (a) individual nodes, (b) nodes representing sets of individuals, and (c) universal or predicate nodes, a semantic network should include proposition nodes: "The smallest unit of information in a semantic net is the atomic proposition. An atomic proposition consists of a proposition node, a PRED link to a predicative node, and links to a suitable number of concept nodes serving as arguments of the predicate. The argument links are marked in some systematic way, e.g. A, B, etc., to distinguish the first, second, etc., arguments" (Schubert, 1976). We would propose exactly the same distinctions among types of nodes with two exceptions: we would introduce an additional node type for mass nouns, and we would keep universal nodes (classes) and predicate nodes distinct. Our purpose here, however, is to show the necessity and usefulness of proposition nodes. What we will do is to examine the main problems of knowledge representation that can be solved by an appropriate use of this type of nodes.

2. PROPOSITION NODES AS ARGUMENTS

The generic node in a network, which we denote with "N", can be specified as being (i) a node that is linked only by argument links (we denote this as an X node), or (ii) a proposition node, i.e. a node from which one (and only one) predicate link is originated along with the argument links as required by the predicate (we denote such nodes as C nodes).

We use the symbol C (for "cognitive unit") in that the expression "proposition" - which however we keep on using in order to establish a continuity with Schubert (1976) - can be too easily incorrectly linked to linguistic form (see, for example, Kintsch's representation scheme (Kintsch, 1974)). A cognitive unit is a mental object which can have a role in very different contexts: representing the meanings of language units, representing knowledge, representing goals, etc.

Of course, any N node including C nodes can be an argument of a predicate. For example in (1)

(1)

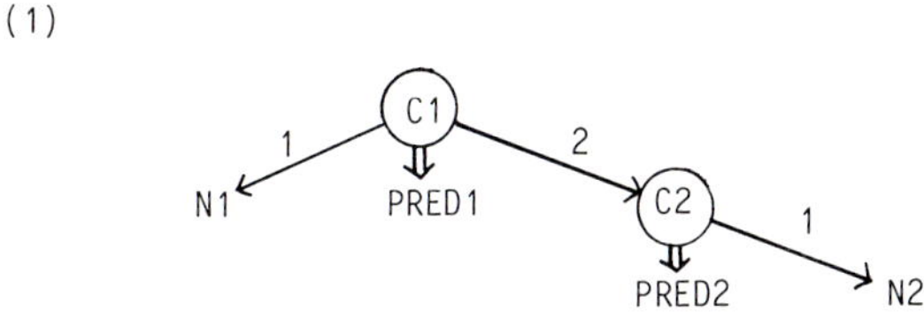

the proposition node C2 is an argument of PRED1, while N1 and N2 are not specified
as being X or C nodes. Predicates may accept both X and C nodes (e.g. NICE, IN),
only C nodes (e.g. NOT, SUPPOSE, TOMORROW), or only X nodes (e.g. GREEN, KISS).

As (1) shows, there are two (and only two) types of arrows. The double arrow
points from a proposition node to its predicate. The single arrow points from a
proposition node to the predicate's argument(s). Single arrows are numbered as
the various arguments of a predicate play different semantic roles.

Predicate nodes are considered as entities lying on a different plane than the
network plane. They constitute a conceptual vocabulary which is used in building
up the network. It is important to note that one and the same predicate can be
considered as a whole in some operations and as something decomposed in smaller
predicates in other operations. From this it follows that: (i) there is no
absolute set of "semantic primitives" but only a conceptual vocabulary which is
appropriate for the current level of operations; (ii) there are two connections
between the network plane and the predicate plane, one connecting each proposition
node to its predicate and the other connecting the predicate to a more detailed
"networked" expressions of the predicate.

Returning to X and C nodes one should not confuse this distinction with the
linguistic distinction between nouns and verbs. In intuitive terms our distinction
could be described as a distinction between "things" and "facts". But we will have
the opportunity to discuss the differences between the two types of nodes later
in the paper. What we want to do in the following sections is to show the
usefulness of proposition nodes as arguments in knowledge representation, with
special reference to knowledge that is acquired or expressed through language.

2.1 <u>Subordination</u>

Proposition nodes are necessary to represent the meaning of syntactically
recursive sentences. E.g. sentence (2)

(2) The child says that he leaves tomorrow

with "child" as antecedent of the pronoun "he", is represented as in (3)

(3)

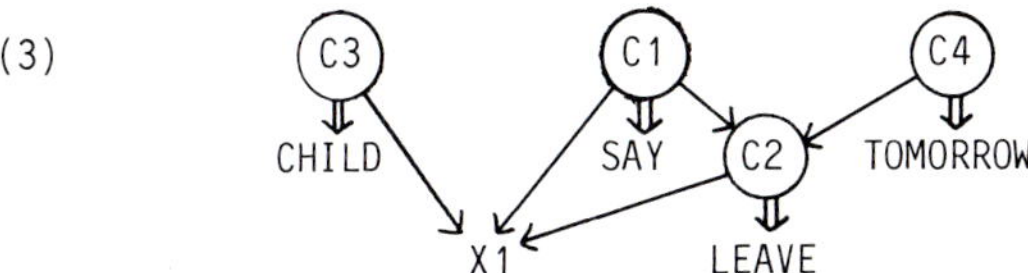

Similarly, sentence (4)

(4) When the child sings he is happy

is represented as in (5)

(5)
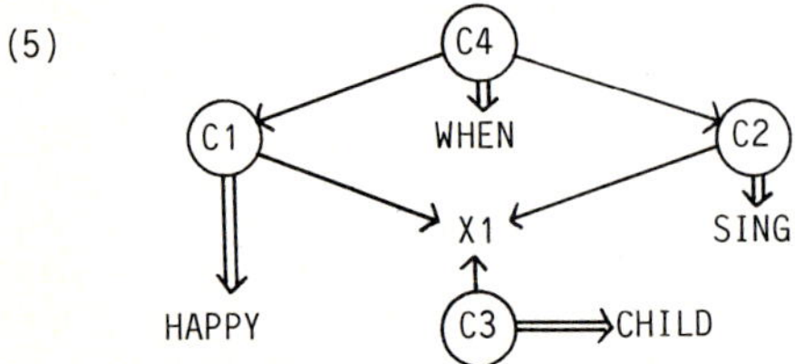

2.2 Adverbials

Proposition nodes as arguments are also necessary to represent adverbials as predicates which modify the sentence's nucleus (the verb with its arguments) (see Parisi and Antinucci, 1976). This has already been shown with sentences (2) and (4) which incorporate two adverbials: "to-morrow" and "when he is happy", respectively.

2.3 Pronominalization

If proposition nodes in addition to "thing"-nodes are available, one can deal in an identical manner (i.e. with a search of a specific node in the memory of the preceding discourse) with the two readings of the pronoun "it". Consider for example the ambiguity of (6)

(6) Bill has killed a dog. Mary saw it.

where Mary may have seen the animal (reading (a)) or the event (reading (b)). We represent reading (a) as (7)

(7)
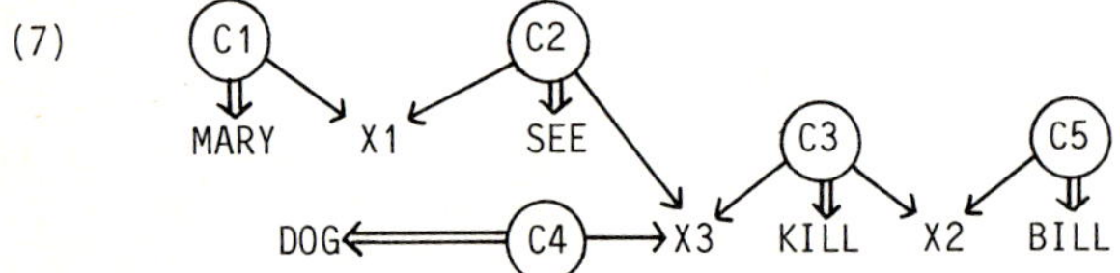

and reading (b) as (8)

(8)
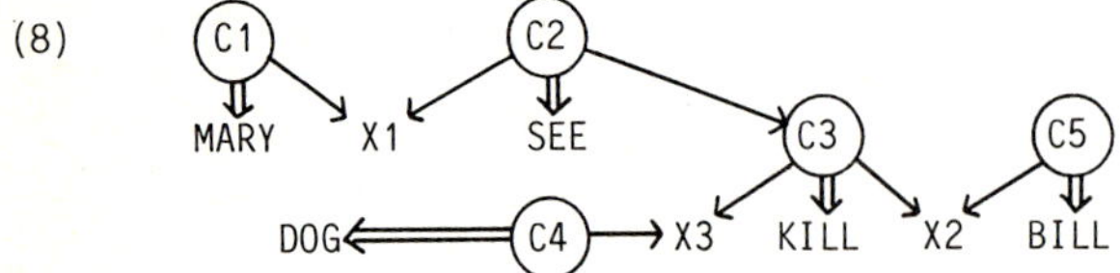

Representation (8) explains why sentence (6) can be a paraphrase of sentence (9)

(9) Mary saw that Bill killed a dog.

2.4 <u>Lexical decomposition</u>

Proposition nodes are necessary for decomposing the meaning of a word in smaller
units that may recur as part of the meaning of other words. Lexical decomposition
is necessary to give an account of implications and paraphrase relations.

We do not only want to decompose (10) into (11)

(10)

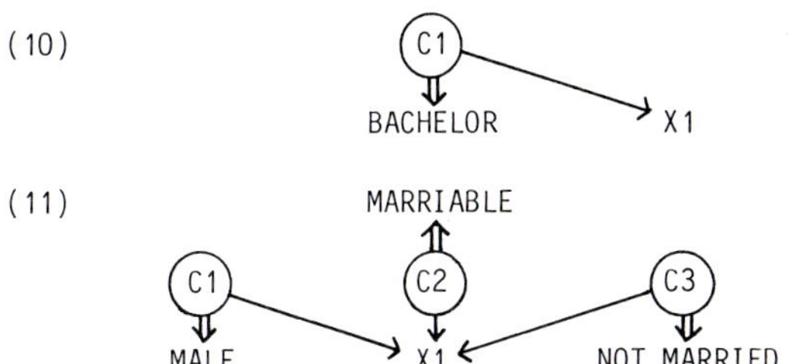

(11)

where we only have a multiplication of properties (propositions) linked together
by their pointing to a single node (X1). We also want to decompose (12) into (13)

(12)

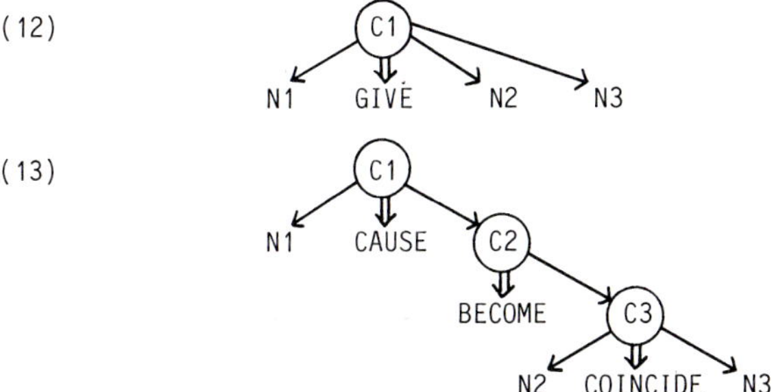

(13)

Among the many advantages of lexical decomposition we will only cite one specific
fact which will make clear the nature of proposition nodes of all C nodes of the
decomposed structure. Consider the difference between the two sentences (14) and
(15)

(14) Bill is cooking the eggs in the kitchen.

(15) Bill is cooking the eggs in the pan.

The verb "to cook" can be decomposed into two proposition nodes with predicates
CAUSE and COOK, respectively. In sentence (14) the adverbial "in the kitchen" is
on the higher node since it qualifies the whole event, whereas in sentence (15)
the adverbial "in the pan" is on the lower node since it only qualifies where the
eggs are cooking. This is shown in (16) (with simplifications):

(16)

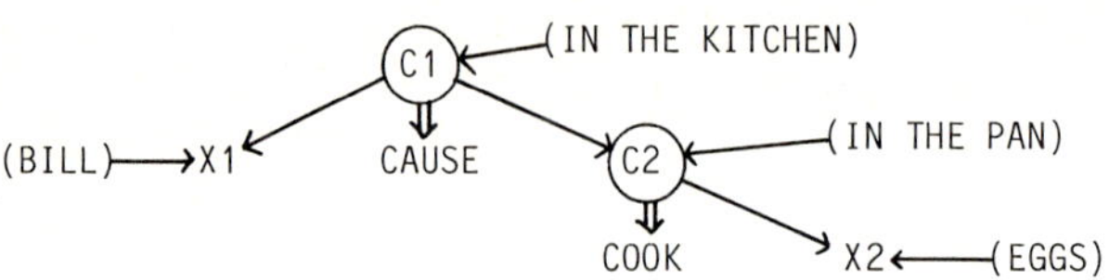

(We will sometimes write

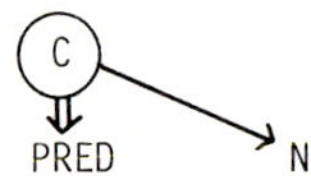

as

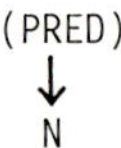

$$(\text{PRED}) \downarrow N$$

to make our representations simpler.)

3. THE STATUS OF PROPOSITIONS IN THE MIND

3.1 Propositions vs. knowledge

As Schubert (1976) has observed, "usually all propositions in the net are assumed to be asserted". This implies a confusion between propositions and knowledge. We believe, by contrast, that a proposition - which is only the content of a possible knowledge - should be clearly distinguished from its status in the mind. Consider the three sentence (17)-(19)

(17) Bill left.
(18) Mary says that Bill left
(19) If Bill left we can also go

If we should examine the knowledge represented in the mind of someone who has produced these three sentences (or of someone who has heard and believed the three sentences), we would find that in all the three corresponding representations there occurs a proposition "X1 LEAVE", where X1 is Bill. However, in the representation for sentence (17) this proposition node must represent something known by the speaker, while in the representations for sentences (18) and (19) it must not represent a knowledge of the speaker but something which is known by another person (Mary) (sentence (18)) or it is only an hypothesis (sentence (19)). As a matter of fact, if we ask the author or the addressee of sentence (17) if Bill actually left, he is entitled to answer Yes, while this would not be the case for sentences (18) and (19).

We conclude that it is necessary to represent the difference in the status of the proposition "X1 LEAVE" for sentence (17) as contrasted with sentences (18) and (19). Propositions can have a variety of statuses in the mind, related not only to what is known and what is not known but also to fictions, stories, hypotheses, dreams, goals, fears, etc. (Castelfranchi, 1977). However, we will limit ourself here to representing the difference between propositions and knowledge.

The availability of proposition nodes offers a basis for finding a solution to this problem. We could introduce either "propositional operators", like Schubert's "V" (= true) and "⎯¬" (= not), or specific predicates which take propositional nodes as their arguments and make them something which is known or negated (or wanted, hypothesized, dreamt of, feared, etc.). Let us examine these two alternatives.

3.2 The predicate NOT

We are not satisfied with Schubert's use of operators V and ⎯¬ and more particularly with his not making explicit the relationship between them. Schubert uses the operator ⎯¬ both to represent an asserted negation (a negative knowledge: I know that something is not true) and to represent the opposite of a proposition. This is shown in (20)

(20)   (a)   "John believes that Mary is happy"
               John⎯⎯ believes⎯⎯→ happy ⎯⎯ Mary

        (b)   "John believes that Mary is happy and she is"
               John⎯⎯ believes⎯⎯→ happy ⎯⎯ Mary
                                    ↑
                                    ¦
                                    ¦
                                    V

        (c)   "John believes that Mary is happy and she isn't"
               John⎯⎯ believes⎯⎯→happy⎯⎯ Mary
                                    ↑
                                    ¦
                                    ¦
                                   ⎯¬

        (d)   "John believes that Mary isn't happy but she is"
               John⎯⎯ believes→ ⎯¬ →happy ⎯⎯⎯⎯ Mary
                                     ↑
                                     ¦
                                     ¦
                                     ¦
                                     V

According to this usage, V always represents the truth (i.e. what is believed by the reference mind. For the concept of a reference mind, see below.). On the other hand ⎯¬ represents falsehood (i.e. what is not believed to be true by the reference mind) if it is not the object of other predicates, while it only represents the opposite proposition if it is the object of other predicates. We might ask why "John believes that Mary is happy" is not represented as (21)

(21) John⎯⎯ believes→ V ⎯⎯→happy⎯⎯ Mary

In fact it seems to us that Schubert is using ⎯¬ as two different things: sometimes as a simple predicate and sometimes as an operator which is the opposite of the operator V. We think that a cleaner solution would be to analyze Schubert's operator in terms of the operator V on a one-argument predicate NOT accepting only C arguments.

That a word like "not" does not always translate into something which is not true (i.e. which is not believed by the reference mind) is clear enough. If I say (22)

(22) Bill believes that Mary is not happy

this does not imply that "Mary is not happy". Therefore, if we introduce the predicate NOT to represent the meaning of sentence (22), i.e. (23)

(23)

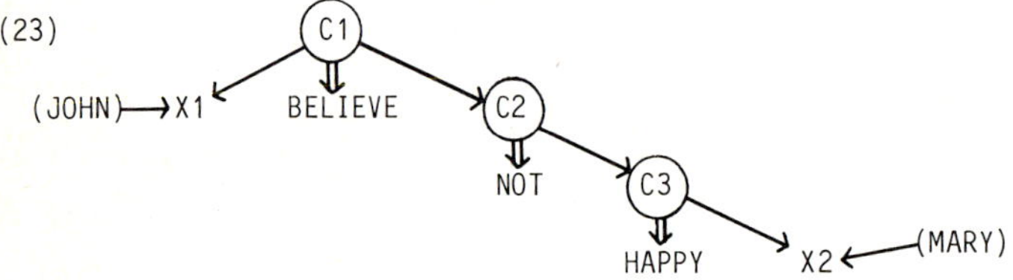

its assertion will be equivalent to applying the operator ¬ to the embedded proposition node, i.e. (24) is equivalent to (25)

(24)

(25)

Structures (24) and (25) represent the same thing; however, (25) has the advantage of using operators uniformly. Moreover, solution (25) can use a single rule "NOT(NOT)⟹NULL" to explain why (26) is at some level of analysis equivalent to (27)

(26) Bill believes that Mary is not fasting
(27) Bill believes that Mary is eating

and (28) is equivalent to (29)

(28) Mary is not fasting
(29) Mary is eating

The representations for (26) and (27) are, respectively, (30) and (31)

(30)

(31)

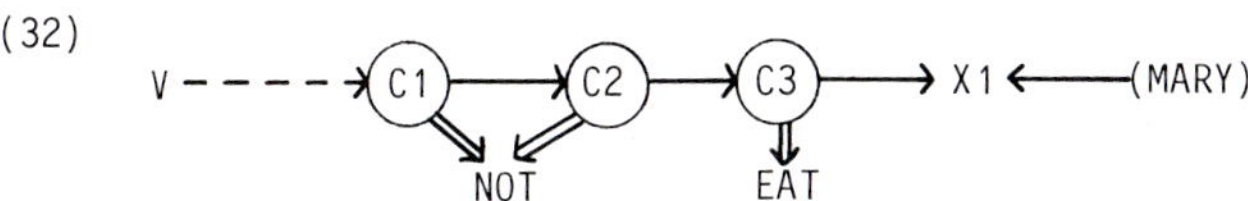

The representations for (28) and (29) are, respectively, (32) and (33)

(32)

(33)

3.3 The predicate ASSUME and the Subject

However, we believe that even Schubert's operator V can be dispensed with and be replaced by a two-argument predicate ASSUME (X, C). In this way we can have a more uniform representation scheme using only predicates and no operators.

In a knowledge representation system it should be possible to represent the knowledge that someone else has, i.e. what is believed by other people. To this purpose we can use the predicate ASSUME as an abstract meaning element shared by verbs like "know", "believe", "suppose", "think", etc. For example, a sentence like (34)

(34) Bill believes that Mary left

would be represented as (35)

(35)

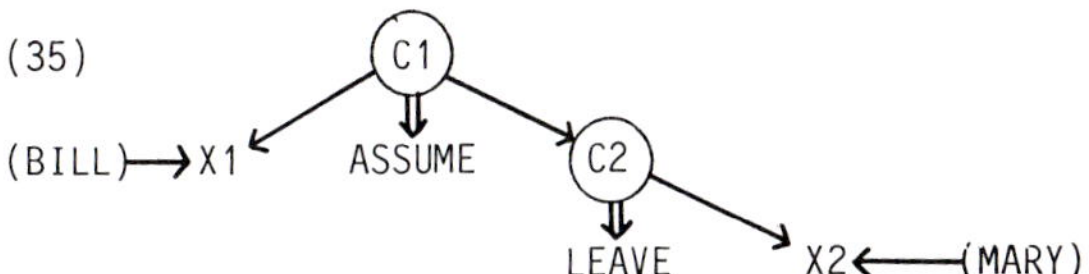

Let us call "Subject" the mind whose knowledge we are modeling. Truth is relative to a Subject, i.e. true propositions are propositions which are believed by Subject. We propose using the predicate ASSUME to represent the fact that a given proposition is believed by Subject. This has a number of advantages. As already noted, it allows us to dispense with operators (in particular, operator V) and gives us a simpler representation scheme. Secondly, our proposed solution more clearly indicates the procedural nature of the predicate ASSUME. If I say that Bill believes C, this means concretely that if I would inspect Bill's mind I would find that C is an object of predicate ASSUME in Bill's mind much as I would find that C is an object of predicate ASSUME in my mind if I believe C (Castelfranchi, Lariccia, and Parisi, 1983).

Thirdly, if we use a predicate (ASSUME) to characterize the fact that a
proposition is "asserted", the corresponding proposition node can be an argument
of adverbial qualifications: "perhaps", "certainly", etc., much as this can happen
with "normal" proposition nodes.

However, we must take care not to confound Subject (the first argument of the
predicate ASSUME used in representing what the mind believes to be true) with a
possible node representing the mind within itself. To make clear this distinction
we will introduce a special node X0 for representing Subject. Hence, the
proposition ASSUME (X0, C) will characterize the status of a proposition (C) as
something which is believed to be true by Subject. X0 distinguishes this
particular use of the predicate ASSUME marking something (a C) as having the
status of an assumption of Subject, from other uses of the same predicate that
are only objects of various statuses.

To see why we need X0 consider sentence (36)

(36) Bill is convinced that I believe that Mary left

which is represented as (37)

(37)

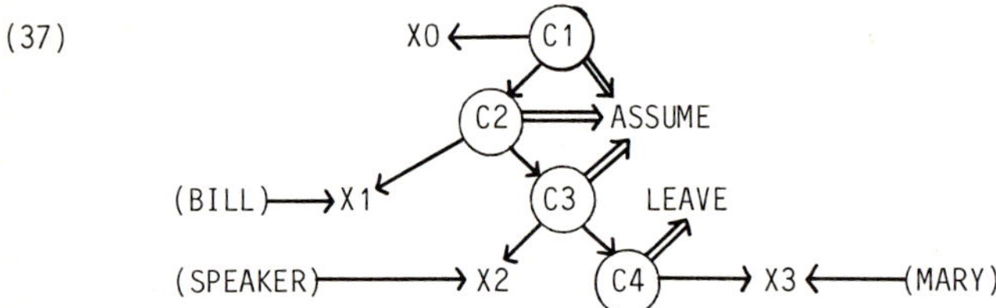

Of course, sentence (36) should not imply that "Mary left". Representation (37)
insures that this implication does not occur by distinguishing a node representing
myself in my mind (X2) from the node "constituting" my mind and governing my
assumptions (X0).

3.4 Meta-knowledge and lying

On the basis of what has been said in the preceding section it becomes possible
to represent the knowledge that a mind has about its own knowledge, i.e. its
meta-knowledge.

If one says (38)

(38) Bill left

he does not simply assumes C1, i.e. that Bill left, but he also assumes C4, i.e.
that he assumes it. In other words, the representation of (38) in its speaker's
mind is (39)

(39)

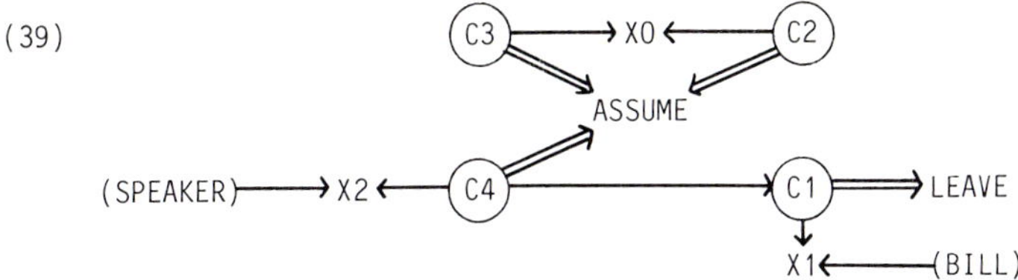

It is a knowledge structure like (39) which gives us the awareness of lying or
saying the truth and therefore constitutes a lie or a sincere declaration. If we
want to represent the knowledge in the mind of someone who says sentence (38) but
is lying, we would have something like (40) - using WANT (XO, C) to represent the
speaker's goal

(40)

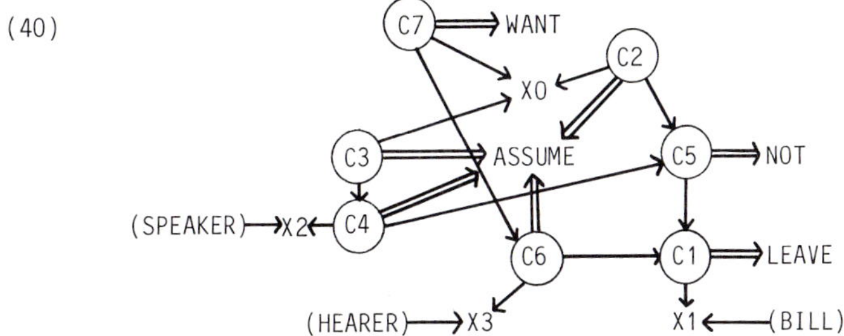

As it is clear from (39) and (40), the representation of meta-knowledge requires
that we distinguish between the node XO (Subject) from the node that represents
that same mind inside itself (the node with SPEAKER as predicate). If we do not
make this distinction the fact that I believe that I believe something would
necessarily imply that I believe it. In other words, it would be impossible to
distinguish between what a system thinks it assumes and what it actually assumes.
(Operationally, a system assumes something if its behavior reflects that
assumption.) This distinction is lacking in Mellor's (1978) analysis of what he
calls "conscious beliefs". In his recursive structure BELIEVE(BELIEVE(C)) - where
the predicate BELIEVE is equivalent to our predicate ASSUME - it is impossible to
say whether C is actually believed or not, although Mellor seems to be perfectly
aware of the possibility of a discrepancy between what is actually believed and
what one only believes to believe.

We shall come back to the idea of using predicate nodes to construct knowledges
when we will have introduced "complex predicate nodes". Combining complex
predicate nodes with the explicit representation of assumptions greatly increases
the representation power in what we will call the "game of who assumes what".

4. PARALLELISM BETWEEN PROPOSITION NODES AND OTHER TYPES OF NODES

Contrary to what Schubert seems to believe, proposition nodes are not a fourth
type of nodes in addition to the three "conceptual" nodes, i.e. individuals, sets,
and predicates. As already mentioned, we believe that there are two basic types
of nodes: X and C nodes. Furthermore there a number of sub-types which however
apply equally to both X and C nodes. This is the principal difference between our

representation scheme and Schubert's. From it we derive the possibility of
introducing sets and classes of propositions, and of making proposition nodes more
abstract and general. We also believe that our approach to proposition nodes leads
to an increase in representation power. The classification that we propose is (41)

(41)

Types of nodes	Count Individuals	Sets	Mass	Classes
X nodes ("things")	"Bill" "New York" "this chair" "one of Mary's children"	"Bill and Mary" "some chairs in this rooms" "Mary's children"	"some wax" "a little bit of vinegar"	"chairs" "wax" "children"
C nodes ("facts" or events")	"Bill' arrival to New York" "that Bill kisses Mary"	"Bill's arrivals to New York" "that Bill kisses Mary and that Mary gets angry"	"some happiness" "a little bit of benevolence"	"arriving" "being happy" "kissing girls" "benevolence"

4.1 Sets of proposition nodes

As we have nodes for sets of X nodes (XS) so we must recognize the existence of
nodes for sets of C nodes (CS). We represent the relationship between a set and
the set's members by using the predicate BELONG. For example, we represent the
meaning of sentences containing sets of X nodes as in (42)-(44)

(42) Bill and John run

(42)

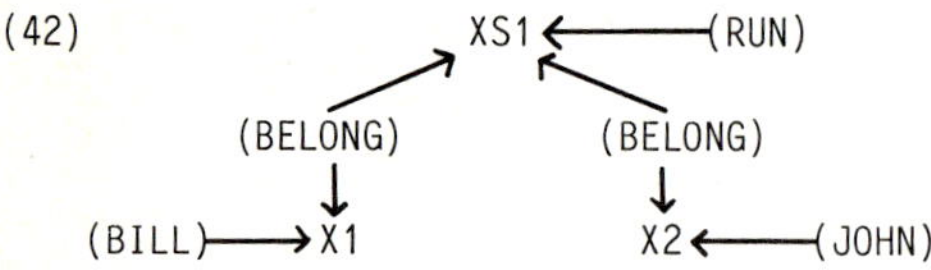

(43) The children play

(43)   (CHILD)————————→ XS1 ←————————(PLAY)

(44) Mary kissed the children, Peter and Louise

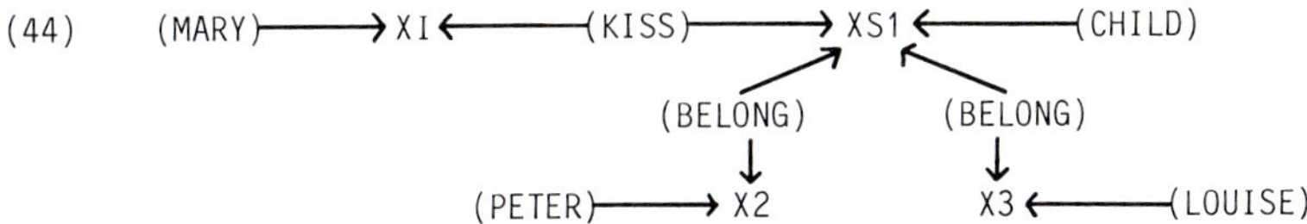

Similarly we will represent the meaning of sentences with sets of C nodes as in (45)

(45) The departure of Bill and the arrival of John delighted Mary

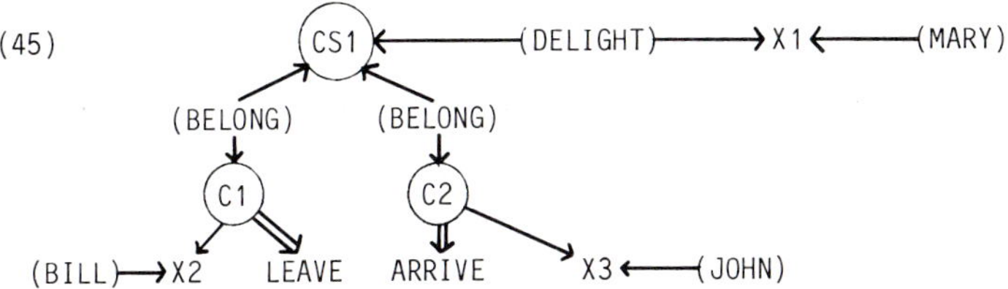

However CS nodes have an important property which is not shared by XS nodes. They may, although not necessarily, point to a predicate and its arguments. Consider the example in (46)

(46) Bill's arrival and John's arrival delighted Mary

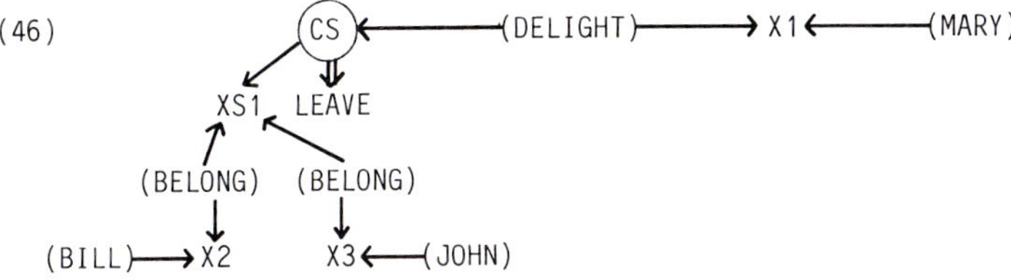

A proposition node which is a set node (CS) points to a predicate when the individual proposition nodes that are its members point to one and the same predicate (e.g. Bill arrives, John arrives). Otherwise, the CS node does not point to a predicate but it behaves like a node which is a set of X nodes (XS). Hence, CS nodes can be constructed in two alternative ways: (a) like XS nodes, i.e. when the member nodes share an "external" property (in (45) "that Bill depart" and "that John arrive" both belong to a CS because they share the property "delights Mary"); (b) in a way which is specific of CS nodes, i.e. when the member propositions contain a shared predicate - and in this case the CS node points to the shared predicate, as in (46).

4.2 <u>Classes of propositions</u>

As an X node - be it an individual, a set, or a mass node - is an instance of a class node (XC), so a C node may be an instance of a class C node (CC). To represent the relationship between a node and the class node the node is an instance of, we will use the predicate ISA.

As it is not necessary to write near an individual X node the property on the basis of which it is an instance of a particular class, e.g. we do not write (47)

(47)   XC ◄————(CHILD)
                 ↑
               (ISA)
                 ↓
                X1 ◄———(CHILD)

but we write (48)

(48)   XC ◄————(CHILD)
                 ↑
               (ISA)
                 ↓
                 X1

in the same way it not necessary to write near an instance C node the predicate that is already written near the class C node it belongs to. To represent a particular event of 'killing' as an instance of the general class of 'killings', we have rerpresentation (49)

(49)   KILL
                           ⇑
                          (CC)
                 XC1 ◄   ↑   ► XC2
                        (ISA)
                          ↓
                         (C1)
                  X1 ◄   ► X2

An important principle applies in this case: "If an individual proposition node is an instance of a proposition class, then its arguments are instances of the respective classes which are arguments of the class node".

Hence, a more complete representation of (49) would be (50)

(50)

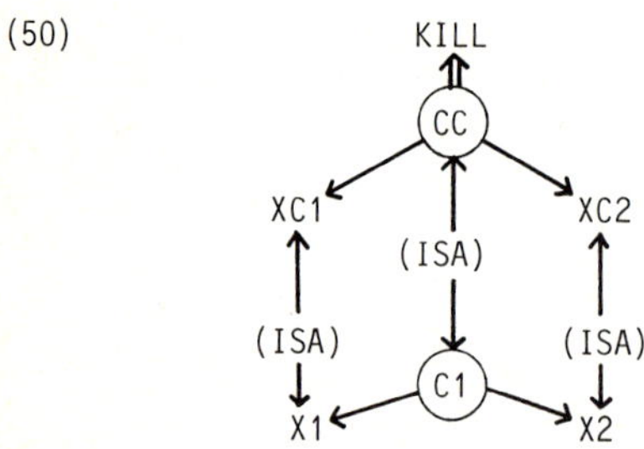

where XC1 is the class of killers and XC2 is the class of killed people.

The ISA link between an individual C and a class C corresponds to "para-individualization" in KL-ONE (Brachman, 1979).

As there are propositional count nodes (individual or sets), so there are propositional mass nodes as well. With regard to X count nodes, we can't say "lots of chair" or "how much chair?", but we can say "lots of chairs" and "how many chairs?". On the contrary, with X mass nodes, we can say "lots of water" and "how much water?", but we can't say "lots of waters" or "how many waters?" (unless we mean types of waters).

The same situation we have with C nodes. With C count nodes we can't say "lots of arrival" or "how much arrival?", whereas we can say "lots of arrivals" and "how many arrivals?". For C mass nodes, we can say "lots of happiness" and "how much happiness?", but we can't say "lots of happiness" or "how many happinesses?".

5. COMPLEX PROPOSITION NODES

We have seen that individual nodes, both X and C, can be grouped into sets (XS and CS) on the basis of a common property, and viceversa a set node can be partitioned into individual nodes which inherit the properties of the set node they belong to.

In a sense even individual nodes can be decomposed into "smaller" nodes, although the nodes which belong to an individual node do not inherit its properties. A chair cannot be decomposed into chairs - this is what distinguishes count from mass nodes. However, a chair can be decomposed into parts: legs, seat, etc., as in (51)

(51)

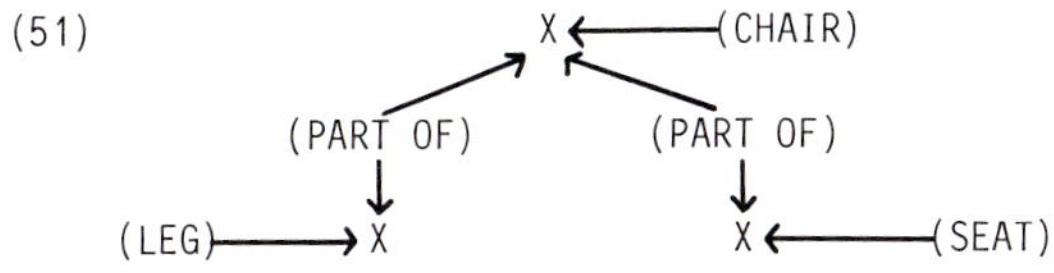

(We will come back to "parts" of individual X nodes in Section 5.6 below.)

In a similar way we can have "parts" of an individual proposition node. If the fight between Achilles and Hector is a event, i.e. an individual proposition node, the various stages of the fight will be "parts" of that node. For this and a number of other reasons that we will discuss in later sections, it is necessary to have "complex proposition nodes", i.e. individual proposition nodes to which other individual proposition nodes belong as parts.

We might represent the relationship between a complex proposition node and its part nodes by stating the relationship in each particular case with an explicit predicate PART. For example, the tale of Little Red Riding Hood would be represented as in (52)

(52)

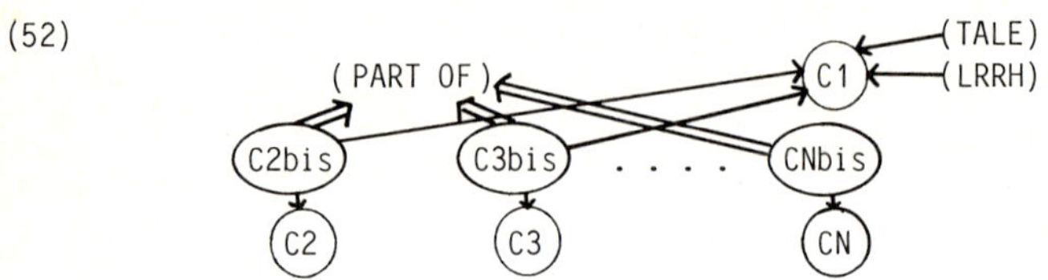

where C1 is the complex node representing the tale of Little Red Riding Hood
(LRRH) and C3, C5, etc. are the various parts of the tale.

This is a very cumbersome representation, however. An alternative that seems
preferable is to represent complex nodes "structurally", by identifying complex
proposition nodes as a special node type and by creating a specific direct link
between complex nodes and their part nodes. The LRRH tale would receive the
representation in (53)

(53)

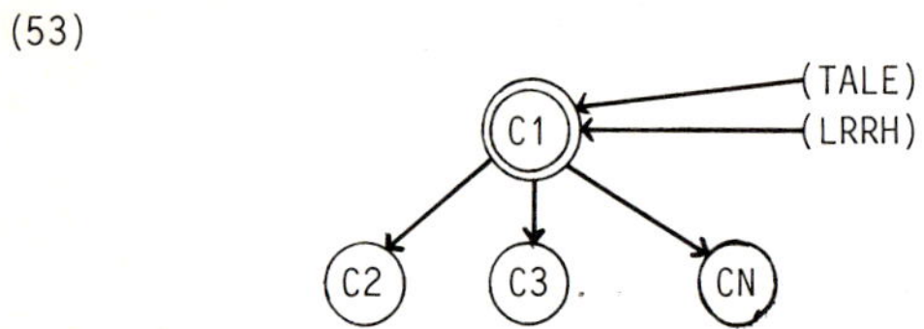

where the double-circled node is a complex node; or in a list format, the
representation in (54)

(54) C1: C2   C3 ... CN

This of course introduces a third type of arrow in our representation scheme,
leading from a complex node to its parts.

This structural representation implies that the "content" of a C node may not
consist of a predicate with its argument(s), as it does normally, but it may be
a list of C nodes. As Schubert has put it, "We need to create graphical entities
which correspond to "composite" sentences, composed by arbitrarily many atomic
sentences. The obvious solution lies in the introduction of explicit nodes for
logical compounds of propositions, with graphical links to components" (Schubert,
1976).

In proposing complex nodes Schubert has in mind sentences and he believes that
complex nodes are useful to represent linguistic coordination. As we will show,
complex nodes are needed for a number of purposes beyond representing the meaning
of sentences. Furthermore, we need both complex nodes and nodes that are sets
of C nodes, and coordination is to be represented by making use of sets of C
nodes (in addition to sets of X nodes) and not of complex nodes. Sets of C nodes
(or sets of X nodes) are created when the component nodes have a shared property
and/or when there is a linguistic signal (coordinating conjunctions, plural
suffixes, such words as "also", "another", etc.) expressing the sharing of a
property. In other cases where a number of propositions behave as a single entity
without sharing a property we make recourse to complex proposition nodes.

Note that as we have represented complex proposition nodes "structurally" we might also represent "structurally" sets and classes and their relationships to members and instances, respectively. This latter solution is adopted in KL-ONE. There are pros and cons in both alternatives but we won't review them here.

5.1 Organization of semantic memory

5.1.1 "Aspects" of entities

All varieties of knowledge can be found attached to a node in a semantic net. For example, around the node of Mr.Smith we can find the following items (here and in other cases below we will use a list format for network representation):

(55)
C1: X1 HUMAN	C9: X1 MARRIED
C2: X1 MALE	C10: X1 FATHER OF X3
C3: X1 ADULT	C11: X3 BILL
C4: X1 HAS X2	C12: X1 WORK AT X4
C5: X2 WATCH	C13: X4 M.I.T.
C6: X2 GOLDEN	C14: X1 BLOND
C7: X1 TALL	C15: X1 HAS X5
C8: X1 RESEARCHER	C16: X5 BEARD

From the point of view of search and retrieval it is implausible that all these knowledge items are just listed in memory with no structure or organization. Hence, we assume that all we know about an entity is grouped into a number of "aspects" of that entity. For example, what we know about Mr. Smith is partitioned in facts about its "physical appearence", about his "job", "family", etc. For example, propositions C7, C14, C15, and C16 are not simply listed along with the other propositions but they costitute a complex proposition which is the "physical appearence" of Mr. Smith. Propositions C8, C12, and C13 will be grouped into another complex proposition which is his "job", and so on.

It should be noted that even propositions which do not directly mention the node X1 (Mr. Smith's node) - e.g. proposition C13 about M.I.T. - may be part of the complex proposition "Mr. Smith's job".

This partitioning of knowledge into separate "aspects of X1" can facilitate research since if we must look for a knowledge item related to X1's physical appearence, e.g. how tall Mr. Smith is, we can avoid visiting knowledge about his job, or family, etc.

Obviously, such an organization of knowledge is not specific to each single case and doesn't concerns only individual nodes. We know in general which "aspects" a person tends to possess and we know which knowledge items constitute his physical appearence, his job, his family, etc. For example, even if we do not possess knowledge about a person's hair, we know that hair is part of his physical appearence. The "aspects" of an entity are predisposed at the level of class nodes and are inherited by individual nodes.

5.1.2 Episodes, narratives, etc.

What we know about Mr. Smith is also grouped into complex propositions according
to a different criterion: what happened in a certain time period. Hence, such
complex propositions represent complex events. In this case, there is a temporal
(and often also a spatial) structure which organizes the various knowledge items
within the complex node. Of course, various individual nodes (Mr. Smith's wife,
his children, his dog, etc.) may be involved in a single episode.

An episode (a temporal complex proposition) can be something which really
happened (i.e. something assumed by the reference mind) or it may be something
that Mary has told me, something dreamt of by Bill, or my dream, a fairy tale,
etc. This may the basis of an interesting distinction between "knowledge OF" a
text, a narrative, a dream, etc., and "knowledge ABOUT" a text, a narrative, a
dream, etc.

When someone reads a piece of news on a newspaper we can ask him two types of
questions: "internal" questions regarding facts OF the text (e.g. Who has escaped?
Where did the child go? Did they find him?) and "external" questions concerning
the text itself (e.g. Where did you read this? When did you learn that? What
does it talk about? Does the text mention a child?). To answer the first type of
questions one must search among the propositions that constitute the text, i.e.
that are part of the complex propositional node. To answer the second type of
questions one must examine the propositions which have the complex node - i.e.
the text - as their argument.

In this case also organization is useful from the point of view of search. To
answer a question I must first identify which episode, text, fairy tale, etc.
(complex node) the questioner has in mind - and then search inside it. If it not
clear which section of memory is being addressed, the questioner must make it
clear, e.g.:

(56) In the Little Red Riding Hood tale, the grandmother was ill?
     The Little Red Riding Hood tale talks about a wolf?
     Does the tale which scares Bill talk about a wolf?

Episodes, texts, stories, etc., play also a role in language production and
comprehension, for example with reference to the use of pronouns and definite
articles. They function as "contexts" (Charniak, 1983). Once we have identified
a context (complex node) we can use a definite noun without any modifiers (e.g.
a restrictive relative clause) since there is only one single individual to
which the noun can be applied within that context.

5.1.3 Topics

The same organization (grouping into complex nodes) that we use for episodes,
texts, tales, "things told yesterday by Mary", etc., can be extended to capture
the fact that our general knowledge appears to be partitioned in distinct
"topics". What we know about soccer is not mingled with what we know about
painting or US politics, etc.

Complex nodes can be part of larger complex nodes. This hierarchical organization

of complex nodes, and hence of "topics" in memory, may be the basis for a
selective activation of what one knows.

5.2 "Definitory" properties: constructive (sets) and categorial (classes)

Set and class nodes have the characteristic that the knowledge items attached to
them do not all play the same role. Some of the knowledge items "define" the set
or class node. These are the items on the basis of which the set or class node
has been created and they are necessary and sufficient conditions for being a
member of the set node or an instance of the class node.

Consider the text in (57):

(57) "A number of boys live in my apartment house. John is tall and redhaired.
     Bill is short and redhaired. Peter is blond and he lives on the 1st floor.
     All the redhaired boys live on the 1st floor.

The last sentence creates a set node whose members are John and Bill. The
properties in terms of which the set has been constructed are BOY and REDHAIRED.
However, if I represent this set without expressly indicating that BOY and
REDHAIRED are its "constructive" properties, I get the representation in (58):

(58)

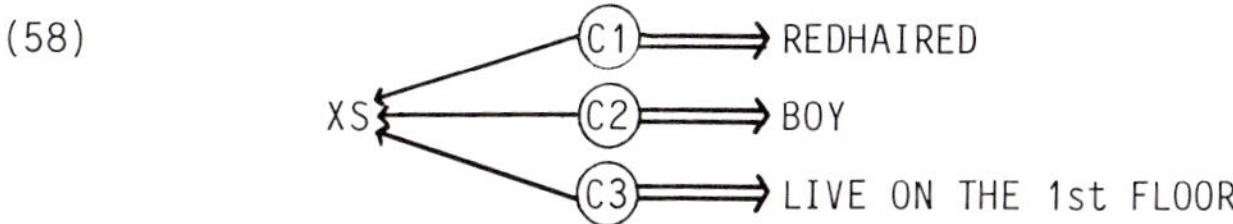

But (58) is not a correct representation of what I know after reading text (57).
As a matter of fact, from representation (58) one might derive a sentence like
(59)

(59) The boys living on the 1st floor are redhaired

which would not be true with respect to text (57).

Representation (58) is not correct also because if I meet another boy living on
the first floor I would be entitled to make him a member of the set and hence to
believe with no grounds that he is redhaired. The properties on the basis of
which the set has been constructed and which one must posses to be a member of
the set, are not BOY and LIVING ON 1st FLOOR but BOY and REDHAIRED.

Finally, consider that sets typically have cardinality (= number of members) and
one and the same set would have different cardinalities unless some of its
properties are set apart from the others as "constructive" properties. The
redhaired boys are 2 but the boys living on the 1st floor are 3.

Complex nodes may be used to group together those properties of a set that are
its defining (constructive) properties (predicate DEF). Hence, the correct
representation for our set is not (58) but (60).

(60)

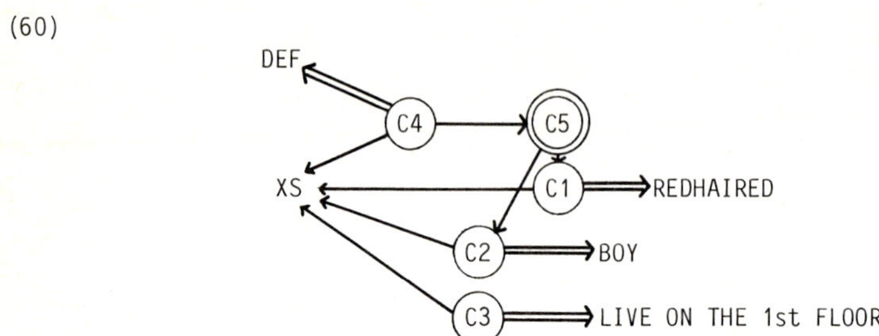

A similar problem is raised by class nodes: the properties or relations in terms
of which individual nodes are categorized, i.e. assigned to class nodes as their
instances, are only a sub-set of all the knowledge items we have on those class
nodes. If we know that "pink diamonds are expensive", this is very different from
knowing that "expensive diamonds are pink". Hence, we need something more than a
simple representation like (61)

(61)

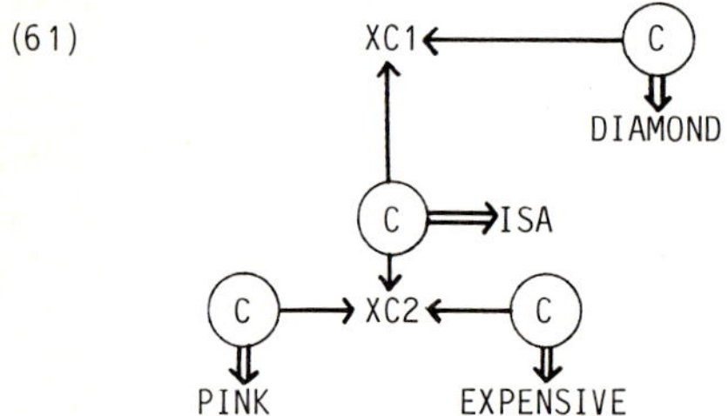

By using complex nodes to identify definitory (categorial) properties of class
nodes, we may arrive at a better representation like (62):

(62)

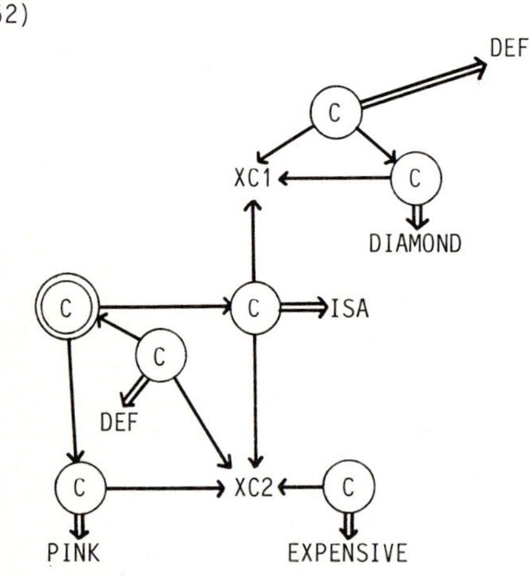

In (62) we have a class (XC1) defined by being a diamond, and another class (XC2)
defined by being a sub-class of diamonds and by being pink. About this second
class of things I have the knowledge that they are expensive.

5.3 Definitory properties and quantifiers

The grouping of the definitory properties of a set or class by means of a complex proposition node may also be necessary to represent the scope of quantifiers. To say that a quantifier has a scope means that the quantifier asserts the quantity of a set (or class) which is defined by certain properties and not others. If we say

(63) Many of the redhaired boys live on the first floor

we are neither asserting that "the boys" are many nor that "the redhaired boys" are many, but that "the redhaired boys who live on the first floor" are many (with reference to some implicit set of redhaired boys). In other words, in order to quantify we must be clear about which properties are being used to construct the quantified set and therefore what belongs to the set and what lies outside it.

We prefer not to use the quantifiers of formal logic to represent the natural language quantifiers, e.g. "many". A complete analysis of sentence (63) would produce a representation that would sound something like "The quantity of the set of redhaired boys living on the first floor is less than the quantity of the superset of redhaired boys but it is more than the norm of (in this case, half) the quantity of this same superset". Without decomposing the predicate MANY, a simplified representation would be

(64)

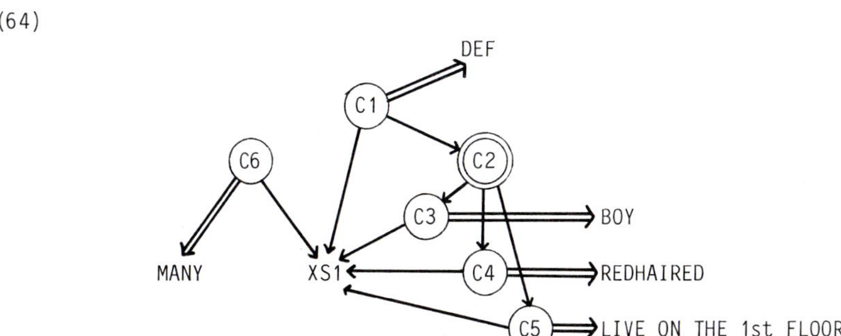

Given that the proposition which define a set can contain other sets, it can happen that the scope of a quantifier contains other quantifiers. Consider the well-known pair of sentences (65) and (66).

(65) Many minerals are contained in all the samples
(66) All the samples contain many minerals

Sentence (65) favors an interpretation which is a paraphrase of "The minerals which are contained in all the samples are many", where one quantifies with "many" a set of minerals defined by "being contained in all the samples", i.e.

(67)

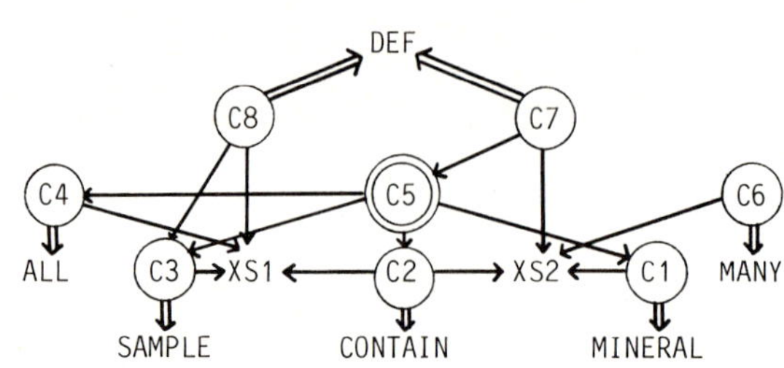

Sentence (66), on the other hand, is interpreted as "The samples which contain
many minerals are all the samples". Here one quantifies with "all" a set of
samples defined by "containing many minerals", i.e.

(68)

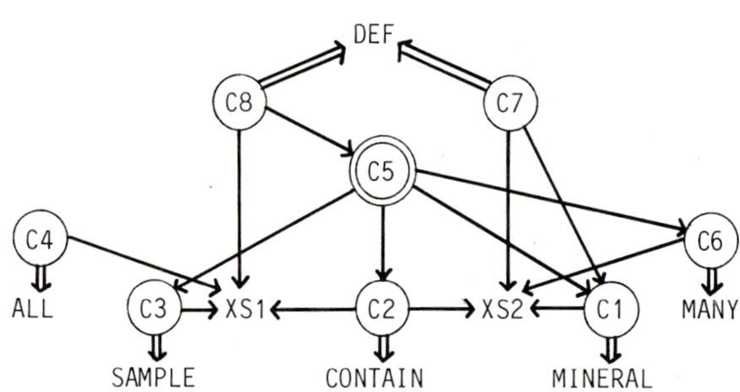

As it is clear, the representations for sentence (65) and (66) are identical
except that in (67) the set XS1 is defined only by "being a sample" (C3) and its
quantifier (C7) is part of the definition of the set XS2, while in (68) the set
XS2 is defined only by "being a mineral" (C1) and the remaining properties (C2,
C3) including the quantifier (C6) are part of the definition of the set XS1. In
other words, the properties are the same in the two cases but they are used
differently.

5.4 Defining classes of C-nodes by grouping

We can use the same method for defining classes of C-nodes (CC). However, classes
of C-nodes can be defined in terms of propositions mentioning them (like the
classes of X-nodes we have considered so far) but they can also be defined by
propositions which "compose" them. In other words, a class of C-nodes can be a
complex C node.

Assume that we want to represent the class of "assassinations". In order to
define an "assassination" we must make use not only of the concept (predicate) of
killing but also of the fact that the killer and the killed are persons. Therefore,
a representation like (69)

(69)

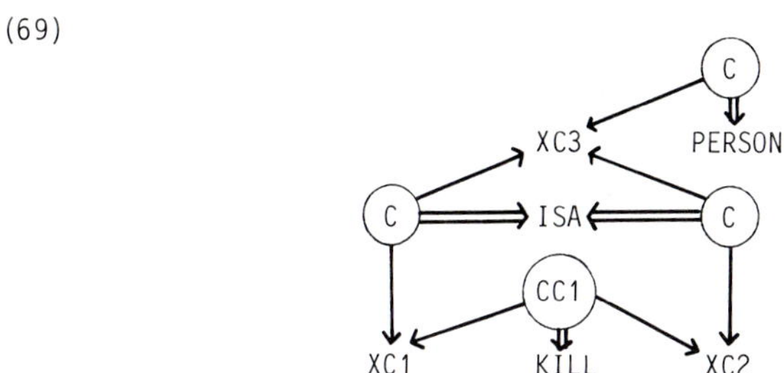

where CC1 is the class of "assassinations", won't be sufficient. What we need is
something like (70)

(70)

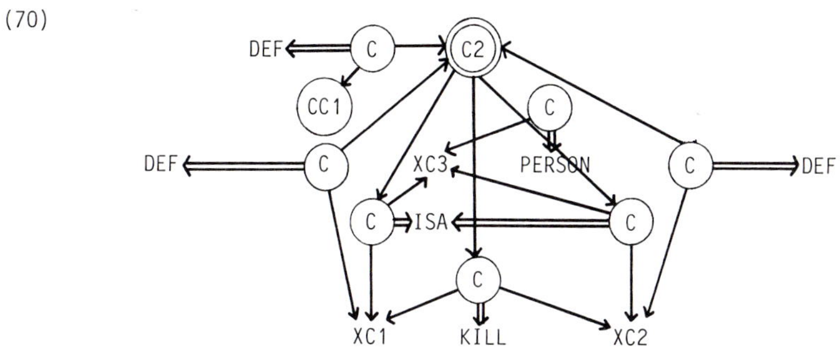

where CC1 is the class of "assassinations", XC1 the class of "assassinators", and
XC2 the class of the "assassinees". All three classes are defined not only by the
predicate KILL but by the fact that both the killer and the killed are persons.
One and the same complex node, C2, defines all three classes.

More generally, complex nodes are useful if we want to represent a complex
predicate as decomposed into simpler predicates. Consider the predicate KILL. We
can represent it as a whole, as in (71)

(71)

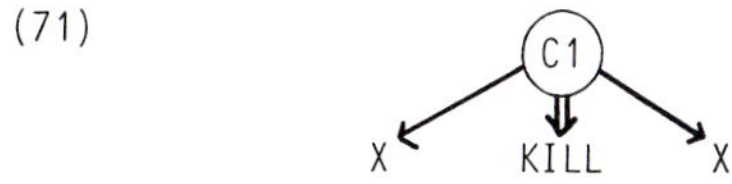

or we may want to represent its internal structure, as in (72):

(72)

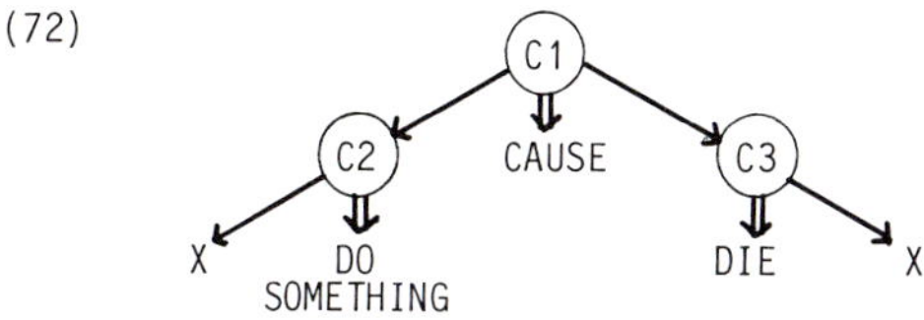

However, in representation (72) what is the node of "killing": C1, C2, or C3?
Clearly none of these three nodes is the node of "killing". "Killing" is the
complex node which groups together C1, C2, and C3, that is C4 in (73)

(73)

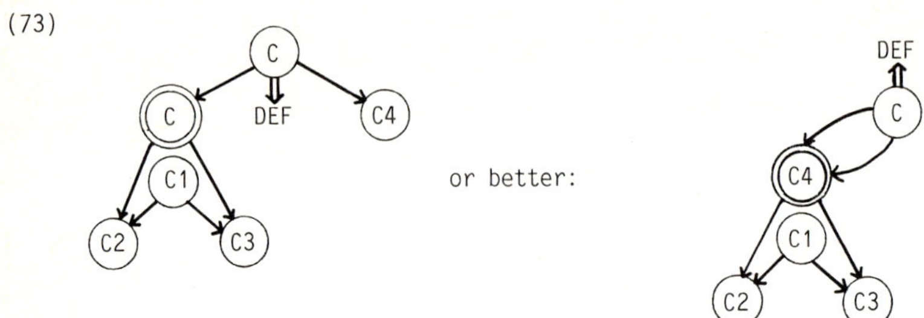

or better:

Of course, predicate decomposition is useful for lexical decomposition. However,
note that the existence of complex nodes implies a two-level representation of
word meanings. The complex node defines a level at which the meaning of a word
like "to kill" is not decomposed, while the predicates of the propositions that
are part of the complex node define a second level where the meaning of "to kill"
is decomposed into three more elementary predicates: DOES SOMETHING, CAUSE, DIE.

5.5 A better representation of linguistic recursivity

Complex propositional nodes can be the basis of a better representation of
knowledge acquired through comprehension of recursive sentences. In Section 2.1
we used simple propositional nodes to represent the meaning of a sentence like
(2)

(2) The child says that he leaves tomorrow

as (3)

(3)

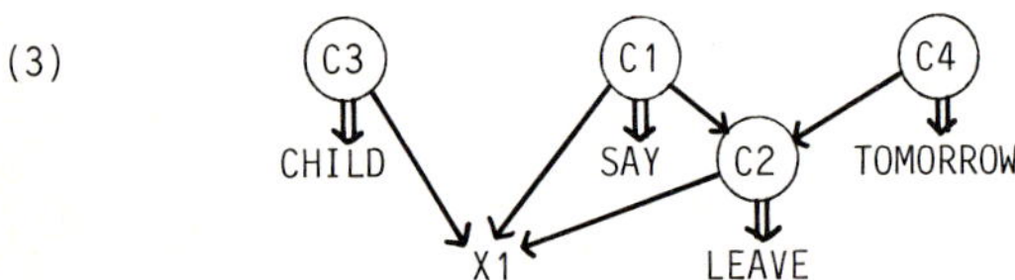

However, representation (3) implies that all the child says is that he leaves but
not that the leaving takes place tomorrow. This is of course inappropriate. If we
want to put more than a single knowledge item under a matrix verb we need complex
nodes. Another and more appropriate representation for sentence (2) would
therefore be (74).

(74)

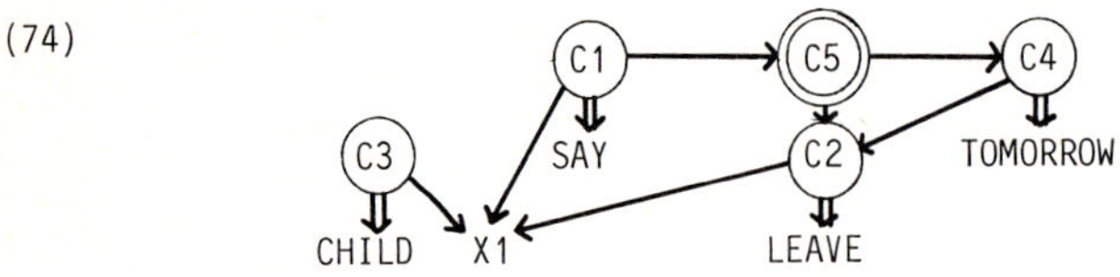

5.6 Complex X nodes

As already mentioned in Section 5, individual X nodes can also be made up of

parts and thus be complex nodes. As a C node can be an episode, a topic, or a
complex of properties to be articulated in its constituting parts, we may have
complex objects which are constituted by more elementary objects (parts). We can
represent the relationship between an object and its parts explicitly, i.e. by
means of a predicate PART (as we did in Section 5), or we may introduce complex
X nodes directly linked to their constituting parts, as in (75)

(75)

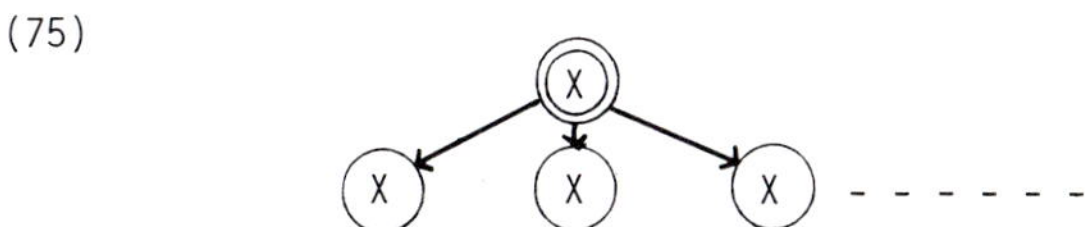

If we apply this notation to the analysis of the concept of, e.g., an arc, we
obtain (76)

(76)

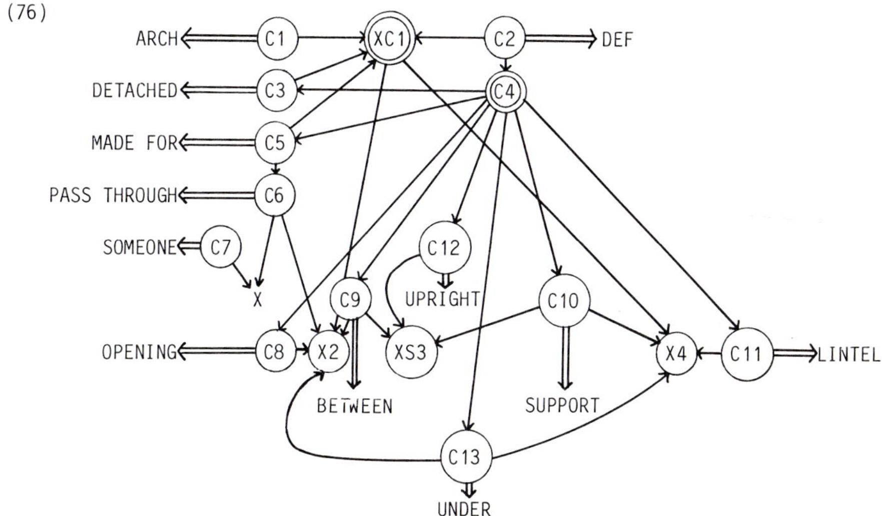

In (76) we have both a complex X node (XC1), with links to the parts of an arc,
and a complex C node (C4), which defines the concept of an arc utilizing among
other properties the relationships among these parts (C9, C10, C11). This complex
C node, therefore, fulfills the same function that in KL-ONE is fulfilled by the
Structural Description.

It can be of some interest to observe that with functional objects, e.g. chairs,
the function of the object is very often nothing more that the complex C node of
the functions of some of its parts. For example, the function of chairs is to
enable somebody to seat above the ground leaning his back on something. A chair
is made up of a seat, legs, and a back. The function of the seat is to enable
somebody to seat; the function of the legs is to keep the seat above the ground;
and the function of the back is to enable the seated person to lean his back on
something.

6. The "Who assumes What" game

By using complex propositional nodes and the devices introduced in Section 3 to
represent assumptions (and other statuses of propositions in the mind), it may be
possible to approach an adequate representation of "who assumes what". This is a
vast area of phenomena variously named by different disciplines: implications,
presuppositions, points of view, beliefs, opacity, possible worlds, etc. All
these phenomena seem to be related to the necessity of distinguishing in our
representations which parts are believed by the speaker, which parts by the
hearer, which parts by a character in the story, etc.

In the following Sections we will discuss briefly how some of these phenomena
might be dealt with in the present framework. We will assume throughout that
assuming a complex node C1 automatically implies assuming the component
propositions (C2, C3, C4).

6.1 Presuppositions

We define (Castelfranchi and Parisi, 1980) presuppositions of sentences as
assumptions of the speaker - which he comunicates to the hearer - concerning
(a) his own assumptions and (b) the assumptions of the hearer, and concerning
the agreements or disagreements between (a) and (b).

Many presuppositions are linked to specific lexical items. For example, "to know"
contains the information that the speaker assumes the content of the subordinate
clause and further assumes that the hearer does the same (factual presupposition).
In the sentence (77):

(77) John knows that the Yankees won

"that the Yankees won" is assumed not only by John (according to the speaker),
but by the speaker himself and by the hearer (again, according to the speaker).
By contrast, in sentence (78)

(78) John believes that the Yankees won

only John is assumed by the speaker to assume "that the Yankees won". The speaker
himself assumes only "that John believes that", and there are no assumptions
attributed to the hearer.

A negative assumption (counterfactual presupposition), often but not necessarily
shared by the hearer, is communicated by a sentence like (79)

(79) John illudes himself that the Yankees won

and counterfactual presuppositions are also contained in counterfactual
conditionals. In sentence (80)

(80) If Bill had eaten the strawberries, he would have seen sick

the speaker assumes that eating strawberries causes being sick but he also
assumes that Bill did not eat strawberries and that he is not sick.

In other cases information about the assumptions of the speaker, hearer, and persons talked about is not carried as a presupposition but asserted by an adverb. This is what happens in a sentence like (81)

(81) Bill wrongly accused John of bumping on his car.

6.2 Opacity

Cases of opacity receive a clearcut treatment in the present framework. Sentence (82)

(82) Oedipus is looking for his mother Jocasta

is odd because to "look for" normally contains the idea that who looks for something X assumes that this something has the property used in the description of X; in our case it is implied Oedipus assumes that the person he is looking for is his mother, which we know to be untrue. Only later in the story Oedipus will gain this particular piece of knowledge. The mind of the knowledgeable speaker of sentence (82) may be represented as (83) if (82) is said at the beginning of the story

    (83)   C1: ASSUME X0 C2
            C2: C3 C4 C5 C6
            C3: OEDIPUS X1
            C4: ASSUME X1 C5
            C5: JOCASTA X2
            C6: MOTHER OF X2 X1
            C7: LOOK FOR X1 X2

and as (84) if (82) is said at the end

    (84)   C1: ASSUME X0 C2
            C2: C3 C4 C5 C6
            C3: OEDIPUS X1
            C4: ASSUME X1 C5
            C5: C6 C7
            C6: JOCASTA X2
            C7: MOTHER OF X2 X1
            C8: LOOK FOR X1 X2

A sentence like (85)

(85) John wants to marry a stupid girl

has the following representation

```
(86)      C1: ASSUME X0 C2
          C2: C3 C4 C5 C8 C9
          C3: JOHN X1
          C4: WANT X1 C6
          C5: ASSUME X1 C6
          C6: C7 C8 C9
          C7: MARRY X1 X2
          C8: GIRL X2
          C9: STUPID X2
```

if what the speaker of (85) intends to communicate is that John want to marry a
girl he himself believes to be stupid. On the other hand, (85) is represented
thus

```
(87)      C1: ASSUME X1 C2
          C2: C3 C4 C5 C8 C9
          C3: JOHN X1
          C4: WANT X1 C6
          C5: ASSUME X1 C6
          C6: C7 C8
          C7: MARRY X1 X2
          C8: GIRL X2
          C9: STUPID X2
```

if only the speaker, but not John, believes that the girl is stupid. "To want",
if the speaker doesn't tell us the opposite, normally contains the idea that who
wants X also assumes that X has the property used in the description of X. This
lexical explanation seems to us to be simpler than the one proposed by Creary
(1979), and also more complete in that it includes the representation of who
assumes that Jocasta is Oedipus' mother or that the girl is stupid.

6.3 "Epistemic" interpretations

Representing assumptions is also necessary for other kinds of sentences and
expressions, for example for "epistemic", causal, or conditional expressions and
for the "epistemic" reading of a verb like "must" (see Antinucci and Parisi,
1971).

Consider sentences (88) and (89)

(88) The street is wet because it rained
(89) It rained because the street is wet

While in sentence (88) a causal relationship is asserted between two events in
the world (the street being wet and the rain), in sentence (89) the causal
relationship is between two assumptions: assuming that the street is wet and
assuming that it rained.

Similarly, sentence (90)

(90) Bill must be gone

is ambiguous. In one reading (deontic "must") there is an obligation on Bill to go. In another reading (epistemic "must") there is an obligation on the speaker to assume that Bill has gone.

6.4 <u>Minds inside minds</u>: "Io credetti ch'ei credesse ch'io credessi"
                           ("I believed that he believed that I believed"
                           Dante, Inferno)

Among phenomena which seems to require complex nodes for their representation is the representation of other minds in a reference mind. We have already touched on this problem marginally when we have discussed sentences which talk about or presuppose other minds (the hearer's mind or the mind of the persons mentioned in the sentence). We want to examine briefly now the problem in its generality.

Let us make it clear first of all that this is a problem going much beyond the representation of the meaning of sentences. If a mind must reach its goals within a social environment (inhabited by other minds) it must be able to represent the content of other minds (their goals and their assumptions). All social exchange is founded on this capacity and the same is true for conversational exchange. Furthermore, very often our assumptions about the world, about other minds, and about ourselves depend on and derive from the assumptions of others, or better, from the assumptions we assume others have.

All this shows that the problem of "minds inside other minds" is a very complex problem which has not yet found a satisfactory solution within artificial intelligence. Robert Moore has referred to the appealing idea of using "the multiple data-base capabilities of advanced A.I. languages to set up a separate data base for each person whose knowledge we have some information about" (Moore, 1977). However, in his larger work (Moore, 1980) Moore himself judges this proposal impracticable.

We think that there should be no separation between what one knows or thinks about, e.g. his child, and what he believes that, e.g., the child's mother knows or think about him. The two bodies of knowledge are tightly interconnected and used to support each other.

In our approach, as we have seen, one and the same proposition (C) in one and the same data-base may belong to what XO believes, to what, according to XO, John believes, to what, according to XO, Bill believes that XO believes and so on.

Does this imply that the beliefs of the various persons are all dispersed and mingled together around specific propositions? If this were the case, there would be no true representation of other minds as unitary entities. However, given the availability of complex nodes, it must not be necessarily so. As we have represented texts, tales, topics, etc. as complex nodes, we can create as well a complex node grouping together all the assumptions of, say, Bill.

An approach not very different to the one proposed here appears to be that of Hendrix (1979) with his "partitioning" of the knowledge base. (This approach has been also used by Cohen (1978)). However, Hendrix' theory seems to imply that the various minds, even if contained in a single data-base, can only be hierarchically "embedded" one in another. This may be applicable to cases where there are no intersections of assumptions or simultaneous and not hierarchical access to the various levels. An example is sentence (91)

(91) John believes that Bill thinks that Mary has left

But consider sentence (92)

(92) John believes that Bill knows that Mary has left

With this sentence we receive not only an information about Bill's mind - according to John - but also an information about the speaker's mind, which is two levels up.

We prefer to think, therefore, that the various minds are not in a necessarily hierarchical relationship but that they should be able to intersect and relate in a variety of ways. A representation using complex propositional nodes and explicit assumptions appears to be sufficient, general, and flexible enough to make this possible.

A related proposal for representing multiple minds within a single mind is Bruce and Newman's (1978). In their scheme, however, what each mind believes to be true is represented separately. In this paper we have described a less redundant and more homogeneous representation in which each different mind converges on a singly represented proposition.

REFERENCES

Antinucci, F., Parisi, D. On English Modal Verbs. Paper presented at the 7th
        Regional Meeting. Chicago: Chicago Linguistic Society, 1971.

Brachman, R.J. On the epistemological status of semantic networks. In N.V.Findler
        (Ed.), Associative networks. New York: Academic Press, 1979.

Bruce, B., Newman, D. Interacting plans. Cognitive Science, 1978, 2, 195-233.

Castelfranchi, C. La regolazione cognitiva. (Rapporto tecnico 191). Roma: Istituto
        di Psicologia C.N.R., 1977

Castelfranchi, C., Lariccia, G., Parisi, D. La ricorsività cognitiva. In B.Bara
        (a cura di), La linguistica computazionale. Milano: Franco Angeli, 1983.

Castelfranchi, C. e Parisi, D. Analisi di alcuni quantificatori italiani in
        termini di rappresentazione delle conoscenze. In Tempo Verbale e Strutture
        Quantificate in forma logica. Firenze: Accademia della Crusca, 1981.

Castelfranchi, C., Parisi, D. Linguaggio, conoscenze e scopi. Bologna: Mulino,
        1980.

Charniak, E. Passing markers: a theory of contextual influence in language
    comprehension. Cognitive Science, 1983, 7, 171-190.

Cohen, P.R. On knowing what to say: planning speech acts. (Technical Report 118).
    University of Toronto: Department of Computer Science, 1978.

Creary, L.C. Propositional attitudes: Fregean representation and simulative
    reasoning. IJCAI-6, 1979.

Hendrix, G.G. Encoding knowledge in partitioned networks. In N.V.Findler (Ed.),
    Associative networks. New York: Academic Press, 1979.

Kintsch, W. The representation of meaning in memory. New York: John Wiley & Sons,
    1974.

Mellor, M. Conscious beliefs. Paper presented at the meeting of the Aristotelian
    Society, 1978.

Moore, R.C. Reasoning about knowledge and action. IJCAI-5, 1977.

Moore, R.C. Reasoning about knowledge and action. (Technical Note 191). Artificial
    Intelligence Center, SRI International, Menlo Park, 1980.

Parisi, D., Antinucci, F. Essentials of grammar. New York: Academic Press, 1976.

Schubert, L.K. Extending the expressive power of semantic networks. Artificial
    Intelligence, 1976, 7, 163-198.

Shapiro, S.C. The SNePS semantic network processing system. In N.V.Findler (Ed.),
    Associative networks. New York: Academic Press, 1979.

Computational Models of Natural Language Processing
B.G. Bara and G. Guida (eds.)
© Elsevier Science Publishers B.V. (North-Holland), 1984

VIEWING PARSING AS WORD SENSE DISCRIMINATION:
A CONNECTIONIST APPROACH

Garrison W. Cottrell*, Steven L. Small°*

*Department of Computer Science
°Department of Psychology
The University of Rochester
Rochester, NY, USA

This paper advocates the interdisciplinary development of a computational theory of human language comprehension and proposes a collection of initial constraints from which to start on such an enterprise. In order to satisfy these constraints, our modelling effort employs an architecture significantly different from the typical computer and closer to that of the human brain. We use a particular spreading activation or active semantic network scheme, called *connectionism*, which entails a massive number of appropriately connected computing units that communicate through weighted levels of excitation and inhibition. While such an architecture does not solve any problems per se, we believe that a number of questions become easier to set forth and more straightforward to solve. This paper surveys a number of fundamental language comprehension issues from the new perspective, and presents some simulation results of a parsing model based on these considerations.

1. INTRODUCTION

The recent history of artificial intelligence has seen the development of many interesting computer programs in the domain of automatic natural language comprehension. These programs and their associated research efforts in knowledge representation and system design are motivated by two interdependent goals. On one hand, researchers are interested in the development of high performance language systems for use in facilitating man-machine communication. On the other hand, they want to understand the mechanisms of human language understanding, and believe that the construction of computer models can shed some light on these processes. In practice, the line between these two research aims has not been clear, and the goals of most particular research efforts not made explicit.

Most research efforts have put forth computational language processing systems as dual experiments in AI engineering and cognitive simulation. After constructing working programs, many of these efforts have pursued computational goals and left to psychologists the task of interpreting, evaluating, and improving upon the systems as cognitive models. Since little was known about the evaluation of such theoretical work, these models all appeared to mesh with existing intuitions and data from experimental psychology. Where experimental data was available, cognitive simulations took no stands; where such simulations seemed to take a stand, there was no data. Recently, there has been increasing interest in bridging this gap (see papers in the *Proceedings of the Cognitive Science Society*, 1982).

1.1 Computational Models

A fundamental premise of this paper is that the time is right for the interdisciplinary development of a computational theory of human language comprehension. Toward that end, we shall propose a collection of initial constraints and considerations from which to start on such an enterprise. These come from several disparate sources, as follows: (1) neurophysiology and neurolinguistics; (2) psychological results in lexical access; and (3) computational plausibility. New architectures for models of the vision process that meet some of these constraints have been proposed by psychologists and artificial intelligence researchers. We review these briefly to motivate our language models. Then we describe a model of word sense disambiguation that obeys the above constraints and present some simulation results. It is necessary first to discuss a second basic premise.

It must be possible to form a clear correspondence between elements of the theory and elements of the world that the theory attempts to explain. It is precisely on this count that existing theories have broken down: how do the symbol structures and symbolic inference schemes of computational models relate to the structures and processing strategies that people use for the same tasks? The answer in many cases is that the correspondence is at a *functional* level. The functions performed by the program must be performed by a human in some way in order to accomplish the same task. We claim that in order to explain the wealth of psychological data on low-level language processing, the correspondence must be at a level below the functional; that the *mechanisms* involved in carrying out these functions must be considered if we are ever to have real explanatory power. This approach has been employed successfully by several researchers (McClelland and Rumelhart (1981); Rumelhart and McClelland (1982); Gigley (1982); Small, Cottrell, and Shastri (1982); Pollack (1982); Dell (1980)). This paper presents our model as one "explanation" of the lexical decision research to be discussed below. These considerations of level of description have led us to reconsider certain of the basic tools and metaphors employed for theory construction in information processing psychology. The principal metaphor to be rejected sees the human being as a conventional computer.

1.2 Constraints

1.2.1 Neurophysiological Constraints

Francis Crick (1979) has pointed out the inherent differences between the conventional sequential computer and the human brain. His comparison is summarized in the following table:

	computer	brain
speed	fast	slow
order	serial	parallel
component reliability	reliable	unreliable
faults	fatal	no degradation
signals	precise, symbolic	imprecise, terse

We draw our first set of constraints from Crick's observations and knowledge of human physiology:

1. The processing units are relatively simple--not more capable than a neuron. This is not too great a constraint. Recent evidence (Levy (1982)) shows that neurons are far from simple linear threshold units, for example. Some computation appears to be going on at

the dendrites, outside the cell body. However, the "cycle time" of a neuron--how fast it responds to input--is about 2 msec, or 10^6 times slower than the fastest computers.

2. Another large constraint is that the brain's connections are *fixed*; very few new pathways are grown in the adult brain. What we may change is weights on the connections, thus developing new pathways (recruitment). Methods for doing this have been outlined by Feldman (1982a). However, this process is necessarily slow. We presume that this accounts for long-term learning, and that short-term associations are handled differently. (One possibility is discussed in Feldman (1982a).)

3. One coinage of the brain is frequency of firing, thus the inputs (and outputs) cannot carry more than a few bits. This is perhaps the greatest departure from the typical information processing paradigm. There are not enough bits in firing frequency to allow symbol passing between individual units.

4. Whereas some locations in the brain may control activity in others, we assume that decisions are completely distributed: each unit computes its output solely based on its inputs; it cannot "look around" to see what others are doing, and no central controller gives it instructions.

5. The model must be noise resistant and robust. Faults in individual units should not (ordinarily) degrade overall performance. While we do not address this constraint in our current implementation, we do assume that redundancy accounts for much of the fault tolerance.

6. The number of processors and connections must be constrained: on the order of 10^{11} processors, with 10^3-10^4 connections each (the approximate number of neurons and connections in the brain).

The first question one might ask is how people can possibly perform multiple tasks (such as walking and talking) at the same time with these constraints. We must, based on the relatively slow speed of neurons, be able to do a lot of computation in a small number of steps. The picture is not so bleak: there are significant advantages in the parallelism and high connectedness of the system, and in that the time-consuming process of encoding and decoding of symbol strings is not required of the processors.

1.2.2 Psychological Constraints

Beyond these general constraints, we draw a design constraint from psychological evidence on human processing characteristics. We refer to recent results in lexical access studies. These are relatively low-level processes, but suggest ways in which the brain may operate at all levels. Recent studies in lexical access have tried to distinguish between what has been termed the Prior and Post Decision Hypotheses. The question is whether the context of a sentence constrains the search for the contextually appropriate meaning of a word, so that only a single meaning is accessed (the Prior Decision Hypothesis), or whether all meanings of the word are initially accessed, and then the proper one selected by context. Early research produced mixed results, some studies supporting one hypothesis, some the other (Conrad (1974); Foss and Jenkins (1973); Holmes (1977); Lackner and Garret (1972); Swinney and Hakes (1976)).

Recent work by Swinney (1979) and others (cf. Tanenhaus, Leiman, and Seidenberg (1979); Seidenberg, Tanenhaus, Leiman, and Bienkowski (1982)) has shown that the time course of these effects is important. Using a lexical priming paradigm, these studies have shown that immediately following an ambiguous word, at least two (the number they tested) meanings are initially active, but by 200 ms later, one has been chosen. In Swinney's experiments, the subject would hear a sentence such as "the carpenter picked up the file". At the end of "file" a string would appear on a screen and the subject would have to press one of two keys depending on whether the string was a word or not (a "lexical decision task"). Decisions are facilitated (reaction times are faster) for words related to *both* meanings of "file" (cabinet or tool) immediately after "file" is heard, but several syllables later, there is facilitation only for the tool sense. Thus, depending on when researchers sampled their subjects, one hypothesis or the other gained support. This result held for words with noun-verb, verb-verb, and noun-noun ambiguities even in a biasing context. One important exception to this result has been found by Tanenhaus. He found prior decision in the case of noun-noun ambiguous words in a highly constraining context. The important thing to note in this result is that there may have been strong lexical priming (rather than contextual influence) by one or more words in the sentence highly related to one of the meanings in the ambiguous word. Another interpretation is that parallel access obtained, but the decision was reached even before the end of the word (Lucas (1983)).

As a constraint on our design, we interpret these results as evidence that for our purposes lexical access occurs independently of the context and then passes all meanings on to be selected from and integrated into the meaning structure for the sentence. The noun-noun results can still be explained in this system as an action of the lexical access system alone, with the priming effect of the context word damping alternate readings of the target word.

1.2.3 Neurolinguistic Constraints

Lastly, we take a constraint from evidence of language processing deficits in aphasics, in particular the localization of syntax and lexical access. Wernicke's aphasics appear to have a disrupted lexical and/or meaning access system, while appearing to have their syntactic systems intact. Broca's aphasics experience syntactic deficits, but are able to name objects correctly. While this is an oversimplification (see Gigley (1982) for a recent review) we interpret this to suggest keeping these systems separate, as opposed to totally integrated as in some other models. Secondly, it is clear that Broca's aphasics do understand some language; the system has not totally degraded, even though part of it is missing. This is in sharp contrast to many computer models that certainly wouldn't run if some procedures were missing. A model of human comprehension should be "lesionable" if it is to be realistic. This is not to say that other computer models cannot be "lesioned", but models like ours (Dell (1980); Gigley (1982); Small, Cottrell, and Shastri (1982); Pollack (1982)) make lesioning possible (depending on the implementation) without reprogramming. Also, we may model degrees of lesioning (by removing only some of the connections involved in a particular function), which would be considerably harder in the PARSIFAL system (Marcus (1979, 1982)), for example. More discussion of this point is given in (Gigley (1982)).

2. OVERVIEW

The type of model we propose is a particular neural network or active semantic network scheme, similar to ones used successfully in modelling visual word or letter recognition (McClelland and Rumelhart (1981); Rumelhart and McClelland (1982)), skilled motor performance (Rumelhart and Norman (1981)), speech errors (Dell (1980)), low and high level visual processing (Feldman (1981, 1982a); Feldman and Ballard (1982); Hinton (1981); Hrechanyk and Ballard (1982)). A particular source of optimism for this approach is the successful work in modelling low-level letter and word recognition by McClelland and Rumelhart. Their model was used to explain a large body of research on the "word superiority" effect. When a letter is presented briefly on a screen, it is recognized faster and more accurately if it is in the context of a word than if it is presented alone. Their model accounted for this difference solely on the basis of feedback connections between a word unit and its constituent letter units, without any specific "context" mechanism built in. Thus, we hope that such models will give us context effects as a side effect of the architecture.

An example, taken from McClelland and Rumelhart (1981), is shown in Figure 1. The network is divided into three levels, the bottom level representing input from the vision system consisting of positionally indexed features of letters, which feed into units representing the letters formed by those features at the next level, which in turn feed into the word units of which they are a part at the next level. Units representing different letters in the same position inhibit one another, and features which are incompatible with units at the next level inhibit those units. As mentioned above, this model is used to explain a large body of psychological results which show that it is easier to detect the presence of letters when they are in the context of words than if they are presented alone (the word superiority effect). The effect is a result of feedback to the letter units from the word units they stimulate, feedback that does not occur when the letter is presented alone. It is an explanatory model in a strong sense: the units involved could correspond to neuronal level units, and some of the effects are a direct result of the architecture used. For example, there is a word superiority effect for pronounceable non-words (such as "mave") which is shown in their model to be a result of a "gang effect". There is a "gang" of word units that are similar to the non-word (such as "have", "make", and "move") which provide the necessary feedback for the superiority effect. The words in the gang all have three letter units partially activating them. The feedback from the many partial activations is equivalent to that of a completely activated word. This is a side effect of the archictecture which may not have occurred to those designing symbol-passing models. The system illustrates an important structuring technique used in designing such networks: division into layers of processing with connections only allowed between adjacent layers and within layers. Within a level, however, mutually exclusive networks may be built, that is, nets with very few interconnections.

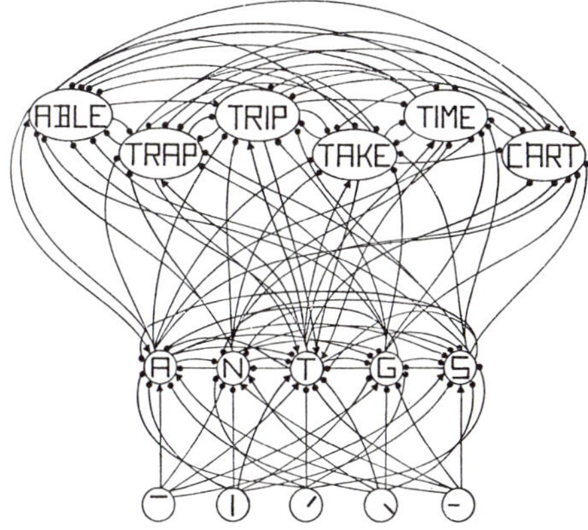

Figure 1: A few of the neighbors of the node for the letter "t" in the first position in a word, and their interconnections (McClelland and Rumelhart (1981)).

2.1 Example

Our model was inspired by the McClelland and Rumelhart model, and we hope to gain as much explanatory power from this approach. As an anchor for this research, we are concentrating on modelling the results of Seidenberg et. al. and Swinney explained above. So far we have designed and simulated an example network that disambiguates four different senses of the word "threw" on the basis of highly specialized case information and frequency of word senses. We present a brief example here to give the flavor of our model.

We start where McClelland and Rumelhart left off; that is, our input level consists of word units. The example sentence is "bob threw the fight". We simulate hearing or reading the sentence by sequentially stimulating the units "bob", "threw", "the", and "fight", so that it takes four steps of the simulation to input this sentence (we have so far not attempted to bring the timing into line with the data). These word units are connected to appropriate "meaning" units at the next level. At this early stage of design, this is simply represented by using an "awkward lexeme" (Wilks (1976)) for each sense of the word we want to represent. The "bob" unit thus stimulates the BOB1 unit at the word sense level. The "threw" unit stimulates PROPEL, GAVE (as in "threw a party"), THREW1 ("threw a fight"), and VOMIT ("threw up") in parallel, modelling the "several meanings active" result of the studies cited above. The next level encodes constraints between these interpretations in the form of highly specific case frames for the verbs. The case frames represent specific types of AGENT, OBJECT, etc. that are "expected" for each verb. Figure 2 shows the relevant subset of the network for this example, including the verb-to-case-frame connections for PROPEL and THREW1. Cases are nominalized by tacking on the first letter of the sense to AGT, OBJ, LOC, etc. Type information is encoded by the connections from noun senses to case roles. For example, "threw" in the "threw a fight" sense expects the object to be some kind of game, so FIGHT1 is connected to TOBJ, but FOOD is not. These links can thus be thought of as the well-known "isa" links. In contrast, a fight is not something one can propel, so there is no connection between FIGHT1 and POBJ.

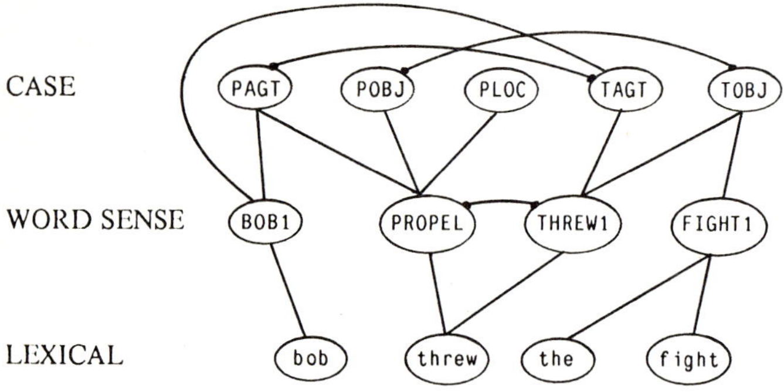

Figure 2: Subset of the network for "bob threw the fight".

When a verb word sense, such as PROPEL becomes active, it sends enough activation to the case frame above it so that the case nodes are just below threshold, and any filler sending them activation will cause them to "fire". When the unit FIGHT1 becomes active, its connection to the case node TOBJ causes TOBJ to fire, which feeds activation back to both FIGHT1 and THREW1. This feedback is what allows THREW1 to defeat the competing senses of "threw" through mutually inhibitory links. The result is a stable coalition (mutually supporting units) between the correct word senses and THREW1's case frame. To paraphrase Hinton (1981), "at the early stages of language processing, individual units can represent hypotheses about how small parts of the sentence should be interpreted, and interactions between units can encode knowledge about the constraints between local interpretations." In our model, the case nodes reflect the constraints between how the verb and nouns can go together.

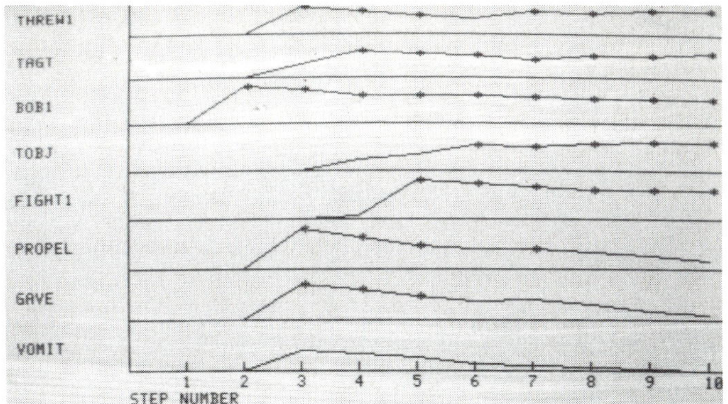

Figure 3: Graph of unit potential over time from the simulation of "bob threw the fight". Scale is 0 to 10 (y-axis).

2.2 <u>Model Organization</u>

We propose a three-level, four component network to represent the parsing system (see Figure 4). This takes as its lowest level the top level of the McClelland and Rumelhart network. An overview of the function of each level follows. More detail is presented later, and forms the bulk of this paper.

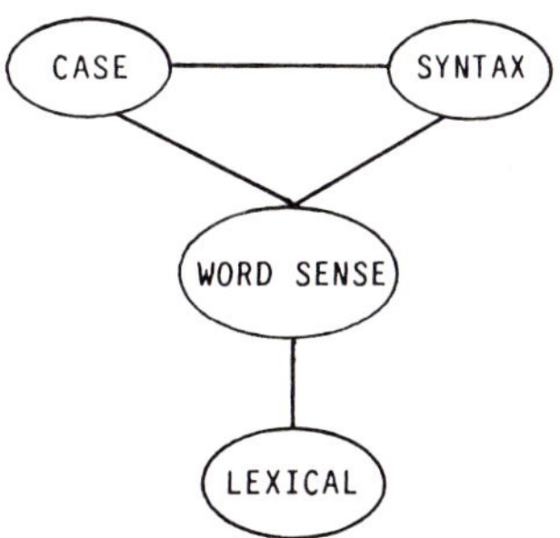

Figure 4: An overview of the system.

The Lexical Level. This is the input level of our network. The units at this level roughly represent morphemes, but as a simplifying assumption, we just have a unit for every word in the language. Future elaboration of the model will include breakdown by morphemes.

The Word Sense Level. All morphemes are connected to their "meaning" nodes at this level. Ambiguous words are connected to all their meanings, which mutually inhibit one another within their subnetworks. There are three subnets at this level, the "noun phrase" or "object" network, the predicate or "action/event" network, and the function word network. Mutual inhibition exists between different noun meanings of the same word, and between different predicate meanings, but not between nouns and verbs as a whole.

The Case Level. This level expresses the possible relationships (bindings) between the predicates and objects. We posit an "exploded case" representation; that is, we use several hundred case roles that are more specific than Agent, Object, etc., but fall into those classes (see Fahlman (1979)). These nodes as a result are connected to fewer word senses than Agent and Object would be, and carry much more information directly.

The Syntax Level. In the current formulation, this network operates on the linkage between word senses and the case roles in order to constrain what bindings may be made, based on sentence structure. For example, if a passive construct is encountered, this would enable certain connections (e.g., between the subject NP and the OBJECT cases) while disabling others, reflecting the passive transformation.

The operation of the model consists of a flow of activation from the lexical items (introduced in sequence) to their meanings. The meaning nodes in turn, activate the case nodes. The relation that fits the input best will then "win." Winning involves the formation of a stable coalition, that is, a group of connected nodes in which the overall excitation exceeds the overall inhibition. Our model can be said to have "worked" if the proper case roles form a coalition with the right meanings and morphemes from the sentence. Since many sentences are ambiguous, the network will have to decide on an interpretation based on word sense frequency and relational knowledge expressed at the case level. We presuppose higher levels in the network for making general inferences and for long term memory. We must leave specifying these to future research. However, these levels provide the famous "context" (aside from local context) and we can simulate their effects by pre-loading the network with different biases.

3. PREVIOUS WORK

3.1 Word Sense Discrimination

The problem of how people understand language has received considerable attention from artificial intelligence researchers in the last 20 years. Natural language understanding is a hard problem in part because of the highly ambiguous nature of natural language. In a recent informal study, Gentner (1981) found that the 20 most frequent nouns have an average of 7.3 (dictionary) word senses each; the 20 most frequent verbs have an average of 12.4 senses each. Small (1978) lists 57 senses for the word "take." We believe that a model which tries to emulate how people understand language must take seriously the ambiguity problem, since whatever process people use to understand language, it handles this problem well (Rieger (1976)). We propose a model that handles ambiguous words in what we believe to be a clean way, and is at the same time neurologically and psychologically plausible.

Only a few researchers have attacked the ambiguity problem in the past, most notably (Wilks (1976); Riesbeck and Schank (1976); Hayes (1977); Small and Rieger (1982)). The answer proposed always involves some notion of "context." Given enough context, the argument goes, nothing is ambiguous. Context is used to constrain the search for the proper meaning of the word. If the wrong one is chosen, a program can backtrack. However, the Swinney and Seidenberg results, noted earlier, suggest that people actually access some meanings in parallel, and then "choose" one. We have designed a model which is in keeping with these results.

In our previous work on Word Expert Parsing (WEP) (Small (1980)), an attempt was made to attack these issues. The principal work upon which WEP was based, the ELI system of Riesbeck (1974) and the PARSIFAL system of Marcus (1979), emphasized the modelling of human language comprehension, but along different dimensions. Riesbeck and Schank (1976) were concerned with the great interdependence of memory and parsing, and attempted to create a program that was able to use syntactic, semantic, and contextual cues present in language to infer the effects of reading on the structure of memory. Marcus used carefully organized data and procedural structures to model the parsing process in a way that fit certain empirical constraints from linguistics and psychology.

In the Word Expert Parser all language knowledge is embodied in word experts, which communicate among themselves until they agree on a mutually satisfying interpretation for the sentence. The model focuses on the irregularities of language rather than the regularities, and therefore views all words as more or less idiomatic. This leads to a word centered approach, in which each expert knows how its word's meaning changes depending on other words occurring to its right or left. Despite the obvious parallelism that could be exploited in such a model, each expert is a sequential process, which runs in a coroutine discipline with the others. A large amount of effort in the WEP was devoted to the problems of coroutines, demons, timeouts, and similar control issues, making the language processing aspects less perspicuous.

While WEP and the work on which it was based have led to interesting results, there are reasons for questioning their underlying assumptions. Psychological data on lexical decision and aphasia, cited above, suggest that the processing mechanisms used in these models are not correct (Small and Lucas (1983)). Physiological evidence shows that the human brain functions in a fundamentally different way than do traditional computers and programs. We claim that the type of model architecture described below has a better chance of matching these kinds of data than does the more traditional symbol passing framework and that it employs a cleaner processing mechanism than WEP.

3.2 Connectionist Models

The archictecture used for our model derives directly from the massively parallel models of the sort currently under development by Feldman and Ballard and others (Feldman and Ballard (1982); Hrechanyk and Ballard (1982); Hinton (1981)), which they call *connectionist models*. While their primary interest has been computer vision, where parallel iterative methods have long been used in low-level processing (Rosenfeld, Hummel, and Zucker (1976)), our hypothesis is that there is much overlap in the underlying implementation of the two processes in the brain.

We follow the formulation of Feldman and Ballard (1982) in outlining the basic characteristics of connectionist models. The basic idea is to design networks of simple computing units that compute by being connected appropriately, and the intent is that these units should correspond roughly to an information processing model of our current understanding of neurons. The definitions are not meant to be minimal or elegant, but loose enough to model anything from a small part of a neuron to the external functionality of a major subsystem.

A unit or node in our world is a computational entity comprising:

$\{q\}$: a set of *discrete states* (less than 10)
p: a continuous value in $[-10,10]$, called *potential*
v: an *output value*, integers $0..10$
i: a vector of *inputs* $i_1,...,i_n$

and functions from old to new values of these:

$$p \leftarrow f(i,p,q)$$
$$q \leftarrow g(i,p,q)$$
$$v \leftarrow h(i,p,q)$$

Since all of our units use the same thresholded potential output function, it is useful to characterize a unit that has output as *firing*. Note that there is no notion of time in this definition, and this is usually handled by requiring all units to remain in synchronization. Also, there is no constraint on the function computed by a unit, although we usually require that it be relatively simple. On the other hand, using more complex functions, we can define units that represent a network of other units, thus giving us the ability to abstract from networks. Note that we are not restricting ourselves to linear units, so we are not resurrecting perceptrons (Minsky and Papert (1972)).

A *connection* (or link) is an identification of an element of a unit's input vector with the output of some unit (possibly the same one), along with a *weight*, a value between 0 and 1 which is multiplied times any value transmitted on the link before it is passed to the unit. This is used to rate the importance of a link to a unit. For example, a word unit will have links to its various senses weighted to reflect the frequency of each sense for that word, so that the most frequent sense will get proportionately more input. As a further example, a verb word sense unit will get more highly weighted feedback from its obligatory case units than from the optional ones, so that if obligatory cases are not filled (and thus not producing output), the verb unit will not get enough feedback to remain firing.

A *network* is a set of units with a definition of these functions for each unit, and the connections between them, exhaustively defining the input vector for each unit.

One *cycle* or iteration of the simulation consists of computing the above functions for each unit in the network. All units are thus kept in lock step.

We may use these definitions to have our units perform logical functions on their inputs. We depart from Feldman and Ballard who found OR-of-AND units useful (corresponding to disjunctive normal form). We have found AND-of-OR units more appropriate for our work. A simple way to describe this in our terms is to define the potential in terms of a sum of separate maximum computations, e.g.,

$$p \leftarrow p + k(\max(i_1, i_2) + \max(i_3, i_4))$$

which is the continuous analog of

$$p \leftarrow p + k(OR(i_1, i_2) \ \& \ OR(i_3, i_4))$$

when combined with appropriate thresholds.

We can think of the arguments to the "max" expressions as corresponding to input *sites* (see Figure 5). For example, in our case units, one site can have all possible "fillers" for that case connected to it, another all possible predicates which use that case. If we use an output function which thresholds the potential, we can make it so that the unit does not fire unless both a filler and a predicate are present. We term such sites *conjunctive sites*.

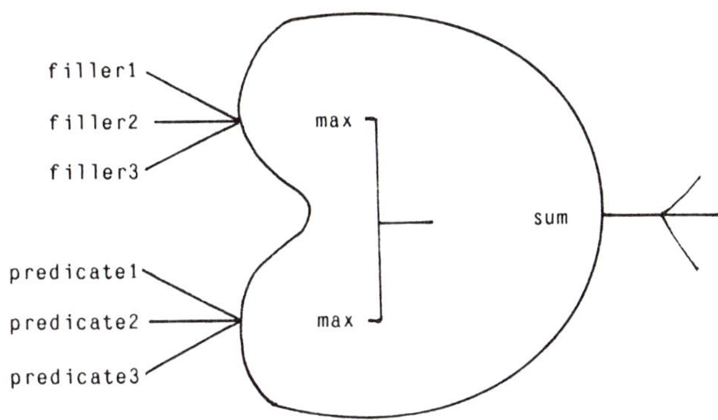

Figure 5: A typical case unit.

A defining feature of the connectionist approach differentiating it from so-called "diffuse" neural network models is the unit/value principle. That is, a unit represents a value of a parameter. If it receives input from other units that provide evidence for this value and this input exceeds the unit's threshold, the unit fires at a rate which expresses its confidence in the value it represents. This is transmitted to all connected units. This was seen in the introductory example in that each unit represented a lexical item, a word sense, or a case role.

A connection machine provides us with a new metaphor for information processing models to replace the Von Neumann machine, which has been used for this purpose since the beginning of the endeavor. This approach is being explored by a number of researchers (see papers in Hinton and Anderson (1981)), who are developing models based on theoretical architectures closer to the human brain in its characteristics. Further, some researchers are developing actual computer hardware to operate with massive parallelism and low degradation of overall behavior in the face of local errors (Hillis (1981); Fahlman (1980)). The development of information processing models under this new framework is already leading to advances (McClelland and Rumelhart (1981); Dell (1980)). We refer the reader to the cited papers for further discussion on why this paradigm might be a valuable new way to pursue the goals of cognitive science.

4. A MORE DETAILED LOOK

The purpose of this section is to outline the preliminary system in more detail. We will approach the description in a bottom-up manner, starting with the lexical level and working our way up to the syntax level.

The Lexical Level. The nodes at this level represent elements of the lexicon of the model, one unit per word. Connections are unidirectional from these units to all their possible senses at the word sense level, so that a lexical unit excites its meanings and then decays rapidly. Connections are weighted according to word sense frequency such that usual senses of a word get more initial activation than unusual senses (evidence from Yates (1978) indicates that this may be in error: subordinate senses seem to get primed just as well as frequent ones). Although we assume that the lexical level is driven by a phoneme perception network and a visual perception network, for our purposes it is the input level: we simulate hearing a sentence such as "John loves Mary" by activating the "John", "loves" and "Mary" units sequentially, with a model-dependent delay between them.

The Word Sense Level. All morphemes at the lexical level are connected to their "meaning" nodes at this level. Currently, we simply have an "awkward lexeme" (Wilks (1976)) for every sense we want to represent. Connections up to the next level vary with syntactic class; verb units prime case frames at the case level, while nouns fill cases. Feedback connections are also different; verbs will not remain firing unless their obligatory cases are filled, while nouns only need feedback from one case node to remain high.

In order to represent order information, every node is duplicated several times for different positions in the sentence. Thus unit BOB1 represents a sense of "bob" at position 1 in the sentence. This is not totally implausible; only noun (object concepts) and verbs (so far we have ignored adjectives and adverbs) are duplicated. We assume that the number of duplicates can be kept at some small fixed number (roughly corresponding to the number of things that can be maintained in short term memory) and that a suitable "chunking" mechanism can be devised to overcome this limitation. Function words have meaning only in their influence on the syntax network and through priming case nodes ("to", for example, will prime all Location case nodes).

All meaning nodes are involved in two mutual inhibition networks. One is a *winner-take-all* (WTA) network which determines which word sense occurs at at a particular position in the input: all word sense nodes representing the same position are mutually inhibiting. This guarantees that we only get one meaning per position in the sentence. The other mutual inhibition network is between the same word senses at different positions. Since it is not known in advance where a meaning will occur in a sentence, the lexical unit stimulates all positions; the winner is determined by extra input from the syntax net which favors the word sense at the current position. The inhibition between these is not as great as within-position inhibition to allow the possibility of repeated words.

The Case Level. We follow Bruce (1975) who defines a case as a binary relation which holds between a predicate (usually a verb) and its argument. For example, in the sentence "John ran home," "ran" is the predicate with two cases showing in this sentence:

>   Agent (ran, John)
>   Dest (ran, home)

Thus, our cases will represent possible relations between the predicate and the noun phrases. General cases such as Agent and Object, however, are not very useful as an aid to parsing. For example, in the sentence "John bought a dog," both John and a dog can be agents (considering only semantic information), so they must both be eventually connected to the Agent node as in Figure 6.

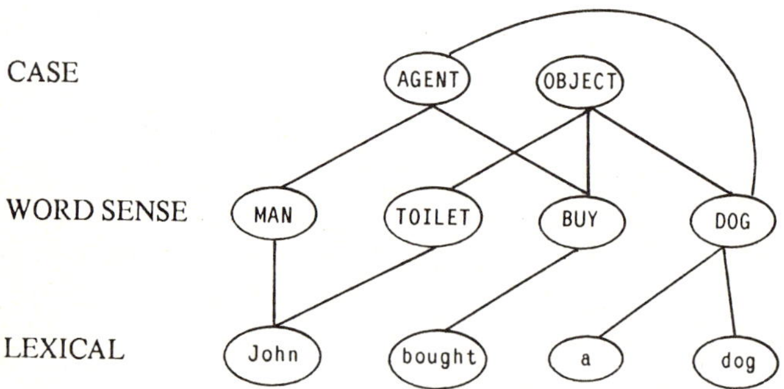

Figure 6: Agent and Object are not good enough.

We need more semantics than this in our case nodes. Given that we have a large number of nodes to work with, it is reasonable to use a large number of more specific relations. We term this representation an *exploded case* representation.

We make our cases specific in two ways. The first is semantic: cases are verb-specific and represent the *type* of Agent, Object, etc. that may be used with the associated verb. In the above example, the predicate would be connected to a BUY-AGENT node that represents agents capable of buying. This allows much more specific connections and more constraints on the role fillers. The SOME-DOG node is not connected to the BUY-AGENT node (see Figure 7), preventing a competing coalition from forming (this implementation of existential quantifiers is a simplification for our first-cut approach). This allows much more specific connections and more constraints on the role fillers (a dog would never be a BUY-AGENT). This also has the advantage of building expectations (through subliminal activation of case frames by their verbs) for the remaining (highly specific) cases to be filled in the sentence, reminiscent of expectation-based parsing systems (Riesbeck & Schank (1976); Small (1980)). Because of the specificity of the cases, these expectations are a strong way of resolving a large number of lexical ambiguities.

We saw an example of this in the "bob threw the fight" example, where THREW1 stimulated TOBJ to just below threshold, and when an appropriate filler came along (FIGHT1), TOBJ fired immediately. Because of the specificity of the cases, these expectations should be a strong way of helping to resolve a large number of lexical ambiguities. This was demonstrated in our initial example in that the correct sense of "threw" was found through feedback from its exploded case frame, i.e., the particular type of object that fit with the "threw the fight" sense (lexicalized as TOBJ in that example) lent activation to that sense. More examples follow this section.

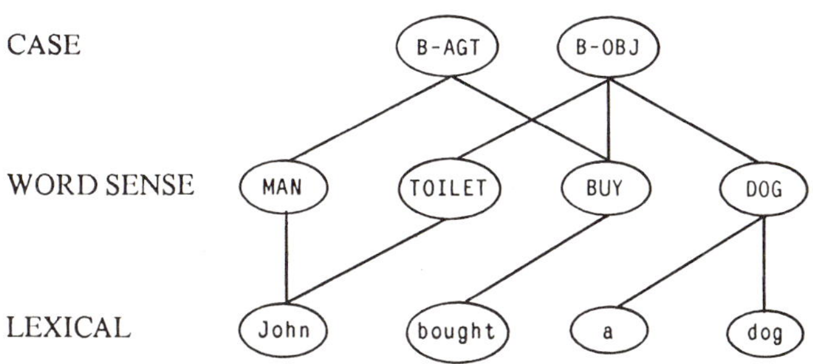

Figure 7: Exploded cases are better.

The second way in which cases are exploded is syntactic: they are indexed by position in correspondence with the positional word senses, so that LOVE-AGENT1, LOVE-AGENT2, etc., represent "the Agent is in position 1", "the Agent is in position 2," and so on. These receive input from the syntax network to drive Agents in position 1 high in active sentences and Objects in position 1 high in passive sentences.

A technical problem that now arises is the "binding problem," that is, how noun phrases become associated with the cases that they fill. In our initial example, the mutually reinforcing units FIGHT1 and TOBJ represent a binding. The exploded case representation thus constitutes a partial solution to this problem, insofar as it does the binding in cases where the binding can be made on semantic grounds. Its advantage is in allowing us to use our relational nodes as type nodes. The usual cases of Agent, Object, Experiencer, etc., can be thought of as implying type restrictions on what can fill them. The Agent case, for example, must usually be filled by an animate object. By using more specific relations, we can require that the filler of the Propel-Object case, for example, be something "capable of being propelled." Thus we have explicit links between fillers and their cases, which encode type relations, as in the above example. The binding is made if a stable coalition arises between the correct interpretation of the word sense (the "right" word sense node) and the case node.

This leaves open the question of how we understand sentences which specify unusual fillers for such cases, as when a tornado "throws" a house through the air. One possible answer involves hierarchical type relations, either in the cases themselves, or in an underlying semantic net. The solution lies in being able to trigger an upward move in this hierarchy, to allow more general fillers for cases.

The Syntax Level. In a parallel language perception network, this problem comes down to the representation of the sequential nature of the input. We describe an abstract representation here, called a *sequence network*, which moves through a sequence in response to incoming data. This representation provides the basic building block for the representation of syntax in our model.

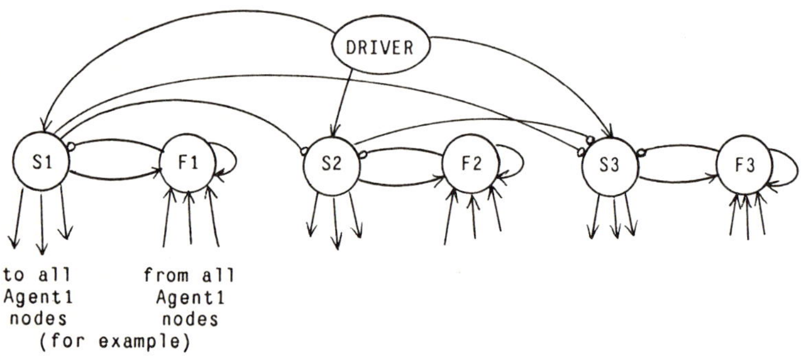

Figure 8: A sequence network.

The sequence network is depicted in Figure 8. Each node is an independent processing unit and thus receives no other information than the firing frequency of the units connected to its input sites. The uppermost unit in the figure is the "driver" of this network; it is assumed to be firing throughout this example. All other units are initially at rest. The driver sends activation to all of the sequence units (s_i's) simultaneously, so that they all begin to fire at the same time. Each sequence unit has inhibitory links (shown with a dot at the end of the arc) to all following units, which causes the first unit to quickly suppress the firing of "later" units (this is inspired by a similar idea used in Rumelhart and Norman (1982) to model motor control). The s_1 unit can then send activation to all units in another network that represent the first element of the sequence (for example, all Agent units). This disposes these units to fire more easily from other input. They are in turn, connected to the f_1 unit, which represents feedback that the first element of the sequence has occurred in the input. The f_1 unit requires input from both s_1 and an Agent unit (for example) in order to fire. This prevents it from firing unless that element of the sequence is expected. It is self-connected so that it remains firing once it starts. The f_1 unit then inhibits the s_1 unit, allowing the other sequence units to begin to fire. The s_2 unit quickly inhibits the others, and the process continues. Note that the network is not allowed to move on to the next element of the sequence until it receives feedback; this keeps it in synchrony with the input independent of the arrival rate of the input (unless the input comes in faster than it can respond). A trace of a simulation of this network is shown in Figure 9. The graphs are of activation levels for each unit over time, placed above one another. The x-axis is time (simulation steps); the y-axes are activation (0 to 10).

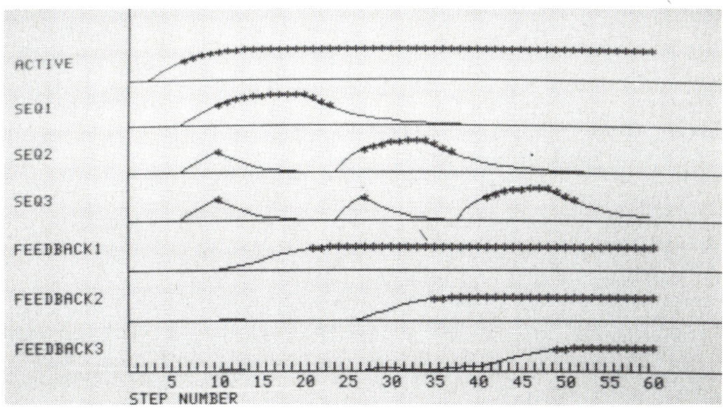

Figure 9: Simulation of the example sequence network.

In the current model, the syntax network operates on the word sense positional WTA networks and the indexed case roles in the order in which they are expected, using these sequence networks. In the second example to follow, we use two of these, one representing a simple active sentence in terms of cases (Agent-Verb-Object), and another for passives (Object-Verb-Agent). The syntax network is set up to expect an active sentence. If a passive construct is encountered, this enables the passive sequence network which inhibits the active one and overcomes incorrect bindings (coalitions). This involves inhibiting all Agent1 ("the Agent is in the first position") units and exciting all Object1 ("the object is in the first position") units, reflecting the passive transformation. To overcome these bindings requires a large amount of inhibition, suggesting why passives are "hard."

Clearly sequence networks do not have to operate strictly in lock step; they can be relaxed to allow skipping optional sequence elements, and they can be arranged in trees (the driver can itself be an element of a higher level sequence), making them suitable for grammar representations. The next section gives an example of word sense discrimination followed by an example of processing an active and passive sentence.

5. EXAMPLE ANALYSES

We present the results of two small networks built with the ISCON network design aid and simulator (Small et al. (1983)). ISCON allows a user to define types of units, create, modify and connect them, and run simulations with or without graphic output. The definition of a type includes specifications of input sites and associated functions, and the functions associated with computing the new state, potential, and output from the results of the site inputs. For example, the predicate node type in the example network has three input sites: word (from lexical level), case (from the unit's case frame) and inhibitory (from other senses of the same verb). All types used the McClelland and Rumelhart (1981) potential function, and output was simply a thresholded potential (no states were used). The simulator allows the user to stop at any point and view the nodes of the network, and modify it if desired. Performance is expected to degrade for networks of over a few hundred nodes, so we are working on a compiler to convert the networks into a faster representation.

Note that the examples are simple, but at the same time illustrate important processing characteristics of the model. The first example illustrates the analysis of a sentence that contains highly ambiguous words, and shows the partial hypotheses of the model at intermediate processing states. The second example shows the use of sequence networks for the analysis of active and passive sentences in such a way that the correct bindings (see discussion above) are made.

5.1 Example: Word Sense Disambiguation

This is a toy example, using only 40 units, but it illustrates several processing characteristics of our model, and two ways in which it can disambiguate verb senses. The syntax portion of the model is not used in this example. This is an illustration of how far we can get without it. The network successfully disambiguates the sense of "threw" (and "ball") in the following sentences:

        1) bob threw a ball.
        2) bob threw a ball for charity.
        3) bob threw a ball to the dog.
        4) bob threw the fight.
        5) bob threw up dinner.
        6) bob threw a ball up.
       *7) bob threw up a ball.
       *8) threw bob ball up.

The last two sentences illustrate what we feel is a desirable property of cognitive models of language understanding: the ability to "make sense" of an ungrammatical input. While syntax must have a role in our model, it should not prevent understanding of these sentences, but only impose constraints on bindings that may be overridden. This is in sharp contrast to many previous AI models, which would most likely "break," or reject such input, without making sense of it.

We will describe a trace of the processing of Sentence 5, keeping in mind the possibility of Sentence 7. Following this we will discuss the processing of Sentence 1, keeping in mind the possibility of Sentence 2, as this will illustrate a different disambiguation process.

Example A: Parsing a Collocation

The relevant subset of the network is shown in Figure 10. Note that typing information is encoded in the connections to the cases. FOOD "isa" VOBJ, but isn't usually a POBJ (recall that exploded cases are lexicalized by tacking on the first letter of the predicate which defines them: PROPEL, VOMIT, THREW1 ("threw the fight") and GAVE ("threw a party")). Obviously, food can be propelled, and a low-weighted connection should be included to reflect this. For this example, we simulate hearing or reading the sentence by stimulating each word at the lexical level sequentially; the next word is introduced at each iteration of the simulation. Figure 11 shows a trace of the potentials of each of the relevant units for this example. (POBJ and PREC are not shown. They do not fire in this example, as neither has a filler.) We see that at iteration 3, BOB1 has primed PAGT and VAGT (along with TAGT and GAGT, not shown). These units will not cross threshold and fire until they get additional input from their associated predicates (at iterations 4 and 5, respectively). This is an example of how we prevent activation from spreading too much: conjunctive sites are used at the case nodes so that both the predicate and a filler must be present (firing) for the case node to fire and feed back to the filler and predicate. Nodes on the word sense level (fillers and predicates) have the feedback connections weighted so they will not fire from top-down feedback alone; they must have bottom-up input first.

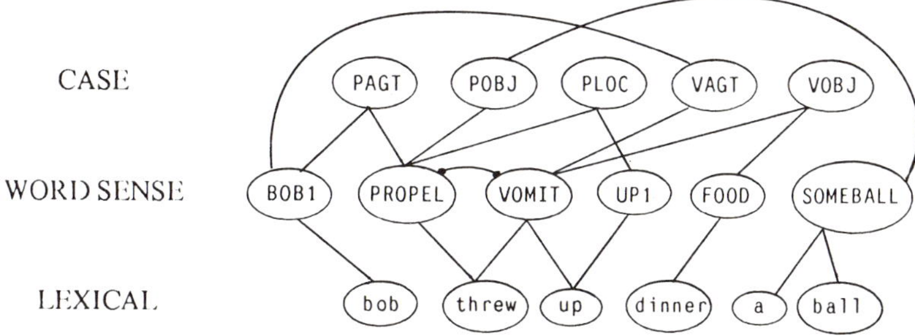

Figure 10: The subset of the connection network for Example A.

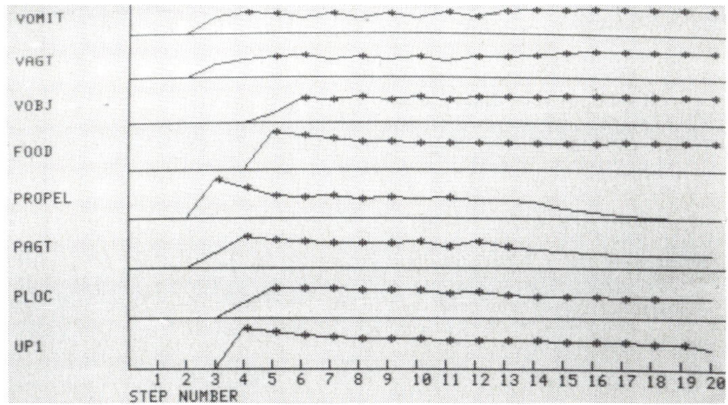

Figure 11: Graph of unit potential over time from the simulation of Example A. Scale is 0 to 10 (y-axis).

Also at iteration 3, the lexical unit for "threw" has excited the four units on the word sense level (not all shown) representing its possible meanings. Figure 12 (from the same simulation) shows how collocations such as "threw up" are handled: there is a conjunctive connection from "threw" and "up" to VOMIT, so that VOMIT does not cross threshold until both are on. This is consistent with some results of Swinney (private communication) which show that the sense of a collocation is not active until all the participating words are heard.

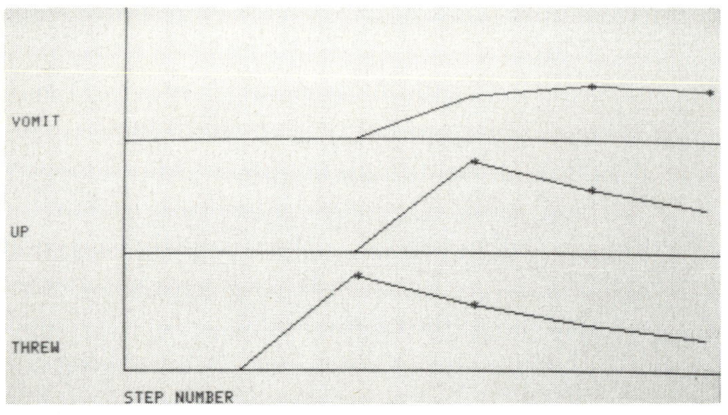

Figure 12: Processing a collocation (from the simulation of Example A).

At iteration 4 in Figure 11 we see parallel activation of multiple hypotheses: both VOMIT and PROPEL are active. A mutually inhibitory connection between them helps insure that one will "win." We also see part of the case frame for PROPEL has been primed (POBJ and PREC, not shown, have also been primed). One case, PAGT, has been "filled"; that is, the PAGT node has crossed threshold and is involved in a mutual feedback coalition with BOB1 and PROPEL. The rest of the cases are basically in "expectation" state: if a filler in the noun network comes along, they will immediately cross threshold, as in the next iteration when activation spreads from UP1 to PLOC.

We skip to iteration 8 (Figure 11). Here we show two cases filled for each predicate; FOOD fills the requirements for a VOBJ, and UP1 fills the PLOC (location) case, while both PAGT and VAGT are filled by BOB1. However, all cases are not created equal. The reason PROPEL is no longer firing by iteration 12 is that weights are set in feedback connections from the case nodes so that obligatory cases, in this example PAGT and POBJ, must be firing in order for the verb to keep firing. Hence VOMIT "wins" here, since both VAGT and VOBJ have been filled. If, instead, "a ball" had been scanned, this would have filled the POBJ case, and the PROPEL coalition would have "won." We can liken this to a "voting" procedure where the cases cast votes for their verb (Ballard (1983)). The dropping off of PROPEL eventually leads to its cases also fading, so that by iteration 20 (Figure 13 shows all the units involved in the coalition) we have a stable coalition showing the result of the parse. This, for us, *is* the result: a pattern of activation on nodes representing the correct interpretation. Note that, since there is still residual activation on PLOC and PAGT, subsequent reinterpretation ("it splattered all over the ceiling") should be easier, although we have not yet investigated mechanisms for effecting this.

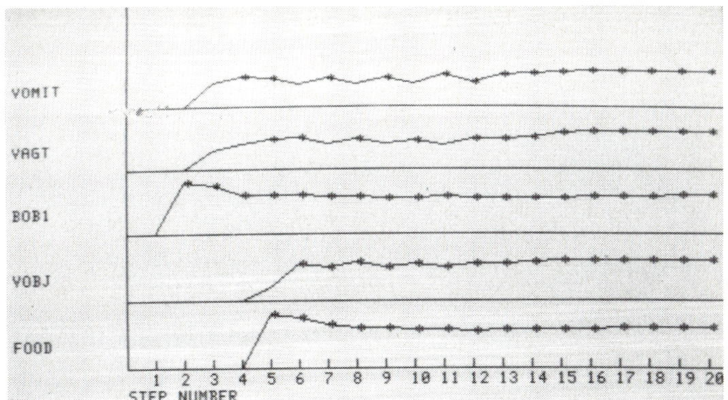

Figure 13: Result of the parse: a stable coalition.

Example B: Verb and Object Disambiguation

The second example will trace the result of the introduction of Sentence 1, "bob threw a ball". Note that in this case, there are two meanings for "ball" represented in the network: the round kind and the "dance" kind. Here we will have two senses of threw with two obligatory cases filled (AGENT and OBJECT), so the disambiguation will depend on word sense frequency alone. This is represented by having different weights on the connections between the lexical nodes and the word sense nodes. Figure 14 shows the relevant subset of the network for this example.

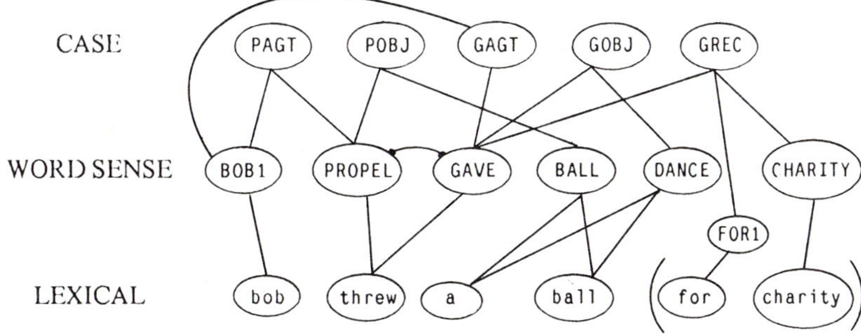

Figure 14: The subset of the connection network for Example B.

Figure 3 from the early example illustrates how connection weights reflect word sense frequency. (Processing is the same for the current example through iteration 3). Here we show the four senses of "threw" we have represented. The activation levels of the verb senses reflect the different weights on connections from "threw"; the senses considered more frequent are thus given proportionately more activation. This activation level difference is the same, although harder to detect, in Figure 15, where we show the case frames for the senses of interest, PROPEL and GAVE (a poorly lexicalized sense representing "gave a party"). Both the POBJ and GOBJ cases will be filled by the different senses of "ball" (SOMEBALL fills the POBJ case and SOMEDANCE fills the GOBJ case), so disambiguation will have to result from the frequency effects.

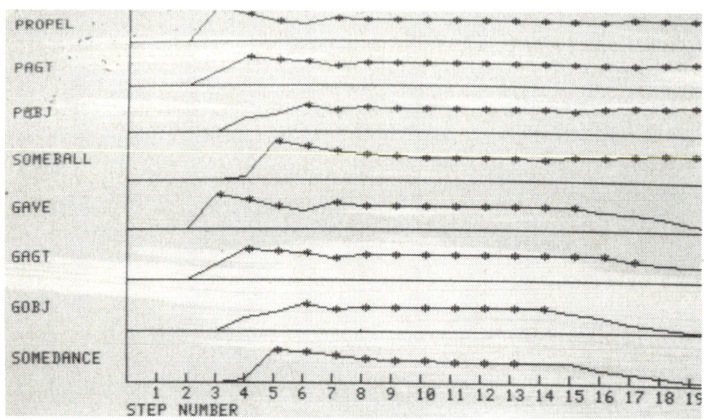

Figure 15: Output from the simulation of Example B, showing the relevant part of the case frames for PROPEL and GAVE. Mutual inhibition of word senses and competing cases, coupled with lower overall initial activation of the second coalition will result in the first "winning".

We see this situation in iteration 7 (Fig. 15). The two senses of ball (SOMEDANCE and SOMEBALL) are mutually inhibiting. The SOMEBALL sense, however, has an initial activation level higher than that of the "dance" sense. This, coupled with the lower initial activation level of the GAVE sense of "threw," enables the coalition involving PROPEL to "beat" down the activation of its competing coalition, so that by iteration 14, the SOMEDANCE unit is no longer firing. Now, with no support for the GOBJ case, it fades in the next iteration, causing GAVE to fade also, since GOBJ is an obligatory case for GAVE. In a domino fashion, the coalition for GAVE collapses, resulting in the proper coalition (the four upper units in Fig. 15, plus BOB1, not shown). Now, if the sentence ends with "for charity", the recipient case of GAVE (GREC) is filled (Fig. 16). The result is that GAVE receives more feedback (from three cases instead of two). GAVE in turn gives more activation to GOBJ, enabling more feedback to SOMEDANCE, which is enough to help it overcome SOMEBALL, resulting in the correct interpretation.

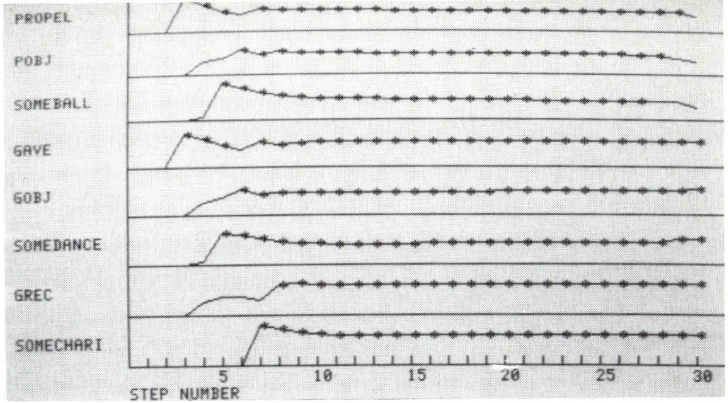

Figure 16: Output from the processing of "bob threw a ball for charity." The third filled case (GREC) helps the GAVE coalition win.

5.2 Example: Active and Passive Voices

We will trace the processing of "bob loves mary", followed by a trace of the processing of "bob is loved by mary". This network was constructed as a first pass test of some of our ideas on the representation of syntax. It is meant only to be suggestive and should not be taken as a theory.

Example A: Active Voice

Initially, all noun meanings in the first position are receiving input from the syntax network, giving them the edge they need to "win" over identical senses in other positions (see Fig. 17). (It is helpful in understanding these figures to know that the number on a word sense or case name indexes position in the sentence.) The result is that BOB1 wins over BOB2 and BOB3 when they are all stimulated equally by the "bob" unit at the lexical level. Another result at this point is that any other word senses in the first position are suppressed through the action of the WTA network they participate in with BOB1. Similarly, LOVE2 and MARY3 will later become successive "winners." We can see that "SEQ1" (part of the "active" sentence sequence network) has subliminally stimulated LAGT1 (LOVE-AGENT in position 1) so that its potential begins to rise by iteration 12, giving it the edge over LOBJ1 (LOVE-OBJECT in position 1) which doesn't start accumulating potential (from BOB1) until iteration 17. When BOB1 fires, it provides feedback to the syntax network, turning off SEQ1 and enabling the step to SEQ2. This in turn enables LOVE2 to "win". The combination of input from BOB1 and LOVE2 causes LAGT1 to fire, representing a part of the final stable coalition. Note that there is a direct link between LAGT1 and BOB1, so that stimulating either one results in a boost to the other (lots of other first-position word sense nodes are connected to LAGT1, but they are suppressed by BOB1). This is suggestive of how we might "read out" this binding to a connectionist semantic network representing long term memory.

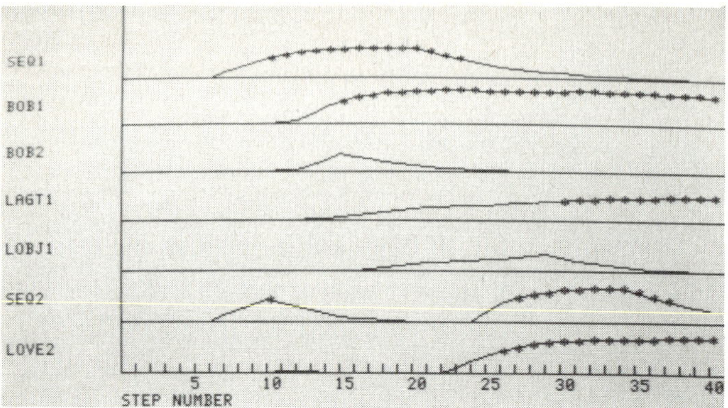

Figure 17: Graph of unit potential over time (history) for processing of "bob loves mary". Note how the model converges on BOB1 and LOVE2.

By iteration 35 (see Fig. 18, also from the simulation for Example A), the LOBJ3 unit is stimulated to just below threshold by LOVE2 and SEQ3. After "mary" has made her presence felt, the LOBJ3 unit crosses threshold due to the additional input the MARY3 unit adds and forms the final part of the stable coalition representing the result of the parse (iteration 60 in Fig. 18). Recall that in connectionist parsing, this *is* the result of the parse: a stable pattern of activation on the "correct" word sense and case nodes.

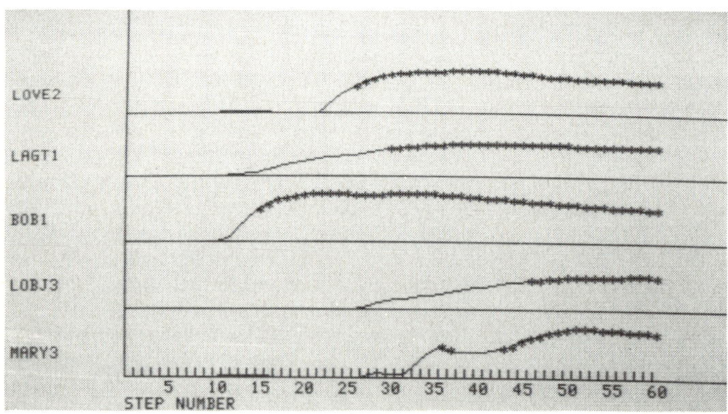

Figure 18: A history for the simulation of Example A showing the model convergence on MARY3 over other choices.

Example B: Passive Voice

The second example traces the result of processing "bob is loved by mary" (see Figs. 19 and 20). Until iteration 20 when the "is" unit begins firing on the lexical level (not shown), processing is the same. The "is," "ed," and "by" units are connected to a PASSIVE node, which is the driver for the passive sequence network. The "is" unit begins to activate this node by iteration 23, but it is not firing until it receives input from "by," (iteration 43), several iterations after the binding of BOB1 to LAGT1 is made. The PASSIVE node not only begins the passive sequence (PSEQ1), but also actively suppresses LAGT1 (and all other "Agent1" nodes) and enhances Object nodes in the first position. This allows LOBJ1 to gain the upper hand, and the proper bindings are made (see Fig. 20).

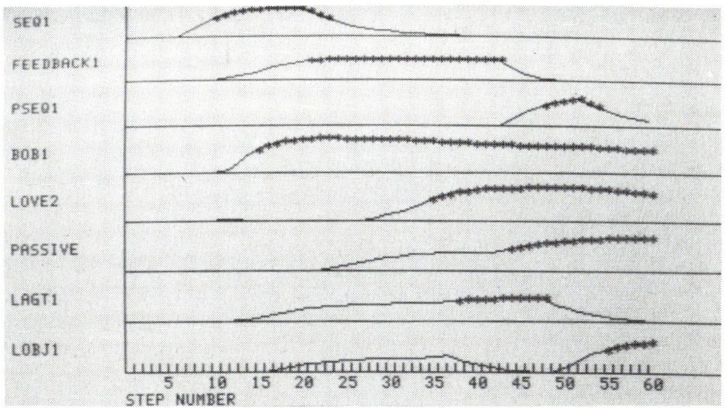

Figure 19: Potential history for passive sentence of Example B. Note suppression of LAGT1 and enhancement of LOBJ1.

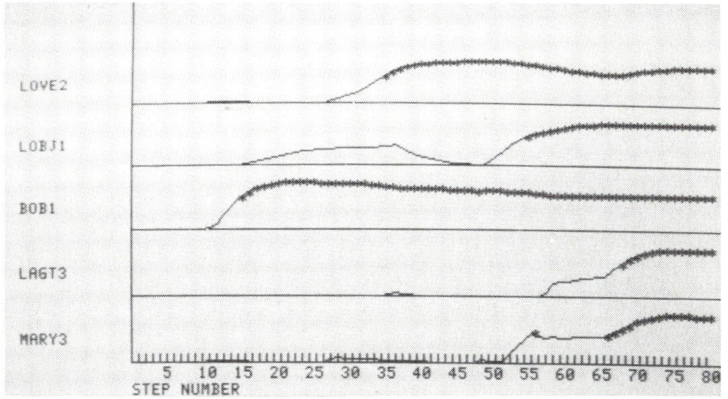

Figure 20: History for Example B showing convergence on LOBJ1 (BOB1) and LAGT3 (MARY3).

This formulation of syntax still leaves much to be desired, but it is a demonstration of the feasibility of such an approach. Future work will concentrate on how to connect this into an "active semantic network" to provide the necessary chunking ability to make the limitation on word sense positions plausible, and will also look into using "dynamic connections" (Feldman (1982b)) as a possibly more flexible alternative to indexing the word sense nodes. The long range goal involves building networks on a much grander scale to process cohesive text. Many issues remain to be solved in this effort. However, the central thesis here is that empirical constraints on neuron-like systems can be taken seriously in the modelling effort.

5.3 Discussion of Examples

Processing Aspects

Parallel processing. All units are updated simultaneously, so processing occurs at all levels at the same time. Bindings are being established between the word sense and case levels while new words are arriving at the lexical level and stimulating their senses at the word sense level.

Parallel activation of multiple hypotheses. The four senses of "threw" all fire simultaneously, while several different agent and object cases fire and compete over several iterations until the most active wins. Many NLP programs will choose an alternative and backtrack if wrong. Note that in this paradigm, it is actually easier to activate all possibilities, with the one that "fits" best winning. We saw this happen in all of the examples with the case nodes moderating the interactions between the senses.

Expectation-based parsing. Cases which are primed fire easily. These are strongly typed case roles so that the expectations are specific to the verb which defined them.

Control Aspects

Distributed decision making. Decisions between competing coalitions are decided by inhibitory links between units of the same type. Case roles of the same type (e.g., all agents) are mutually inhibiting. This is a general technique in connectionist models: incompatible value units are in a "Winner Take All" network (Feldman and Ballard (1982)) that will always settle to only one unit highly active. Note that no homunculus appeared to force decisions.

Word sense disambiguation. The structure does this in two ways: (a) Obligatory cases provide more feedback than optional ones, so that a predicate with all of its obligatory cases filled will defeat any other predicates that do not. This is the way in which VOMIT defeated PROPEL in "bob threw up dinner". Even though both verbs had two cases filled, the missing POBJ case caused PROPEL to fade out. (b) When two verbs have their obligatory cases filled, the decision is made based on word sense frequency differences. The more frequent senses get more initial activation, and this edge is enough to defeat the competing coalition.

6. RESEARCH ISSUES

In this section we discuss several issues involved in extending the model and building reasonably sized networks. Some of these can be seen as problems of scale. A small network, as illustrated above, can always be adjusted until it works. The problem is keeping things under control when large numbers of words and word senses are represented, and maintaining proper behavior when incrementally adding new words to the network. Large numbers of connections and units may also introduce unwanted crosstalk. We consider these and other issues in turn.

6.1 <u>Current Problems</u>

Semantic Priming. An important feature of the sketch presented so far is the ability to model some semantic priming effects. If two word sense nodes share the same case, the activation of one should give some activation to the other through feedback from the case node. In the model as presented, however, this only happens if a verb associated with the case is also active. An adequate representation of meaning, e.g., an active semantic network, would rectify this failing. There are two traditional approaches to this problem: semantic networks (Collins and Loftus (1975)) and shared features (Smith, Shoben, and Rips (1974)). In the first approach, related words are primed by being connected by relations in a semantic net. For example, if two nodes are of the same type, a member of the same set may be primed by activation spreading up to the type node, and back down to other members of the same type. Weights on connections would be used to reflect natural categories and exemplars (Rosch (1973); Lakoff (to appear)). Part-of relations are another kind of link through which priming can occur. We plan to explore this by building a subset of a semantic network involving one or more types of relations, such as isa or part-of, to test these these ideas. Another approach is componential analysis of meaning. In this scenario, the meaning of a word is represented by activating sets of primitive features. Words which share features will prime one another simply by the fact that some of the features for related words will be activated when all the features for the target word are also activated. These approaches are not necessarily incompatible, and we intend to explore both.

Sharing. A problem introduced by sharing features or types is keeping stable coalitions distinct; that is, preventing activation from "bleeding" too much. This problem didn't arise in our example because for every new meaning we simply introduced a new node, with no connection (except inhibitory) with other meanings. We already have seen one technique for controlling activation in the above examples; different weights on connections prevent nodes without bottom-up input from becoming activated by top-down feedback. Whether this type of control will be adequate in all cases remains to be seen.

Unwanted Side Effects. As the network size increases, side effects may arise simply through the complexity of the network; activation may spread in unplanned ways, giving spurious results. One problem arose in designing the example network: more than one stable coalition persisted without converging to one, forcing us to add more inhibitory connections between competing parts of the coalitions. Mutual inhibition of competing hypotheses is necessary for decisions to be made, but how much is plausible? Although the brain is characterized by massive inhibition, we want to avoid arbitrarily forming inhibitory links (e.g., having FOOD inhibit BALL), and therefore adopt a conservative approach.

One factor which has considerably reduced the effect of new units on previous network behavior is the widespread use of functions such as maximum and minimum at input sites. These functions don't care about how many arguments they have, and if input from the new units is within the range of previous inputs, no change in behavior results. For example, adding less frequent verb senses of throw, which get less initial excitation, has no effect on processing of sentences which use more frequent meanings. Even though these senses are mutually inhibiting, the inhibitory input to all senses other than the most frequent (PROPEL) come from PROPEL, since it produces the maximum inhibition. Thus, mutual inhibition between verb senses is constant with respect to the number of senses known.

Another aspect of adding new words to an existing network is the necessity of discovering rules for what connections should be made and what new units need to be created. Without this, we do not have an adequate theory. The example network was hand built, but already rules are emerging; by connecting corresponding case roles in a mutually inhibiting network, we can prevent more than one stable coalition from persisting. The goal is to have new units and connections generated semi-automatically when adding new words. This will also prevent errors in construction when the networks get more complex.

Numbers. At this point, we might consider our constraint on the number of units and connections available. If we imagine a network large enough to duplicate a person's vocabulary, are we still within bounds on the number of units? A rough estimate is on the order of 10^4 lexical units X 10 senses each X 10 case nodes each (exaggerating slightly) X 10 "slop" factor = 10^7, still comfortably below the limit of 10^{11}, leaving some units for walking, seeing, and eating. This assumes no sharing, which should cut these numbers considerably.

The careful reader will have noticed that we have not considered issues in high level representation such as schema representation and inference, representing additional constraints from current knowledge representation ideas. For a discussion of these issues, see Small (1982).

6.2 Current Plan

The specific direction we are taking is to model the Swinney and Seidenberg et. al. results in parallel lexical access. A statement of the problem is thus: to produce a working simulation which qualitatively (i.e., we won't worry about timing) behaves in agreement with these results. This means it should disambiguate word senses on the basis of semantics and/or syntax, that several meanings will be initially active, and that after a settling period, one meaning will remain active. Our initial results in semantically based disambiguation and syntax are encouraging. We also want to model the aberration in these results, which is the prior decision found in the case of noun-noun ambiguities. We hypothesize that this anomaly is due to semantic priming by a word in the sentence that is highly related to one of the interpretations of the ambiguous word. Therefore we will have to account for semantic priming in our model.

7. SUMMARY AND CONCLUSIONS

The research program we are commencing--the construction of a computer model of human language comprehension--represents an interdisciplinary effort in cognitive science. The long range plan involves connecting up a large number of neuron-level computing units to process cohesive text. Many issues remain to be resolved in this effort. However, the central thesis here is that the empirical constraints on the organization of the active network, consisting of processing evidence from psychology, physiological evidence about the brain, and computational plausibility, can be taken seriously in the modelling effort. Our initial results in the parsing subsystem, while certainly preliminary, demonstrate this possibility.

REFERENCES

[1]   Ballard, D.H., Parameter nets, Artificial Intelligence (to appear, 1983.)

[2]   Bruce, B.C., Case systems for natural language, Artificial Intelligence 6 (1975) 327-360.

[3]   Collins, A.M. and Loftus, E.F., A spreading activation theory of semantic processing, Psychological Review 82 (1975) 407-428.

[4]   Conrad, C., Context effects in sentence comprehension: A study of the subjective lexicon, Memory and Cognition 2, No. 1A (1974) 130-138.

[5]   Cottrell, G.W. and Small, S.L., A connectionist scheme for modelling word sense disambiguation, Cognition and Brain Theory 6, 1 (1983) 89-120.

[6]   Crick, F., Thinking about the brain, Scientific American 241 (1979) 219-232.

[7]   Dell, G.S., Phonological and lexical encoding in speech production, Ph.D. dissertation, Dept. of Psych., Univ. Toronto (1980).

[8]   Fahlman, S.A., NETL, A system for representing and using real knowledge (MIT Press, Boston, MA, 1979).

[9]   Fahlman, S.A., The Hashnet interconnection scheme, Technical Report, Dept. of Comp. Sc., Carnegie-Mellon Univ. (June 1980).

[10] Feldman, J.A., A connectionist model of visual memory, in: Hinton, G.E. and Anderson, J.A. (eds.), Parallel models of associative memory (Lawrence Erlbaum Assoc., Hillsdale, NJ, 1981).

[11] Feldman, J.A., Dynamic connections in neural networks, Biol. Cybernetics 46 (1982a).

[12] Feldman, J.A., Four frames suffice, TR 99, Dept of Comp. Sc., Univ. Rochester (1982b).

[13] Feldman, J.A. and Ballard, D.H., Connectionist models and their properties, Cognitive Science 6 (1982) 205-254.

[14] Foss, D. and Jenkins, C., Some effects of context on the comprehension of ambiguous sentences, Journal of Verbal Learning and Verbal Behavior 12 (1973) 577-589.

[15] Gentner, D., Some interesting differences between nouns and verbs, Cognition and Brain Theory 4 (1981) 161-177.

[16] Gigley, H.M., Neurolinguistically constrained simulation of sentence comprehension: Integrating artificial intelligence and brain theory, Ph.D. Thesis, Dept of Comp. and Inf. Sc., Univ. Massachusetts (September 1982).

[17] Hayes, P.J., Some association-based techniques for lexical disambiguation by machine, TR 25, Dept. of Comp. Sc., Univ. Rochester (June 1977).

[18] Hillis, W.D., The connection machine (computer architecture for the New Wave), Memo 646, Artif. Intell. Lab., Massachusetts Inst. Tech. (1981).

[19] Hinton, G.E., Shape representation in parallel systems, in: Proc., 7th International Joint Conf. on Artificial Intelligence (Vancouver, BC, August 1981).

[20] Hinton, G.E. and Anderson, J.A. (eds.), Parallel models of associative memory (Lawrence Erlbaum Assoc., Hillsdale, NJ, 1981).

[21] Holmes, V.M., Prior context and the perception of lexically ambiguous sentences, Memory and Cognition 5 (1977) 103-110.

[22] Hrechanyk, L.M. and Ballard, D.H., A connectionist model of form perception, in: Proc., IEEE Workshop on Computer Vision (Ringde, NH, August 1982).

[23] Lackner, J.R. and Garret, M.F., Resolving ambiguity: Effects of biasing context in the unattended ear, Cognition 1 (1972) 359-372.

[24] Lakoff, G., Categories: An essay in cognitive linguistics, in: In-Seiok Yang (ed.), Linguistics in the morning calm (Hanshin, Seoul, Korea, 1982).

[25] Levy, W.B., Associative encoding at synapses, in: Proc., 4th Annual Conf., Cognitive Science Society (Ann Arbor, MI, August 1982).

[26] Lucas, M., "Lexical access during sentence comprehension: Context effects, frequency effects, and decision processes," Ph.D. Thesis, Dept. Psych., Univ. Rochester (1983).

[27] Marcus, M.P., An overview of a theory of syntactic recognition for natural language, Memo 531, Artif. Intell. Lab., Massachusetts Inst. Tech. (1979).

[28] Marcus, M.P., Consequences of functional deficits in a parsing model: Implications for Broca's aphasia, in: Arbib, M.A., Caplan, D., and Marshall, J.C. (eds.), Neural Models of Language Processes (Academic Press, New York, 1982).

[29] McClelland, J.L. and Rumelhart, D.E., An interactive activation model of context effects in letter perception, Part 1, An account of basic findings, Psych. Review 88 (1981) 375-407.

[30] Minsky, M. and Papert, S., Perceptrons (MIT Press, Cambridge, MA, 1972).

[31] Pollack, J., Natural language processing using spreading activation and lateral inhibition, in: Proc., 4th Annual Conf., Cognitive Science Society (Ann Arbor, MI, August 1982).

[32] Proc., 4th Annual Conf., Cognitive Science Society (Ann Arbor, MI, August 1982).

[33] Rieger, C.J., Viewing Parsing as Word Sense Discrimination, in: Dingwall (ed.), Surveys of Linguistic Science (Greylock Publishers, 1976).

[34] Riesbeck, C.K., Computational understanding: Analysis of sentences and context, Memo 238, Artif. Intell. Lab., Stanford Univ. (1974).

[35] Riesbeck, C.K. and Schank, R.C., Comprehension by computer: Expectation-based analysis of sentences in context, Research Report 78, Dept. of Comp. Sc., Yale Univ. (1976).

[36] Rosch, E., Natural categories, Cognitive Psychology, 7 (1973) 532-547.

[37] Rosenfeld, A., Hummel, R.A., and Zucker, S.W., Scene labelling by relaxation operations, IEEE Trans. on Systems, Man, and Cybernetics 6 (1976) 420-433.

[38] Rumelhart, D.E. and McClelland, J.L., An interactive activation model of context effects in letter perception, Part 2, The contextual enhancement effect and some tests and extensions of the model, Psych. Review 89 (1982) 60-94.

[39] Rumelhart, D.E. and Norman, D.A., Simulating a skilled typist: A study of skilled cognitive-motor performance, Cognitive Science 6 (1982) 1-36.

[40] Seidenberg, M.S., Tanenhaus, M., Leiman, J., and Bienkowski, M., Automatic access of the meanings of ambiguous words in context: Some limitations of knowledge-based processing, Cognitive Psychology 14 (1982) 489-537.

[41] Small, S.L., Conceptual language analysis for story comprehension, TR 663, Dept. of Comp. Sc., Univ. Maryland (1978).

[42] Small, S.L., Word expert parsing: A theory of distributed word-based natural language understanding, Ph.D. dissertation and TR 954, Dept. of Comp. Sc., Univ. Maryland (1980).

[43] Small, S.L., Exploded connections: Unchunking schematic knowledge, in: Proc., 4th Annual Conf., Cognitive Science Society (Ann Arbor, MI, August 1982).

[44] Small, S.L., Cottrell, G.W., and Shastri, L., Toward connectionist parsing, in: Proc., National Conf. on Artificial Intelligence (Pittsburgh, PA, August 1982).

[45] Small, S.L. and Lucas, M., A computer model of sentence comprehension, Ricerche di Psicologia, Special Issue on Artificial Intelligence (1983); TR 1, Cognitive Science Program, Univ. Rochester (1983).

[46] Small, S.L. and Rieger, C., Parsing and comprehending with word experts (A theory and its realization), in: Lehnert, W. and Ringle, M. (eds.), Strategies for Natural Language Processing (Lawrence Erlbaum Assoc., Hillsdale, NJ, 1982).

[47] Small, S.L., Shastri, L., Brucks, M., and Kaufman, S., ISCON: An interactive simulator for connectionist networks, TR 109, Dept. of Comp. Sc., Univ. Rochester (December 1982).

[48] Smith, E.E., Shoben, E.J., and Rips, L.J., Structure and process in semantic memory: A featural model for semantic decision, Psychological Review 81 (1974) 214-241.

[49] Swinney, D.A., personal communication, Rochester, NY (April 1982).

[50] Swinney, D.A., Lexical access during sentence comprehension: (Re) consideration of context effects, Journal of Verbal Learning and Verbal Behavior 18 (1979) 645-660.

[51] Swinney, D.A. and Hakes, D.T., Effects of prior context upon lexical access during sentence comprehension, Journal of Verbal Learning and Verbal Behavior 15 (1976) 681-689.

[52] Tanenhaus, M., Leiman, J., and Seidenberg, M.S., Evidence for multiple stages in the processing of ambiguous words in syntactic contexts, Journal of Verbal Learning and Verbal Behavior 18 (1979) 427-440.

[53] Wilks, Y., Parsing English II, in: Charniak, E. and Wilks, Y. (eds.), Computational Semantics (North-Holland, 1976).

[54] Yates, J., Priming dominant and unusual senses of ambiguous words, Memory and Cognition 6 (1978) 636-643.

ACKNOWLEDGEMENTS

This research has been supported in part by the National Science Foundation under Grants IST-8208571 and MCS-8209971. The title of this paper comes from the article by Rieger (1976), which advanced a different view with the same underlying goals. This paper represents a slightly expanded version of Cottrell and Small (1983).

We would like to thank Jerry Feldman and James Allen for helpful comments on this paper. We would also like to thank Lokendra Shastri, Mark Brucks, Steve Kaufman, and Roger Meike for their work on the simulator and graphics, and Peggy Meeker for her help in preparing the manuscript.

Computational Models of Natural Language Processing
B.G. Bara and G. Guida (eds.)
© Elsevier Science Publishers B.V. (North-Holland), 1984

A PROPOSITIONAL LANGUAGE
FOR TEXT REPRESENTATION

Danilo Fum*, Giovanni Guida°⁺ , Carlo Tasso°

° Istituto di Matematica, Informatica e Sistemistica
Università di Udine
Udine, Italy

*Laboratorio di Psicologia E.E.
Università di Trieste
Trieste, Italy

⁺ Progetto di Intelligenza Artificiale
Politecnico di Milano
Milano, Italy

In the paper a new formalism for representing a natural
language text, developed in the framework of the SUSY
project currently carried on at the University of Udine,
(Italy), is presented. The main constituents of the
formalism, called basic linear representation (BLR), are
entities and relations which are utilized to build up the
sequence of propositions into which the text is mapped.
The BLR language is described both from the point of view
of its notational aspects and of its expressive adequacy.
Particular attention is focused on the topics of
quantification, reference, time, place, and manner.
Details about a parser able to map natural language into
the BLR form are provided.

1. INTRODUCTION

The work reported in this paper is part of a project presently ongoing at the
University of Udine (Italy) in the field of text comprehension and automatic
abstracting (Fum, Guida, Tasso, 1982; 1984; to appear). In order to precisely
situate the theme of this paper it is appropriate to have first an overall look at
the general aims and scope of the whole project.

The project has a very ambitious long-run objective: constructing an intelligent
system (SUSY: SUmmarizing SYstem) capable of understanding the meaning of a
descriptive text (for example a scientific paper), and of generating an
appropriate summary of it. The computational study of narrative texts (stories)
is explicitly left out of the focus of our interest.

Text comprehension is a very complex and demanding task which includes, in our
approach, several kinds of activities, namely: understanding the literal meaning
of the elementary components (single sentences) of the text, connecting the
meaning of single sentences together and assigning a coherent meaning to the
entire text, evaluating the relative importance of the elementary parts of the
text and ranking them according to their relevance to a given goal. These
activities require a robust linguistic competence as a prerequisite, and they
involve, moreover, several skills (e.g. reasoning on world knowledge,
inferencing, analysing goals, etc) which are far beyond mere linguistic
competence. The task of understanding and representing the meaning of a natural
language text has been split in SUSY into three phases: (i) sentence
understanding, (ii) structure capturing, and (iii) importance ranking.

(i) – The <u>sentence understanding</u> phase works on the natural language input text
and   maps   it   into   a   propositional   representation,   called <u>Basic Linear
Representation (BLR)</u>. A powerful parser is devoted to understand the literal
meaning of each sentence, and to construct the corresponding BLR. The parser is
also requested to solve all references within and between sentences.   The   output
of sentence undestanding is therefore a formal explicit sentence-by-sentence
representation of the meaning of the input text.

(ii) – The <u>structure capturing</u> phase accepts in input   the   BLR   supplied   by   the
preceding step, and goes deeper in the understanding activity focusing on the
overall logic and rethoric organization of the text.   It   produces   an   augmented
version of the BLR, called <u>Extended Linear Representation (ELR)</u>, which contains
explicit representation of:
  - the logical structure of the text, which accounts for the conceptual
    connection between sentences;
  - the rethoric structure of the text, which explains how the flow of ideas
    and the arguments of the writer have been organized and implemented in
    the text.

(iii) – The <u>importance ranking</u> phase is aimed at giving a hierarchical ordering to
the elements of the ELR, which can account for the relative importance of the
single parts that constitute the input text.   Importance ranking produces a
(partial) labeling of the ELR with appropriate importance weights, called
<u>Hierarchical Propositional Network (HPN)</u> which represents   the   deepest   level   of
understanding of the input text.

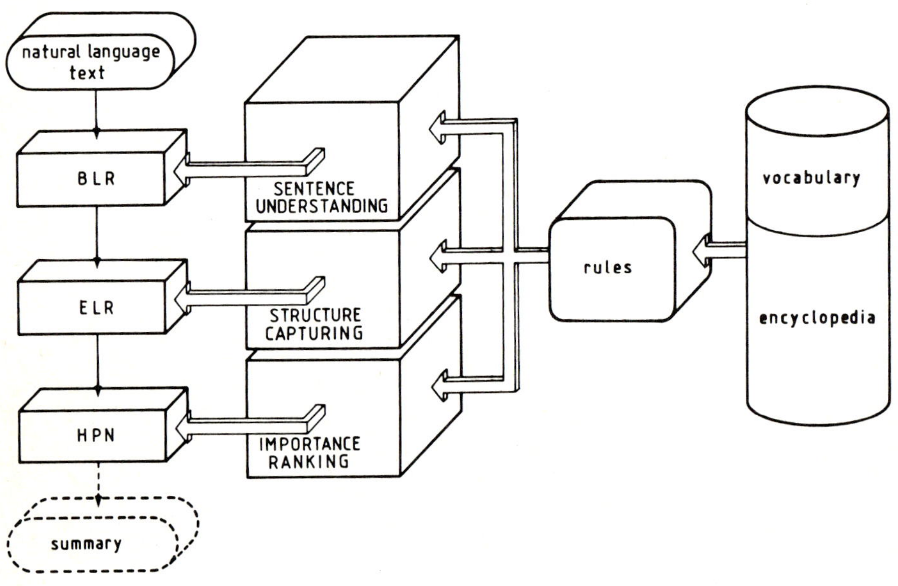

Figure 1. Overall Architecture of SUSY

The above activities are designed in such a way as to be performed by means   of   a
set of rule-based systems competent in the different knowledge domains involved in
the understanding process. A vocabulary and an encyclopedia (see section 8)

contain the basic linguistic and world knowledge necessary for system operation. Once the HPN representation of a text has been obtained, summarizing becomes a reasonable task which mainly consists in pruning those parts of the representation which convey unimportant information. The pruning strategy can easily be made dependent on specific goals and needs of the user, and several summaries tailored to different classes of exigencies can be obtained. Clearly, summarizing is only an example of the possible use of the text comprehension paradigm above proposed; it can serve several other applications, including translation, indexing, question-answering, document processing, and knowledge acquisition.

Figure 1 gives a graphical illustration of the overall design of the project.

The SUSY project covers several areas of scientific interest for research in natural language processing. In this paper we will focus on one specific problem which is, in a sense, a prerequisite for the entire research: the design of a suitable language (and of its parser) for representing the meaning of a text, i.e. a notation for the BLR. A set of specifications for such a language should include:
- a precise and, as far as possible, formal definition of both syntax and semantics;
- a good degree of expressive adequacy, i.e. the capability to explicitly represent all the details and nuances proper of natural language utterances;
- the property of being sufficiently lucid and transparent to an intuitive interpretation, i.e. of being reasonably clear and explicit;
- the suitability to effectively support the further processing that will be done on the BLR in order to obtain the ELR and HPN.

A straightforward choice for the design of the BLR language could be to adopt some classic tools for knowledge representation, such as semantic nets, and to extend it to meet the above requirements. This opportunity has been discarded in favor of a new language, sharing several features with existing knowledge representation formalisms, but explicitly designed for the text understanding paradigm above outlined. Starting from the basic work of Kintsch (1974; 1982), and Kintsch and van Dijk (1978), we have developed a complete propositional representation language and we have sketched the main lines for the implementation of a parser capable of mapping a natural language text into BLR. In the paper, the main features of the BLR language are illustrated and an evaluation of its expressive adequacy is provided. A description of the general architecture and mode of operation of the parser is given as well.

2. THE REPRESENTATION LANGUAGE: BASIC NOTIONS

In this section we introduce the propositional formalism developed for representing the meaning of a natural language text. By the term BLR we will denote here both the language used for building up the basic linear representation, and the representation itself. We will first illustrate the most basic elements of BLR, discarding for the moment any consideration of more advanced issues such as quantification, reference, time, place, and manner. These topics, although fundamental, will be dealt with only in subsequent sections, in order to provide a step-wise illustration of all the rather complex features of the BLR language. This section is divided into two parts: in the first, the basic notions of BLR are informally presented through examples; in the second, more detailed and rigorous definitions are introduced.

The BLR representation of a text is constituted by a sequence of labeled propositions, each of them built up by a predicate with instantiated arguments. Consider for example the sentence:

(1) "John is eating an apple".

The action expressed by the verb "to eat" is represented through the predicate EAT
(EATER, EATABLE), which takes two arguments: the first (EATER) refers to any
living being able to eat, the second (EATABLE) refers to any thing that can be
eated.   Sentence (1) is represented by a proposition obtained from the predicate
EAT by instantiating the first argument (EATER) with JOHN and the second argument
(EATABLE) with APPLE.   The BLR of (1) is therefore:

        10 EAT (JOHN, APPLE).

This example is very simple since it gives raise to a BLR composed by just one
proposition.   A sligthly more complicated example is:

        (2) "John is eating a red apple".

The corresponding BLR results:

        20 EAT (JOHN, APPLE)
        30 RED (APPLE).

Both predicates and arguments are built up by concepts, the smallest semantic unit
of the BLR representation.   Linguistic components of a natural language text (such
as nouns, verbs, adjectives, adverbs, idioms, etc.) are mapped into concepts
through a correspondence supplied by a vocabulary, as described in section 8.   As
shown in Figure 2, the set of all possible concepts (in a given application
domain) can be partitioned into two subclasses in two different ways.

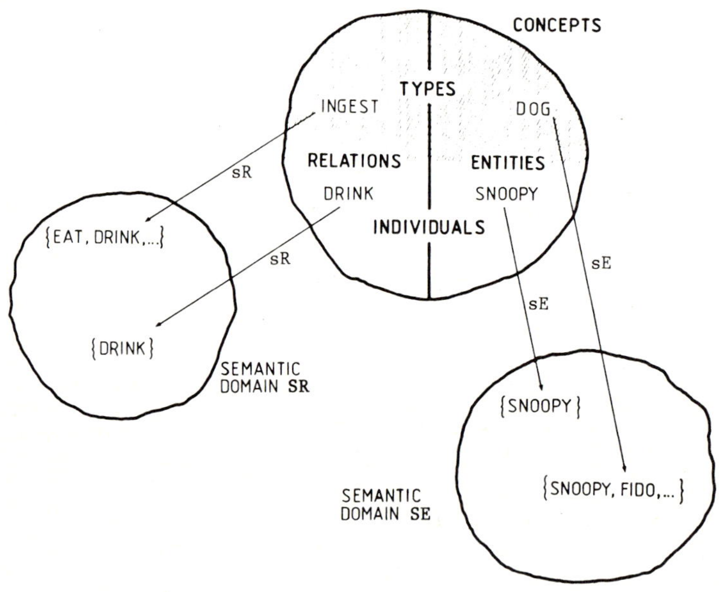

Figure 2. The set of Concepts C and its Characterization

First of all we can distinguish entities from relations.   Entities refer to
specific objects or classes of objects or persons or things, whereas relations
assert a property of a concept or express a relationship among concepts.
Instances of entities are MAN, JOHN, APPLE, EMPIRE-STATE-BUILDING; examples of

relations are EAT, INGEST, RED, SLOWLY.

The other way of partitioning the set of concepts is according to the criterion which distinguishes individuals from types, the former referring to individual objects, and the latter to groups or classes of individual objects. As an example, consider the individual entity JOHN-SMITH, which refers to a specific man, and the type entity MAN, which can be understood as the class of all men, including also JOHN-SMITH. Individual entities sharing some common property can obviuosly be grouped together to form classes which may be directly referred to by type concepts. So, for instance, the type DOG globally refers to the individuals SNOOPY, PLUTO, FIDO, etc. The same distinction between individuals and types holds for relations as well. Consider, for instance, the concepts EAT and DRINK, and the concept INGEST: the latter is considered a type relation being more comprehensive than the former ones, since it is used to denote the more general situation of taking into the mouth something that could be either a solid food or a liquid. These refinements of the meaning of INGEST are in fact captured by the two concepts EAT and DRINK, respectively.

The process of grouping concepts together, and of referring to the whole class by a type concept, can be repeatedly applied to types themselves. So, for example, a class of entities such as {DOG, CAT, BIRD, HORSE} can be referred to by the superordinate type ANIMAL, while, on the other hand, WALK, RUN, DRIVE, etc. are instances of the more general type relation MOVE. In this way we can define extensionally the semantics of a type concept by listing all concepts belonging to the class globally referred to by that type concept. This can be done also for individual concepts: in this case the enumeration would comprehend just the individual concept itself.

On the basis of the above introduced notion of individual and type concepts we can define a binary relation between concepts, called ISA relation. With reference to the above examples, we may have:

    JOHN-SMITH ISA MAN
    CAT ISA ANIMAL
    DRINK ISA INGEST,

where the left-hand concept refers (directly or indirectly through intermediate type concepts) to a class of individual concepts which is included in the class referred to by the right-hand concept. The relation ISA is transitive, since it is based on set inclusion between classes of concepts. From the two instances:

    SNOOPY ISA DOG
    DOG ISA ANIMAL

it can therefore be inferred that

    SNOOPY ISA ANIMAL

holds as well.

Instances of the ISA relation constitute the other possible way – in addition to the use of predicates illustrated above – of building up propositions. More in detail, any instance A ISA B, can be used to generate a proposition of the kind B(A). The above three instances, for example, can supply the following propositions:

    40 DOG (SNOOPY)

    50 ANIMAL (DOG)

    60 ANIMAL (SNOOPY).

Note that in the structure built up on the set of concepts by grouping concepts together to form types, different sets of concepts can overlap. Consider for example the following two instances of the ISA relation:

    TOMATO ISA PLANT
    TOMATO ISA FOOD

Here TOMATO belongs at the same time to the classes (type concepts) PLANT and FOOD.

Having introduced this first characterization of concepts, we turn again our attention to predicates and propositions. A predicate is built up by appending to a relation concept one or more arguments, which are specified through type concepts. When we build up a proposition, we have to substitute each argument in the predicate, say X, by an individual or type concept, say A, such that A ISA X. For example, the sentence:

    (3) "Motorists drive cars"

contains the verb "to drive" which is represented by the predicate DRIVE (DRIVER, DRIVABLE) with the two arguments DRIVER and DRIVABLE. The one-proposition BLR of (3) is obtained by instantiating the first argument with the concept MOTORIST (since MOTORIST ISA DRIVER), and the second argument with CAR (since, for example, CAR ISA VEHICLE and VEHICLE ISA DRIVABLE). We therefore obtain:

    70 DRIVE (MOTORIST, CAR).

It can also be the case that an argument of a predicate in a proposition is instantiated by a reference to another proposition. Consider for example the sentence

    (4) "It's hard to drive a big truck",

which is represented by:

     80 HARD (90)
     90 DRIVE (NIL, TRUCK)
    100 BIG (TRUCK),

where NIL means that the first argument of the predicate DRIVE is not instantiated, since missing in the natural language text. Another example is

    (5) "Mary is teaching Bob and Julie",

which is represented by:

    110 TEACH (MARY, 120)
    120 AND (BOB, JULIE).

Here the conjunction "and" is mapped into the relation concept AND, which can be used to form a predicate with a variable number of arguments of any possible type. A fragment of text like:

    (6) "Bob said that Mary was eating an apple while driving the car"

would be represented by

    130 SAY (JOHN, 140)
    140 WHILE (150, 160)
    150 EAT (MARY, APPLE)
    160 DRIVE (MARY, CAR),

where the arguments of WHILE are instanciated with references to the appropriate propositions.

The basic notions concerning the BLR language introduced so far deserve a few comments. First of all we have to notice that the ISA relation is clearly and univocally defined through set inclusion properties among classes of concepts. This definition aims at precisely identifying the real meaning that the BLR language attaches to the ISA relation, avoiding in such a way any problem that could arise from an ambiguous definition (consider, for example, the case of ISA intended both as set membership and set inclusion: Brachman 1979; 1983). Moreover, the ISA relation provides a rigorous way for defining the semantics of a generic entity or relation concept. We can in fact list all the individuals that ISA a concept, giving the extensional semantics of that concept. Or, alternatively, we can identify all types which "contain" a concept, providing an intensional definition. Furthermore, the semantics of a relation can also be recognized through the number and type of the arguments of the corresponding predicate, and in this way a predicate is attached a meaning not necessarily by means of decomposition into a small set of very general primitives (cfr. Schank's work on conceptual dependency: Schank 1972; 1975).

The taxonomy introduced by the ISA relation in the set of concepts allows utilizing property inheritance, which represents one of the most common features of the several IS-A links proposed in the literature (Findler, 1979). However, in the BLR formalism two different kinds of property inheritance coexist:

1. inheritance among entities, concerning the fact that all properties of an entity can be inherited by all concepts that ISA that entity;
2. inheritance among relations (and therefore predicates) since the ISA relation is defined also among this kind of concepts; we name it "inference inheritance" since it consists in the possibility of inheriting all the inferences drawable for a relation X by all the relations that ISA X.

In the second part of this section we give a more formal and detailed illustration of the BLR language.
Let C be a set of concepts {c1,c2,...,cn}, such that C=EC U RC, where EC and RC are disjoint non-empty sets whose elements are called <u>entities</u> and <u>relations</u>, respectively.

Both EC and RC are partitioned into <u>individuals</u> and <u>types</u>, i.e. EC=IE U TE (and RC=IR U TR), where IE (IR) is the non-empty set of individual entities (individual relations), and TE (TR) is the non-empty set of type entities (type relations).
Let us now introduce a few definitions.

<u>Definition-1</u>. Given a set of entity concepts EC=IE U TE, the power set of IE is called the <u>semantic domain</u> SE of EC.

<u>Definition-2</u>. A <u>semantic interpretation</u> of EC on SE is a one-to-one mapping sE of EC onto SE, such that:
   - each individual X is mapped into the singleton {X} of SE;
   - each type is mapped into an element of SE with cardinality greater than one.

Similarly, we can define the <u>semantic domain</u> SR for RC as the power set of IR, and the <u>semantic interpretation</u> sR as a one-to-one mapping of RC onto SR, with the same properties as sE.

The semantic interpretations sE and sR provide a formal way to extensionally define the semantics of both entities and relations.

<u>Definition-3</u>. Given a set of entities EC, a semantic domain SE for EC, and a semantic interpretation sE, for any two concepts X and Y in EC we say that X <u>ISA</u> Y (or alternatively that X <u>is of type</u> Y, or X <u>belongs to</u> Y) if sE(X) is included in sE(Y).

In the same way we define the ISA relation between relation concepts. The situation is graphically illustrated in Figure 2.

<u>Definition-4</u>. Given a set of concepts C=EC U RC, a <u>basic predicate</u> on C is a (n+1)-tuple X(X1,X2,...,Xn), where X belongs to RC and is named <u>constitutive relation</u>, and X1, X2,...,Xn belong to TE U {ANY} and are called <u>arguments</u> of X. ANY is a special type concept such that for any X belonging to TE U TR, X ISA ANY.

<u>Definition-5</u>. A <u>subject domain</u> D is a quadruple D=(C,sE,sR,P), where C is a set of concepts, sE and sR are the semantic interpretations of EC and RC, and P is a set of basic predicates on C.

The notion of subject domain formalizes the knowledge necessary to deal with a given subject. Clearly the design of D is not fixed a-priori, but depends on the goal of the application, and on the desired level of refinement.

The next definition concerns the concept of proposition, and it does not embody the treatment devised for quantification and aggregate concepts, which will be illustrated in detail in the following sections.

<u>Definition-6</u>. (Preliminary version). Given a subject domain D=(C,sE,sR,P), a <u>proposition</u> is a labeled (n+1)-tuple

$$N \; X(X1,X2,...,Xn),$$

where the <u>label</u> N is a positive integer number and the (n+1)-tuple can be obtained from:

1. a basic predicate Y(Y1,Y2,...,Yn), where X=Y and each argument Yj (j=1,2,...n) is substituted in one of the following ways:
   - by a type or an individual entity Xj, such that Xj ISA Yj;
   - by a label of another proposition, if Yj= ANY;
   - by the dummy argument NIL;

2. an instance of the ISA relation between two entities A and B, such that A ISA B, A=X1, B=X, if n=1.

<u>Definition-7</u>. Given a subject domain D=(C,sE,sR,P), a <u>basic linear representation</u> (<u>BLR</u>) of a natural language text is a finite sequence of propositions.

We remind againg the reader that we have intentionally chosen not to illustrate so far such fundamental problems as quantification, reference, time, place, and manner, which represent indeed one of the most critical topics to be treated when dealing with natural language texts. A consequence of this choice is that all the BLR's and the definitions presented are missing the parts concerning these topics, which will be focused on later.

After having presented the main features of BLR in the following sections we shall evaluate its adequacy for representing the meaning of natural language expressions. A suitable representation formalism, in fact, must be able to carry all the information expressed in the text structure, i.e. the representation must be able to encode any conception which a human being is capable of. In the following, in absence of an explicit and agreed-upon metric against which to compare the expressive power of the formalism, we shall concentrate our attention on some critical topics (such as definite vs. indefinite noun phrases, opaque vs.

transparent references, number, quantification, time and locative expression, etc.) and shall examine how these aspects of the language are dealt with by BLR.

3. QUANTIFICATION

3.1 <u>Universal</u> <u>and</u> <u>Existential</u> Quantification

One of the most pervasive problems that must be tackled in dealing with natural language representation is the treatment of quantifiers. Almost every statement of ordinary discourse involves in fact quantification, and several other natural language features are closely connected to it. Let us examine with the help of some examples how quantification is treated within BLR.
A simple sentence like:

(7) "Man is mortal"

(i.e. all men are mortal) is represented in our formalism by:

170 MORTAL (MAN).

This constitutes a case of <u>universal</u> quantification and is represented in BLR by instantiating the argument of a predicate by a type. Proposition 170 is interpreted as stating that the predicate MORTAL applies to every member of the type MAN that appears as its argument (that is MORTAL is predicated of every entity of the type MAN). A particular case of universal quantification appears in the following sentence:

(8) "John likes flowers",

which is represented by

180 LIKE (JOHN, FLOWER).

Proposition 180 is interpreted as stating that all the members of the first argument (JOHN) LIKE all the members of the second argument (FLOWER). The point is that, whereas FLOWER is a type (there are several entities that ISA FLOWER: e.g. DAISY, DAFFODIL, ROSE, etc.), JOHN is an individual: the only element for which it is possible to assert that ISA JOHN is ... JOHN itself. Proposition 180 then predicates that every entity that ISA JOHN (i.e. only the individual JOHN) LIKEs every entity that ISA FLOWER. We call this quantification, obtained by instantiating a predicate argument with an individual, <u>individual</u> <u>quantification</u>. From a formal point of view, there is no difference between universal and individual quantification, and in fact they are represented in the same way, as individual quantification is a special case of universal quantification on a singleton set.

The other usual way of quantifying is <u>existential</u> <u>quantification</u>. The sentence:

(9) "John is eating an apple"

is represented in BLR by the proposition:

190 EAT (JOHN, V1:APPLE)

in which the symbol V1 (and, more generally, Vn where n is a positive integer) is a variable identifier. Every variable must be of (at least) a type, and the notation V1:APPLE declares a variable V1 of type APPLE. Proposition 190 is interpreted as representing the fact that JOHN (individually quantified) is eating an individual, labeled V1, that ISA APPLE. The notation V1:APPLE is in fact a short-hand for the extended notation:

```
200 EAT (JOHN, V1)
210 APPLE (V1).
```

In the above propositions the variable V1 is given by default the type of the corresponding arguments of the predicates it instantiates. Assuming, as we have done above, that the arguments of EAT are EATER and EATABLE, respectively, V1 is then declared being of type EATABLE in proposition 200, and V1 stands for an individual that ISA APPLE in proposition 210. The extended notation allows more finely-grained representations and, generally, more expressive power than the short-hand. This is evident, for example, in expressing the scope of negations. Let us consider the sentence:

(10) "John is not eating an apple".

This sentence is semantically ambiguous since it may have in fact two meanings:

(i) "It is not the case that John is eating an apple"

(ii) "What John is eating is not an apple".

While the former sentence can be easily represented by the short-hand form

```
220 NOT (230)
230 EAT (JOHN, V1:APPLE),
```

the meaning of the latter can be represented only through the extended notation:

```
240 EAT (JOHN, V1)
250 NOT (260)
260 APPLE (V1).
```

3.2 Existential (Singular and) Plural Quantification

The problem of representing the number of nouns is treated in BLR as a particular case of quantification. Singular nouns can be given both universal and existential quantification in natural language expressions. Sentences like:

(11) "The dog barks"
(12) "A dog barks"

are interpreted as meaning that all dogs bark, and are represented by

```
270 BARK (DOG).
```

The sentence

(13) "A dog is barking"

suggests, on the other hand, an existential interpretation and is represented by

```
280 BARK (V1:DOG).
```

In our opinion, the correct meaning of an existentially quantified singular noun like that contained in (13) is that one and only one dog is barking. Let us consider, for example, the following fragment of text:

(14) "There are two dogs in the courtyard. A dog is barking".

We claim that it would be uncooperative and misleading to use (14) if both dogs are really barking.

The interpretation of the generic existential expression Vn:<type> (or simply Vn, in the extended notation), is "there exists one and only one individual Vn of type <type>", and this kind of quantification can fit only concepts which are represented in the sentence surface structure by singular nouns. A singular noun phrase therefore either is universally quantified or it identifies one and only one element in the domain of discourse, i.e. it is existentially quantified. The problem of which interpretation to give to a singular noun phrase is, of course, a parsing problem that is not always easily solvable.

Similarly, a plural noun can be quantified universally as in

(15) "The dogs bark",

that expresses the fact that all dogs (i.e. all entities that ISA DOG) bark, or existentially as in

(16) "The boys are playing tennis",

that states that some members of the type BOY are playing tennis at a given moment. We assume that plural nouns are existentially quantified in a different way from singular ones, and we call this kind of quantification _existential plural_. In BLR, sentence (16) is represented by

290 PLAY (VV1:BOY, TENNIS),

where the expression VV1:BOY denotes a set of entities of type BOY whose cardinality is greater than one (i.e. a subset of two or more boys). Let us stress that existential plural quantification conveys a rather complex meaning. The notation VV1:<type> denotes that "there exists a subset VV1 of <type> such that, for each individual X belonging to VV1...". Existential plural quantification therefore embeds the power of both existential and universal quantification. The very deep consequences of this feature will be explicitly utilized for example, in dealing with temporal variables (see proposition 760 in section 5.1).

Summing up, we have two different kinds of existential quantification:

(i) _singular_, expressing the fact that there exists one and only one individual of a given type, used only with singular nouns, and represented by Vn:<type> in the short-hand form or by Vn in the extended notation;
(ii) _plural_, indicating that there exists a subset of at least two elements of a given type, obviously used only with plural nouns, and represented by VVn:<type> in the short-hand form or by VVn in the extended notation.

3.3 Mass Quantification

Both universal and existential quantification implicitly entail the concept of number (and indeed the number of nouns is treated in BLR using quantificational features): i.e., they can be applied only to concepts that can be enumerated. There is however another common way of quantifying in natural language which is used to individuate not single entities, or groups of entities, but a specified amount, weight, extent, supply, etc. of an entity. Let us consider for instance:

(17) "John is drinking some Cabernet",

which means that the individual JOHN is drinking a certain quantity of the entity CABERNET. We represent the meaning of (17) by:

300 DRINK (JOHN, Q1:CABERNET),

where the expression Q1:CABERNET, used to indicate a certain quantity of the wine

Cabernet, represents an instance of what we call <u>mass quantification</u>.

It is necessary to add some comments about mass quantification. First of all, this kind of quantification can be used only with mass concepts, that is concepts that refer to an extended substance rather then to each element of a set of isolable individuals, i.e., to objects that can be only taken in pieces having a certain mass, weight etc. Moreover, mass quantification makes sense only when used with individuals. It is possible to utilize mass quantification with types as in:

        310 DRINK (JOHN, Q1:WINE),

but the interpretation of proposition 310 is that John is drinking a certain quantity of a not specified kind of wine (Cabernet, Tokay, Champagne?). Finally, it should be noted that, in addition to mass quantification, it is obviously possible to use universal, individual, or existential quantification with mass entities. For example:

        320 LIKE (JOHN, CABERNET)

means that John likes (every piece of) Cabernet, i.e. Cabernet in general;

        330 LIKE (JOHN, WINE)

means that John likes every kind of wine, i.e. wine in general, and

        340 DRINK (JOHN, V1:WINE)

that John drinks a particular kind of wine.

3.4 <u>Quantification Scope</u>

The conceptual tools herewith developed are not sufficient to represent some cases of quantification that occur quite often in natural language sentences. Let us consider for instance:

        (18) "Every man loves a woman".

This sentence is ambiguous since it can be interpreted in two ways. According to one interpretation, every man loves a woman who is not necessarily the same for all men. According to the other, there exists a woman who is loved by every man. While the former interpretation is easily represented in BLR by:

        350 LOVE (MAN, V1:WOMAN),

there is no way, up to now, to represent the latter meaning of sentence (18). The quantification symbols in the BLR are in fact attached directly to the arguments of the predicates and, since the order of the arguments of every predicate is fixed, it is impossible to change the scope of quantifiers by simply swapping their position. We therefore need a suitable way of expressing quantification scope. We represent the second meaning of sentence (18) by:

        360 LOVE (MAN, (V1:WOMAN)).

In BLR, embedding arguments in parentheses means to change the scope of quantification from left-to-right to most-parenthesized-first criterion. In proposition 350 quantification scope is interpreted as left-to-right, i.e., existential quantifier within the scope of universal quantifier. In proposition 360, since the argument WOMAN (existentially quantified) is enclosed between parentheses and MAN (universally quantified) is not, MAN is within the scope of WOMAN. In this way, without complicated and cumbersome notation, it is possible

to express all possible cases of quantification over predicates with a variable
number of arguments. By using different levels of parentheses it is in fact
possible to denote any ordering between quantifiers and, therefore, to adjust
scoping according to any exigency of representation. Clearly a great number of
parentheses makes representation less perspicuous. Limiting our attention to
binary predicates – e.g. LOVE (LOVER, LOVEE) – we have (Scragg, 1976) the
following cases:

```
370 LOVE (MAN, WOMAN)          "Every man loves every woman"
380 LOVE (MAN, V1:WOMAN)       "Every man loves a woman ( = his woman,
                                  not  necessarily the same for all men)
390 LOVE (V1:MAN, WOMAN)       "Every  woman is  loved by a man ( = the
                                  same for all women)"
400 LOVE (V1:MAN, V2:WOMAN)    "A man loves a woman"
410 LOVE (V1:MAN, (WOMAN))     "Every woman is  loved by a man ( = her
                                  man, not  necessarily the same for all
                                  women)"
420 LOVE (MAN, (V1:WOMAN))     "Every man  loves a  woman ( = the same
                                  for all men)"
```

Note that, as a consequence of quantification scope, the variable V1 has a very
different meaning in proposition 380 and 420: in the latter V1 denotes a <u>specific</u>
(fixed) individual of type MAN, in the former V1 represents the <u>generic</u> (variable)
individual of type WOMAN which can be related to each individual of type MAN –
i.e., for each element belonging to MAN, V1 denotes here a generally different
element of type WOMAN. This distinction between specific and generic role of a
variable will be crucial in the treatment of references (see section 4.1).
It is possible to treat analogously the cases of existential plural quantification
and to represent, for example, the different meanings that are intuitively
assigned to the sentences:

```
(19) "All philosophers read some books"
(20) "Some books are read by all philosophers".
```

While (19) is normally interpreted as stating that, if a man is a philosopher,
than he reads a certain number of books (more than one, we assume), sentence (20)
conveys the idea that there exists a certain number of books that all philosophers
read. The different meanings of (19) and (20) are captured by the following two
BLR propositions, respectively:

```
430 READ (PHILOSOPHER, VV1:BOOK)

440 READ (PHILOSOPHER, (VV1:BOOK)).
```

3.5 <u>Fuzzy</u> <u>Quantification</u>

To conclude our presentation of the treatment of quantifiers, it is necessary to
illustrate the way fuzzy quantifiers are represented in BLR. With the term <u>fuzzy</u>
<u>quantifiers</u> we mean expressions like "a lot of", "plenty of", "a few", "many",
"almost all", and so on, that do not have a standard representation in logic. It
is necessary to notice that these specifications are used only in connection with
arguments wich have an existential plural or mass quantification. Fuzzy
quantifiers are treated in BLR as normal predicates, and sentences like

```
(21) "A lot of girls are screaming"
(22) "Few boys are reading"
```

are represented, respectively, by:

```
450 SCREAM (VV1:GIRL)
460 LOT (VV1)
```

and

```
    470 READ (VV1:BOY)
    480 FEW (VV1).
```

It is similarly possible to indicate specific amounts, measures, volumes, and so
on with mass quantified concepts. The meaning of:

```
    (23) "John is drinking a pint of beer"
```

is then represented by:

```
    490 DRINK (JOHN, Q1:BEER)
    500 QUANTITY-OF (Q1, PINT, 1)
```

The interpretation of fuzzy quantifiers relies on a huge amount of encyclopedic
knowledge.   The expression "a lot", for instance, has completely different
meanings (i.e., indicates a different order of magnitude) when it is used to refer
to the number of cars or to the number of books an individual has. "A lot of
cars" could signify four or five cars, while "a lot of books" could indicate
hundreds or even thousands of books.   "A lot of books", furthermore, means
different things if it is used to quantify the number of books possessed by a
student or, instead, by a library.   The meaning of fuzzy quantifiers is,
therefore, heavily context-dependent, and their interpretation is demanded to the
parsing routines which use encyclopedic knowledge.

4.   REFERENCE

4.1 Referencing Entities

Reference to the same entity in different propositions is a basic point in the BLR
language. Three major cases of reference are worth to be dealt with in detail.

(i) - The first case occurs with existentially (singular and plural) and mass
quantified variables wich are used with a <u>specific</u> role. Here differently
numbered variables are assumed to refer to different entities (or groups, or
amounts of entities), while different occurrences of the same variable refer to
the same entity. Consider for example:

```
    (24) "The man who is crossing the street is John's father"
```

which, leaving the temporal features aside, is represented by:

```
    510 CROSS (V1:MAN, V2:STREET)
    520 FATHER-OF (V1, JOHN).
```

Here V1 is existentially quantified both in 510 and 520 and has a specific role,
i.e. it refers to a fixed individual of type MAN. The occurrence in 510 and 520
of the same variable V1 denotes that both predicates CROSS and FATHER-OF apply to
the same individual labeled V1. More precisely, as a consequence of the shared
variable V1, we interpret the pair 510 and 520 as a single statement containing
two predicates but having a unique definition of quantifier scope: i.e. we
interpret 520 as an extension of 510.

(ii) - Let us consider now a slightly more complex example:

```
    (25) "Every man loves a ( = his) woman who loves a man (not necessarily
          the  man  who  loves her, and  not  necessarily the  same for all
          women)"
```

which is represented by:

        530 LOVE (MAN, V1:WOMAN)
        540 LOVE (V1, V2:MAN).

Here the interpretation of proposition 530 is straightforward; proposition 540 instead deserves a few comments. If we first consider 540 alone, we note that it contains the two existentially quantified variables V1 and V2, and its meaning is that "someone (V1) loves a man (V2)". But now is crucial to note that the variable V1 is shared by both 530 and 540, and in 530 it has a <u>generic role</u>, i.e. it denotes a generic individual of the type WOMAN, as it is within the scope of a universal quantification (MAN). Interpreting 540 as an extension of 530 through the shared variable V1, V2 falls within the scope of the universal quantification (MAN) too, and it denotes a generic individual of the type MAN, which is generally different for each element belonging to MAN (and then for each instance of V1). This is exactly the meaning of (25). This second case of reference, where existentially quantified variables are used with generic role, is very subtle and contains a lot of expressive power.

Let us consider another example:

        (26) "Every man loves a woman who loves all men".

This sentence can be represented by:

        550 LOVE (MAN, V1:WOMAN)
        560 LOVE (V1, MAN).

Here we have three quantifications: MAN (universal), V1 (existential), and MAN (universal again); each of them is within the scope of all preceding quantifiers.

As a last example, to sum up the first two cases of reference so far introduced, consider the sentence:

        (27) "Every man loves a (=his) woman who loves a man (not necessarily
             the same mentioned above) who loves her"

Sentence (27) can be easily represented by:

        570 LOVE (MAN, V1:WOMAN)
        580 LOVE (V1, V2:MAN)
        590 LOVE (V2, V1).

(iii) — Let us consider now the sentence:

        (28) "Every man loves a (= his) woman who loves him"

If we try to represent it using the tools so far developed we get:

        600 LOVE (MAN, V1:WOMAN)
        610 LOVE (V1, ...?)

i.e. we are unable to represent the fact that in 610 V1 LOVEs the same element of MAN to which it refers in 600 (where it has a generic role). The problem, encountered here for the first time, is that we have no sign to denote the generic element of universal quantification. Universal quantification in BLR is simply represented by the name of the type over it ranges. We introduce therefore the notation <type>:X1 (and, more generally, Xn where n is a positive integer) to represent universal quantification over the type <type> where the generic individual belonging to <type> is given the label X1. We can represent now sentence (28) by:

```
        620 LOVE (MAN:X1, V1:WOMAN)
        630 LOVE (V1, X1).
```

Interpreting 620 and 630 according to the rules stated above for shared variables, we get the exact meaning of sentence (28). In fact, 630 (which contains two existentially quantified variables and means "Someone (V1) loves somebody (X1)") extends 620 and, as the shared variable V1 has a generic role in 620, both V1 and X1 fall within the scope of the universal quantification (MAN:X1).

This third case of reference, which involves universally quantified variables, allows us to gain a more general look at universal quantification itself. The notation of universal quantification used so far (<type>) can be considered as a useful short-hand of the extended notation (<type>:Xn), where the generic variable is assigned a precise label. The short-hand form is sufficient to deal with a lot of usual cases but has less expressive power than the extended notation which is, in turn, necessary to represent complex cases.

4.2 Definite and Indefinite Reference

Through the numbering of variables involved in existential quantification it is possible to represent the definiteness and indefiniteness of reference (Kintsch, 1974). The first occurrence of a variable in the text representation is considered indefinite; the successive occurrences of the same variable are considered as definite expressions.

4.3 Transparent and Opaque Reference

Let us consider the sentence:

        (29) "John wants to marry a blonde."

Sentence (29) can be interpreted according to the following readings: (i) John knows a girl who is blonde, and John wants to marry her; (ii) John does not know yet the girl he will marry some day but, in any case, his future wife should be blonde. The subtle semantic distinction between a transparent (reading (i)) and opaque (reading (ii)) reference is easily captured in BLR. In the first case, the speaker knows who is the girl John wants to marry, her identity is known even if it is not explicitly revealed. We can represent this particular meaning of sentence (29) by the following BLR:

```
        640 WANT (JOHN, 650)
        650 MARRY (JOHN, V1)
        660 BLONDE (V1)
        670 KNOWN (V1).
```

The opaque sense is given by omitting proposition 670 in the above representation.

A more embarassing problem is posed by:

        (30) "Someone calls Mary every day".

This sentence can be interpreted in different ways: (i) there is a person, always the same, that calls Mary every day and his/her identity is unknown; (ii) there is a person, always the same, that calls Mary every day and whose identity is known but not revealed; (iii) there is someone, but not necessarily the same person, that calls Mary every day. The first two readings represent the classic opaque and transparent references and, leaving for the moment aside the representation of temporal expressions such as "every day", they are expressed by:

```
        680 CALL (V1:PERSON, MARY)
        690 KNOWN (V1)
```

in case of transparent reference, and by omitting proposition 690 in case of opaque reference. It is difficult, instead, to represent the third reading of sentence (30). The problem is that, every time MARY is called, the variable indicator must assume a new value because the caller can be every time a different person. We assumed anyway that a variable identifier can be used for designating a single element of a certain type and it is therefore impossible to indicate with the same identifier different elements. The difficulty of this representation relies in the time specification "every day" whose meaning cannot be made explicit with the tools so far introduced. This case will be resumed and thoroughly solved in the following section.

5. TIME, PLACE, AND MANNER

5.1 <u>Time</u>

In this section we will augment the expressive power of our formalism by describing how verb tenses and temporal expressions are dealt with in BLR. Natural language shows a "tiresome bias" (Quine, 1960) towards the treatment of time, and the importance of a powerful and reliable time representation in artificial intelligence systems cannot be overestimated (McDermott, 1982). The fact that ordinary sentences are tensed implies that reference to time is inextricably bound to the syntax of natural languages. So, for example:

　　　(31) "John is eating an apple"

asserts something about John which refers to a particular point on the temporal axis: i.e. sentence (31) concerns what John is doing <u>now</u>. On the other hand,

　　　(32) "John ate an apple"

says something about John that concerns some moment in time <u>before now</u>.
In addition to tense, natural language sentences can contain explicit time expressions that specify and delimit more precisely the temporal scope of verb phrases. Let us consider, for example:

　　　(33) "John ate an apple yesterday"
　　　(34) "John will visit France next summer"
　　　(35) "John plays the piano all the day".

In BLR, propositions are considered time-dependent, i.e. it is generally necessary to state the time limits to which a proposition refers. Verb tenses and explicit time specifications are represented in BLR by an additional argument, expressing the temporal features of the proposition, that joins the arguments taken by the predicate from which the proposion derives. This additional temporal argument is supposed to occupy the right-most place in the proposition. The BLR representations of sentences (31) to (35) are given by the following propositions, respectively:

　　　700 EAT (JOHN, V1:APPLE, NOW)

　　　710 EAT (JOHN, V1:APPLE, T2:PAST)

　　　720 EAT (JOHN, V1:APPLE, T2:YESTERDAY)

　　　730 VISIT (JOHN, FRANCE, T1:NEXT-SUMMER)

　　　740 PLAY (JOHN, V1:PIANO, DAY)

Note that variables referring to temporal specifications have been identified through Tn (where n is a positive integer) in order to make BLR's more readable.

Several points have to be discussed about the proposed representation. Temporal expressions can enter into a proposition in three different ways (Schubert, 1976): as specifications of moments of time, as time intervals, and in what has been called permanent mode.

In BLR time moments are considered, in accordance with the general philosophy of the representation language, individual entities. Time is considered a continuous axis and single points have no representation in BLR; temporal individuals are considered time snapshots (called moments) and each of them is used to indicate a particular state of the world. Moments in BLR can therefore refer to time intervals of varying length within which the state of the world does not change. Let us stress that, since moments represent time intervals, the extent of different moments can overlap.

Temporal individuals can be grouped together to form types. All temporal entities belong to the type TIME, i.e. the set of time entities can be defined as the set of all concepts X such that X ISA TIME. Quite general temporal types are, for example, PAST (i.e. the set of all moments X such that X<NOW) and FUTURE (i.e. the set of all moments X such that X>NOW). NOW, on the other hand, is a singleton set containing only the moment used to represent the present state of the world.

By representing moments of time through individual entities, and collections of moments through types, it is possible to take advantage of the BLR quantificational features and to use them to express temporal specifications. The interpretation of sentence (31) is therefore that John eats an apple in every moment of the (individually quantified) type NOW, i.e. that John is presently eating an apple. Sentence (32) says, on the other hand, that John eated an apple in a (not furtherly specified) moment in the past (T1). Temporal entities can have also existential plural quantification as in:

       750 VISIT (JOHN, FRANCE, TT1:PAST)

that represents the fact that John visited France several times in the past. The fact that existentially quantified variables embed the power of both existential and universal quantification is explicitly utilized in :

       760 EAT (((JOHN)), VV1:APPLE, (T2:PAST))

that is interpreted as stating that there were several occasions in the past for each of them it is possible to assert that John eated some apples. It is analogously possible to use universal quantification with temporal arguments, and proposition 740 is accordingly interpreted as stating that John plays the piano in every moment that belongs to the temporal type DAY. Moreover, temporal variables resulting from existential quantification can be used in the definition of other existentially quantified moments (see propositions 1010 and 1030 in section 6.1).

Other concepts can be used to express the ideas of past and future more specificly. Types for the past are, for example, LAST-MONTH, YESTERDAY, A-WEEK-AGO. These types specify time in a relative way, i.e. their meaning is different depending on the specific moment to which NOW refers. Absolute temporal types are exemplified by YEAR-1789 which indicates all the moments (i.e. all the temporal individuals) pertaining to the specific year 1789.

While the general idea of the present is conveyed in BLR by NOW, utilized to express the precise moment in which an action is happening and to represent situations that are true only in relation to the present state of the world, PERMANENT is used for situations not strictly dependent on a precise moment of time. Some situations are in fact relatively timeless being usual and/or permanent. Focusing on this point, it is evident that

       (36) "Gold is a metal"

asserts something about gold that is independent from time parameters. In general, every proposition built up through an ISA relation expresses something that is considered as PERMANENT. The BLR of sentence (6) is therefore given by:

        770 METAL (GOLD, PERMANENT).

Sometimes it is necessary to represent explicitly the time features also of propositions expressing general facts or situations. Let us consider, for example, (Kintsch, 1974):

        (37) "The Chinese are communist"
        (38) "The (= some) Chinese invented porcelain".

The respective representations must be temporally marked:

        780 COMMUNIST (CHINESE, NOW)
        790 INVENT (VV1:CHINESE, PORCELAIN, T2:PAST))

since otherwise we could legitimately infer that

        (39) "Some communists invented porcelain".

The distinction between PERMANENT and NOW is classicly captured by the representation of the sentences:

        (40) "John is playing the piano"
        (41) "John plays the piano"

given by:

        800 PLAY (JOHN, V1:PIANO, NOW)

        810 PLAY (JOHN, V1:PIANO, PERMANENT).

In dealing with temporal expressions it is necessary to be able to explicitly represent <u>intervals</u> of time. Let us consider:

        (42) "Yesterday John played the piano for three hours"
        (43) "Yesterday John played the piano from 4 to 6 p.m.".

We do not need any additional mechanism to represent intervals of time. As we have said before, a moment in BLR is considered an interval by itself, more precisely, it corresponds to an interval of (physical) time during which the state of the world does not change. To represent sentences (42) and (43) is only necessary to predicate the exact extension or the time limits of the moments. This is done in the following couples of sentences:

        820 PLAY (JOHN, V1:PIANO, T2:YESTERDAY)
        830 EXTENSION-OF (T2, HOUR, 3)

        840 PLAY (JOHN, V1:PIANO, T2:YESTERDAY)
        850 LIMITS-OF (T2, 4PM, 6PM).

It is also possible to utilize fuzzy temporal arguments (e.g. SELDOM, RARELY, OFTEN, USUALLY, EVERY-DAY, etc.) to specify the temporal features of sentences. The BLR's of:

        (44) "John seldom plays the piano"

and

(45) "John plays the piano every day"

are therefore given, respectively, by

        860 PLAY (JOHN, V1:PIANO, SELDOM)

        870 PLAY (JOHN, V1:PIANO, EVERY-DAY).

The semantics of fuzzy temporal types (like that of fuzzy quantifiers) is defined in the encyclopedia and their interpretation is strongly context-dependent. What is important to note is that fuzzy temporal types denote a set of moments upon which it is possible to quantify universally or existentially.

It is now possible to resume a point left unsettled in section 4 and show how it is possible to capture the complete meaning of the sentence:

        (30)"Someone calls Mary every day".

By simply changing the scope of the fuzzy temporal argument, it is easy to distinguish among the cases in which the same person calls Mary every day:

        880 CALL (V1:PERSON, MARY, EVERY-DAY);

and the case in which every day it is a possible different person who calls Mary:

        890 CALL (V1:PERSON, MARY, (EVERY-DAY)).

Finally, in dealing with natural language expressions it is necessary to specify the _sequence_ of two or more events in time. For instance,

        (46) "John left after shutting the door"

denotes the successive happening of two distinct actions both in the past. We represent the meaning of (11) by:

        900 SHUT (JOHN, V1:DOOR, T2:PAST)
        910 LEAVE (JOHN, NIL, T3:PAST)
        920 AFTER (910, 900)

where the predicate AFTER takes a variable number of arguments (entire propositions) each of them indicating an action that is considered happening after that/those indicated by the following one/s: in our example the action described in proposition 910 follows that described in proposition 900. Time relations like AFTER, BEFORE, WHILE, DURING, etc. are used to indicate the temporal relationships between two or more events. As it is evident in proposition 920, not all BLR propositions are marked by temporal arguments. In particular, propositions that take another proposition as their first (or only) argument cannot be temporally specified.

5.2 _Place_ and _Manner_

Differently from time, specifications of place, manner, and, in general, all the adverbs that appear in the sentence surface structure are represented in BLR through separate propositions. A few examples will suffice to clear the point and give the flavor of the BLR's thus obtained.

        (47) "John is running slowly"

is represented by:

        930 RUN (JOHN, NOW)

        940 SLOWLY (930)

Proposition 940 modifies the meaning of proposition 930 which constitutes its sole
argument and, accordingly, proposition 940 is not temporally marked.

        (48) "John is running in the woods"

has the following BLR:

        950 RUN (JOHN, NOW)
        960 IN (950, VV1:WOOD)

Proposition 960 specifies the spatial location of the event described in
proposition 950 and, since its first argument is constituted by another
proposition, is not temporally marked. On the other hand, the representation of:

        (49) "There were some apples on a table"

constituted by:

        970 ON (VV1:APPLE, V2:TABLE, T3:PAST)

must be temporally specified since the first argument of 970 is an existentially
plural quantified variable. Proposition 970 in fact specifies the spatial
location not of an event (that is temporally marked by itself) but of some objects
and it is therefore necessary to state explicitly the time moment to which the
spatial specification refers. Further examples of propositions expressing place,
manner, etc. are given in the following section.

6. REFERENCING CLASSES OF ENTITIES

6.1 Extending the Use of Existential Plural

We illustrate here another aspect of BLR, namely quantification of variables.
Consider the following fragment of a natural launguage text:

        (50) "There were some red apples on the table. One of them was ripe.
              John grasped it and ate it".

In the first sentence of (50) something is predicated about some apples, and in
the remaining part these apples are referenced. We can notice that the
construction of the BLR for the first sentence is straightforward, while the same
is not true for the other two sentences. In fact, the reference "One of them"
should be treated as an existential quantification not referring (as usual) to a
type concept, but to a set of objects which have been just defined through an
existential plural quantification. For this reason, in the BLR representation
language it is possible to use a set of entities defined through existential
plural quantification (e.g. VV1:<type>) as a new type.

The BLR of (50) is therefore:

         980 ON (VV1:APPLE, V2:TABLE, T3:PAST)
         990 RED (VV1, T3:PAST)
        1000 RIPE (V4:VV1, T3:PAST)
        1010 GRASP (JOHN, V4, T4:T3)
        1020 AND-SEQ (1010, 1030)
        1030 EAT (JOHN, V4, T5:T3).

It is interesting to focus on the following critical point: in (50) the topic of
discourse are a few apples. About these apples it is predicated both that they
are on a table and that they are red, but these properties are somehow secondary

with respect to the fact that these objects are apples, and the subsequent
reference are indeed concerned mainly with the property of being apples.
Sometimes, however, it happens that the role of some predicates cannot be
considered secondary, but, on the contrary, it is fundamental in order to identify
specific classes of objects, called aggregate concepts.

6.2 <u>Aggregate Concepts</u>

Aggregate concepts share many features with type concepts, but, differently from
them, they are generated only with respect to a specific natural language text
since they are not contained in the vocabulary (the knowledge base devoted to
store what, in Definition 5 (section 2), was called the semantic domain). More
specifically, an aggregate concept denotes a class of individuals, which are
identified through a certain number of predicates appearing in the natural
language text. Consider for example the following fragment of text:

> (51) "Some motorists prefer to drive fast cars.
>   Even though these cars are produced only limitedly,
>   some of them are not very expensive".

The situation is quite similar to (50), however there is a difference: "these
cars" and "some of them" do not refer just to cars, but exclusively to those which
are fast. We say that "fast cars" constitutes an <u>aggregate</u> <u>concept</u> (or simply
<u>aggregate</u>), i.e. a new unitary notion defined through some predicates and which
can be treated and referenced directly as a whole. Aggregate concepts are denoted
by the generic symbol An, which is considered as the class of concepts which
satisfy some predicates. As a class of concepts, an aggregate concept is utilized
exactly as a type, and, in particular, it can be quantified. Futhermore, it can
be semantically characterized by the ISA relation.

The BLR language utilizes three alternative ways for specifying an aggregate
concept, depending on the information supplied in the natural language text from
which the aggregate derives.
The <u>predicational specification</u> is the most general and most commonly utilized.
The information provided for identifying a generic aggregate is the following:

1. an identifier of the kind An (with n=1,2,...);

2. the linguistic items contained in the text, which refer to An;

3. a list of types to which An belongs;

4. a list of the predicates which have to be satisfied by all individuals or
    types belonging to An.

The second way is called <u>enumerational specification</u>, and it is utilized whenever
the text contains an exhaustive list of the individuals or types belonging to the
aggregate. The information provided in this case for the specification is the
same as in the predicational case, except for point 4., which is substituted by:

4'. the exhaustive list of all concepts which build up An.

The third way stems from the consideration that it is possible to operate on
classes of concepts (types) through set operators such as union, intersection, and
complement, building up in such a way new classes, that can be denoted by means of
an aggregate. This last way of identifying an aggregate concept is called <u>set</u>
<u>operator specification</u>, and consists in substituting points 3. and 4. of the
predicational specification as follows:

3'. an expression built up by set operators applied to type or
     individual concepts.

It has to be noticed that the enumerational specification is just a particular instance of the set operator specification.

With reference to (2), we can introduce the aggregate Al through the following predicational specification:

```
AGGREGATE SPECIFICATION
        Id        : Al
        Linguist  : fast cars
        ISAtypes  : Al ISA CAR
        Pred      : FAST (Al)
END SPECIFICATION.
```

This specification has to be attached to the the BLR of (2), which therefore results:

```
        1040 PREFER (VV1:MOTORISTS, 1050, PERMANENT)
        1050 DRIVE (VV1, Al, PERMANENT)
        1060 EVEN-THOUGH (1080, 1090)
        1070 PRODUCE (NIL, Al, PERMANENT)
        1080 LIMITEDLY (1070)
        1090 NOT (1100)
        1100 VERY (1110)
        1110 EXPENSIVE (VV3:Al, PERMANENT),
```

where in propositions 1050, 1070, and 1110 there is an existential quantification referred to the aggregate concept Al ("fast cars").

7. FINAL VERSION OF DEFINITION 6

We present here the final version of Definition 6, taking into account also the BLR features introduced in the previous sections, mainly concerned with quantification and aggregate concepts.

Definition-6. Given a subject domain $D=(C,sE,sR,P)$, a _proposition_ is a labeled $(n+1)$-tuple

$$M \ X(X1,X2,\ldots,Xn),$$

where the _label_ M is an integer positive number and the $(n+1)$-tuple is obtained from :

1. a basic predicate $Y(Y1,Y2,\ldots,Yn-1)$, where $X=Y$ and each argument Yj $(j=1,2,\ldots,n-1)$ is substituted in one of the following ways:

    1. by an individual entity Xj, such that Xj ISA Yj;
    2. by a type entity Xj, such that Xj ISA Yj, optionally followed by $:Xk$, with $k=1,2\ldots$;
    3. by an aggregate concept identifier Ak, with $k=1,2,\ldots$, such that Ak ISA Yj;
    4. by a variable identifier Vk, with $k=1,2,\ldots$, such that Vk ISA Yj;
    5. by a variable identifier VVk, with $k=1,2,\ldots$, such that VVk ISA Yj;
    6. by a pair $V:\langle type\rangle$, where V is a variable identifier Vk, VVk or Qk with $k=1,2,\ldots$, and $\langle type\rangle$ is obtained from Yj through a substitution of the kind 1.1, 1.3, or 1.5, in such a way that V ISA $\langle type\rangle$ and $\langle type\rangle$ ISA Yj;
    7. by a label of another proposition, if $Yj=ANY$;
    8. by the dummy argument NIL;

    Each substituted argument Xj $(j=1,2,\ldots n)$ may be enclosed in k $(\langle=n)$ pairs of brackets.

Xn is optional and it is utilized for temporal specification.

2. an instance of the ISA relation between two entities A and B, such that A
    ISA B, A=X1, B=X, if n=1.

8. SKETCH OF AN IMPLEMENTATION

This section is devoted to discuss the main lines for the implementation of a
parser capable of understanding a text and of constructing a formal representation
of its meaning, according to the BLR formalism introduced above.

The main capabilities requested to a parser which can construct the BLR of a
natural language text are:

1. identifying the relevant predicates to be used to build up propositions;

2. correctly instantiating the arguments of the selected predicates with the
    relevant concepts, variable identifiers, or proposition labels;

3. building up appropriate aggregate types, whenever necessary;

4. dealing with quantification;

5. solving references;

6. assigning correct and complete time specifications.

These requirements demand for several linguistic capabilities (lexical, syntactic,
semantic, and pragmatic) and also for the ability to reason on common-sense and
world knowledge. Moreover, a precise definition of both the syntax and semantics
of the BLR formalism is needed to direct the construction phase.

The first task to tackle in designing quite a complex parser, as the BLR parser is
expected to be, is to devise a neat functional organization, i.e. to define a
suitable architecture. The task of parsing, i.e. mapping a natural language text
into the corresponding BLR representation, involves two main capabilities: (a)
analyzing the input text and extracting from it a set of formal knowledge, and
(ii) using this knowledge to construct the BLR. Analysis and construction can
operate in a strictly sequential way or can be designed in such a way as to
interact during operation. The latter approach seems, in principle, more flexible
and, moreover, it can better match the requirements of the analysis phase which
can hardly be thought of as a one-step process. Therefore we will focus on a
highly interactive structure.

The parsing process can be organized into two co-operating components: a
construction module which manages the process of building up the BLR, and a set of
specialists devoted to analyze the input text (each one being concerned with a
specific feature of natural language understanding) and to supply the information
necessary to the construction module. The construction module has also the
responsability of controlling the overall operation of the system and of directing
the activity of the specialists towards the construction of the BLR. Parsing is
therefore managed as a goal-directed process: at each step of the system
operation only those specialists are activated which can directly contribute to
the achievement of the current task of the construction module. Co-operation
between the construction module and the specialists involves the management of a
complex process, since the activation of the specialists is not a purely
sequential process: contributions of different specialists are generally needed
to solve parsing problems and their interaction can not be planned in a fixed way.

The operation of the construction module is based on the iteration of the following cycle until the construction of the BLR is completed:

1. examine the current configuration of the BLR and individuate a list of possible actions useful to carry out the construction;

2. select from the above defined list the (most promising) first action to do;

3. activate the relevant specialist, capable of supplying the information necessary to perform the selected action;

4. get from the activated specialist the needed information (in the case the specialist fails, go back to step 1);

5. perform the selected action.

The construction module is implemented as a rule-based system (Hayes-Roth, Watermann and Lenat 1978; Davis and King, 1977) and utilizes a set of construction rules, which represent knowledge about the BLR (both its syntax and semantics), about the use of the specialists, and about the use of the information supplied by the specialists for the construction and validation of the BLR. Communication between the construction module and the specialists takes place through a mail box for exchanging both control messages and information. Both the construction module and the specialists can read and write in the mail box and can access the input text and the current BLR (this can be updated only by the construction module). The mail box is used as follows:

1. when the construction module wants to activate a specialist, it puts in the mail box a message directed to the selected specialist (a call with parameters which specifies what the construction module is requesting from the specialist);

2. each specialist reads in turn in the mail box messages coming from the construction module and, when a relevant message is found, it becomes active;

3. when the active specialist has completed its task, it leaves in the mail box a return message and the obtained results to be utilized for the construction module.

Specialists cannot, therefore, interact with each other directly: their co-operation takes place only through the construction module. In particular, when a specialist fails in the execution of its task and the help of another specialist is requested, it is the responsability of the construction module to analyze the causes of the failure and activate another specialist. Figure 3 illustrates the overall architecture of the parser.

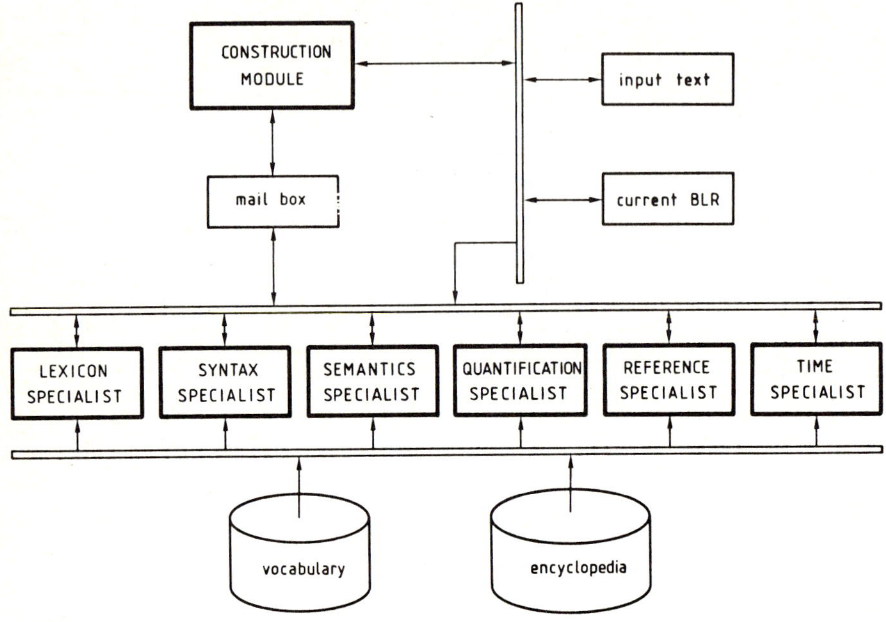

Figure 3. Overall Architecture of the Parser

The specialists available to the system are supposed to be competent in each one of the several domains which are involved in the comprehension activity and to cover the wide spectrum of different capabilities required to build up the BLR. The following specialist are needed:

1. lexicon specialist

2. syntax specialist

3. semantics specialist

4. quantification specialist

5. reference specialist

6. time specialist.

In order to analyze the specific competence and the mode of operation of each specialist, it is necessary to preliminarily examine the knowledge bases available to the parser: namely, the vocabulary and the encyclopedia.

The vocabulary is a list of the words recognized by the parser and, for each of them, it supplies the related morphologic and semantic knowledge. A record of the vocabulary includes four fields:

1. word: the natural language word (or idiom) represented in the form <stem + standard ending> (such as nominative singular for nouns, nominative, masculine, singular for adjectives, and infinite present for verbs; for irregular verbs or nouns with changing radicals cross pointers are provided);

2. morphologic classification: the morphologic type and fixed morphologic features (masculine noun, verb, adjective, etc.);

3. morphologic model: the morphologic pattern/s to be used for the morphologic analysis of the word;

4. meaning: the meaning/s of the word expressed through one or more concepts.

The word-field is used as the entry key for accessing the vocabulary file during the scanning of a natural language text. Ambiguity and polysemy are dealth with by having several records with the same word-field and different meaning-fields, and several records with different word-fields and the same meaning-field, respectively.

The encyclopedia contains further semantic, pragmatic, and real-world knowledge necessary for the operation of the parser. More specifically, it is organized into two parts:

1. concept-knowledge: for each concept the following information is provided: (a) the class it belongs to, e.g., individual entity, individual relation, type entity, type relation concept; (b) a subset of the types it belongs to; (c) the list of its possible arguments (in the case of a relation concept), of their type, and of their syntactic case.

2. world-knowledge: represented through a network of propositions, connected through directed arcs.

The encyclopedia can be accessed from the vocabulary through entry pointers which connect each concept to the relevant concept-knowledge and to the nodes of the world knowledge in which the concept is directly referred to.

It is worth noting that the part of the concept knowledge which contains a subset of the types a given concept belongs to, provides an explicit representation of (part of) the ISA relation. For each concept X, this subset (say $\overline{ISAx}$) does not generally include all types Y such that X ISA Y (call this set ISAx). $\overline{ISAx}$ is generally a small subset of ISAx, but it contains at least all those types which are sufficient to derive ISAx by transitivity. In addition to this necessary kernel of types, $\overline{ISAx}$ may contain of course other types which, because of their frequent use or basic importance, it is preferable to store explicitly rather than to derive them whenever needed.

Concept-knowledge will be mainly used by the semantics specialist to build up propositions, and world-knowledge will be used by the quantification and reference specialists.

We can now go further in analyzing the specific mode of operation of each of the specialists which are devoted to carry out the single tasks of the analysis process.

The lexicon specialist is devoted to recognize the words (and idioms) of the input text, to retrieve them in the vocabulary, and to perform a complete morphological analysis of them. For each word the appropriate morphologic type (e.g., noun, adjective, verb, adverb, etc.) and morphologic features (gender, number, and case for nouns and adjectives, mode, tense, and person for verbs, etc.) are identified. The lexicon specialist can be implemented through a finite-state recognizer, which uses a base of <u>lexical models</u> that specify the rules governing inflection and conjugation of words (Courtin, 1977). The recognizer can produce all lexically consistent interpretations of each input words. The role of the lexical specialist is to supply basic linguistic information necessary for the operation of several of the other specialists (mainly syntax, semantics, and time specialists).

The <u>syntax specialist</u> is devoted to analyze the surface structure of each sentence and to recognize its functional organization which is often a prerequisite for a correct semantic interpretation. The model for the syntactic analysis we adopt is based on the notions of case (Fillmore, 1968) and constituent. By the term <u>case</u> we mean the functional role that a fragment of text plays in the context of a sentence (e.g.: agent, object, qualifier, instrument, etc.). A <u>constituent</u> is a fragment of text that can receive a case assignement, i.e. which constitutes an elementary building block of a sentence. In order to construct a correct syntactic representation of a sentence, i.e. a tree which specifies the structural and functional dependencies between constituents, it is necessary to carry on several steps of a classic syntactic analysis involving <u>syntactic types</u> (verb phrase, noun phrase, etc.) The syntax specialist needs for operation the linguistic information supplied by the lexicon specialist, and operates bottom-up by utilizing a base of production rules called <u>syntactic rules</u>. Our approach to syntactic analysis shares several features with augmented phrase structure grammars (Heidorn, 1975), activation-based parsing (Jones, 1983), and word expert parsing (Small and Rieger, 1982).

The <u>semantic specialist</u> is aimed at constructing the first kernel of the BLR which will be completed, checked, and refined by other specialists. Semantic analysis includes the following main steps:

1. recognizing the predicates which are candidate for the construction of the propositions;

2. searching for the correct actual values to be assigned to the arguments of the predicates (including semantic type checking between formal arguments and corresponding values);

3. building up tentative propositions (including preliminary quantification);

4. organizing propositions into one or more plausible BLR's to be checked and refined by the other specialists.

The <u>quantification specialist</u> operates on the partial BLR constructed by the semantic specialist, and checks and adjusts the use of quantifiers. It operates as a rule-based system and utilizes a set of <pattern-action> rules called <u>quantification rules</u> to check quantification.

The <u>reference specialist</u> is devoted to solve references involving existentially (singular, plural and mass) and universally quantified variables. It operates on the output of the quantification specialist, and very often in strict interaction with it. It utilizes a set of <pattern-action> rules called <u>reference rules</u>, which express conditions for unification of different variables which share the same referent. Different types of knowledge are utilized by the reference specialist: lexical knowledge (e.g., for resolving or cheking references with possessive and relative pronouns), concept-knowledge of the encyclopedia (e.g., in the case of element-class references such as car-vehicle, dog-animal, etc.), world-knowledge for inferring complex references.

The _time_ _specialist_ analyzes the time specifications contained in the text (both
implicit in the tense of verbs and explicit in time adverbs and expressions) and
completes the current BLR in such a way as to give a correct and complete
representation of time relations.   It mainly utilizes lexical and syntactic
knowledge and operates through a set of <pattern-action> rules called _time_ _rules_,
which direct its operation towards the goal of expliciting as much as _possible_ the
temporal organization of the text.

8. CONCLUSION

In this paper we have presented the BLR formalism for natural language text
representation developed in the framework of the SUSY project. The representation
language has been illustrated both for what concerns notational aspects and
expressive adequacy.   A sketchy description of the BLR parser, able to map texts
into BLR form, has been presented as well.

At the end, it is worthy to punctuate the overall status of the SUSY project
currently ongoing at the University of Udine:

- the experimental activity is now focused on the implementation of the BLR
  parser. Franz LISP running under UNIX on a VAX 11/780 will be utilized;
- the ELR and HPN representations already developed (Fum, Guida, Tasso, to
  appear) are now under refinement in order to formalize their definifion;
- we are also focusing on what we consider to be the most original and new
  topic in the whole project, i.e.   the definition of a Theory of
  Importance suitable for tackling the importance ranking task to be
  executed in order to summarize a text;
- a comparison of the BLR formalism with other logical formal systems is
  planned.

REFERENCES

1. Brachman, R.J., On the Epistemological Status of Semantic Networks, in:
    Findler, N.V.   (ed.), _Associative_ Networks: _Representation_ _and_ _Use_ _of_
    Knowledge _by_ _Computers_, (Academic Press, New York, 1979).

2. Brachman, R.J., What IS-A Is and Isn't: An Analysis of Taxonomic Links
    in Semantic Networks, _Computer_ 16 (1983) 30-36.

3. Courtin, J., Algoritmes pour le traitement interactif des languages
    naturelles, _These_ d'Etat: _Universite_ _Scientifique_ _et_ _Medicale_ _de_
    Grenoble, Grenoble, France, 1977.

4. Davis, R. and King, I., An Overview of Production Systems, in: Elcock,
    E.W. and Michie, D.   (eds.), _Machine_ _Intelligence_ _8_, (Ellisworth
    Horwood, Chichester: UK, 1977).

5. Fillmore, C., The Case for Case, in: Bach, E. and Harms, R.T.,
    Universals _in_ _Linguistic_ _Theory._, (Holt, Rinehart and Winston, Chicago,
    1968).

6. Findler, N.V. (ed.), _Associative_ Networks: _Representation_ _and_ _Use_ _of_
    Knowledge _by_ _Computers_, (Academic Press, New York, 1979).

7. Fum, D., Guida, G., and Tasso, C., Forward and Backward Reasoning in
    Automatic Abstracting, in: Horecky, J. (ed.), _Coling_ _82:_ _Proceedings_
    Ninth _Intern._ _Confer._ _on_ _Computational_ _Linguistics_, Prague,

Czechoslovakia, (North-Holland, Amsterdam, 1982).

8. Fum, D., Guida, G., and Tasso, C., A Rule-Based Approach to Natural Language Text Representation and Comprehension, in: Trappl, R. (ed.), Cybernetics and Systems Research 2: Proceedings Seventh European Meeting on Cybernetics and Systems Research, Vienna, Austria, (North Holland, Amsterdam, 1984).

9. Fum, D., Guida, G., and Tasso, C., Capturing Importance in Natural Language Texts: an HPN-Based Approach, Proceedings Second International Colloquium on Meaning and Lexicon, Kleve, Germany, (to appear).

10. Hayes-Roth, F., Waterman, D.A., and Lenat, D.B., Principles of Pattern-Directed Inference Systems, in: Waterman, D.A. and Hayes-Roth, F. (eds.), Pattern Directed Inference Systems, (Academic Press, New York, 1978).

11. Heidorn, G.E., Augmented Phrase Structure Grammars, in: Nash-Webber, B.L. and Schank, R.C. (eds.), Theoretical Issues in Natural Language Processing, (Association for Computational Linguistics, Menlo Park:CA, 1975).

12. Jones, M.A., Activation Based Parsing, Proceedings Eighth Intern. Joint Confer. on Artificial Intelligence, Karlsruhe, Germany, (Kaufmann, Los Altos:CA, 1983).

13. Kintsch, W., The Representation of Meaning in Memory (Erlbaum, Hillsdale: NJ., 1974).

14. Kintsch, W., Aspects of Text Comprehension, in: Le Ny, J.F. and Kintsch, W. (eds.), Language and Comprehension, (North-Holland, Amsterdam, 1982).

15. Kintsch, W. and van Dijk, T., Toward a Model of Text Comprehension, Psychological Review 85 (1978) 363-394.

16. Quine, W., Word and Object, (Wiley: New York, 1960).

17. McDermott, D., A Temporal Logic for Reasoning about Processes and Plans, Cognitive Science, 1982 (6), 101-155.

18. Schank, R.C., Conceptual Dependency: A Theory of Natural Language Understanding, Cognitive Psychology 3 (1972), 552-631.

19. Schank, R.C., Conceptual Information Processing, (North-Holland, Amsterdam, 1975).

20. Schubert, L.K., Extending the Expressive Power of Semantic Networks, Artificial Intelligence 7 (1976) 163-198.

21. Scragg, G., Semantic Nets as Memory Models, in: Charniak, E. and Wilks, Y. (eds), Computational Semantics, (North Holland, Amsterdam, 1976).

22. Small, S. and Rieger, C., Parsing and Comprehending with Word Experts, in: Lehnert, W.G. and Ringle, M.H. (eds.), Strategies for Natural Language Processing, (Erlbaum, Hillsdale, NJ, 1982).

Computational Models of Natural Language Processing
B.G. Bara and G. Guida (eds.)
© Elsevier Science Publishers B.V. (North-Holland), 1984

FROM TOPIC AND FOCUS OF A SENTENCE TO LINKING IN A TEXT

Eva Hajičová, Petr Sgall

Faculty of Mathematics and Physics
Charles University
Prague, Czechoslovakia

The present paper points out the means by which
topic-focus articulation (TFA) can be described
as one of the main hierarchies of meaning in a
sentence. We briefly characterize and evaluate
several attempts to bring this articulation into
an immediate connection with the structure of a
text. In Section 4 we establish a connection
between TFA and coreference as one of the issues
concerning linking in a text; our formulation is
based on an account of the degrees of salience
among the elements in the stock of knowledge
shared by the speaker and the hearer. We assume
that such an account can be used within a system
of automatic comprehension of natural language
texts.

1. INTRODUCTION: THE STATE OF THE ART IN TFA

Only marginal attention was paid to TFA for many decades. The Prague
School, as one exception, has shown an interest in this question
since the 1930's. Only after Chomsky (1971) did the questions of
topic (theme) and focus (comment) shift their position from a rarely
discussed issue to one of the central problems of linguistics.
Numerous analyses of TFA were presented in connection with transformational grammar or other frameworks. However, far less numerous are
the attempts at a systematic description that would take into account
the recursive properties of the syntactic structure and the composition of topic and focus from units corresponding to phrases or
syntagms, clauses, etc. Is it a realistic task to construct a
procedure assigning to a sentence a set of representations indicating possible repartitions of topic and focus?

It may be considered a necessary precondition of this task to first
find out how topic and focus should be adequately described in the
underlying structures of sentences. One of the earliest attempts at
such a formulation was connected with dependency syntax (Sgall,
1967) and characterized the main structuring of the underlying or
tectogrammatical representations (TR ̄s), in which the hierarchy of
communicative dynamism (CD) could be rendered by the left-to-right
ordering of the nodes of the dependency tree.

Other trends have been connected with transformational grammar
(Jackendoff, 1972) and, more recently, with intensional semantics
(Stechow, 1980; Klein and Stechow, 1982). The empirical questions

have not yet been fully explored, however; it seems that a more
thorough study of intonation patterns is necessary as a first step.
In many approaches the importance of these patterns is either under-
estimated, or viewed too simplistically. It is important to notice
that (a) and (b) are two different sentences in (1) and (2) as well
as in (3), though the semantic difference is much more important in
(3) than in (1); with (1) the two sets of propositions to which the
two sentences correspond assign the value 'true' to the same subsets
of possible worlds, which is not the case with (3).

      (1)(a) Mother is COMING.
         (b) MOTHER is coming.

      (2)(a) Napoleon ruled on ELBA.
         (b) NAPOLEON ruled on Elba.

      (3)(a) Many men read few BOOKS.
         (b) Few books are read by many MEN.

In (3) the relations between the scopes of the quantifiers play an
important role: (3)(a) speaks (in its primary meaning) about a single
set of men, to each element of which a set of books is assigned,
while in (the primary meaning of) (3)(b) this relationship is revers-
ed. However, it is not quite clear what the differences are between
the truth conditional structures of sentences (2)(a) and (2)(b),
which do not contain any overt quantifiers as are found in (3).
Though the meanings of the sentences clearly differ, (2)(a) may be
primarily evaluated as true for the months between the two Empires,
whereas (2)(b) covers these two epochs. Furthermore, the interplay
between primary and secondary meanings, as well as the relationships
between sentence meanings (TR's) and semantic interpretations are
still connected with many unresolved questions for which it is
necessary to find at least a relatively safe basis of description.

Thus it is not surprising that many specialists still continue to
analyze TFA in the context of 'soft' syntax and semantics, without
using an explicit framework. This approach is certainly useful in
connection with such difficult tasks as is the study of the structure
of a text (see Section 3), or the comparative study of TFA in
languages which are typologically very different. Kuno (1972) presented significant insights into this problem when he compared Japanese
with English.

2.1. How to describe topic and focus

One of the main points still seems to concern the very nature of TFA
and its position in the structure of language.Seeking an answer to
this question, we attempted to connect the results of the classical
Prague School analyses, based on the use of testable empirical
criteria, with the methodological requirements of Chomskyan linguistics and also with what was achieved in intensional semantics. Our
approach, which can be only briefly characterized here, is presented
in more detail in Hajičová and Sgall (1980) and Sgall, Hajičová and
Panevová (in prep.). This approach may have a certain significance
for a procedural understanding of the meaning of the sentence.

The sentence should not be viewed only statically, but it should be
understood as an instruction given by the speaker to the hearer, i.e.
as an elementary structure adapted to functioning in communication.
Not only the speaker's intention "to tell someone something" by
linguistic means (Searle, 1970, 42ff) should be taken into account,
but also the speaker's intention to use means which would help the

hearer to find the interpretation relatively easily. Much effort
would be necessary if the meaning and reference of the expressions
contained in the sentence had to be found by the hearer in the vast
domain of her/his memory without any aids, without distinguishing
between what the hearer already knows or immediately perceives, and
what s/he has to look for or to learn as a new piece of information.

The sentence, as a systemic form of an elementary communicative
linguistic act, is organized in such a way as to minimize this effort
on the part of the hearer. In uttering a declarative sentence, the
speaker specifies the items of information s/he shares with the
hearer and considers to be easily accessible to the latter at the
given time point of the discourse (topic), and s/he specifies,
further, what properties should be assigned to them by the hearer,
in what relationships with what other items they should be introduced, or what other modifications they should undergo (focus).

In sentences with such a simple structure as (1)(a) the valency-based
syntactic relations coincide with TFA; i.e. the terms subject and
predicate may be used here both in their grammatical as well as in
their philosophical (Aristotelian) sense. Other cases are not so
simple; either the relationship of the two elements is inverted, as
in (1)(b), the sentence includes more than two elements, as in (2),
(3), or deeper embeddings, as in the following example:

    (4) Jim came to the house that he wanted to BUY.

In (4) there are unstressed pronominal elements within the focus,
which denote items readily accessible in the hearer's memory (coreferential with nouns occurring in the preceding part of the
sentence). This points to the necessity of distinguishing between
the dichotomy of the topic and the focus of the sentence and the *contextually bound* and *non-bound* character of the individual nodes
(occurrences of lexical units); the former correspond to the so-called *given* elements, chosen by the speaker among the items s/he assumes
to be easily accessible in the hearer's memory, i.e. salient, activated over an upper threshold in the stock of shared knowledge, or
recoverable, in the sense of Halliday (1967); see also Chafe's (1976)
term 'identifiable'.

We assume that a meaning of a sentence (its tectogrammatical representation, TR) can have the form of a dependency tree (with complex
symbols occurring as labels of the nodes, the main verb constituting
the root of the tree, and the left-to-right order of the nodes representing the hierarchy of CD),[1] and we work with two rather strong
hypotheses:

(a) The verb occupies such a position in the TR that it is more (less)
dynamic than every other element of the clause that belongs to the
topic (focus) of that clause. In the primary case the verb itself
belongs to the focus, but it is also possible that the verb is contextually bound and included in the topic. There are also such
examples as:

    (5) I met the teacher of LATIN.

    (6) Which teacher have you met?

Here(with at least one of the meanings of (5), e.g. if it is used as
an answer to (6) or similarly) all complementations of the verb (its
daughter nodes) belong to the topic, the focus consists only of one
or more nodes subordinated to the most dynamic of these complementations.

(b) The hierarchy of CD within focus is determined by an ordering
of the kinds of complementations (types of dependency relation, deep
cases and adverbials), which is given by the grammar; we call this
relation *systemic ordering*. In individual sentences, this scale is
"modified" within their hierarchy of CD by contextually bound
elements being removed to the left; the hierarchy of CD within topic
is not determined by the grammar.

We assume, furthermore, that every sentence has a focus (since otherwise it would convey no information relevant for communication, it
would lack any illocutionary force), but that there are sentences
without any topic (corresponding to thetic judgments).

The notion of contextual boundness should not be understood as
immediately connected with the not altogether clear difference
between given (known) and new information. The difference between
contextually bound and non-bound elements of a TR has its specific
position in the patterning of the system of language. A contextually
bound element need not be assumed by the speaker to be actually
known to the hearer, as example (7) shows;[2] it may even be considered by the speaker not to exist in the actual world (not taking place,
etc.), see sentence (8).

    (7) Who is Peter? - Peter I don't KNOW.

    (8) Their arrival is very IMPROBABLE now.

Also in such a sentence as (3)(b) above, *Few books are read by many
MEN*, the set of few books need not be directly known to the hearer;
it is enough if e.g. the reading of books (or just the level of
cultural background) was mentioned in the preceding co-text.

It is necessary to avoid such assumptions as that regarding topic or
focus as a single (deep or surface) constituent of the sentence. On
the contrary, it is possible that e.g. two noun phrases (functioning
as different complementations of the main verb - adverbials, or deep
subject, deep object, etc.) are both included in the focus (or that
both belong to the topic). Let us consider the following examples:[3]

    (9) What trip did you take? - I went for a week to the MOUNTAINS
        (... and not for a month to CANNES).

    (10) This spring John has been writing a new MONOGRAPH.

    (11) Jerome ATE it last night.

    (12) She lost it on a TRIP.

In (9) the time adverbial (*for a week*) as well as the directional
belong to the focus; the actor (deep subject) along with the verb
constitute the topic. In (10) - when answering such a question as
What is John doing? - the actor and the time adverbial are in the
topic, the verb and the deep object - in the focus. If (11) is uttered, e.g. as an answer to *What happened to the cake?*, its verb constitutes the focus, and the situation is similar with (12), which can
answer e.g. such a question as *Does Helen still like her old neck-
lace?*, where also the locative is included in the focus. In (11) and
in (12) the subject as well as the object clearly belong to the topic,
so that there is no hope that the sentence could be analyzed into
topic and focus as two constituents of any level whatsoever. Dependency syntax seems to be better suited to accounting for the fact

that neither topic nor focus is necessarily simple from whatever point of view.

It is important to distinguish between *contextually bound* and *presupposed*, since non-bound items may also be connected with presuppositions, see Hajičová (1974) and Dahl (1974).

As we have already noted, the degrees of CD within the focus are distributed in accordance with systemic ordering. A criterion for discovering the relationship between two types of modifications under this ordering may be formulated as follows: if a governing word can be expanded by two different modifications, A and B, occurring in this order in the surface representation (with normal intonation), neither of them being contextually bound, whereas the surface word order B A (or placement of the intonation centre on A if preceding B) is possible only if B *is* contextually bound, then A precedes B under systemic ordering.

This can be verified by means of such examples as (13) to (15), in which the position of the deep object before the instrument (13), origin (14) and locative (15) in the scale of CD of the (a) examples (corresponding, in these sentences with normal intonation, to the surface word order) is not conditioned by contextual boundness. No higher frequency is concerned here, but the fact that the object can be non-bound, since each of the (a) examples can answer such a question as *What did he do?*; these examples are ambiguous in that the object is non-bound in some of their readings, while it is contextually-bound in others (a similar ambiguity also concerns the verb). On the other hand, the (b) examples, with marked intonation (or changed word order), can not be used as answers to the quoted question; they correspond rather to a question which contains their final noun phrase (e.g. *What does he use these hoes (logs) for?*). This shows that the lower degree of CD of these NP's in (b) - expressed by marked intonation or by inversion - is conditioned by the fact that they are contextually bound.

> (13)(a) He dug a hole with a HOE.
>
> (b) He dug a HOLE with a hoe.

> (14)(a) He made a canoe out of a LOG.
>
> (b) He made a CANOE out of a log (*or* He made a log into a CANOE.)

> (15)(a) He dug a hole in the GARDEN.
> (b) He dug a HOLE in the garden (*or* In the garden he dug a HOLE.)

An examination of Czech in comparison with English and several other languages has led to the conclusion that the systemic ordering of some of the main participants is identical for many languages, having the form: Actor - Addressee - Objective (deep object). As for Instrument, Origin, Locative, it seems that English differs from Czech in that these three participants follow Objective in English, though they precede it in Czech.

Examples show that a change in the order of the relevant modifications in each of the examples, if not accompanied by a transfer of the intonation centre from the end of the sentence, leads to the expected effect, namely that the modification transported to the left (or the loss of pitch) is then understood as being contextually bound.

Another point concerns the role of topic and the so-called logical subject (i.e. the item that is assigned - or predicated - some quality by the sentence). As we have seen, topic need not consist of a single constituent in the sentence. Kuroda (1972, 159) gives this feature of the topic as a reason why topic should not be identified with subject "in a logical sense", though he does not state why he is convinced that logical subject (of a categorical judgment) must consist of a single syntactic constituent.

2.2 How to determine topic and focus

Among the operational criteria for determining TFA, the question test is often used. The question test is based on the assumption that the contexts in which a sentence may be appropriately used can be characterized by a set of questions that can be immediately (and fully) answered by this sentence.[4]

The following rules may be understood as underlying the question test:

(a) If the set of all those questions for which the given sentence can serve as an immediate answer (called the set of relevant quest- ions in the sequel) is such that (aa) for some such phrases A and B included in the given sentence, that (the referent of) A is (referr- ed to by a phrase) included in every question from the set of relev- ant questions in which B is included, and also (ab) in such a quest- ion (from the set) that does not include B, then in (all TR's of) the given sentence the (source of the) phrase A is less dynamic than the (source of the) phrase B;

(b) if A (from the given sentence) occurs in no element of the set of relevant questions, it is the focus proper of the given sentence;

(c) if A occurs in every element of the set of relevant questions, then it belongs to the topic of the given sentence;

(d) if (a) is met by A and B, but either A or B breaks (b) and also (c), then the sentence is ambiguous in that the phrase breaking these two conditions belongs to its topic in some of its TR's and to its focus in some other(s);

(e) if there is a pair of phrases A, B, in the given sentence, such that A and B break (aa) and neither A nor B meets (c), then the sentence is ambiguous not only with respect to the position of the boundary between topic and focus - cf. (d) and Chomsky's (1971) *range of permissible focus* - but also in that A is less dynamic than B in some of its TR's and more dynamic in some others; at most in one of these two cases both A and B belong to the focus (this case can be determined on the basis of systemic ordering).

According to these rules e.g. the phrase *my sister* belongs to the topic in all TR's of (16), while *from the garden* belongs to the focus in all of them, and each of the words *brought* and *some fruits* belong to the topic in some of them, but to the focus in others.

(16) My sister brought some fruits from the GARDEN.

One of the approaches using a test with negation is based on the
properties of negative sentences, in which (see Hajičová, 1973)
primarily it is the focus (in its relationship to the topic) that
is negated, so that e.g. the (a) sentences in (17) and (18) are more
properly paraphrased by the (b) than by the (c) sentences.

    (17)(a) Many arrows didn't hit the TARGET.

         (b) About many arrows it is not true that they hit the
            TARGET.

         (c) It is not true that many arrows hit the TARGET.

    (18)(a) Every Sunday one doesn't WORK.

         (b) About every Sunday it is not true that one (then)
            WORKS.

         (c) It is not true that every Sunday one WORKS.

This kind of negation test can be used to show that - as for the
primary readings - in (17)(a) the subject and in (18)(a) the temporal
adverbial belong to the topic.

Another negation test is known from Chomsky (1971), who uses the
possible natural responses to show which parts of the sentence can
- in some readings - belong to its focus. Other variants of the test
using a negative continuation have been elaborated rather systematically by Posner (1972a) in his *Kommentartest* and by Bogusławski (1977).
The former also pays due attention to the different positions of
the intonation centre, and makes use of the different positions of
the negative particle in German. Zemb (1968) discussed the relevance
of this approach for TFA with deep insight.

It seems important that in those situations where more than one of
the above mentioned tests can be applied, the results of the test
coincide. This coincidence corroborates the view according to which
the bipartition of the sentence into topic and focus, based on contextual boundness, is relevant for the semantic function of linguistic
negation in a sentence, as well as for the role of the sentence in
the structure of a text. The interplay of contextual boundness with
the dependency structure of a TR determines which parts of the TR
are included in its topic and which of its parts belong to its focus,
though the way in which this is determined is not simple; a more
detailed discussion and a formal definition of topic and focus is
contained in Sgall (1979).

The tests with questions and negation can be used in a linguistic
analysis of texts; as for the procedures relating to an automatic
identification of topic and focus, some hints that can serve as a
starting point were formulated in Hajičová and Sgall (1980, 101-106).

3. TOPIC, FOCUS AND TEXT

It is often argued that a thematic organization essentially similar
to that of the sentence also underlies the structuring of any text.
However, it can be shown that the structure of a text obeys different principles than that of a sentence.

It is not precise to characterize a text or a discourse as a sequence
(or string) of sentences. The constituent parts of a text correspond
to sentence tokens (utterances) rather than to sentence types; the

reference assignment, i.e. the specification of the objects referred
to by referring expressions, is crucial for the structuring of a
text, especially for its coherence based on the linking of its
elements. Different tokens (occurrences) of a single sentence may
differ in the reference assignment, so that it is an utterance rather
than a sentence that constitutes a part of the text. Utterances may
be of other than sentential (or even linguistic) form (e.g. the nod
in answering a question is an appropriate part of a dialogue, though
it is not a sentence). This point is connected with the fact that
discourse or text belongs to the domain of communication (language
use, a kind of human activity) rather than to the system of language.

Questions of the internal structuring of a text cannot be answered
by general statements concerning the structure of every possible
text (in a given language). Instead of *text grammars* it is preferable
to construct a *theory of coherence* (Petöfi, 1978, 366), and it is
known that different kinds of text structuring can be described as
being characteristic for texts of different types (these types of
texts themselves can be supposed to correspond in a certain way to
the forms of human cognition). The differences of the structure of
different kinds or types of texts, as studied by Hausenblas (1964),
Posner (1972b) and others, corroborate the view that the regularities
connected with the patterning of texts are of a different character
than the regularities dealt with in the description of languages.
Conversation, as well as other kinds of discourse, is well known to
have rules of its own, quite different from rules of grammar (see
Mey, 1981).

Also apparent in the domain of linking, especially in coreference,
is the difference between the structure of a sentence and the patterning of a text. Within a sentence there are several points by which
coreference is determined grammatically. This holds for the reflexive pronouns (though esp. with the reflexive possessives the situation is not always as clear-cut as might be assumed, see Bílý (1981)
and the writings quoted there). Also in such cases as *They allowed
him to do it* the coreference of the Actor of the infinitive with the
Objective of the governing clause is conditioned by grammar. On the
other hand, if crossing the boundaries between sentences, coreference
perhaps always is indistinct (Halliday and Hasan, 1976, 311n), and
pragmatic inferencing is involved in the resolution of anaphoric
expressions (Reinhart, 1981, § 4.2). Thus in *Henry goes to a theatre
with his wife every week; John does so only rarely* it is not clear
whether John does so with his wife or not, perhaps he may be a bache-
lor. This concerns also most cases of optional deletion, be they of
an intersentential character, or in coordinated clauses, cf. *John
met Jim. He didn't say hello.* (The subject is indistinct, and so is
the deleted Addressee.)

If discourse is viewed as a kind of human action, then text linguistics should be developed within the theory of communication rather
than parallel to the linguistics of the sentence (or even instead of
the latter). There are then different possible approaches to the
relationship between the relatively well known TFA of a sentence and
the corresponding aspects of the patterning of a text. If one uses
the term *topic* (or *theme*) as a technical term from the sphere of
TFA, rather than in its colloquial meaning, then "thematic progressions" described by Daneš (1970; 1974) constitute the aspect of linking in text that is most closely related to TFA: the first type of
thematic progressions consists in the focus (comment) of a given
utterance U_1 reappearing as the topic of the immediately following

utterance U_2, as e.g. in *Last week I visited LUND. It is a nice university town...*; in the second type the topic of U_1 is identical[5] to that of U_2, as e.g. in *Charlie came to his AUNT. He wanted first of all to show his POLITENESS*; the two utterances of the third type derive their topics (themes) from a hypertheme, such as *the apartment* in *Three of the four rooms are rather large. The windows lead into a garden.* However, often the progressions contain different combinations of the elements of topic and focus (Juganov, 1979), so that only relatively rarely the topic of an utterance as a whole is coreferential either with the topic or with the focus of the preceding uterance.

However, "topic" is often understood as "topic of the discourse" or in a similar way (which corresponds to the everyday usage rather than to the technical meaning the term *topic* has acquired in connection with TFA). Then it seems typical that it is not maintained that every text or discourse has a single topic. It was pointed out already by Marty (1897, p. 346) that what we now call TFA is characteristic of a sentence, and not of a text. Several authors who have undertaken an empirical investigation that perhaps was intended to lead to a general characterization of "the topic of the text" have concluded that smaller segments of a text regularly have topics of their own. This has been stated by Marciszewski (1976, pp. 21ff); also van Dijk (1977, pp. 132 ff) prefers to speak of "the topic for this passage", "topic of (a part of) a discourse", etc., instead of presenting arguments in favour of the view that every text has a single topic. Most of the more recent approaches to "discourse topic" are of a similar character, see the survey given by Reinhart (1981). A thorough characterization of different approaches concerning the dialogue was presented by Carlson (1983), who himself analyzes the structure of the dialogue from the viewpoint of Hintikka's game theoretical semantics.

4. TOPIC AND LINKING IN TEXT

As we have seen, the relationship between TFA and the structure of a text is by no means straightforward. However, it may be of interest to consider some of the characteristic relations between contextually bound elements and their antecedents in a text. These relations are based on the hierarchy of salience of the elements of the stock of shared knowledge. This hierarchy was studied by Hajičová and Vrbová (1982), who analyzed segments of text from the viewpoint of the changes of salience and its role in linking. Their results can be briefly summarized as follows.

Let us introduce a tentative notation:

x_a denotes an expression x referring to an object a;

$a(X;Y)$ denotes that the object a is salient to degree X in the stock of shared knowledge in the given time point; we denote by M the maximal degree of salience and by $M-m$, m being a positive integer, the lower degrees (we are aware that numerical degrees can be understood only as a first approximation); Y denotes the low (L) or high (H) *permanence* of salience, i.e. it is assumed that an object assigned H retains its salience in the subsequent portion of the discourse longer than that assigned L;

$P(x_a)$ denotes that x has either the form of a weak (unstressed)

anaphoric pronoun or a zero form, i.e. is deleted in the
given sentence S, though being present in the underlying
structure of S;

$D(x_a)$ denotes that x is a definite noun phrase (including such
expressions as *one of the ...*); to the left (right) of the
arrow we indicate the state immediately preceding (following)
the utterance of the sentence S in which x occurs.

Now the following preliminary rules concerning the degree and the
permanence of salience can be formulated, where $n \geq 0$.

(A)   If $P(x_a)$, then $a(X;Y) \rightarrow a(X;Y)$.

(B)   If x_a is contextually non-bound and belongs to the focus of S,
then $a(X;Y) \rightarrow a(M;Y)$.

(C)   If $D(x_y)$ is in the topic of S, then $a(X;Y) \rightarrow a(M-1;H)$.

(D)   If $a(X;Y)$, then $b(X-2;Y)$ obtains for every object b that is
not itself referred to in the TR of S, but is immediately
associated with an item contained there (e.g. *room* and *ceiling,
school* and *pupils*).

(E)   If *as for x_a, concerning x_a* is the leftmost expression of S,
then $a(X;Y) \rightarrow a(M-1;H)$; it is probable that X is rather a low
degree in this case.

(F)   If no x_a is included in S and no associated object is referred
to (see rule (D) above), then $a(X;Y) \rightarrow a(X-2;L)$.

(G)   If x_b is contained in a heading, then $a(X;Y) \rightarrow a(M;H)$; for
every b for which no x_b is contained in a heading,
$b(X;Y) \rightarrow b(X-2;L)$.

These rules can be understood as a starting point for a procedure
that may serve to identify the reference of expressions in a discourse. The contextually bound parts of sentences (i.e. first of all
their topics) refer to objects which either have the highest degree
of salience (among the objects that can be referred to by the given
expression), or have a relatively high degree and a high permanence
of salience. The difference between $n = \emptyset$ and $n = 1$ is too small to
make the reference assignment univocal if a weak pronoun is used in
the utterance following S. It can be assumed that a difference
larger than 1 is sufficient in this respect (though our use of
numerical values is meant only as a first approximation). Thus e.g.
after two such sentences as *The school garden was full of CHILDREN.
Outside PARENTS were waiting,* an utterance of *Most of them seemed
to be quite SATISFIED* can be used with *them* referring clearly to
the parents. On the other hand, the same utterance following after
*Many parents used to send their children to our COURSES. The children
LIKED it here* clearly refers to the children.

Several issues are treated only in a very preliminary way by the
rules in their present form. More thorough formulations should be
found in the following areas:

It should be reflected whether in the given case a single element of
a set of objects that can be denominated by a certain expression is
activated to a sufficiently higher degree than other objects belonging to this set; if this condition is not met the simple denominat-

tion would not be connected with univocal reference and a specific
denomination is required by the given point of linking: thus if only
a single male human being was mentioned in the preceding two utterances, *he* is sufficient to recall the referent; if two such beings
do not sufficiently differ in the corresponding degrees of activation, then *the teacher* might be univocal; if both of them share this
qualification, an expanded NP such as *the teacher of chemistry* or
a similar denomination will be used in the next utterance.

Certain other scales or hierarchies should be taken into account;
e.g. that concerning the more or less immediate relationships of
association, cf. Rule (D). The permanence of salience should be described in a more subtle way, taking into account also the more or
less prominent positions of the utterances described (sentences
metatextually opening a narration or a portion of it are more prominent than others in that the objects introduced in them retain their
activation to a higher degree than others), different degrees of
headings, etc.

These lines of further research should be pursued to gain the possibility of characterizing a token of a sentence (with its sense) as a
procedural instruction aiming at certain changes in the hearer's
image of the world.⁶

FOOTNOTES

1.   There are certain advantages in defining CD as a partial ordering,
where the sister nodes are always ordered with respect to each other
and to their common mother, but the relationship between other nodes
remains undefined. It should also be noted that the relation of
coordination (conjunction) requires a more complex framework than
that of dependency trees, see Plátek, Sgall and Sgall (in prep.).

2.   Cf. Jacobs (1977), who was mistakenly convinced that the opposit-
ion between "known" and "new" information played an immediate role
in our framework.

3.   Also some disadvantages of Firbas' (1957, 1975) approach (defining 'theme' and 'rheme' on the basis of CD) may be overcome in this
way; e.g. the existence of topicless sentences can be accounted for,
while in the other case even a sentence consisting only of an im-
personal verb (e.g. Lat. *Pluit* - *It rains,* or Czech *Nelze POKRAČO-
VAT* - It is not possible to CONTINUE) would have a topic; cf. Wollmann's (1981, esp. 155) treatment of similar sentences, which -
though subscribing to Firbas' views - does not fully respect the
definition based on CD: he characterizes e.g. *ale nelze říci (but it
is impossible to tell)* in his (4) as topicless.

4.   By an immediate answer we denote e.g. *Mary has thrown them into
the wastebasket* as an answer to *What has Mary done with the flowers?*
rather than to *What happened with the flowers?*, since in the latter
case (at least on one reading) the answer includes *Mary* as contextually bound, though its referent is not referred to in the question
(i.e. is activated enough by the situation).

5.   A full identity is not required here; such associative links as
that between a whole and its parts, or those concerning hyponyms,
etc., are relevant.

6. The changes are carried out as soon as possible, some of them
do not wait until the hearer decodes the utterance as a whole.

REFERENCES

Bogusławski, A. *Problems of the Thematic-Rhematic Structure of
    Sentences*. Warsaw: PWN, 1977.
Carlson, L. H. *Dialogue Games: An Approach to Discourse Analysis*,
    Dordrecht: Reidel, 1983.
Chafe, W. L. Giveness, contrastiveness, definiteness, subjects,
    topics and point of view. In C. N. Li (Ed.), *Subject and Topic*.
    New York: Academic Press, 1967.
Chomsky, N. Deep structure, surface structure and semantic interpret-
    ation. In D. D. Steinberg & L. A. Jakobovits (Eds.), *An Inter-
    disciplinary Reader*. Cambridge, U.K.: Cambridge University Press,
    1971.
Dahl, Ö. Topic-comment structure revisited. In Ö. Dahl (Ed.), *Topic
    and Comment, Contextual Boundness and Focus*. Hamburg: Buske
    Verlag, 1974.
Daneš, F. Zur linguistischen Analyse der Textstruktur. *Folia linguis-
    tica* IV, 1970, 72-78.
Daneš, F. Functional sentence perspective and the organization of
    the text. In F. Daneš (Ed.), *Papers on FSP*. Prague: Academia,
    1974.
Dijk, T. A. v. *Text and Context*. London and New York: Longman, 1977.
Firbas, J. Some thoughts on the function of word-order in old
    English and modern English. *Sborník prací filos. fakulty brněn-
    ské university*, A5, 1957, 72-100.
Firbas, J. On the thematic and the non-thematic section of the sent-
    ence. In H. Ringbom et al. (Ed.), *Style and Text, Studies
    presented to N. E. Enkvist*. Stockholm: Skriptor, 1975.
Hajičová, E. Negation and topic vs. comment. *Philologica Pragensia*
    16, 1973, 81-93.
Hajičová, E. Meaning, presupposition and allegation. *Philologica
    Pragensia* 17, 1974, 18-25. Reprinted in W. Klein & A. v. Stechow
    (Eds.), *Functional Generative Grammar in Prague*. Kronberg/Taunus:
    Scriptor, 1974.
Hajičová, E. & Sgall, P. A dependency based specification of topic
    and focus. *SMIL – Journal of Linguistic Calculus* 1/2, 1980,
    93-140.
Hajičová, E. & Vrbová, J. On the role of the hierarchy of activation
    in the process of natural language understanding. In J. Horec-
    ký (Ed.), *COLING 82*. Amsterdam: North Holland, 1982.
Halliday, M. A. K. Notes on transitivity and theme in English.
    Journal of Linguistics 3, 1967, 37-81, 199-244; 4, 1968, 179-
    215.
Halliday, M. A. K. & Hasan, R. *Cohesion in English*. London: Longman
    Group, 1976.
Hausenblas, K. On characterization and classification of discourses.
    Travaux linguistiques de Prague 1, 1964, 67-84.
Jackendoff, R. S. *Semantic Interpretation in Generative Grammar*.
    Cambridge: Mass.: M. I. T. Press, 1972.
Jacobs, J. review of P. Sgall, E. Hajičová & E. Benešová, Topic,
    focus, and generative semantics. *Lingua* 43, 1977, 77-91.
Juganov, V. J. Tekst i tipy tematičeskich progressij. In *Značenije i
    smysl rečevych obrazovanij*. Kalinin: Kalininskij gos. universi-
    tet, 1979.
Klein, W. & Stechow, A. v. *Intonation und Bedeutung von Fokus*.
    Konstanz Universität, mimeo, 1982.

Kuno, S. Functional sentence perspective. *Linguistic Inquiry* 3, 1972, 463-487.

Kuroda, S.-Y. The categorical and the thetic judgment. *Foundations of Language* 9, 1972, 153-185.

Marciszewski, W. Ot ponjatija temy predloženija do ponjatija ključevogo slova. *Naučno-techničeskaja informacija* 2, 1976, 18-25.

Marty, A. Über die Scheidung von grammatischem, logischem und psychologischen Subject resp. Prädicat. *Archiv f. system. Philosophie* 3, No. 2, 1897, 174-190; No. 3, 294-333; reprinted in and quoted from his *Gesammelte Schriften* II, Part 1, Halle a. S. 1918.

Mey, J. General editor's preface. In F. Coulmas (Ed.), *Conversational Routine*, The Hague - Paris - New York: Mouton, 1981.

Petöfi, J. S. A few comments on the methodology of text-theoretical research. *Journal of Pragmatics* 2, 1978, 365-372.

Plátek, M., Sgall, J. & Sgall, P. A dependency base for a linguistic description. To appear in P. Sgall (Ed.), *Contributions to Functional Syntax, Semantics and Language Comprehension*. Prague: Academia & Amsterdam: John Benjamins. (in prep.)

Posner, R. *Theorie des Kommentierens*. Frankfurt/M., 1972. (a).

Posner, R. Dialogsorten - Die Verwendung von Mikrostrukturen zur Textklassifizierung. In E. Gülich & W. Raible (Eds.), *Textsorten*. Frankfurt/M.: Athenäum, 1972.(b)

Reinhart, T. Pragmatics and linguistics; An analysis of sentence topics. *Philosophica* 27, 1981, 53-93.

Searle, J. R. *Speech Acts*, Cambridge: Cambridge Univ. Press, 1970.

Sgall, P. Functional sentence perspective in a generative description. *Prague Studies in Mathematical Linguistics* 2, 1967, 203-225.

Sgall, P. Towards a definition of focus and topic. *Prague Bulletin of Mathematical Linguistics* 31, 1979, 3-25;32, 24-32.

Sgall, P., Hajičová, E. & Panevová, J. *The Meaning of the Sentence in Its Semantic and Pragmatic Aspects*. Prague: Academia, & Dordrecht: Reidel. (in prep.)

Stechow, A. v. *Notes on Topic and Focus of Interrogatives and Indicatives.* Konstanz Universität, mimeo, 1980.

Wollmann, A. Wortstellung und kommunikative Gliederung in Übersetzungsäquivalenten Sätzen. In J. Esser & A. Hübler (Eds.), *Forms and Functions*. Tübingen:Gunter Narr, 1981.

Zemb, J.-M. *Les structures logiques de la proposition allemande*. Paris: O.C.D.L., 1968.

Computational Models of Natural Language Processing
B.G. Bara and G. Guida (eds.)
© Elsevier Science Publishers B.V. (North-Holland), 1984

LANGUAGE GENERATION BY COMPUTER

Eduard H. Hovy, Roger C. Schank

Department of Computer Science
Yale University
New Haven, CT, USA

This paper describes a natural language generator program that has knowledge about social and psychological aspects of conversation such as relative social statuses of speaker and hearer, models of the various hearers, some perception of the hearers' interests and sympathies, as well as its own purposes with the conversation. The program contains a set of strategies that govern the decisions made during the generation process to produce text tailored to each hearer.

1 THE PROBLEM

1.1 The Pragmatic Elements of Generation

Human language exhibits an amazing variability. We do not tell different people the same idea in the same way, nor is our speech unaffected by the atmosphere and social setting of the conversation. This variability is a reflection of the incorporation of more than the mere literal meaning of the facts we set out to communicate. The extra information derives from the speaker's goals, reflects social factors, or expresses the speaker's emotional state ... in fact, it may serve a whole range of purposes that are neither syntactic nor strictly semantic. Rather, these purposes are pragmatic, and pertain to conceptual entities such as the speaker's goals and plans (for himself and for the hearer), and affective entities such as emotions and self-assurance.

Pragmatic considerations pervade our language: "I'm sorry, officer, I didn't realize I was speeding..." when what you really want to say is unprintable. Two kinds of pragmatic considerations play a role in language: the speaker's own concerns (to learn, to understand better, to affect his self-image); and his concerns *vis-a-vis* the hearer (to provide knowledge, to convince, to affect the hearer's self-image, to manipulate the hearer's future actions). To converse well and effectively, the speaker must know at least the following about the hearer:

- the extent of the hearer's knowledge

- the hearer's interests, sympathies and antipathies

- the hearer's self-image vs the speaker's self-image

- the hearer's emotional state

1.2 Traditional Approaches

In the past, various approaches have been tried in order to gain a better understanding of human language generation. No attempts have been made, however, to address pragmatic considerations as well as syntactic ones within a single program. We mention here three such approaches and point out where they fall short, in order to give some idea of the range and complexity of the issues involved.

1.2.1 Transformational Grammar

Transformational linguists have suggested various systems which at first glance seem eminently suitable for use in computer language generation. Chomsky suggested a sophisticated system in [Chomsky65]. However, he and his direct followers construct a purely descriptive model, not a functional (in the sense of procedural) one. Chomsky realizes this:

> "... it seems absurd to suppose that the speaker first forms a generalized Phrase-marker by base rules and then tests it for well-formedness by applying transformational rules to see if it gives, finally, a well-formed sentence. But this absurdity is simply a corrollary to the deeper absurdity of regarding the system of generative rules as a point-by-point model for the actual construction of a sentence by a speaker." (p. 139)

Thus, regardless whether transformational grammarians have succeeded in correctly characterizing a large part of the structure of language or not, their characterizations are not suited as a basis for a process model of language generation.

There are various reasons for rejecting some procedurally stated variant of these models as serious models of the way people actually generate language. One reason is the fact that the relationship between syntax and semantics is left completely unspecified. In a *descriptive system* the game is "you give me a sentence and I'll give you its derivational structure, or else show that it is ungrammatical"; but in a *generation process* the sentence is to be built up, not analyzed. A transformational grammar system provides no way of constructing a deep structure (a syntactic entity) corresponding to whatever the speaker wants to say (which by its nature is semantic). (See [Gross79].) Seen in this light, the system loses much of its force as a model of human language and becomes merely a tool for abstract analysis, so far removed from actual generation that it has no more than occasional significance. (Furthermore, work done at Yale on request-based parsing suggests that, for parsing, the system is of secondary practical significance and definitely no plausible model for human performance. Our interest, after all, is *how people make and understand* language, not how they judge the grammaticality of sentences. See [Schank&Birnbaum83].)

1.2.2 ATN Generators

Most of the existing *process* models of language generation are only concerned with the latter half of the six considerations given above: the set of decisions determining the expression of a concept once the overall sentential structure (i.e. phrase, topic, verb and mode) has been decided upon. What remains to be done is a low-level template filling job. Many such generators have been written: for instance, [Simmons&Slocum72] and [Goldman73].

As for almost all other cognitive processes, the linearization process can be achieved by computer science techniques using very efficient and highly unhumanlike ways (just as for, say, multiplication). It is possible to express the contents of some semantic frame in linear form using an ATN mechanism that simply traverses the frame, generating output where applicable.

Simmons and Slocum used the following mechanism as their generator:

- the concept to be expressed is represented in a semantic net with a set of well-defined case relations (ACTOR, OBJECT, etc.).

- a grammar is defined which can generate syntactically well-formed sentences. When implemented as an ATN, it exhaustively searches the semantic net to produce an acceptable, meaningful sentence. The richer the grammar implemented as the ATN, the more kinds of sentences it can say. That is, given various sentential forms and knowledge about what information each can convey, the ATN can base its choice process on what is contained in the net in order to find a satisfactorily powerful sentence template to expand.

This approach is mentioned here only in order to illustrate that language generation by computer is feasible *and indeed quite simple* when there is no serious attempt at modelling (in some significant sense) human language generation. Nobody would entertain the idea that an ATN generator embodies such a model -- according to it, we would never produce ungrammatical sentences nor have any reason to generate different sentences for some concept under different circumstances. Furthermore, there is no mention of pragmatic factors such as speaker-hearer relationships, or speaker goals, etc.; it is not even clear how such notions would be incorporated into an ATN model of human language generation.

1.2.3 Template Generators

The linearization process can be implemented as a production system, where the syntax is expressed as a set of production (TEST-ACTION) rules. The tests check on semantic conditions; when they fire, actions instantiate fixed templates which are then expanded, piece by piece (depending again on the content of the frame), until they finally become a normal natural language sentence (see [Danlos83] and [McDonald81]). This process can loosely be called *breadth-first expansion*, as it resembles the breadth-first traversal of the decision tree which leads from representation to ultimate text. [McKeown82] has done work on selecting appropriate templates, depending on what type of question the generator has to answer.

Template-based generators are relatively simple to write and produce very impressive output, depending on their flexibility. While language probably does consist of thousands of templates and template templates (ranging in length from two units to several), the temptation simply to store a precompiled full sentence form with each verb must be resisted -- such generators never make a mistake, or come up with novel sentence combinations!

1.3 Decisions, Decisions

One of the fundamental assumptions we make for language generation is that the representation we start with captures the meaning of the story uniquely. If, now, a speaker produces two versions of the same story, the differences arise not from differences in underlying representation, but from differences in intent. Using this hint, we examined the types of decisions a speaker has to make in uttering the thoughts in his head. Starting with some general topic, a speaker must

- select a next topic of conversation

- select and delimit the content of a sentence

- select the phrasal forms and focused element that determine sentence structure

- select words to fill out phrasal templates

- modify certain elements due to grammatical rules

because human language exhibits variations in any of these aspects.

None of the generators described above take note of the pragmatic issues we mentioned earlier, even though the issues clearly influence the language produced by people. The question is: how can we integrate grammatical and pragmatic issues into one process? The answer lies in the decisions that take place during the generation process: *Each of the five decision types mentioned above can be shown to depend, at least partially, upon the pragmatic considerations.* These issues augment the normal rules of discourse and rules of grammar to form the criteria by which the decisions are made. A generator[1] that uses these criteria when deciding how to

---

[1]The generator will often be anthropomorphised as the *speaker* and the interlocutor will be called the *hearer*, whether the communication (the *conversation*) be verbal, one-sided, human or not. That which is to be generated will often be called the *story* or the *representation*, and the output the *text*.

expand story representations into text will therefore model human performance more closely than one that is purely syntax-based.

1.3.1 An Example

An example, tracing the decisions made in the generation of a simple sentence, will illustrate the effects of the pragmatic criteria. We discuss the decisions in hierarchical order, bearing in mind that a generation process can make whatever decisions are necessary at any time. Consider the following story:

```
PROPEL
    ACTOR : ARMED-PERSON
            POLITICAL-ORGANIZATION : PLO
    OBJECT : KNIFE
    TO : WOMAN
         OCCUPATION : HOUSEWIFE
         CHILDREN : 6
         AGE : 48
    LOC : CITY
          NAME : Paris
    TIME : YESTERDAY
    RESULT : STATE-CHANGE
                ACTOR : WOMAN
                TO-STATE : DEAD
                RESULT : SEARCH
                         ACTOR : POLICE
                         OBJECT : ARMED-PERSON
                         TIME : PRESENT
```

This story can be generated in various ways:

(i) "A PLO terrorist stabbed a housewife in Paris yesterday. The police are searching for him."

(ii) "A 48-year-old housewife with six children died in Paris yesterday. Police are searching for a PLO terrorist."

(iii) "Police are seaching for a terrorist who stabbed a housewife in Paris yesterday."

(iv) "A freedom-fighter is being searched for because he stabbed a mother of six in Paris yesterday."

(v) "Paris was the scene of the killing of a housewife. The police are searching for an armed man."

(vi) "A knife was used by an armed man to kill a mother of six in Paris yesterday."

(vii) "A 48-year-old woman was killed by a man with a knife in Paris yesterday. She died. Police are searching for the man now."

1.3.2 Level 1 Decisions: Story Content

We do not want to say exactly the same things to all hearers at all times. *Our task here is to delimit the extent of the story*, (i.e., to select the next topic), including only what we deem applicable in the current context to the current hearer. As the story is defined in terms of the concepts that form the memory, it may not always be clear what is explicitly part of the story and what is not. Thus it is necessary, before starting a new sentence (or sentential part), to check which concepts we want to generate. However, this does not imply that we have some kind of global overview of the story, and can edit and prune it as we like -- such capability would violate the constraint that we generate language in "left-to-right" fashion. We make the decisions of this level of the decision hierarchy dynamically *during* the generation process. The result: we may at any such decision point decide to abandon the current topic and pursue a new, related, one (for example, when we perceive that the hearer is very interested in something we had originally planned just to mention briefly).

One pragmatic reason we may decide to include or omit some part of the story is the consideration of the hearer's sympathies. In the example, someone strongly opposed to terrorism may be especially interested to hear about the search, whereas the woman's family may only care about her death. If the speaker's goal is to strengthen these sympathies, he must include the relevant parts of the story. Different decisions about what to include would eventually result in sentences: (i) about the killing; (ii) about the death; (iii) about the search.

1.3.3 Level 2 Decisions: Sentence Content

The next level of decisions in the hierarchy is now: given that we know *what* we want to say, *how* do we go about saying it? Where do we start? How do we continue after that? It is possible that at some point during the traversal of the story configuration we "find" something new and consider it worth saying. In such cases we have the option of saying it immediately, as part of the current sentence (if that is at all possible), or of starting it as a new sentence, or of finishing off the current topic and only then starting the new one. *Decisions on this level can be characterized as the choice of the next sentence topic.*

On this level, as before, the important criteria for sentence content decisions concern the speaker's goal and his perception of the hearer's interests and sympathies. If the speaker's goal is to support the police, he can decide to link explicitly the search and the killing, resulting in sentence (iv); otherwise implicitly: (ii) and (iii). If the speaker's goal is to win sympathy, he can accentuate the death by making it a separate sentence: (vii).

1.3.4 Level 3 Decisions: Sentence Structure

Having delimited the content of our story and chosen a sentence topic, we must now plan the structure of the sentence. *Here we have to choose a subject, a verb, an object; we must decide on mode and tense; we must decide how many prepositional phrases (if any at all) to include; we must decide on the order they must appear.*

Different **choices of subject** at this point produce sentences such as: normal active mode (i); passive mode (vii) and (iv); focusing on the location (v); and on the instrument (vi). As the sentence subject carries some implicit focus, pragmatic criteria can be used to select it from among the aspects of the story. For example, if the hearer is interested in the PLO, sentences (i) or (iv) (about the terrorist or the scene of the stabbing, repectively) are more suitable to catch his interest than, say (ii) (which focuses on the mother).

An important decision is the **choice of a verb**, because of the role it plays in determining subsequent decisions. This is the case because the verb acts as the repository for such sentence-building information as associated prepositions, special case markings, preferred or obligatory phrases and mode, etc. Here various *modi operandi* are possible, ranging from picking any suitable verb and perhaps not saying quite what the representation contains, to searching for an exactly appropriate verb, which requires some planning and scanning of the story representation. The difference here is illustrated by sentences (i) and (vii), where the choice of "stab" makes mentioning the knife unnecessary. In general, when the verb prescribes the use of any phrasal units, the pragmatic desirability of including such phrases must be checked first.

Building up noun groups and prepositional phrases can also be affected by pragmatic considerations. Typical decisions involve whether or not to pronominalize, and if not, which attribute of the concept to select as head noun; whether to include, and how to order, other attributes such as adjectives. Usually, the concept to be expressed as a noun phrase is an object, where almost any of its attributive aspects can fill the head noun position. Thus the woman in our example (a very sparse example) can variously be expressed as:

> "a forty-eight-year-old woman"
> "a forty-eight-year-old mother of six"
> "a female forty-eight-year-old"
> "a mother of six"
> "a woman"

When there is much information, it can be rationed out in newspaper style:

> "A woman ..... The forty-eight year old, ..."

The criteria affecting these decisions are the previous occurrence of an aspect as well as hearer interest and sympathy and the speaker's goal. For example, assuming that the head noun carries some focus, one strategy may be to fill in the head noun position with whatever aspect the hearer finds most interesting. In the example, sentence (i) contains no additional information, in contrast to (ii); the former is suited in a report of many killings, among which it is not especially interesting; the latter in a tabloid, where maximum gore must be extracted.

1.3.5 Level 4 Decisions: Words

The final level of decisions: *the choice of specific words*. As before, hearer interest and sympathy and speaker goal play a critical discriminatory role. In our example, we would want to say "terrorist" to a pacifist, but not to a PLO sympathiser, to whom "freedom-fighter" would sound far better; and a reporter may prefer the word "armed man" to either of the other alternatives: see sentences (i), (iv) and (vi).

2 THE PROGRAM

2.1 Overview

In this section we describe a program that interleaves the pragmatic criteria that play a role at each of the decision points with syntactic considerations in order to produce language. It is a complex mechanism which can most easily be explained in terms of four separate parts that each have a different functional role in the generation process. (This is not to imply that the four parts are indeed separate: after all, the ultimate goal is to generate language in the way people do it, and that is in integrated fashion.)

Memory and Representation :

- **Memory** : a property inheritance net in which hierarchies of concepts and domain knowledge have been defined.

- **The Representation** : the representation of the story, inextricably embedded into memory (so much so that the generation routines can examine both the story episode and the memory concepts equally easily, and decide what to include in the text).

A Model of the Hearer : The generator's model of the hearer's interests, disinterests, relative social status, emotional state, likes, dislikes, etc. -- defined in the memory.

The Strategies : When the speaker has a definite goal with the conversation (i.e., when he wants to have some specific effect on the hearer) then the corresponding strategies examine both the story itself and what is known about the hearer in order to tailor the output accordingly. This examination process returns guidelines that aid the generation routines in making decisions.

The Generation Routines : The generation routines are the central kernel of the generator that traverse the story representation and memory in order to express what is contained there in natural language. Wherever decision points exist, the strategies provide guidance.

2.2 Domain

We have chosen terrorism as the domain of discourse for this generator, chiefly for two reasons: firstly, the kinds of acts found in terrorism stories are all variants of two quite general structures (in fact, there is only a limited number of probable events), yet the domain is large, subtle and contentious enough to be interesting for generation; secondly, much work has been done in parsing terrorism stories, and so existing programs provide a lot of information and memory structure already.

3 MEMORY AND THE REPRESENTATION

3.1 A Hierarchy of Concepts

The representation used to model memory is a property inheritance net that organizes a hierarchy of tokens that represent objects and actions. The token structure and organization scheme is based on the systems [Schank72] and [Fillmore68]. The computer implementation of that scheme is performed in the frame manipulation language YRL, a variant of KRL (see [Charniak&Riesbeck&McDermott80]).

This property inheritance net is the world knowledge of the speaker: a collection of particular instances of some of these pre-existing nodes containing some specifically filled slots (typically, the ACTOR, OBJECT, TIME, LOC slots). The story is defined in terms of the elements of this net.

These are the types of tokens:

- LEVEL 1 : MOPs[2] (Memory Organization Packets) represent stereotypical fixed
  sequences of events, where each event may be a MOP itself, or a single action, or even
  a primitive (CD) act. An action is usually not represented as a single conceptual

---

[2]For a simple exposition of MOPs see [Lytinen&Schank82]; see [Schank82] for the original theory.

entity but as a set sequence of primitive acts. Each action is thus part of an action
hierarchy, and, just as for tokens, the parent and children acts help define it. Actions
contain information about the types that typical actors, objects, etc., belong to, as
well as syntactic information such as dependent prepositional clauses and word
ordering. MOP scenes are linked together in their normal temporal sequence as well
as by the following three types of causal links, each in two directions:

- ▸ PRECOND and RESULT : immediate causal result / precondition

- ▸ IR-FROM and IR-TO : initiating reason (the link between a state that causes
  some act and the act itself)

- ▸ LEAD-FROM and LEAD-TO : eventual (indirect causal) result / precondition

Each type of link results in a unique characteristic generated phrase.

- LEVEL 2 : simpler events: actions (MOP scenes, CD acts[3]), state changes

- LEVEL 3 : persons, objects, states, places, measurements

- LEVEL 4 : literals, predefined concepts

3.2 Definition of Domain Knowledge

In this section we describe part of a taxonomy of the concepts and words the program needs
to understand events in the domain of terrorism.

There are three classes of concepts/words: EVENTS, OBJECTS and the rest. EVENTS
represent actions, OBJECTS things, and the rest the syntactic flags and indicators such as
prepositions, auxiliary verbs, etc. EVENTS have the most complex structures. They are
subdivided into MOPs, scenes and CD acts. Examples are M-TERRORISM, SHOOT and
ATRANS respectively.

The following are some **MOPs** of the terrorism domain:

---

[3]See [Schank&Abelson77] for a discussion of Conceptual Dependency.

M-ASSASSINATE	**M-KIDNAP**	**M-HIJACK**
S1 - AMBUSH	S1 - PLAN	S1 - PTRANS
S2 - SHOOT	S2 - KIDNAP	S2 - THREATEN
S3 - ESCAPE	S3 - DEMAND	S3 - DEMAND
S4 - DEMAND	S4 - RELEASE / KILL	S4 - RELEASE / KILL

SCENES :

THREATEN -- (SAY (HARM to party) to party)
DEMAND -- (SAY object of party to party)
RELEASE -- (MOVEO from actor)
KILL -- (HARM to-state dead)
KIDNAP -- (MOVEO party to actor)
RECEIVE -- (TAKE object to actor)
PLAN -- (PREPARE **MOP**)
SHOOT -- (HARM party INSTR gun)
ESCAPE -- (MOVEA from loc)

ACTIONS :

PREPARE -- (AC MBUILD **MOP**)	plan, prepare, setup
HARM -- (AC DO OB to-state NEG)	harm, damage, kill, hurt
SAY -- (AC MTRANS to PA)	say, demand
MOVEA -- (AC PTRANS AC)	go, board, move
MOVEO -- (AC PTRANS OB)	free, release, push
TAKE -- (PA ATRANS OB to AC)	take, receive, accept
EXPLODE -- (**bomb** DO to-state NEG)	explode, destroy

OBJECTS are also organised in hierarchical fashion. Some of the higher level entities are:

AGENT ORGANIZATION PERSON MAN WOMAN ANIMAL BUILDING HOSPITAL

AIRPORT COUNTRY SPAIN BRITAIN VEHICLE CAR PLANE WEAPON RIFLE GUN

KNIFE

4 INTERPERSONAL KNOWLEDGE AND SPEAKER GOALS

4.1 Knowledge about the Hearer

The aspects of a hearer that can affect a speaker's language are many and varied. The following classification of some aspects that typically play a role here focuses mainly on positive cooperative conversations, not negative ones such as arguments.

4.1.1 What the Hearer Knows

Depending on what MOPs and other structures the hearer knows, decide how much to expand a story or excise from it, and in what detail to express concepts. Knowledge of the hearer's vocabulary aids word selection, for example when adults speak to children or people not fluent in the language. For simplicity, the generator developed in this paper assumes that the hearer has the same general world knowledge -- though perhaps more or less detailed -- as it has itself. Thus it can make use of its own knowledge structures during generation.

4.1.2 What the Hearer considers Interesting and Uninteresting

Using a knowledge of the hearer's interests, catch and keep his attention by explicitly mentioning or expanding on interesting aspects of the story, and leaving out what he considers boring. The generator combines its knowledge of the hearer's interests with knowledge about what concepts seem to be intrinsically interesting; see [Schank78].

4.1.3 What the Hearer is Sympathetic and Unsympathetic with

Create sympathetic or antipathetic emotions in the hearer by expanding or excising parts of the story that he is sympathetic with, and by using nouns and adjectives that have (for him) the appropriate affective values. Both sympathies and antipathies are assumed to be of general interest to the hearer; as such they merit the same treatment in general conversation. The program, when addressing the sympathies of the hearer, focuses on the parts of the story related to concepts he finds sympathetic; this causes some variation in sentence order, detail of description of objects or people, and word choice: see the relevant part in the example.

4.1.4 The Hearer's Image in the Conversational Setting

An aspect that plays a large role in the specific forms of language generated is the relative social status of speaker and hearer, on a scale ranging from dominant to equal to inferior. This relative social status is important in certain kinds of conversations only -- in others, like newspaper stories, formulae of neutral expression are used -- and can be influenced by the tone or atmosphere of the conversation. Typically, when the speaker is inferior to the hearer, generated text is shorter, can be interspersed with affirmatory questions, and includes less material that is only slightly relevant. When the speaker is dominant over the hearer, the generated text can be extremely curt and to the point, or it can be more expansive. A relaxed conversational setting like a party or golf game would tend to loosen the constraints of strict topicality that bind the generator; and a formal setting, like an interview, tighten them.

A generator taking this aspect into account would have to decide on the phraseology, degree of effusion, etc. that is appropriate when speaking to the hearer with his social status. (Should the decision be wrong, the hearer's behaviour would quickly signal that. This, however, is not only a generation issue, but requires a parser with knowledge of interpersonal address forms. For this reason this aspect of generation is not incorporated in the current version of the generator.) The generator described here employs a newspaper-like, neutral style of address to all four hearers.

4.1.5 The Hearer's Current Emotional State

One of the most difficult aspects to model, or even to discuss, is emotion. This aspect is completely ignored in the generator at present. However, a generator must be able to assess the emotional state of the hearer -- friendly, neutral, irritated, angry -- in order to decide how much tolerance the hearer has for demands on his sympathy, and then to adjust text length, word choice, etc., accordingly.

4.2 Four Characters

In order to model how a generator would produce different versions of a story to different hearers, four characters were defined. This definition simply consists of a list of the typical characteristics of each person under the categories discussed above. The generator takes the characteristics into account when formulating its sentences, using strategies that will be explained in the next section. The generator (the speaker) is to be seen as some neutral person (such as a TV reporter) who knows all the characters rather superficially. As the domain of discourse here is terrorism (specifically in Northern Ireland), the four hearers are:

- An IRA terrorist :

```
interests    : British losses
sympathies   : IRA successes
antipathies  : anything British, authorities
emotion      : tense, angry
knowledge    : terrorism in detail
```

- The terrorist's wife :

```
interests    : nursing, children
sympathies   : children
antipathies  : killing, war
emotion      : tense, unhappy
knowledge    : nursing, terrorism in general
```

- A British soldier :

```
interests    : weaponry
sympathies   : British successes, authorities
antipathies  : IRA successes
emotion      : tense, irritated
knowledge    : military action in detail
```

- An American person :

```
interests    : politics
sympathies   : peace
antipathies  : killing, war
emotion      : relaxed, neutral
knowledge    : terrorism in general
```

The various hearers are defined in terms of the world knowledge and concept definitions that exist in the generator, for the reasons given before. To this extent, then, shared cultural nuances will be assumed, implicit in the representations and in the generated sentences.

4.3 Goals and Strategies

Just having some model of the hearer is not sufficient for successful generation: the generated output can vary considerably depending on the speaker's purpose with the conversation. For example, some categories of conversation goals are:[4]

- Create interest/disinterest in the hearer

- Disseminate information

- Create a specific emotion in the hearer

- Reinforce/undermine the hearer's perceived social status

Each goal is embodied by a set of strategies which guide the generator at decision points during its traversal of the representation. The eventual output is thus the result of what was contained in the representation as well as the goal of the generator and its knowledge of the character of the hearer. The generator currently implements only strategies concerned with creating and maintaining hearer interest or sympathy. As such, these strategies select and order the concepts to be said as well as the various parts of each sentence; control the amount of detail generated about objects and people; and select specific words.

4.3.1 Create Interest or Disinterest

- select concepts and use words that are (for the hearer) linked with strong emotions (like happy/sad) rather than with neutral ones. (This requires examining the model of the hearer and finding whether the concept to be expressed is related to something he finds interesting. For example, a terrorist would be interested in acts of terrorism, which are violent acts; a story about shooting is a story about a violent act and thus should be interesting.)

- if the hearer knows all about some fact or event, just refer to it to keep his interest; otherwise, describe it in full detail

- if the hearer knows some aspects of an event (e.g., the time and place) but not others, say the aspects he doesn't know to keep his interest; otherwise, describe it in full

- if the hearer knows some aspects of an event but not others, place the aspects he doesn't know in focussed positions in the sentence to keep his interest; otherwise, focus on the known aspects

- if the hearer doesn't know about the topic, focus on aspects he does know about, if any, unless he is interested in hearing more

- if the hearer knows some aspects of an event (e.g., the time and place) but not others,

---

[4]See [Schank&Lehnert79] for a more detailed fleshing out of the goals extant during a conversation.

and if the goal is to antagonize the hearer, say only the aspects he does know

4.3.2 Create Sympathy and Antipathy

- if the hearer is sympathetic to some aspect of the topic, and the goal is to win his sympathy, then say the topic
- if the hearer is unsympathetic to some aspect of the topic, and the goal is to interest him, then say the topic
- if the hearer is sympathetic to some aspect of the topic, and the goal is to win his sympathy, then place that aspect in a focussed position in the sentence
- if the hearer is sympathetic to a concept, and the goal is to win his sympathy, then use words and adjectives with the same affective value

(The program, when addressing the sympathies of the hearer, focuses on the parts of the story related to concepts he finds sympathetic; this causes some variation in sentence order, detail of description of objects or people, and word choice: see the relevant part in the example.)

4.3.3 Reinforce/Undermine the Hearer's Perceived Social Status

- Use deferential or abusive phrases: formulae of expression that apply to a hearer with a higher or lower self-image than that of the current hearer (for instance, confirmatory questions ("if you don't mind") or conciliatory address forms ("sir") to an equal, and curt phraseology or overly familiar address forms to a superior, respectively)
- Intersperse affirmatory instructions/questions ("You're doing fine" and "Is this ok?")

5 GENERATION ROUTINES

5.1 The Expansion Process

This section describes how the strategies use the pragmatic knowledge to guide the generation processes at decision points. Generation can be achieved by using four levels of expansion rules. These levels form a natural hierarchy in terms of the complexity of the knowledge they organize as well as in capturing the dependency of lower-level rules on higher-level ones. *They embody the hierarchy of decisions discussed in section 1.*

Here are the four sets of expansion rules, in hierarchical order:

```
1)    TOPIC          --->    TOPICS
                             POINTS
2)    POINT          --->    SENTENCE-FORM
                             nothing
3)    SAY-FUNCTION    --->    words
                             SAY-FUNCTIONS
                             POINTS (here as relative clauses)
4)    word           --->    output
```

Each left hand side produces zero or more of *each of* its right hand side options. Rules of any level may precede or follow rules of any other level as long as they are independent of each other.

The main generator data structure is a stream[5] -- this is the natural way to implement the left-to-right generation of language using a mixed breadth-first and depth-first expansion policy. The top-level function is a simple loop that loads the stream with the concepts that must be said. The main evaluation then consists of expanding the head element of the stream according to a rule from one of the four levels of rules given above and returning the result to be replaced at the stream head. (The use of this programming device as particularly suited to generation was suggested by McGuire [McGuire75].)

To make the following paragraphs clearer, we will trace the expansion of three stories from the example given in the next section. We will discuss the effects of making different decisions at the different levels on the text generated to the IRA terrorist, to his wife, and to the British soldier.

5.2 Level 1: Choosing a Topic

The decision that the generator has to make is: what is a good next topic? The strategies for choosing a topic take into account high-level knowledge like a model of the hearer and what goal the speaker has with the conversation. *Level 1 rules embody the mainly semantic considerations which determine the overall structure of the conversation,* as described earlier.

---

[5]A *stream* is a list of units of which always only the first (the stream *head*) is evaluated. Typically each unit is either a word or a function; in the former case the word is output and removed from the stream and in the latter the function is evaluated and its results replaced as the stream head.

A TOPIC denotes the single unit that represents a specific whole episode or concept in memory. Generally it becomes a topic of the conversation, engendering one or more sentences. Typically, TOPICs are MOPs; as such, a TOPIC may consist of one or more POINTs, where a POINT is a MOP scene that expands into a single sentence (or perhaps an independent phrase). TOPICs and POINTs are interchangable in the sense that the same unit can be a TOPIC in one conversation and only a POINT in another; in fact, the speaker may initially consider something only a POINT and then decide later to concentrate on it and make it a TOPIC (which is, of course, how the subject of a conversation changes dynamically).

In the example: when speaking to the IRA terrorist, the generator finds that he is interested in killing British and sympathetic to IRA causes. Thus the first topic to say to him is the shooting of the British soldier (or, when addressing his sympathies, the escape of the gunmen). The wife is interested in nursing; to her, the wounding, hospital treatment and subsequent release of the girl would become the first topic. Speaking to the British soldier, the generator would talk of the killing of his comrade first, and then mention the killing of the innocent bystander.

5.3 Level 2: Forming a Sentence

The decisions that the generator has to make are: what to include in the sentence, and in what order to put the clauses. (For example, the pragmatic strategies play a role in determining the sentence subject. Assuming that there is an implicit focus on the subject in most sentences, a passive sentence will be generated whenever the semantic OBJECT of the event is deemed more significant than the ACTOR. Other strategies are concerned with lower-level knowledge, such as the dictates of the specific verb chosen (some verbs require a direct object whereas other equivalent ones do not).) *Level 2 rules are dependent on level 1 decisions and give form to individual sentences.*

A POINT generally expands into a full sentence via an intermediate SENTENCE-FORM. (Exceptions are: when the POINT has already been said (as part of another, perhaps), it is simply removed; and when the POINT is actually part of another (i.e. when a sentence has been started and the current POINT has been deemed worthy of forming part of it), then it is expanded to become a relative clause (or some equivalent semi-independent sentential unit).) A SENTENCE-FORM is a general sentential template indicating the positions of the different parts of speech in the sentence. It takes the form of an ordered list of SAY-FUNCTIONS and normal natural language words. (Note that this generator is not a template-based generator as discussed in section 1 -- each SENTENCE-FORM is *dynamically* constructed from an applicable template stored under the verb (if any), together with any additional slots present in the POINT; the default is S-V-O (or copula sentence).) The templates are used here to indicate typical phrase order and prepositions, but not used as a rigid formula for sentence structure.

In the example: When making a sentence about the shooting of the soldier, one can mention the soldier, the place, the time, the instrument, and the gunmen. The most interesting aspect to the terrorist is the soldier; and to the British soldier (because he is interested in weaponry), the rifle. Thus choose to say the soldier as sentence subject when speaking to the IRA man, and the rifle when speaking to the soldier. Similarly, start with the girl when speaking to the woman.

5.4 Level 3: Phrases and Noun Groups

The decisions that the generator has to make are: what to include in each sentence group, in what order to build it up, and (in the case of objects) which feature to choose as head noun and how to order the modifiers. One issue is the amount to be said about a person or object. If the hearer is interested or sympathetic, a full description (all known attributes) can be generated; if not, only (perhaps) a single attribute; if antipathetic, nothing. Strategies applying hearer sympathy to choose a head noun and include and order adjectives play a large role here. *Level 3 rules are the low-level syntactic rules which differ from language to language and are only present as a result of decisions on higher levels.*

Each SAY-FUNCTION expresses one slot (i.e., one aspect) of a POINT. A SAY-FUNCTION may expand into zero or more words, SAY-FUNCTIONs, POINTs, or combinations of them. Different SAY-FUNCTIONs can expand the same token into different forms: a sentence subject, simply an adjective, or even a verb. Typically each high-level SAY-FUNCTION accepts its input token, pushes it (together with any relevant information, such as tense and mode in the case of verbs and gender and case in the case of noun groups) onto a stack as the current token of interest and expands into a series of lower-level SAY-FUNCTIONs. Some higher-level SAY-FUNCTIONs are: SAY-SUBJECT, SAY-VERB, SAY-OBJECT. The intermediate-level SAY-FUNCTIONs (such as SAY-LOC, SAY-MEASURE, SAY-TIME, SAY-INSTR) examine their input token and expand into a series of words and low-level SAY-FUNCTIONs, which then find appropriate word(s) and expand into a series of words and other SAY-FUNCTIONs. These include: SAY-AGE, SAY-NUMBER, SAY-GENDER, SAY-NATION, SAY-NAME, SAY-DESCRIP, SAY-ARTICLE, SAY-NOUN, SAY-PRONOUN.

In the example, say more or less about the rifle, depending on the hearer: to the British soldier give all the information: "a semi-automatic seventy calibre Belgian rifle"; to the woman say only "a seventy calibre rifle". When making conversation with the terrorist, choose to say "Englishman" as the head noun, but when addressing his interests, say "soldier".

5.5 Level 4: Word Access

The decision that the generator has to make is: which word to use. Concepts are usually referenced by various words, and for word selection hearer interest and sympathy and speaker goal must be taken into account. The concept ARMED-PERSON is defined as follows:
- if the action is political violence and the hearer is interested in political freedom, then use FREEDOM-FIGHTER
- if the action is political violence and the hearer is interested in maintaining peace, then use TERRORIST
- otherwise use GUNMAN

In the example, compare the use these words to the soldier, the terrorist, and the neutral person, respectively.

Words are defined in terms of memory concepts and thus are indexed from them. Associated with the word is such syntactic information as tense forms and idiosyncratic prepositional phrases for verbs and plurals for nouns. Words appearing on the stream are simply uttered.

6 AN EXAMPLE

6.1 Story Representation and Text

This section contains an example of the program output. A story, SHOOTING1, was defined as an instance of the MOP M-SHOOTING. The generator produced output to each of the four characters described earlier. Capital letters denote concepts defined in memory; small letters denote literals.

```
(SHOOTING1 = (M-SHOOTING)
 (ACTOR : GUNMEN1  =  (ARMED-PERSON)
         (NUMBER : TWO  =  (NUMBER)
                  (NUMBER : 2)))

 (OBJECT : SOLDIER1  =  (SOLDIER)
          (NAME : (Bill Smith))
          (NATION : BRITAIN  =  (COUNTRY))
          (AGE : AGE2  =  (AGE)
                (UNIT : YEAR  =  (DURATION))
                (NUMBER : FORTY  =  (NUMBER)
                         (NUMBER : 40)))
          (RESID : LEEDS1  =  (CITY)
                  (NAME : Leeds))
          (TITLE : SERGEANT  =  (SOLDIER)))

        : WOMAN1  =  (WOMAN)
          (NAME : (Rosie Areas))
          (AGE : AGE1  =  (AGE)
                (UNIT : YEAR)
                (NUMBER : TWENTY-FIVE  =  (NUMBER)
                         (NUMBER : 25)))
          (DESCRIP : passerby))

        : DAUGHTER1  =  (GIRL)
          (NAME : Mary)
          (AGE : AGE3  =  (AGE)
                (UNIT : YEAR)
                (NUMBER : TWELVE  =  (NUMBER)
                         (NUMBER : 12))))

(TIME : TIME1  =  (YESTERDAY))
(LOC : STADIUM1  =  (STADIUM)
      (NAME : (Belfast Football Stadium)))
```

```
(SCENE2 : SHOOT1  =  (SHOOT)
         (ACTOR : GUNMEN1)
         (OBJECT : SOLDIER1)
         (INSTR : RIFLE1  =  (RIFLE)
                  (NATION : BELGIUM  =  (COUNTRY))
                  (SIZE : CALIB1  =  (MEASURE)
                          (NUMBER : SEVENTY  =  (NUMBER)
                                    (NUMBER : 70))
                          (UNIT : CALIBRE  =  (MEASURE)))
                  (DESCRIP : semi-automatic))

         (RESULT : DIE1  =  (DEATH)
                   (OBJECT : SOLDIER1)
                   (TO-STATE : DEAD  =  (BAD-STATE))
                   (TIME : TIME1)
                   (LD-TO : BURY1  =  (BURY)
                            (OBJECT : SOLDIER1)
                            (LOC : LEEDS1)
                            (TIME : TIME2  =  (TOMORROW)))))

       : SHOOT2  =  (SHOOT)
         (ACTOR : GUNMEN1)
         (OBJECT : WOMAN1)
         (INSTR : RIFLE1)
         (RESULT : DIE2  =  (DEATH)
                   (OBJECT : WOMAN1)
                   (TO-STATE : DEAD)
                   (TIME : TIME1)

                   (LD-TO : BURY2  =  (BURY)
                            (OBJECT : WOMAN1)
                            (LOC : CEMETARY1  =  (CEMETARY)
                                   (NAME : (Belfast Cemetary)))
                            (TIME : TIME4  =  (AFTER)
                                    (UNIT : DAY  =  (DURATION))
                                    (NUMBER : THREE  =  (NUMBER)
                                              (NUMBER : 3)))))

         SHOOT3  =  (SHOOT)
         (ACTOR : GUNMEN1)
         (OBJECT : DAUGHTER1)
         (INSTR : RIFLE1)
         (RESULT : WOUND1  =  (HARM)
                   (OBJECT : DAUGHTER1)
                   (TO-STATE : HURT)
                   (TIME : TIME1)
```

```
        (LD-TO : HOSPITAL1 = (M-HOSPITAL)
                (ACTOR : DAUGHTER1)
                (TIME : TIME1)
                (SCENE1 : G01 = (PTRANS)
                        (OBJECT : DAUGHTER1)
                        (INSTR : AMBULANCE = (VEHICLE))
                        (FROM : STADIUM1)
                        (TO : HOSPITAL2 = (HOSPITAL)
                                (NAME : (Mary Magdalene
                                            Hospital))))

                (SCENE2 : TREAT1 = (TREAT)
                        (OBJECT : DAUGHTER1))
                (SCENE3 : DISCHARGE1 = (DISCHARGE)
                        (OBJECT : DAUGHTER1)
                        (FROM : HOSPITAL2)
                        (RESULT : ORPHAN1 = (ORPHAN)
                                (ACTOR : DAUGHTER1)
                                (TIME : TIME5 =
                                            (PRESENT)))
                (TIME : TIME1)))))

(SCENE3 : ESCAPE1 = (ESCAPE)
        (ACTOR : GUNMEN1)
        (INSTR : CAR1 = (CAR)
                (DESCRIP : Austin))
        (FROM : STADIUM1)
        (TIME : TIME1)
        (LD-TO : SEARCH1 = (SEARCH)
                (ACTOR : AUTHORITIES = (ORGANIZATION)
                        (NUMBER : PLUR))
                (OBJECT : GUNMEN1)
                (TIME : TIME3 = (NOW)))))
```

This is the text generated from this story to the characters: the IRA terrorist (Sean O'Flanahan), the terrorist's wife (Mary O'Flanahan), the British soldier (John Brown), and the neutral American (Pete Piascyk).

```
    Hearer is :  (Sean O'Flanahan)
    Input concepts are :  (SHOOTING1)
    Concentrating on :  INTERESTS


    Final generation is :
 A forty year old British soldier from Leeds, a city, Bill Smith, was shot
and killed with a seventy calibre rifle at Belfast Football Stadium yesterday.
He will be buried tomorrow. Two freedom-fighters shot and wounded a twelve
year old girl, Mary. She was taken to Mary Magdalene Hospital and treated
and discharged. She is an orphan at present. A twenty-five year old passerby
woman, Rosie Areas, was shot and killed. She will be buried in Belfast
Cemetary three days from now. They escaped with an Austin car.
```

```
    ===========================================================
```

```
    Hearer is :  (Sean O'Flanahan)
    Input concepts are :  (SHOOTING1)
    Concentrating on :  SYMPATHY
```

```
    Final generation is :
```
 An Austin car was used by two freedom-fighters to escape from Belfast
Football Stadium yesterday. A twelve year old girl, Mary, was shot and
wounded with a seventy calibre rifle. She was taken to Mary Magdalene
Hospital and treated and discharged. She is an orphan at present. A forty
year old British soldier from Leeds, a city, Bill Smith, was shot and killed.
He will be buried tomorrow. A twenty-five year old passerby woman, Rosie
Areas, was shot and killed. She will be buried in Belfast Cemetary three
days from now.

```
        ===========================================================
```

```
    Hearer is :  (John Brown)
    Input concepts are :  (SHOOTING1)
    Concentrating on :  INTERESTS
```

```
    Final generation is :
```
 A seventy calibre semi-automatic Belgian rifle was used by two gunmen
to shoot and to kill a forty year old British soldier from Leeds, a city,
Bill Smith. He will be buried tomorrow. The rifle was used by them to shoot
and to wound a twelve year old girl, Mary, yesterday at Belfast Football
Stadium. She was taken to Mary Magdalene Hospital and treated and discharged.
She is an orphan at present. The rifle was used by them to shoot and to kill
a twenty-five year old passerby woman, Rosie Areas. She will be buried in
Belfast Cemetary three days from now. An Austin car was used by them to escape.

```
        ===========================================================
```

```
    Hearer is :  (John Brown)
    Input concepts are :  (SHOOTING1)
    Concentrating on :  SYMPATHY
```

```
    Final generation is :
```
 A forty year old Englishman from Leeds, a city, Bill Smith, was shot and
killed with a seventy calibre rifle at Belfast Football Stadium yesterday. The
soldier will be buried tomorrow. A twelve year old girl, Mary, was shot and
wounded. She was taken to Mary Magdalene Hospital and treated and discharged.
She is an orphan at present. A twenty-five year old passerby woman, Rosie
Areas, was shot and killed. She will be buried in Belfast Cemetary three
days from now. An Austin car was used by two gunmen to escape.

```
================================================================

  Hearer is :  (Mary O'Flanahan)
  Input concepts are :  (SHOOTING1)
  Concentrating on :  CONVERSATION


  Final generation is :
 A twelve year old girl, Mary, was shot and wounded with a seventy calibre
 rifle at Belfast Football Stadium yesterday. She was taken to Mary Magdalene
 Hospital and treated and discharged. She is an orphan at present. A forty
 year old British soldier from Leeds, a city, Bill Smith, was shot and killed.
 He will be buried tomorrow. A twenty-five year old passerby woman, Rosie
 Areas, was shot and killed. She will be buried in Belfast Cemetary three days
 from now. An Austin car was used by two gunmen to escape.

                ================================================================

  Hearer is :  (Pete Piascyk)
  Input concepts are :  (SHOOTING1)
  Concentrating on :  CONVERSATION


  Final generation is :
 An Austin car was used by two terrorists to escape from Belfast Football
 Stadium yesterday. A twelve year old girl, Mary, was shot and wounded with a
 seventy calibre rifle. She was taken to Mary Magdalene Hospital and treated
 and discharged. She is an orphan at present. A forty year old British
 soldier from Leeds, a city, Bill Smith, was shot and killed. He will be
 buried tomorrow. A twenty-five year old passerby woman, Rosie Areas, was
 shot and killed. She will be buried in Belfast Cemetary three days from now.
```

6.2 Discussion

Clearly the text is not as polished as that which a simple template-based generator would produce. However, this does illustrate to some extent what we wanted to show: the ordering of the sentences reflects the hearer's interest in or sympathy with the topic, as does the choice of subject within sentences.

Note that when addressing the terrorist's interests, the generator speaks about the killing of the British soldier first; when addressing his sympathies, it chooses to start with the escape of the gunmen -- a direct result of the fact that the terrorist's interests are killing British and his sympathies are with the IRA. Because the British soldier is known to be interested in weapons, a full description of the rifle used is the subject of the first sentence to him. Also compare the omission of any mention of the IRA gunmen when addressing the sympathies of the British soldier with the text generated when just conversing with him. Furthermore, compare the order and relative importance of the various topics when speaking to the woman and to the American: to the wife, the fate of the girl is considered more interesting, and is thus said first; to the American, the final escape is selected as first topic. Finally, note the choice of head noun in noun groups, and the choice of the alternatives for the word "terrorist" where applicable. All these aspects combine to help make plausible text.

The program is written in CLISP, an extension of TLISP, a dialect of UCILisp, at Yale. Code and basic memory form some 4000 lines; the program needs just over 65K bytes of memory to run. The example shown takes about 1 minute to generate (incl. trace output).

7 CONCLUSION: FURTHER WORK

An ideal generator program would be able to plan and deliver a speech about a sensitive topic like abortion to a hostile audience -- say, a church group -- and then to a contrasting audience -- say, feminists -- appropriately. Doing this requires a very rich representation of the subject and a detailed knowledge of the affectual values of various topic-related keywords and key concepts, in addition to the full development of the issues discussed in this paper. As it is, the paper is an introductory study: it identifies the various pragmatic aspects pertinent to language generation, points out some interrelationships, and describes a program which is an incomplete implementation of the theory. On extending the theory and representation, the generator could produce a greater variation in its output to various hearers, giving text which is increasingly plausible in the circumstances.

A consistent and psychologically plausible process-based theory of language generation will contain answers to questions that have been plaguing linguists for a long time. Some of these questions concern the relation of a performance theory (which of course a generator program expresses) to a competence theory; the relationship between syntax and semantics; the nature of the representation that will capture semantic information and yet permit syntactic processes to apply to them; the performance nature of phenomena like pronominalization and anaphora.

Language generation is a powerful tool for studying the issues concerning the affective values of words, concepts and interpersonal relations, by judging the applicability of generated text in given circumstances. Knowledge about affect can be systematized and incorporated into theories about goals and motivations. (Some work in this regard has been done by [Lehnert&Ringle82]: *plot units* contain affective values and embody a rudimentary theory of their interactions.)

ACKNOWLEDGEMENT

The authors wish to thank Larry Birnbaum, Laurence Danlos, Natalie Dehn, Abraham Gutman, Rod McGuire, David J Littleboy and Steven Salzberg for many discussions and suggestions.

References

[1]   Charniak E., Riesbeck C.K., McDermott D.V.
        Artificial Intelligence Programming.
        Lawrence Erlbaum Associates, 1980.

[2]   Chomsky N.
        Aspects of the Theory of Syntax.
        MIT Press, 1965.

[3]   Danlos L.
        Some Issues in Generation from a Semantic Representation.
        In *Proceedings of 8th IJCAI.* 1983.

[4]   Fillmore C.J.
        The Case for Case.
        In Bach & Harms (editor), *Universals in Linguistic Theory*, . New York, Holt, Reinhart
            & Winston, 1968.

[5]   Goldman N.M.
        Sentence Paraphrasing from a Conceptual Base.
        Technical Report, Stanford University, 1973.

[6]   Gross M.
        On the Failure of Generative Grammar.
        Language (55), 1979.

[7]   Lehnert W.G.
        Plot Units: A Narrative Summarization Strategy.
        In Lehnert W.G. and Ringle M.H. (editor), *Strategies for Natural Language Processing*, .
            Lawrence Erlbaum Associates, 1982.

[8]   Lytinen S.L. and Schank R.C.
        Representation and Translation.
        Technical Report 234, Yale University, 1982.

[9]   McDonald D.
        Natural Language Generation as a Computational Problem: an Introduction.
        Technical Report, COINS, 1981.

[10]   McGuire R.
        Political Primaries and Words of Pain.
        1975.

[11]   McKeown K.R.
        Generating Natural Language Text in Response to Questions about Database Queries.
        PhD thesis, University Of Pennsylvania, 1982.

[12]   Schank R.C.
        "Semantics" in Conceptual Analysis.
        Lingua 30(2), 1972.

[13]   Schank R.C.
        Interestingness: Controlling Inferences.
        Artificial Intelligence 12(3), 1979.

[14] Schank, R.C.
      Dynamic Memory: A Theory of Reminding and Learning in Computers and People.
      Cambridge University Press, 1982.

[15] Schank R. & Abelson R.
      Scripts Plans Goals and Understanding.
      Lawrence Erlbaum Associates, 1977.

[16] Schank R.C. & Birnbaum L.
      Memory, Meaning and Syntax.
      In Bever, Carroll & Miller (editor), *Talking Minds: Studies in the Cognitive Sciences,* .
          MIT Press, 1983.

[17] Schank R.C. & Lehnert W.
      The Conceptual Content of Conversation.
      Technical Report 160, Yale University, 1979.

[18] Simmons R. & Slocum J.
      Generating English Discourse from Semantic Networks.
      CACM , October, 1972.
      University of Texas.

Computational Models of Natural Language Processing
B.G. Bara and G. Guida (eds.)
© Elsevier Science Publishers B.V. (North-Holland), 1984

UNDERSTANDING THE CHINESE LANGUAGE

Jiang Xinsong, Li Yingtan, Chen Yu

Shenyang Institute of Automation
Academia Sinica
Shenyang, Liaoning, China

The machine understanding of Chinese is a hard topic for AI
researchers. This paper discusses the peculiarities of Chinese,
the goals and open problems in the area, and introduces some
research results so far achieved. The paper consists of three
parts: introduction to Chinese and Chinese characters; some
research results in Chinese computer processing and understanding; the goals and open problems of Chinese understanding.

1. INTRODUCTION TO CHINESE CHARACTERS AND LANGUAGE

Chinese is the language used by the largest population in the world (see Table
1); it was appointed as one of the official international languages (the others
are English, Russian, French and Spanish) by the United Nations in 1973.

Chinese is different from Western languages in pronunciation, written form,
vocabulary, and grammar; it has its own unique system.

In ancient times, Chinese was a language with monosyllabic words; actually,
most modern Chinese words have two syllables, while Chinese morphemes remain
monosyllabic.

Chinese characters, or Chinese written form, are something strange to Western
people. Each Chinese character has only one syllable with one or more independent pronunciation(s). Historically, there were about fifty thousand Chinese
characters altogether. At present, according to the National Standards, there
are 23,000 Chinese characters, among them 3,755 are in G0 class, 3,008 in G1
class, and 16,000 in G2 class. The characters in G0 class are used most frequently. In modern Chinese, in correspondence with 23,000 characters there
are only 1,332 syllables pronunciation altogether; therefore most characters
have homonyms. Chinese characters belong to ideographs.

Chinese is a root-isolated and analytic language without inflection. The logical
relationship between character and character, or word and word, or sentence
and sentence, in Chinese depends on their order, their meaning and some function
words (function words or empty words are one important feature of Chinese).
Words have no inflection, no matter what position they have in the sentence.
A written Chinese sentence is a line of evenly arranged Chinese characters.
Chinese has no marks helping to segment words and phrases except punctuation
marks. The main way to segment words or phrases is parsing them using a grammar
and a dictionary. All of these peculiarities make Chinese very difficult for
computer processing.

As mentioned above there is a close relation of Chinese characters to sentence
understanding. Now we will discuss some of its peculiarities in detail.

features	languages				
	Chinese	English	Russian	French	Spanish
lingui-stic system	Sino-Tibe-tian	Indo-European			
written form	Chinese characters (ideograph)	alphabetic writing -- Latin alphabet	alphabetic writing -- Cyrillic alphabet	alphabetic writing -- Latin alphabet	alphabetic writing -- Latin alphabet
typo-logical class	root-isolated and analytic language	semi-inflected and semi-analytic language	inflected and synthetic language	inflected and synthetic language	inflected and synthetic language
written form history	from 3,500 to 6,000 years	less than 2,900 years	less than 2,900 years	less than 2,900 years	less than 2,900 years
number of people using	1,000 million	350 million	180 million	80 million	80 million

Table 1. Main features of Chinese, English, Russian, French and Spanish.

Chinese characters came into being at least three thousand and five hundred years ago during the Shang (商) and Yin (殷) Dynasties. The earliest Chinese characters are Jiaguwen (甲骨文) ---inscriptions on bones or tortoise shells in the Shang Dynasty (16th-11th century B.C.). There are about 4,500 Jiaguwen that have been found till now.

Jiaguwen are already a kind of rather mature characters; they contain all the basic Chinese characters building methods:

    1. Xiangxing (象形)   Pictographic
    2. Zhishi (指事)   Self-explanatory
    3. Huiyi (会意)   Associative Compounds
    4. Xingsheng (形声)   Pictophonetic

In the Appendix, several typical Jiaguwen are listed and classified according to the character building methods. In modern Chinese 90% of characters are built up using the pictophonetic method (in Jiaguwen only 20%).

As the Appendix shows, pictophonetic characters have two parts: form part and sound part, the former decides general meaning and the latter gives the sound and the specific meaning. For example:

杆 gan / pole   杠 gang / thick stick   杖 zhang / weaponry   板 ban / board   柜 gui / cupboard   架 jia / fram, rack, shelf

All these words have a common form part: 木 (mu); this means that all are things made of wood (in ancient times). Yet all these words have their own sound part , so they have their own particular meaning and pronunciation.

Generally speaking, the radicals in Chinese characters are used as form part of characters (words). There are 540 radicals in ancient Chinese and 188 radicals in modern Chinese. The sound part of Chinese characters is important as well: there are about one hundred different sound parts to correspond to every radical; a lot of radicals do correspond to the same sound part.

For example:

烈 (Lie) strong , violent, intense   裂 (Lie) split
洌 (Lie) clear, (of water or wine)   趔 (Lie) reel, stagger
冽 (Lie) cold   鴷 (Lie) woodpecker

Here, 列 (Lie) is the common sound part of all the above words, these have different radicals and different meanings although they have the same pronunciation (Lie).

Chinese characters are different from other ideograph characters in history, such as, for example, ancient Egyptian characters and cuneiforms (a kind of syllabic language). All these forms died out long ago. Chinese characters still keep their basic feature of ideographs, and make Chinese a root-isolated language.

As most commonly used Chinese characters have powerful word-building abilities, and every Chinese character keeps its form invariable, a Chinese character is therefore a basic meaning unit. By combining two or more of these meaning units, hundreds of thousands of Chinese words can be built (some characters are words themselves). Chinese characters are powerful in intelligent information transmission and expression as well. Children, who have learned about 4,000 characters in common use, would be able to understand Chinese texts without any difficulty even though they have no further knowledge. For example, an overseas Chinese, American Prof. Tang Degang (唐德刚) of the New York City University, presented the same idea about Chinese characters at a symposium sponsored by the Chinese association of Chinatown of New York in 1981.
He said, every Chinese high school student can understand newspapers without any difficulty, while there are more than 50 per cent of newly-enrolled American university students who can not understand the New York Times. Students who have learned about 4,000-5,000 Chinese characters can understand any chinese text, while an American student should know about 50,000 English words to understand the New York Times (Tang Yan, 1982). Chinese characters make Chinese a powerful language, since they ensure a high efficiency in communication.

Of course it is difficult to judge if one language is more efficient than another, but it is a fact that Chinese language has lasted for thousands of years, and is now being spoken daily by more than 1/4 of the world's population.

To make learning and processing Chinese characters convenient, a lot of schemas about Chinese characters coding have been proposed and used in computers. The best one of them has got 60 to 100 characters a minute input rate. In paragraph 2-2, we will analyze the state-of-the-art of Chinese character coding.

2. SOME RESEARCH RESULTS IN CHINESE COMPUTER PROCESSING AND UNDERSTANDING

Besides its own aims, Chinese character processing is the first step to understanding Chinese. Many researchers have worked in this area for years with some results. Other works concern machine translation.

As early as in 1958, research work on machine translations from Russian and English to Chinese started and after several years of suspension it was restarted in 1975. In the last few years research work on Chinese understanding from the viewpoint of A.I. was started at some Institutes and Universities. Now, we will introduce some recent works in this area in China.

2-1. WD-XYZC Language and characters processing system

WD-XYZC system (the Research Group of Language Auto-processing of Wuhan University, 1982)was developed in Wuhan University from 1978 to 1982. Here, WD-XYZC is a abbreviation of its Chinese name in the Chinese phonetic alphabet: Wuhan Daxue -- Xiandai Yuyan Zidong Chuli Xitong, i.e. the modern language automatic processing system of the Wuhan University. This system adopts the Chinese character coding system S-Y-D-X designed in the same University, that gives every Chinese character a code comprehensive of the following features: Sheng (声) ---- consonant of syllable, Yun (韵) ---- vowel of syllable, Diao (调) ---- intonation, and Xing (形) ---- form. The code in this system is longer than in other coding systems but more convenient for computer processing. This is because the code contains all the information about character sound and form. The shortcoming of this coding system is low input rate: 20 characters per minute (the highest input rate of the best coding systems is about 60-90 characters per minute). A complete code of this system is, for instance:

焕 (Huan) ---- HUAN4DHJ   蒋 (Jiang) ---- JIAM3PCT

A computational linguistic analysis of the novel Loutuo Xiangzi (骆驼祥子) written by the late famous writer Laoshe (老 舍) was performed using the WD--WYZC system. Here, we list the frequency of Chinese characters in Loutuo Xiangzi, comparing them to the frequency of common characters at Table 2.

amount to character number	11%	15%	20%	30%	40%	50%	60%	70%	80%	90%	95%	99%	100%
Loutuo Xiangzi	4	6	1 1	2 3	4 1	6 7	112	187	317	621	957	1608	2413
common literature books	/	9	1 5	2 8	5 3	9 6	195	279	473	860	1268	2179	3965

Table 2. Chinese characters frequency list in novel
Loutuo Xiangzi and common literature books.

The WD-XYZC system at present is able to look for all the sentences which contain certain characters. Figure 1 is the result of looking for all the sentences which contain the character 把 (ba) in Loutou Xiangzi.

The researchers are now continuing their work. Their goal is to give the system the ability to search sentences for certain words, phrases, or sentence patterns. Their plan is to process all modern famous writers' works and to compile the data about character frequency and more detailed information for each book, to generate a <u>Modern Chinese Language Materials Index.</u>

① 把P1H2

我们所要介绍的是祥子，不是骆驼，因为"骆驼"只是个外号；那么，我们就先说祥子，随手儿把骆驼与祥子那点关系说过去，也就算了·

② 把 P2H16

这一些是以前决没想到自己能与洋车发生关系，而到了生和死的界限已经不甚分明，才抄起车把来的·

③ 把 P2H17

被撤差的巡警或校役，把本钱吃光的小贩，或是失业的工匠，到了卖无可卖，当无可当的时候，咬着牙，含着泪，上了这条死亡之路·

④ 把……

Figure 1. The sentences which contain character 把 (ba)
in the novel Loutuo Xiangzi processed by WD-XYZC.

(Here P1H2 means page 1 row 2, P2H2 means page 2 row 2,and so on)

<u>2-2.The coding schemas and implementation of Chinese characters</u>

Coding is one of the most important steps in the computer processing of Chinese. Chinese character coding is the transformation of Chinese characters into a group of alphabet letter or numbers.

In fact, there are already several Chinese character coding systems, for example, the Standard Telegram Coding of Chinese characters, this is a system transforming Chinese characters to four-digit-numbers or to triplets-letters. There is no duplicated code in this system, but this system is hard for people to learn, as there is no association between code and character sound or form.

In 1981,the National Standard GB 2312-80 was issued (see STATE BUREAU OF STANDAR-DIZATION OF THE PEOPLE'S REPUBLIC OF CHINA, 1981), that stipulates all Chinese characters in class GO and G1 (amounting to 7,445 pieces) coding into a two--section code i.e. Quwei Suma (区位数码) ---- region-place-number-coding, and each section has 7 bits of information. This system has coded all the Latin, Russian and Japanese syllables and Kana and Greek, puctuation marks along with other useful signs. This system is also called the National Standard Coding.

Both Standard Telegram Coding and National Standard Coding are not convenient for ordinary people to use and memorize.

After several years of efforts since 1976, several excellent schemas of Chinese character coding have been developed. Chinese character coding has become a

new and specific discipline (there are now about 30 schemas of Chinese character
coding in Taiwan Province of China) (see CHINESE LANGUAGE INFORMATION SOCIETY,
1983).

Those schemas which use common computer keyboard or ASCII Code keyboard to code
Chinese characters and have close relations between code and sound and form
of a character are the best ones.

Correspondingly many Chinese character computer terminals have come into use
and a list of them includes   (see CHINESE LANGUAGE INFORMATION SOCIETY,
1983):

Model HZ-80 small Chinese character information processing system. Its basic
hardware is: microcomputer TRS-80 I, an extended interface, a 4" disc driver.
This system has a HZDOS Chinese operation system, a great ability to compile
Chinese characters, and also a pin-Chinese - character-printer that makes characters more attractive.

Model GF-20/11-A Chinese character microcomputer system. Chinese characters
in eight different coding schemes, including Standard Telegram Coding, International Interchange Coding, and so on, can be processed by this system. This
system has 512 KB addressing ability and provides two sets of 8" floppy disks;
all the languages of this system supported to Chinese characters are: BASIC,
COBOL, FORTRAN, PASCAL and so on. Genereally speaking, this system is the most
advanced system at present in China.

Model ZD-2000 Micro Chinese Computer. This computer uses Z-80A as its CPU, its
ROM contains a characters base of 160 KB, there are 4,000 Chinese characters
available in this system, in BASIC, COBOL FORTRAN and with several input means.
This model computer is now being produced in batches.

Model 1011 Chinese character automatic typewriter. This typewriter adopts a
coding system developed by Dr. Zhi Bingyi and has got an input rate of 100
Chinese characters per minute that is probably the highest one up to now.

Concerning Chinese character input rate, four wellknown companies ---- CDC,
Great Base, Wan'an Electronic Brain and IBM, announced the evaluated results
of four schemas of theirs, on Feb. 6, 1983 (see Guo Yefang, 1983):

        CDC: 56.7 characters/minute
        Great Base: 43.7 characters/minute
        Wan'an E.B.:   42.2 characters/minute
        IBM: 14.9 characters/minute.

There are still at present some computers with Chinese terminals:

        IP 5460 Chinese terminal manufactured by G.E. Company of America.

        Model NCRI-8290c Chinese Computer System by NCR (Hongkong)of America.

        Model MLTP-360 Chinese Processing System.

        HONEYWELL Chinese Computer System.

2-3. Translating English reference headlines into Chinese
       ____

This research work was developed by several units which were engaged in machine
translation in the early years of 1950, and was sponsored by STIIC (The Scientific and Technical Information Institute of China) during the period from 1976
to 1981 (see Jiang Yunpeng, 1982). The original materials were 5,000 items of
English reference headlines on metallurgy.

This system has a 4,200 words dictionary including 740 idiomatic ones, 150 "syntactic polysemants " and 200 "semantic polysemants". Here, so-called "syntactic polysemants" and "semantic polysemants" denote words with many meanings; we will analyze them later.

This system uses a computer having internal store of 64 KB with 16 bit length and computational rate of 830,000 times/second; a Chinese character output system which has 7,000 characters co-operates with the computer.

All of the translation rules and programs were worked out under the guidance of Prof. Liu Yongquan, who is now the vice director of the Language Institute of Social Academy of China. The programs were written in BOL language which is a simplified kind of COBOL. Because of the small internal store, programs have had to be enlarged. Its program in syntactic aspect amounted to 10,500 items, with a dictionary compiling 5,100 items.

This system parses English facing target language ---- Chinese. Every English word is interpreted directly by Chinese words. Every English word in the dictionary has a special number, which concerns semantic features and contains information about whether the word is idiomatic, a polysemant or not. Every common word in the dictionary has a 18-digit number, and there is some more information in the idiomatic and the polysemant dictionaries.

The polysemants in this system are divided into syntactic polysemant and semantic polysemant according to Chinese. Syntactic polysemant in this system means those English words that dominate one or more succeeding prepositions, semantic polysemant means word whose Chinese meaning will be changed by changing their antecedent word or succeeding word. To parse a syntactic polysemant means to decide not only its constituent for itself, but also the constitutent(s) of its preposition phrase(s). For example, "effect" is a syntactic polysemant(it belongs to class " 多 11"), it is one kind of so-called strong government (强支配词 qiang zhipei chi). There is some information about "effect" in the polysemant dictionary:

<pre>
          If: the context is as "effect of ## on **",
          Then: [effect] is a partial predicate (偏谓 , pian wei) and its
                     Chinese meaning is "影响" yingxiang.
                [of ##] is forward-preposition-subject-B, a logic subject.
                [on **] is forward-preposition-object-C, a logic object.
                Whole Chinese meaning is "## 对 ** 的影响".
          If: the context is ......
          Then: ......
                ......
                ......
</pre>

The information about a semantic one in the polysemant dictionary is as following for the word "base":

<pre>
          If: its antecedent word belongs to metal material and its succeeding
              word belongs to metal material too ,
          Then: its Chinese meaning is "基" (ji).
          If: its antecedent word belongs to steelmaking equipment,
          Then: its Chinese meaning is "碱性" (jianxing, alkalinity).
for the word "bearing":
          If: its antecedent word belongs to chemical element or material,
              and its succeeding word belongs to material,
          Then: its Chinese meaning is "含" (han, contain),
                its constituent is "前定" qianding, forward attribute.
          Else: its Chinese meaning is "轴承" (zhoucheng).
</pre>

By using the information of each word in dictionary to first interpret idiomatic ones and polysemants beforehand, and then parsing the text, it is thus possible to avoid complex word analysis.

The analysis of words in this system is divided into four steps:
    1)   to segment the English sentence, finding out idiomatic words, polysemants, and verb phrases;
    2)   parsing noun phrases in English, especially finding out phrases having any of the following features:

```
N+Ved+N
Ving+Pr+N
N+V+Adv
N+A+N
N+Ving+N
N+N
N+Ving
N+Ved
```

    and so on;
    3)   parsing verb phrases;
    4)   parsing prepositions and synthesizing the translated text.

This system uses about 30 nonterminal symbols for parsing work as Table 3 shows.

These nonterminal symbols contain information about position moving, structure form and syntactic relation. For example, Qian Jie Shou Zhuang (前 介 首 状) ---- forward-preposition-first-adverbial means: this constituent is a preposition structure and should move forward in target language and should be used in the target language as a first-place-adverbial.

Except the predicate, all the other constituents in a sentence should put A or B or C after their nonterminal symbol as their structure level information. A represents the first level, B represents the second level, and C represents the third level.

For example, a nonterminal symbol 介宾 B (Jie Bin B, preposition-object B) means the structure form of this constituent is the preposition structure, its syntactic function is object, its structure level is the second.

Now, let us take an English phrase, to show how the system translates it into Chinese:

       Production of copper by the Noranda process

      偏 谓   介 宾 B   前 介 首 状 C

    Pian Wei   Jie Bin B   Qian Jie Shou Zhuang

Partial pred. Prep. obj.B Forward prep. first adv.C

      Target language: 用 Noranda 方 法 生 产 铜

Here, Noranda is a proper noun. It is obvious that either dictionary or grammar in this system are all worked out under particular target and domain conditions, therefore if the situation changes, many things will go wrong.

This system perhaps is the first experimental machine translation system in China, its correct-rate is about 80%. It is hard to say to what degree this system has any relation to Chinese understanding, although, what we have seen from this system is that the target language in this system is really a kind of simplified Chinese.

2-4. ECAT System

ECAT ---- English-Chinese Automatic Translation ---- was developed by a post-

	Chinese	phonetic alphabet	English interpreted
1	主	zhu	subject
2	前 主	Qian Zhu	forward-subject
3	前介主	Qian Jie Zhu	forward-preposition-subject
4	前介宾	Qian Jie Bin	forward-preposition-object
5	后 宾	Hou Bin	backward-object
6	状	Zhuang	adverbial
7	前 状	Qian Zhuang	forward-adverbial
8	前介状	Qian Jie Zhuang	forward-preposition-adverbial
9	前介首状	Qian Jie Shou Zhuang	forward - preposition-first-adverbial
10	前方法状	Qian Fang Fa Zhuang	forward-means-adverbial
11	介首状	Jie Shou Zhuang	preposition-first-adverbial
12	首 状	Shou Zhuang	first-adverbial
13	前首状	Qian Shou Zhuang	forward-first-adverbial
14	宾	Bin	object
15	介宾	Jie Bin	preposition-object
16	前 宾	Qian Bin	forward-object
17	定	Ding	attribute
18	前 定	Qian Ding	forward-attribute
19	前介定	Qian Jie Ding	forward-preposition-attribute
20	前介复定 I	Qian Jie Fu Ding I	forward-preposition-complex-attribute
21	前介复定 II	Qian Jie Fu Ding II	forward-preposition-complex-attribute
22	同位定	Tongwei Ding	appositive-attribute
23	介同位定	Jie Tongwei Ding	preposition-appositive-attribute
24	谓 语	Wei Yu	predicate
25	表 语	Biao Yu	predicative
26	付谓语	Fu Wei Yu	assist-predicate
27	零成分	Ling Chengfen	zero-constituent
28	偏 谓	Pian Wei	partial-predicate

Table 3. Some nonterminal symbols in English machine translation.

graduate student Li Weidong (李卫东) under the guidance of Prof. Liu Yongquan (see Li Weidong, 1982).

There are some similarities between this system and the one described above. Both are written in BOL language and implemented on the same computer. This system has translated an English text containing 3,600 words into Chinese with a correct-rate of 91% in 1981. The result was directly in Chinese characters.

Sentence segmentation marks in this system are divided into three classes:

    1) absolute segmentation marks: punctuation;
    2) relative segmentation marks: preposition, conjunction;
    3) conditional segmentation marks: pronoun, article, number, first verb of predicate.

2-5. A multi-target language translation system from Chinese

This system was developed by a research associate Fong Zhiwei at ARIANE-78 SYSTEM of G.E.T.A in France, in 1981 (see Fong Zhiwei, 1983).

The system is a multi language automatic translator of Chinese into French, English, German, Japanese and Russian simultaneously, it has translated 108 sentences from Chinese scientific and technical texts involving physics, biology, petroleum, archaeology, astromony, scientific history, chemistry, chemical industry and microcarving art. The words of the text amount to 1,114 altogether.

The results showed that the ARIANE-78 system is available not only for Indo--European linguistic system, but also for Chinese.

ARIANE-78 system consists of four program algorithmic blocks: ATEF, ROBRA, TRANSF and SYSGMOR. The first two blocks are used to get a tree with multi--labels which contain logic-semantic relation information, syntactic function information and syntactic form information from the original language. The last two blocks are used to transform and generate target language.

ARIANE-78 is a system that is independent of any special language: either the dictionary or the grammar of that language. So , in this system, the dictionary and grammar rules all are data of the system.

Fong's work has made available a lot of data of grammmar and dictionary in special languages ---- source language and target languages for ARIANE-78. As analysis is independent of generating, as much information as possible could be gained from analysing the source language. This is an important progress.

The source language in Fong's work is Chinese. The information got from analysing Chinese contains six aspects:

    1) information about word order in Chinese sentences
    2) information about level of constituents
    3) syntactic and semantic information of words
    4) information about syntactic function of constituents
    5) logic relation information between words and constituents
    6) semantic relation information between words and constituents.

The first two items above are called geometric values and the last four items are called algebraic values.

Comparing this information with what would be got from analysing by traditional Chinese grammar or structural grammar, we can find out: both traditional and structural grammar are not enough for this kind of analysis.

Fong called this analysis method a multi-label and multi-branch tree analysis method.

In fact, multi-label means that every node of a tree has not only been labeled as S or NP or VP and so on, but also been labeled with other signs which represent other information.

For example, let X be a node, and Y a label function L of X, namely:

$$Y = L(X)$$

the value of L(X) can be one of the following:

$$\left\{ \begin{array}{l} \text{noun phrase} \\ \text{subject} \\ \sim \\ \text{topic} \\ \sim \end{array} \right\} \quad \text{or} \quad \left\{ \begin{array}{l} \text{verb} \\ \text{predicate} \\ \sim \\ \text{belong} \\ \sim \end{array} \right\}$$

$$\left\{ \begin{array}{l} \text{noun} \\ \sim \\ \sim \\ \text{chemical element} \end{array} \right\} \quad \text{or} \quad \left\{ \begin{array}{l} \text{number phrase} \\ \text{attribute} \\ \sim \\ \text{restrict} \\ \sim \end{array} \right\}$$

2-6. A recursive model of Chinese syntactic structure and its implementation

This work was developed by postgraduate student Guo Yuanxing under the guidance of Huang Changning in 1981, at Qinghua University (see Guo Yuanxing, 1981).

The model of sentence structure divides a sentence into four levels: sentence, constituent, structure (phrase) and word.

For example, the sentence:

王　敏　的　弟弟　将　在　北京　学　半　年　英语
Wang Min de didi jiang zhai Beijing xue bannian Yingyu

could be divided into the tree showed in Figure 2.

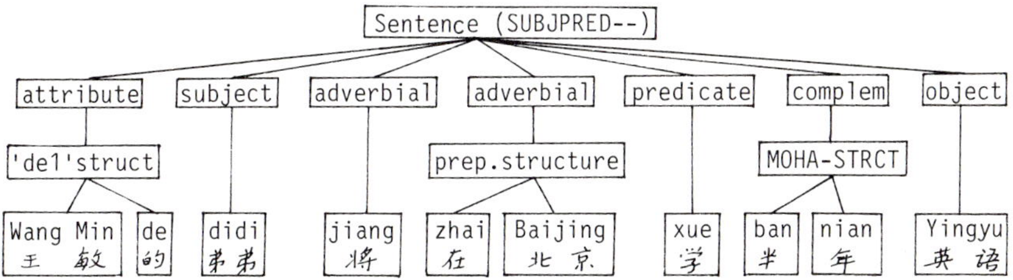

Wang Min of young brother will to be Beijing learn **half** year English

Wang Min's young brother will learn English for half a year at Beijing

Figure 2. Sentence structure

This model is a recursive model, a phrase can consist not only of words, but also of other structures. For example, a " 的 " structure can consist of a SUBJPRED--STRCT and "的 " character, as showed in Figure 3.

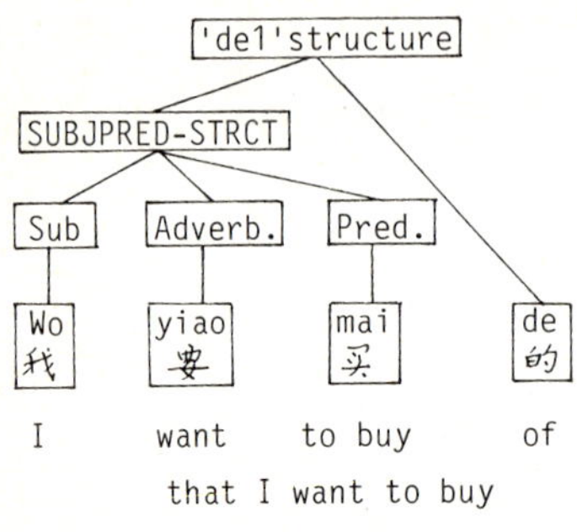

Figure 3. 'de1' structure.

This model classifies a Chinese sentence as subject-predicate structural sentence, verb-object structural sentence (sentence subject omitted), compound structural sentence. In fact, these are only parts of the Chinese sentence.

This model has not considered an important factor of the sentence ---- sentence pattern.

At the level of syntactic constituent, this model has seven different constituents: subject, predicate, object, complement, attribute, adverbial, and concurrent constituent.

The last one means that the constituent is used as object and subject in sub-sentence. For example,the sentence "I call him to go to school" goes as following in Chinese:

Wo   Jiao   ta   dao   xuexiao   qu

我   叫   他   到   学校   去

I   call   he   to   school   go to

Here 他 (ta, he) is the object of the sentence and the subject of clause "ta dao xuexiao qu", so 他 is a concurrent constituent.

At the level of phrase (structure), this model has ten kinds of phrases:

1) Modifier-Head structure (MOHA-STRCT)
2) Unite structure (ASSOCA-STRCT)
3) Subject-predicate structure (SUBJPRED-STRCT)
4) Verb- object structure (VOCS-STRCT)
5) Preposition-object structure (POBJ-STRCT)
6) Localizer structure
7) Tense (verb-tenseword) structure (TENSE-STRCT)
8) "的" structure (or 'de1' structure)
9) "地" structure (or 'de2' structure)
10) "得" structure (or 'de3' structure)

Such classifications are mostly for convenience in computer processing.

At the level of words, this model divided Chinese words into ten kinds, which is the same as in traditional grammar: 1) noun, 2) verb, 3) adjective, 4) pronoun, 5) number, 6)measure word, 7) adverb, 8) preposition, 9) conjunction, and 10) auxiliary word.

Based on syntax parsing program, Guo has made a SPMCT system ---- a transformation program from syntactic structure to conceptual dependency structure. This program made use of R.C. Schank's conceptual dependency theory. What is called conceptual dependence structure is just the semantic structure. Mr. Guo used a figure to show the conceptual dependency. The figure consists of twelve primitive action words presented by Shank (INGEST, EXPEL, PROPEL, MOVE, GRASP, PTRANS, ATRANS, SPEAK, ATTEND, MTRANS, MBUILD, DO) a series of case name and dependency relation words or marks as following:

ACTOR, OWNER, NUM, TENSE,

$\Leftarrow\Rightarrow$	or	$\Longleftrightarrow$	two directional dependency chain
$\langle 0--$	or	$\xleftarrow{0}$	object dependency chain
$\langle R--\rightarrow$	or	$\xleftarrow{R}$	accepter
$\langle R--\prec$	or		doner

of give and accept case

$\langle D--\rightarrow$	or	$\xleftarrow{D}$	end of direction case
$\langle D--\prec$	or		beginning of direction case
$\langle I--$	or	$\xleftarrow{I}$	instruction
$\langle\equiv-\equiv\rangle$	or	$\Longrightarrow$	state dependency chain
$\langle\equiv-\rangle$	or		end state
$\langle\equiv-\prec$	or		beginning state
$\langle---\equiv$	or	$\Longleftarrow$	causality
$\langle--\rightarrow$	or	$\longleftrightarrow$	nominal dependency chain
$\langle--\rightarrow$	or	$\longleftarrow$	action dependency chain

$\wedge$: and V : or

Let us discuss the system with a few practical examples.

Example one: 王敏和张水都是学生。

```
INPUT: WANGMIN HE ZHANGSHUI DOU SHI XUESHENG
SYNTAX STRUCTURE:
(SUBJPRED-STRCT (SUBJ (ASSOCA-STRCT (WANGMIN HE ZHANGSHUI)))
(ADVB DOU) (PRED SHI) (OBJ XUESHENG)*))
CONCEPT STRUCTURE:
((ACTOR (AND WANGMIN XHANGSHUI) <=-=> XUESHENG))
```

The input is a sentence in Chinese phoneic alphabet, its meaning is: both Wangmin
and Zhangshui are students. Its conceptual dependency figure from concept structure above is as following:

```
*王敏*
Wangmin
   ∧               ⟸⟹              *学生*
*张水*
Zhangshui                          xuesheng
                                   student
```

Example two: 书 被 我 扔 到 桌 子 上

```
(Books are threwn on the desk by me)
INPUT: SHU BEI WO RENG DAO ZHUOZI SHANG.
SYNTAX STRUCTURE:
(SUBJPRED-STRCT (SUBJ SHU) (ADVB (POBJ-STRCT (BEI (OBJ WO))))
(PRED RENG) (COMP (POBJ-STRCT (DAO (OBJ ZHUOZI) SHANG)))*))
```

```
CONCEPT STRUCTURE:
((ACTOR WO  <=-=> * PROPEL * <O -- SHU <D --<  Y <D -->  (ON ZHUOZI)))
```

Here, Y stands for an unknown item, (the system has no word to process such a situation). In fact, it means a certain place. So the conceptual dependency figure will be as following:

$$\star \text{我} \star \Longleftrightarrow \star \text{PROPEL} \star \xleftarrow{\quad O \quad} \star \text{书} \star \xleftarrow{\quad D \quad}$$

(Zhuozi Shang)
$\to \star$ 桌子上 $\star$
on the desk
$\to \star$ 某处 $\star$
a certain place
(mou chu)

(Wo)   (Shu)

Note that: the main verb ---- RENG 扔 (throw) ---- has been substituted by a primary action PROPEL without any additional information. Sometimes it would be too simple to be understood by computer, this is because of that: PROPEL only means "application of a physical force to an object", so it will make a group of verbs have the same meaning without any differeces: 扔 (throw) 放 (put) 堆 (push) 拉 (pull) ....

All programs of the systems were written in LISP, and implemented on a microcomputer. Its dictionary has a word frame structure and is able to add new words by means of man-machine interaction.

2-7. RJD-80 Man-machine Dialogue System

This system was developed by Prof. Fan Jiyan with Xu Zhimin in 1981 (see Fan Jiyan, et.al., 1982).

It involved 250 words altogether, among those words, there are 214 nouns, most of these are proper nouns: 34 writers' names, 139 book names, 4 persons' names, and 14 common nouns.

The other words in the system are as following:
  1) 9 pronouns:
       3 personal pronouns: Wo (我) - I or me, Ni (你) - you,
                            Ta (他) - he, him, she, her;
       1 interrogative pronoun: Shui (谁) - who, whom ;
       1 demomstrative pronoun: Na (那) - that;
       2 interrogative nominal pronouns: Shenme (什么) - what,
                                Naxie (那些) - what, which, who;
       2 interrogative adverbs (in English): Zhenme (怎么) - how
                     Duoshao (多少) - how many or how much.

  2) 11 verbs:
       Shi (是) -- to be;   You (有) -- to have;
       Dui (对) -- to be true;   Kan (看) -- to look;
       Xie (写) -- to write;   Daying (打赢) -- to win;
       Dabai (打败) -- to defeat;   Zhidao (知道) -- to know;
       Shugei (输给) -- to be defeated by;
       Xihuan (喜欢) -- to like, to be fond of, to love;
       Renwei (认为) -- to consider, to hold, to think.

  3) 2 adjective:
       Zhuming (著名) -- famous, well-known;
       Henduo (很多) -- very much, very many.

  4) 8 adverbs:

Bu (不) -- not;   Mei (没) -- not yet, not have ;
Meiyou (没有) -- not have;   Dou (都) -- in all cases, all;
Hai (还) -- still, yet;   You (又) -- again;
Yi (已) -- already;   Jiu (就) -- at once, right away.

5) 2 prepositions:
   Bei (被) -- by;   Ba (把) -- taking hold of.

6) 4 conjunctions:
   He (和) -- and, with;   Haishi (还是) -- or;
   Shuyi (所以) -- so, therefore, as a result;
   Yaoshi (要是) -- if, in case.

7) 7 auxilary words:
   De (的);   Liao 1 (了1);
   Liao 2 (了2);   Guo (过);
   Ma (吗);   Ba (吧);
   Ne (呢).

8) 2 interjunctive words:
   O (哦);   A (啊).

Many other kinds of Chinese words are not comprehended in this system, for example: number words, measure words or unit words (量词 , these kind of words are something special in Chinese), optative verb or auxiliary verb and so on. Even so, the words used compose many fairly natural sentences.

This system has put syntactic rules and word dictionary into one program, and the words and rules are all restricted in a common program, so one can only type into the computer certain sentences composed by these words.

This system is the first man-machine dialogue system having some understanding ability in China. Experiments with this system have showed how to make a computer more powerful in natural language understanding.

Because of its restricted vocabulary and other factors, this system can only deal with certain sentences and the system can not be furtherly enlarged.

All programs are written in LISP and implemented on a microcomputer.

2-8. ACLUS ---- Ancient Chinese language understanding system

Based on his former work in natural language understanding, Prof. Li Jiazhi at the Psychology Institute of Academia Sinica proposed the ancient Chinese understanding subject in 1981 and worked out a primary program called ACLUS (see Li Jiazhi, 1983).

Ancient Chinese language or ancient Chinese has the same word order as modern Chinese, i.e. subject- predicate-object (if any). ACLUS is a parsing program for getting syntactic structure from input sentences written in the Chinese phonetic alphabet. It involves a small dictionary which now has 65 words (in frame form).

Example 1.
   Input sentence: "人曰: 何不试之以足?"
     (A man says: "Why do you not try it with your foot?")
   Its deep structure (syntactic structure) is:
     (S (NP (N 人)) (VP (V 曰) (S (AP (ADV 何) (ADV 不))
     (VP (V 试) (NP (PRO 之))) (PP (PRE 以) (N 足))))

Its tree form figure from the above syntactic structure is showed in figure 4.

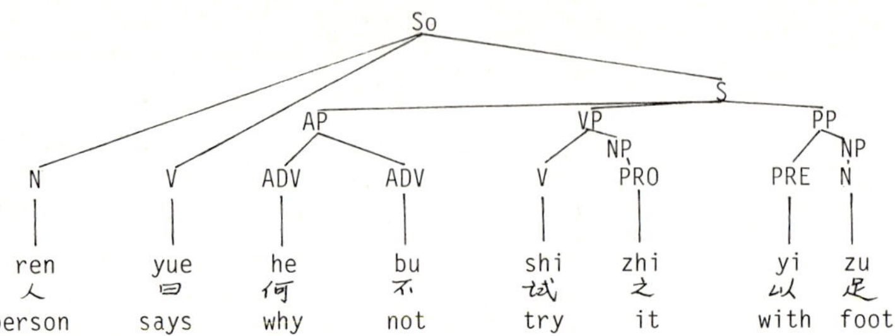

Figure 4. Example 1.
            (Here: Ap ---- Adverb-phrase, Np ---- Noun phrase,
            Vp ---- Verb-phrase,   Pp ---- Preposition phrase)

Example 2.
    Input sentence: "至之市而忘操之."
        (When he got to the fair he forgot to bring it.)
    Its syntactic structure:
        (S (VP 至) (VP (V 之) (NP (N 市)))) (AP (CONJ 而)
        (VP (V 忘) (VP (V 操) (NP (PRO 之)))))).

Figure 5 shows its tree form figure.

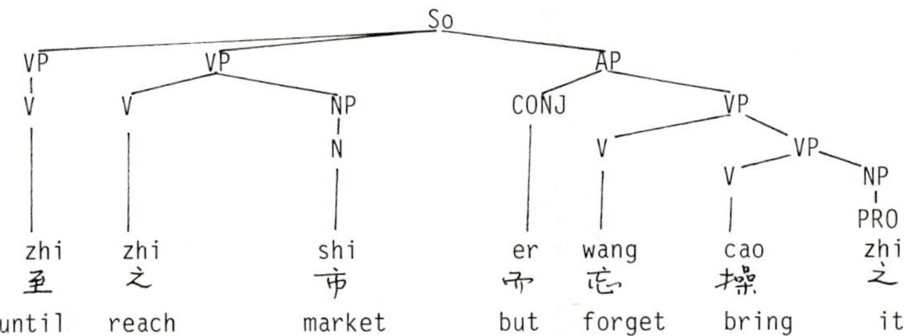

Figure 5. Example 2.

Example 3.
    Input sentence: "楚人以手度自足."
        (A man from Chu measures his own foot with his hand).
    Syntactic structure:
        (S (NP (DET 楚) (N 人)) (PP (PRE 以) (N 手))
        (VP (V 度) (NP (DET 自) (N 足)))).

Figure 6 shows its tree form structure.

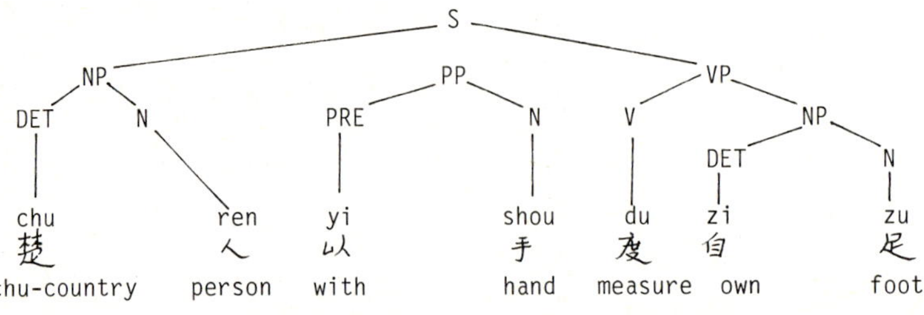

Figure 6. Example 3.

All that we have introduced above are some of the main reseach work on Chinese
processing and understanding in China.

3. THE GOALS, APPROACHES AND OPEN PROBLEMS OF CHINESE UNDERSTANDING

3.1 The broad-sense and narrow-sense goals of Chinese understanding

The efforts in natural language understanding research from the viewpoint of
AI lasted more than 20 years, however, there is no system so far that can really
understand natural language without a lot of restrictions.

We might say that all the existing systems for natural language understanding
are one of the following:
    -- a machine translation system on a particular and limited special field
from one language to other language or languages;
    -- an interface between a knowledge base, a data base and man (in this kind
of system every word has a special meaning which is interpreted by knowledge
base or data base, and can be retrieved from them);
    -- a robot system which can answer questions and respond to commands;
    -- a special system which can understand a story, a text or something simi-
lar.

As for Chinese understanding, there might be an even longer way to go. This
is because of the fact : Chinese, from the viewpoint of linguistics, is a kind
of language which has not been thoroughly investigated. What we mean is that
there are still a lot of unclear phenomena in Chinese. For example, the classification of verbs in Chinese is still an open problem, but it is expected to
be solved in the next five-year-plan.

Our long term program is to build a general parsing program which can deal with
every Chinese sentence, i.e. we would set up a general formal grammar for natural
Chinese. We found Chinese sentences can be as simple as only a content word,
and can be as complex as a short text. As in other languages a natural sentence
is not independent in meaning and closely depends on the context or language
environment. Without context, no one, including computers, could understand
a sentence. So the problem is not how to build a general parsing program for
every Chinese sentence, but how to build a system which can make the meaning
of any sentence clear (see Li Yingtan, 1983).

The works finished by some linguists can only tell us which word or phrase
is the subject, or predicate, or object and so on, but can not tell us what
kind of logic relation those words or phrases have. Nevertheless, in Chinese,
between the subject and predicate, sometimes there is no actor ---- action relation (suppose predicate is an action verb). For example:

Che   qi   chu   qu   le

车   骑   出   去   了

bike ride   out   (perfect tense)

This is a common Chinese sentence. Even in such a simple sentence, Chinese linguists have been arguing for many years without any conclusions. In our opinion,
no matter whether Che (车) is the subject or something else, a bike can only
be ridden by a person, which is common sense. In the above sentence, although
the actor is not explicit, in certain contexts it is clear. If a computer understands sentence like the above one, that would be quite well. If the computer
tells us: "Here CHE (车) is the subject, but I do not know if CHE (车) is
the actor of Qi (骑).", that would be quite bad, even a nonsense!

Prof. Ma Xiwen in Beijing University has proposed an idea in a discussion with Li Yingtan laterly: "These basic Chines grammar problems have been argued for more than twenty years. Almost every grammar rule has its own restrictions.". Prof. Zhu Dexi (a well-known Chinese grammarian in Beijing University) has the same idea: "a grammar book can only be written in proper detail and need not to be complete, otherwise difficulties would be discovered immediately." It seems that natural language might be recursive but not without any limit. Natural language may have no more rules. It would be possible that what we are looking for is not a natural language but an artificial language; from the viewpoint of pragmatics, natural language is much more indefinite and we would have no way to grasp it.

For example, "I am hungry" is a simple sentence that may mean:

    1) I want to eat something;
    2) I have worked too hard or for a too long time, thus I should deserve
       your praising;
    3) I want to stop the work;
    4) I want to take a rest.

Of course, this is really an understanding problem, but there is no relation at all between it and language itself.

What we should do and can do is to be able to understand the meaning of the sentence "I am hungry" from its three words: I, am, hungry.

So, understanding in the final analysis, should consider context, but, before that, understanding should start from language ifself but not context.

Natural language itself is a human phenomenom with many practical restrictions. No matter whether Chinese or English, everybody speaks his native language with his own personal special grammar and dialect. What is called unrestrictive understanding in fact is under the condition that everybody knows a lot of information in advance about the topic. So, to the computer, a restrictive natural language understanding task is always valuable.

The general goal of Chinese understanding research should be to build a system which can extract information from a sentence written in Chinese characters and then this system can transform the sentence into a new form with the same meaning. These new forms may be in another language, or still in Chinese, or in a kind of metalanguage. And by that, the system can answer any question if it is needed. Only then will people admit that the system has really understood the meaning of that Chinese sentence.

Obviously such a system itself needs interaction with man.

Correspondingly, we should have a narrow-sense goal, a restricted Chinese robot system. This kind of system would work with natural sentences in a small limited area, as the robot world would be rather small. This kind of system is in the same kind of T. Winograd's SHRDLU (1972).

A restricted Chinese system for knowledge engineering may be taken as another example of narrow-sense goal.

It must be noted that in all restrictive Chinese systems a sentence consists of words but not characters, so that, the system can cancel the difficult work of segmentation. We will discuss this problem in detail later.

3-2. <u>State of the art of Chinese linguistics and its relation with Chinese understanding</u>

There are still many open problems in Chinese linguistics which are expected to be solved in Chinese understanding.

We assume that the reason why a language can be understood or translated is that there are universal semantic concepts belonging to the human intelligence system, which governs many actions including language action. So, this kind of universal semantic concepts are something superlinguistic. However, for any language, the meaning of its words should be stable, therefore, every special language can not be supersemantic. What are called universal semantic concepts are in fact just what everybody has. Sometimes we call this intelligent information or meta-knowledge.

One person puts the intended intelligent information into language, and another gets that intelligent information from language, that is all.

Natural Chinese understanding demands that Chinese linguistics builds a formal Chinese grammar-dictionary system which can tell the computer how it can get the logical form from the text (see Li Yingtan, 1983).

Fortunately there are some Chinese linguists engaged in this kind of work. For example, a scholar from Taiwan Province named Huang C.T.James has written a book Logical Relations In Chinese And The Theory Of Grammar as his doctoral dissertation at MIT in 1982 (see Huang C.T.J. 1982). Huang's work pays attention to the logical form. Huang points out: any comprehensive grammar theory must show how to map a sentence strcture into predicate calculus logical form. Huang has researched the relation between the sentence superficial structure and the domain of logic components. As Huang pointed out, many things in Chinese are still unclear.

Now a word about Montague grammar. Up to now, though we have not found any example of its use for Chinese, we still believe Montague grammar is a powerful theory for Chinese understanding. This is because it links directly sentence superficial structure and logic form.

However, we do not think any existing theory could solve Chinese formal grammar problems without great difficulty.

An overseas Chinese American and well-known Chinese grammarian Yuen Ren Chao (趙元任) in the book A Grammar of Spoken Chinese reported many Chinese language habits which make the superficial structures of a Chinese sentence nearly to have no subject-predicate form, but topic-comment form. It seems that Chinese should have a high level grammar that do not deal only with sentence form but also with meaning (see Yuen Ren Chao, 1970).

Let us take some examples:

1) 饭我吃了，菜我没吃。   (Fan wo chi le, cai wo mei chi)
2) 我饭吃了，菜没吃。   (Wo fan chi le, cai mei chi)
3) 我吃饭了，没吃菜。   (Wo chi fan le, mei chi cai)

All these three sentences have different word orders, but have the same meaning: I have eaten the rice, but not the dish. The object 饭 (fan, cooked rice) has a different position in the sentences but the actor 我 (wo, I) and action 吃 (chi, eat) have a fixed order relation to each other. Comparing 1) with 2), we can see there is no information which implies whether 饭 or 我 must be the actor or object in the sentence form. The information is contained in the words 饭 and 我 themselves. Besides this, there is still a common knowledge: 我 must be the actor of 吃.

These kind of facts are quite common in Chinese, people could say that Chinese

has no grammar; even if this idea is not correct, it has taken interesting points.
The second parts of the second and third sentences have no actor which is omitted
because it is known from the first part of the sentences.These kinds of phenomena
appear quite often in Chinese.

4) 我 有 本 领 开 飞 机   (Wo you ben ling kai feiji)
   I am able to pilot a plane   (I have ability pilot plane)

5) 我 有 朋 友 开 飞 机   (Wo you pengyou kai feiiji)
   I have a friend who pilots a plane   (I have friend pilot plane)

In these two sentences, according to general grammar, both 本领 and 朋友 are
nouns, and therefore sentences 4) and 5) should have the same superficial structure, but in fact the two sentences have entirely different deep structures
and logic relation.

Sentence 4) means: I have the ability to pilot a plane.
Sentence 5) means: I have a friend who pilots a plane
In sentence 4) "I" is the "actor" of "to pilot a plane".
In sentence 5) "friend" is the actor of "to pilot a plane".

We can find out this kind of difference from the meaning of the words, but not
from the syntactic form or superficial word order and syntactic features.

6) 行 人 走 便 道
   Xing ren zou bian dao
   pedestrian walk pavement

7) 便 道 走 行 人
   Bian dao zou xing ren
   pavement walk pedestrian

8) 雨 布 蓋 着 汽 车
   Yu bu   gai zhe   qiche
   waterproof be covering car

9) 汽 车 蓋 着 雨 布
   Qiche gai zhe   yu bu
   car be covering waterproof

10) 我 打 了 杯 子
   Wo da le beizi
   I broken cup

11) 杯 子 打 了 我
   Beizi da le wo
   cup hit me

The six example sentences above show that there is no rule from the word order
and syntactic feature to determine their logical relation. Sentence 6) and 7)
have the same meaning even if 行 人 (xingren ---- pedestrian) and 便道 (bian
dao ---- pavement) have exchanged their mutual order. Sentences 8) and 9) are
the same case as in sentences 6) and 7). However, the situation is different
in sentence 10) and 11) they have different meanings, i.e. to change the word
order of two sentences will change their logical relation:

我 (wo, I) is actor in 10) but object in 11);

杯子(beizi, cup) is object in 10) but actor in 11).

Such a case can be found only in Chinese. In Chinese, if it will not bring confusion, word order can be changed and the passive mark word 被 (bei, by) can

be omitted. These pecularities make Chinese sentences more simple and flexible but less formal in syntactic information than English.

What we have described above tells us: to understand a Chinese sentence, we must consider not only the word features of their syntax and order, but also their meaning and context together.

So, traditional and structuralistic Chinese grammar do not meet our needs.

We need to build a new complete grammar system based on researching all existing grammar systems including generative grammar. And this is an important task to be faced by AI researchers and linguists.

3-3. <u>Other open problems</u>

Besides what we have discussed above, there are still a lot of open problems in Chinese understanding.

3-3.1. <u>Segmentation</u>

In the written form, all the Chinese sentences are composed of separated Chinese characters, one by one evenly arranged, without any superficial marks for segmentation.

The problem of sentence segmentation is not separated but is closely related with the analysis and parsing of the sentence superficial structure. And the segmentation and structure analysis are interdependent one each other. Therefore the sentence segmentation procedure is really a sentence analysis procedure.

Now we will take an example to show the importance of sentence segmentation. In ancient Chinese texts, there were no punctuation marks. For that reason, many jokes occurred, one among them goes like this: a man went to visit his friend and suddenly it began to rain, so the man wanted to stay there overnight and wrote a line of characters:

下 雨 天 留 客
xia yu tian liu ke
(As it is raining the guest should be put up overnight)

His friend did not expect him to stay any longer and wrote another five characters after the first five:

下 雨 天 留 客　　天 留 我 不 留
xia yu tian liu ke　　tian liu wo bu liu
(As it is raining the guest should be put up overnight;
heaven wants to put up the guest, but I do not.)

The man thought about it over for a moment and put some punctuation marks on it:

下 雨 天 ， 留 客 天 ， 留 我 不 ？ 留 ！
xia yu tian, liu ke tian, liu wo bu? liu!
(It is raining, heaven wants to put up the guest,
should the guest be put up? Yes!)

Then its meaning has changed again.

This is only a joke. But from the joke, we can see how flexible Chinese is!

Therefore, modern Chinese has a complete set of punctuation marks to segment sentences.

Generally speaking every Chinese sentence has more than one kind of segmentation scheme.

Now let us discuss this feature with a simple example of a three characters phrase:

炸　　油　　条
zha　　you　　tiao
fry　fried dough　sticks

It can be segmented in two ways: 1) 炸油条 is only a word that means fried dough sticks; 2) it is an event: 炸 is a verb or action ---- to fry, and 油条 is a noun, means fried dough sticks, as an object of "fry", in Chinese traditional grammar, this is a verb- object phrase.

When we insert the phrase in a longer sentence, this ambiguity may be eliminated, but in different way depending on the context.

In the following sentences:

1) 我 炸 油 条   (I fry dough sticks)
　　wo　zha　youtiao

2) 炸 油 条 了   (Dough sticks are being fried)
　　zha　youtiao　le

3) 不 炸 油 条   (Do not fry dough sticks)
　　bu　zha　youtiao

The phrase 炸油条 (zha youtiao) in sentences 1), 2), 3) is only a verb-object phrase. In the following sentences:

4) 炸 油 条 好 吃   (Fried dough sticks are delicious)
　　zha　youtiao　hao　chi

5) 我 吃 炸 油 条   (I eat fried dough sticks)
　　wo　chi　zha　youtiao

6) 这 是 炸 油 条   (These are fried dough sticks)
　　zhe　shi　zha　youtiao

7) 我 吃 炸 油 条 了   (I have eaten fried dough sticks)
　　wo　chi　zha　youtiao　le

the three characters 炸油条 are a single noun.

We have seen that: " 炸油条了 " in 2) and in 7) have different meanings as they are in different contexts.

We can not look for the correct segmentation in a dictionary either. As an example, we use the sentence introduced by Xie Mingpei of Fudan University in 1982 at the third conference of Chinese Artifjcial Intelligence Society in Beijing.

计 算 机 是 金 计 算 题 目 的 机 器

By segmenting the sentence in all the various possible ways we can obtain 15 different words, but only the following segmentation is correct:

计算机　是　会　计算　题目　的　机器.
Jisuanji　shi　hui　jisuan　timo　de　jiqi

As Chinese texts have no distiguishing marks for each word, sentence parsing is much more complex than in other languages, yet, on the other hand, just this peculiarity makes Chinese sentences more simple and flexible.

To segment a sentence a series of special characters can be used as segmenting marks:

1) punctuation marks, these are a kind of absolute mark.

2) fixed position characters: in Chinese, there are 380 forward fixed position characters and 134 back fixed position characters. What is called fixed position characters are an absolute mark of words. However, the number of these words that contain fixed position characters is too small to solve the segmentation problem (they amount only to 2.5% of words).

3) auxiliary verb and adverb of affirmation, negation, time, contingency, scope and evaluation can be considered as a mark of a verb word. Following are the most common examples of this kind words:

neng 能	ying 应	yao 要	xiang 想	ke 可
xu 须	bu 不	gan 敢	yuan 愿	mei 没
mei you 没有	dou 都	zhi 只	jiu 就	ye 也
hai 还	zai 再	que 却	dao 倒	cai 才
changchang 常常		yijing 已经	cengjing 曾经	ganggang 刚刚
zao yi 早已	zheng zhai 正在		zheng 真	yi ding 一定
da gai 大概		ji hu 几乎.		

4) suffixes of verb, for example:

了 (le) the perfective aspect

着 (zhe) the progressive suffix

过 (guo) the indefinite past aspect

起来 (qi lai) the inchoative aspect

下去 (xia qu) the successive aspect.

5) suffixes of noun, for example:

meng 们	zi 子	hua 化	yan 炎	xing 性
jia 家	yuan 员	fa 法	er 儿	lu
jie 界	shi	lun 论	guan 观	tou 头.

6) preposition and localizer; these words can be the mark of a noun phrase. Following are some examples of this words:

zhai 在	he 和	tong 同	wang 往	xiang 向
dui 对	cong 从	yan 沿	guan yu 关于	wei 为
you yu 由于	yi 依	gen ju 根据	yong 用	ba 把
bei 被	dao 到	cu le 除了	bi 比	gei 给.

shang 上	zhong 中	xia 下	qian 前	hou 后.

zuo 左   you 右   dong 东   nan 南   xi 西
bei 北   bian 边   pang 旁   wai 外   li 里 .

7) 的 (de), 地 (de), 得 (de), 是 (shi), 有 (you), 这 (zhe), 那 (na), and
   number, these words are most common segmentation marks.

Chinese sentence segmentation will become an attractive problem and this problem
is really a challenge to AI research. To solve this problem, we should build up
several data bases, including a Chinese word-building dictionary (see Fu Xing -
ling, 1981 and a word-succeeding-character dictionary.

3-3.2. The continuous ability of transformation of Chinese sentences

Every Chinese sentence can generally accept   some new constituents at its end
and receive a new structure relation.

We shall explain this feature with an example.

Let us see in Figure 7, the sentence: 他 死 了   (ta si le, he was dead) -->

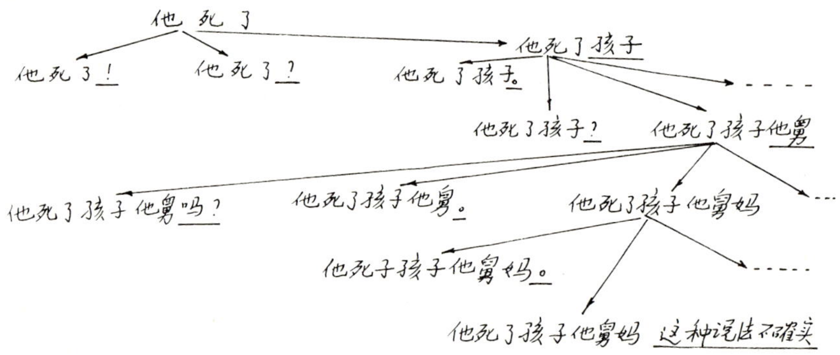

Figure 7. An example of   the continuous ability of transformation
          of Chinese sentences.

他死了? (Was he dead?) or --> 他死了孩子 (ta si le haizi, His son was
dead). This sentence can become --> 他死了孩子? (Did his son die?) or -
--> 他死了孩子他舅 (ta si le haizi ta jiu, His son's mother's brother has
died) --> 他死了孩子他舅妈 (ta si le haizi ta jiuma, His son's mother's
brother's wife has died) ---> 他死了孩子他舅妈这种说法不确实 (ta
si le hai zi ta jiuma zhezong suofa bu queshi, It is not correct that someone
says that his son's mother's brother's wife has died).

Figure 8 shows another example :

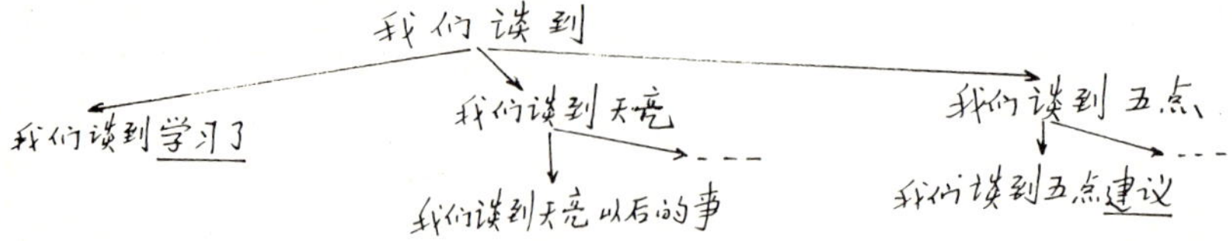

Figure 8. A second example of   the continuous ability of trans-
          formation of Chinese sentences.

我们谈到 (we talk about) --→ 我们谈到学习了 (women tan dao suexi le, We talked about learning) or --→ 我们谈到五点 (women tan dao wudian, We have talked until 5 o'clock) --→ 我们谈到五点建议 (women tan dao wudian jianyi, We have talked about five proposals) --→ ...

From the two examples, we can get this idea: until a Chinese sentence has stopped, you can not be sure whether your suppositions about the sentence meaning is correct or not.

4. CONCLUSION

We can conclude from the above discussion as follows:

1. There is a close relation between Chinese and Chinese characters. Each Chinese character is a basic unit of meaning in Chinese. So in an actual chinese understanding system Chinese characters should be considered.   Are Chinese characters what makes   Chinese a powerful and flexible language.

2. To segment a word in Chinese sentences may be a very hard task during parsing Chinese sentences. The whole sentence and context must be considered. It seems that a procedure to segment a word is actually the procedure to understand a sentence.

3. The results we have gained so far in Chinese understanding are only a first step. Generally speaking, we need to build an understanding oriented Chinese dictionary-grammar and Montague grammar. The main goal of this kind of understanding grammar is looking for the best way from superficial sentence forms to logic forms of meaning.

4. Chinese understanding is really a hard subject facing rearchers, but might be a most attractive problem.

REFERENCES

CHINESE LANGUAGE INFORMATION SOCIETY
中文信息研究会
Papers of the Second Annual Conference, Wuhan City, 6, 1983.
第二次年会论文集

FAN JIYAN & XU ZHIMIN
花继淹   徐志敏
Model RJD-80 artificial dialogue system. Hangzhou Conference of Artificial Intelligence Society Group of the Chinese Computer Society, 4, 1982.
RJD-80 人工对话系统

FONG ZHIWEI
冯志伟
A multi-mark and multi-branch tree method of parsing Chinese sentences. Fourth Annual Conference of Artificial Intelligence of the All-China Institutions of Higher Learning, Guangzhou City, 3, 1983.
汉语句子的多标记·多叉树形图分析法

FU XINGLIAN & CHENG ZHANGHUAN
傅兴岭 陈章焕
The word-building dictionary in common use. The Press of the Chinese People University, 1, 1981.
常用构词词典.   中国人民大学出版社

GUO YEFANG
郭治方

The general situation and its development of the research on coding   Chinese characters.
                                    Second Annual Conference of the Chinese Language Information Society, Wuhan, 5, 1983.
汉字编码研究情况及其发展

GUO YUANXING
郭元兴

A recursive model of the syntactic structure of Chinese and its application to the language process system, Master thesis of Qinghua University, 1981.
汉语句法结构的一种递归模型及其在语言处理系统中的应用   清华大学硕士论文

HUANG, C.T.J.
黄正德

Logic relation in Chinese and the theory of grammar.
Doctoral dissertation, MIT, Cambridge, MA, 1982.

JIANG YINGPENG
蒋 映 鹏

The experimental report on machine translation of reference headline from English to Chinese.
                                    Second Conference of Machine Translation Society, Shanghai, 3, 1982.
英汉题录机叫翻译试验报告
第二届机叫翻译学会议论文   上海

LI JIAZHI
李家治

Ancient Chinese understanding.
                                    Fourth Annual Conference of Artificial Intelligence   of All-China Institutions of Higher Learning, Guangzhou City, 3,1983.
古汉语理解

LI WEIDONG
李 卫东

The analysis and synthesis of ECAT system .
                                    Second Annual Conference of Machine Translation Society, Shanghai, 3, 1982.
ECAT系统的分析与综合

LI YINGTAN
李应潭

An approach to Chinese dictionary-grammar system from the point of view of generative grammar and knowledge representation.
                                    Harbin Generative Grammar Conference, 6, 1983.

RESEARCH GROUP OF
LANGUAGE AUTO--
PROCESSING OF
WUHAN UNIVERSITY
武汉大学语言自动
  处理研究组

Collected papers of Chinese characters processing system WD-XYZC Language automatic processing.
                                    Conference of WD-XYZC System, Wuhan, 10, 1982.
WD-XYZC 语言自动处理文字处理系统论文集，鉴定会议资料

STATE BUREAU OF
STANDARDIZATION
OF THE PEOPLE'S
REPUBLIC OF CHINA
中国国家标准总局

Code of Chinese graphic character set for information interchange primary set GB2312-80. 1981.
GB 2312-80 信息交换用汉字编码 字符集 基本集

TANG YAN
汤晏

The American scholar Tang Degang's opinion to the latinization of Chinese characters.
Zhongbao monthly, Hong Kong, 4, 1982.
美国学者唐德刚 对汉字拉丁化 的意见
香港《中报》月刊 82年4月号

YUEN REN CHAO
赵元任

A grammar of spoken Chinese.
University of California Press, Berkeley and Los Angeles, 1968.

APPENDIX

Jia guwen -- the earliest kind of Chinese characters -- and its building methods

method	Jia guwen	sound	English	illustration
象形 (Xiang-xing) Picto-graphic		shi	pig	a pattern of a pig
		ren	man	like a man kneeling on the ground
		ri	sun	the dot in the center means the sunspot
		yue	moon	a pattern of the moon
		mu	eye	this is just a brief picture of an eye
		niu	ox	this is just the front view of an ox, it is like the horns of an ox
		shou	hand	it represents fingers
		shi	arrow	a pattern of an arrow
		yang	sheep	this is just a front view of a sheep like the horns of a sheep
		nu	woman	it symbolizes a woman going down on her knees and crossing her hands
		fu	jar	it symbolizes a jar and its cover
		bing	ill	it is like a bed, like a man lying on a bed
		dao	knife	a pattern of a knife

Continued

method	Jia guwen	sound	English	illustration
(Xiang-xing) Picto-graphic		車 che 车	vehicle	a pattern of a vehicle
		min 皿	utensil	a pattern of an utensil
		zhui 佳	short tail-bird	a pattern of a short tail-bird
		yu 羽	feather	a pattern of a feather
		zhou	boat	a pattern of a boat
		舟 jiao	horn	a pattern of a horn
		泉 quan	spring	a pattern of spring
		雨 yu	rain	a pattern of rain
		气 qi	gas	a pattern of gas
(Zhi-shi) Self-expla natory		上 shang	above	the short horizontal stroke points out what the below means
		下 xia	below	the short horizontal stroke points out what the below means
		一 yi	one	one horizontal stroke means the number one
		二 er	two	two horizontal strokes mean the number two
		寸 cun	wrist	the short horizontal stroke points out the place where the wrist is
		亦 yi	armpit	two short strokes point out the armpit, it is the front view of man
		交 jiao	intersect	a man crossing his legs
		咩 mie	baa	the "v" means the voice being uttered by the sheep
(Huiyi) Associ-ative compounds		wu 武	military	戈 (ge) means an ancient weapon dagger-axe, 止 means on foot. It means a man holding a weapon and walking -- a military action
		bing 兵	weapons	斤 is namely an axe, 廾 廾 is two hands. It means military weapons
		明 ming	bright	sun and moon for brightness
		莫 mu → 暮	sunset	屮 屮 means rank grass, 日 means the sun. Compound meaning: the sun setting in rank grass.
		涉 she	wade	～ means a river, 止 止 means 2 feet ---- wade across a river
		jiang 各 → 降	fall down	夅 and 阝 symbolizes two feet walking down
		彭 peng	drum-sound	壴 is a drum, 彡 symbolizes sound
		chen 沉	sink	symbolizes a man with wooden collar and a river ---- put a man with wooden collar in water: to make him sink

Continued

method	Jia guwen	sound	English	illustration
形声 (Xing sheng) Picto-phonetic	𦥯	shi 食	food	A is the sound part, it decides the sound of this word, its original sound is Ji and means a set. 𠂤 is the form part, it decides meaning, symbolizes grain (θ) on and in the pot (几) so it means food.
	𡴀	yan 言	speech	∪ is a form part, it means a mouth speaking. 𢆶 is a sound part, the original sound is Qian.
	𣪊	qi 契	engrave	⟩ is a form part, it means to engrave with a knife, 㓞 is a sound part, its original sound is Jian.

ACKNOWLEDGEMENTS

Authors would like to thank Proff.Bruno Bara and Giovanni Guida for their suggestions to this paper;   Mr. Zhu Jingguo, Mr. Lu yucang and Mr. Zhang Pu for their materials;   miss Zhao Cong for her excellent typing,   Mrs. Ling Yinghong and Prof. Hou Ziqiang and many others for their help.

Computational Models of Natural Language Processing
B.G. Bara and G. Guida (eds.)
© Elsevier Science Publishers B.V. (North-Holland), 1984

SEMANTIC PRIMITIVES OR MEANING POSTULATES:
MENTAL MODELS OR PROPOSITIONAL REPRESENTATIONS?

Philip N. Johnson-Laird

MRC Applied Psychology Unit
Cambridge, UK

The controversy over whether images are equivalent to sets
of propositions, and the controversy over whether semantic
primitives are equivalent to sets of meaning postulates,
are currently conducted independently. This article brings
them together in relation to the problematical nature of
the transitivity of spatial relations. Both controversies
can be resolved by assuming that spatial relations are
represented as mental models constructed by a procedural
semantics that decomposes the meanings of words into more
primitive notions.

1. INTRODUCTION

This paper confronts two controversies with one phenomenon. The first controversy
concerns the nature of mental representations and whether there is any essential
difference between an image and a set of propositions. The second controversy
concerns the meanings of words and whether they are represented by semantic
primitives, or by meaning postulates that specify the semantic relations that hold
between them. Both controversies are currently in progress and both are primarily
matters of theory rather than fact. They have not previously been related to one
another; yet, if the fundamental argument of this paper is sound, they can both be
resolved by confronting them with one and the same phenomenon -- a seemingly
trivial aspect of everyday inference: the transitivity of certain spatial
relations. A necessary preliminary, however, is to lay out the two controversies
in more detail.

2. THE FIRST CONTROVERSY: IMAGES VERSUS PROPOSITIONS

Many human beings claim to be able to form and to manipulate mental images in the
absence of corresponding visual stimuli. The phenomenon has been studied ever
since Galton's questionnaire on his correspondent's ability to imagine their
breakfast tables (Galton, 1928, originally published in 1880). More recent
investigations have examined a variety of aspects of images, incluiding their use
as mnemonics (Bower, 1972; Paivio, 1971), their mental rotation and transformation
(Cooper, 1975; Shepard, 1975), their suppression by other tasks (Brooks, 1967;
Byrne, 1974), and their use in retrieving information about objects (Hayes, 1973;
Holyoak, 1977; Kosslyn, 1975, 1980; Moyer, 1973; Paivio, 1975). No one seriously
doubts the existence of the subjective experience of imagery. What is
problematical, however, is the explanation of the experience and the ultimate
nature of images as mental representations. It seems unlikely that they are
simple pictures in the head, because this conjecture leads to a number of
undesirable consequences including the need for an homunculus to perceive the
pictures, and accordingly to the imminent danger of an infinite regress (Dennett,
1969). There remain two schools of thought.

On the one hand, there are those who argue that an image is distinct from a propositional representation (Bugelski, 1970; Kosslyn and Pomerantz, 1977; Paivio, 1971, 1977; Shepard, 1975, 1978; Sloman, 1971). These authors attribute a variety of properties to images. The most important are as follows:

1. The brain processes underlying an image are similar to those underlying the perception of an object or picture.

2. An image is a coherent and integrated representation in which each element of a represented object occurs only once.

3. An image is amenable to apparently continuous mental transformations, such as rotations or expansions, in which intermediate states correspond to intermediate states or views of an actual object undergoing the same transformation. Hence, a small change in the image corresponds to a small change in the object or its appearance.

4. Images represent objects. They are <u>analogical</u> in that the structural relations between their parts correspond to those between the parts of the objects represented. There may indeed be an isomorphism between an image and an object, though this claim only makes sense with respect to an object viewed as decomposed into parts with particular relations between them.

On the other hand, there are theorists who argue that the subjective experience of an image is epiphenomenal and that its underlying representation is propositional in form (Anderson and Bower, 1973; Baylor, 1971; Kieras, 1978; Moran, 1973; Palmer, 1975; Pylyshyn, 1973). These authors attribute a variety of properties to propositional representations. The most important are as follows:

1. The brain processes underlying a propositional representation are similar to those underlying the perception of an object or picture; as Norman and Rumelhart (1975) remark, "the first stage of conscious awareness is already in the form of propositions."

2. The same element or part of an object may be referred to by many of the different propositions that constitute the description of the object. However, when propositions are represented in the form of a semantic network, then the representation can be thought of as coherent and integrated, with each element of the represented object occurring only once with all its relations to other elements readily accessible.

3. A propositional representation is discrete and digital rather than continuous. However, it can represent continuous processes by small successive increments of the relevant variable(s), such as the angle of an object's major axis to a frame of reference. Hence, a small change in the representation can correspond to a small change in the object.

4. Propositions are true or false of objects. Their representations are <u>abstract</u> in that they do not resemble either words or pictures, though they may be needed to provide an interlingua[1] between words and pictures (Chase and Clark, 1972). Their content carries the significant information about what they represent.

The critics of imagery often allow that an image can be constructed from its propositional description, but such an image does not introduce any new information, it merely makes the stored description more accessible and easier to manipulate. Gelernter's (1963) program for proving geometric theorems, and Funt's (1977) program for making inferences about the stability of arrangements of blocks, are both considerably enhanced by the use of procedures that operate on diagrammatic representations. However, Pylyshyn (1973) argues that picture-like representations are not necessary for such purposes: the same function can be served by propositional descriptions. This view has been pushed still further by Palmer (1975):

> The arguments in favor of analogical representations tend to emphasize the relative ease with which certain operations can be performed on them compared to the difficulty in performing the same operations on propositional representations. These arguments, however, generally overlook the fact that propositions can encode quantitative as well as qualitative information. In addition, it is not often recognized that propositions are capable of encoding an analog image.

Palmer then goes on to establish both a way in which a shape such as a triangle can be encoded propositionally and a method for rotating such representations once they have been decomposed into their propositional constituents.

Evidently, the two sorts of representation share a number of properties; they differ mainly on the fourth of the characteristics listed above, i.e. whether they represent objects or describe them. This apparent similarity and the view that they are readily transformed into one another has indeed led some commentators to conclude that the controversy is neither fundamental (Norman and Rumelhart, 1975) nor resolvable (Anderson, 1976, 1978). In particular, Anderson (1978) argues that "any claim for a particular representation is impossible to evaluate unless one specifies the processes that will operate on this representation." He shows that given certain assumptions a theory based on images can be mimicked by one based on propositions. As we shall see, however, there are some important exceptions to the principle.

3. THE SECOND CONTROVERSY: SEMANTIC DECOMPOSITION VERSUS MEANING POSTULATES

Semantic theorists are generally agreed that a major burden for the meanings of words is to account for the relation between such assertions as "Polly is a parrot" and "Polly is a bird". If the first assertion is true, then plainly, so is the second. There is a major disagreement between theorists about the nature of the semantic machinery needed to explain such relations. One school of thought, whose recent ancestry can be traced back to the work of Katz and Fodor (1963) -- though it has a much longer history reaching back into antiquity -- holds that the meaning of a word such as "parrot" is represented in the mental lexicon as a set of semantic elements that includes, amongst others, those corresponding to "bird". The relation between the two sentences is accordingly captured by the semantic primitives in the entries of the mental lexicon. A wide variety of psychological theories of meaning are committed to some sort of semantic primitives (Clark and Clark, 1977; Collins and Quillian, 1972; Miller and Johnson-Laird, 1976; Norman and Rumelhart, 1975; Schank, 1975; Smith, Shoben and Rips, 1974).

An alternative view is that there are no semantic primitives (Fodor, 1976; Fodor, 1977; Fodor, Fodor and Garrett, 1975; Kintsch, 1974; Lyons, 1977). Entailments that depend upon the meanings of words are, according to these theorists, captured by meaning postulates. A meaning postulate as formulated by Carnap (1956) is an assertion that stipulates the semantic relations between words of a language, generally a formal one, e.g. <u>for any x, if x is a parrot then x is a bird</u>. Such rules are introduced into a model-theoretic semantics of a language in order to render some models inadmissible, namely, those for which the meaning postulates are not true. Latterly, the idea has been cut loose from formal semantics and imported into psychological theory. Fodor <u>et al</u> (1975) assume that sentences in a natural language are translated into a corresponding mental language, and that meaning postulates couched in the mental vocabulary are used to make inferences from the translated sentences.

Although there have been attempts to resolve the controversy experimentally, the results so far are equivocal. There is evidence against the idea that comprehension depends on a process of semantic decomposition (Kintsch, 1974; Fodor <u>et al</u>, 1975); there is evidence against the idea that it depends on meaning postulates (Clark and Clark, 1977; Johnson-Laird, Gibbs, and de Mowbray, 1978). But, as yet, there are no results to resolve the issue of whether or not the mental representations of meaning depend on semantic primitives. Indeed, there has been a tendency to accept the view of Katz and Nagel (1974) that there is no fundamental distinction between semantic primitives and meaning postulates. There are, in fact, several arguments that could be made to establish a difference in their psychological plausibility. I shall present only one: it is the argument that will also resolve the controversy about images and propositions.

4. TRANSITIVITY IN EVERYDAY INFERENCE

My central thesis concerns simple inferences based on premises in ordinary language. Consider the following argument about a pencil, a box, and an envelope:

> The pencil is in the box.
>
> The box is in the envelope.
> ______________________________
>
> ∴ The pencil is in the envelope.

Is this inference valid? Before we can answer this question, it would be as well to remind ourselves that an inference is valid if it is impossible for its premises to be true and its conclusion false. Obviously, the present inference <u>is</u> valid since given that the premises are true, the conclusion must be true, too.

Meaning postulates provide an initially plausible basis for a psychological mechanism that makes such an inference. The premises are translated into a propositional representation, which according to Kintsch (1974) might take the following sort of form:

> (IN, PENCIL, BOX)
>
> (IN, BOX, ENVELOPE)

and then the meaning postulate that captures the transitivity of "in":

> For any x, y, z (If (IN, x, y) & (IN, y, z)) then (IN, x, z)

is applied to the representation of the premises to yield the conclusion:

> (IN, PENCIL, ENVELOPE).

And this propositional representation can, if necessary, be translated back into natural language.

Although the details of the various processes of translation have not been formulated explicitly by any theorist, they are not at issue as far as the present paper is concerned. Its argument applies to any processes that lead parsimoniously to propositional representations and to the application of meaning postulates to them. There is nothing privileged about meaning postulates here, they may be replaced by any rules of inference that apply to propositional representations.

The heart of my argument depends on the following sort of inference:

> Luke is on Mark's right.
>
> Mark is on Matthew's right.
> ______________________________
>
> ∴ Luke in on Matthew's right.

It is not immediately clear whether this inference is valid. If the three
individuals are sitting in a straight line on one side of a table, then the
relation denoted by "on X's right" is transitive, and the inference is valid. But
if they are sitting at equal intervals round a small circular table, then the
relation denoted by "on X's right" is not transitive, and the inference is
invalid.

A natural way to try to accommodate this phenomenon within the framework of a
propositional theory is to propose two different meanings for "on the right" and
its cognates, one to which a meaning postulate expressing transitivity applies,
and one to which a meaning postulate expressing intransitivity applies. Indeed,
only this manoeuvre will save the theory if it is to account for the way that
ordinary inferences are made and evaluated. However, if a number of people are
seated round a large circular table, then the previous inference could be valid,
but one might have doubts about the following one:

 John is on Luke's right.

 Luke in on Mark's right.

 Mark is on Matthew's right.
 ————————————————————

∴ John is on Matthew's right.

As more and more individuals are added round the table, there will inevitably come
a point where transitivity breaks down. (As a matter of fact, there is likely to
be a region of uncertainty, but this possibility merely exacerbates the problems
of a meaning postulate theory). In general, "on X's right" may denote an intransitive relation, or relations with a transitivity that varies over any number of
items from three to an arbitrarily large number. Each of these extents requires
its own separate meaning postulate with the number of premises in its antecedent
directly correlated with the number of items over which transitivity holds -- two
premises for transitivity over three items, three premises for transitivity over
four items, and so on ad infinitum. Because there is no limit to the number of
items at which transitivity ceases to hold, there is no limit to the number of
separate meaning postulates that are required to cope with the semantics of this
single relation. This conclusion is psychologically unacceptable on the reasonable criterion, decisive in other contexts (e.g. Miller and Chomsky, 1963), that
human beings do not have an unlimited capacity for learning or for storing
information.

It should be emphasized that these difficulties are not peculiar to "right" and
"left". English vocabulary is plagued by the same sorts of problem, and it is
hard to find any simple spatial term that has an unequivocal logic.

A proponent of meaning postulates might argue that once the transitivity of "on
the right" ranges over some large number of items, say, 100, then it can be taken
to have an unlimited extent. This ad hoc proposal has at least the virtue of
limiting the required meaning postulates to a finite number. Yet, it does not
solve the problem: no matter how large the radius of a circle and how densely the
individuals are packed around it, it is a circle and transitivity must break down.
Another way to save the meaning postulate theory is to assume that there is some
machinery for generating meaning postulates. However, this proposal highlights
another difficulty. It is clear that any feasible system will depend on some
mechanism for determining the nature of the situation referred to explicitly or
implicitly by the premises. In the case of our examples, it will depend on information about the table and the seating arrangements, which in turn will be used to
select the appropriate meaning postulate.

Once the need to deal with reference situations is admitted, a still more obvious,
though deliberate, gap in the meaning postulate theory of semantics becomes
apparent. It is again best illustrated by a simple example. Given the following

arrangement of letters:

       B   A

any competent speaker of English knows that it is true to say of them, "A is on
the right of B" and false to say of them, "A is on the left of B". This
distinction reflects the difference in meaning between "right" and "left"; yet,
there is no way to capture it using meaning postulates. One can, of course,
establish that there is a difference in meaning between the two terms, e.g. for
any x and y, x is on the right of y if and only if y is on the left of x, and for
any x and y, if x is on the right of y then x is not on the left of y. Such
postulates establish that a difference exists, but they do not specify its nature.
For that, it is necessary to make explicit what it is that underlies our knowledge
that A is indeed on the right of B in the example above.

The idea lying behind the psychological exploitation of meaning postulates, and
indeed most psychological theories of meaning, is that it is feasible to specify
the semantic relations between words without considering how they relate to the
world (see Johnson-Laird and Herrmann, 1983, for the implications of this
assumption for semantic network theory). Intensions can be profitably pursued
independently from extensions. The principle seems plausible for meaning
postulates in their original context of formal semantics, where the real world is
replaced by a model, or a set of models, in which the extensions of terms are
assigned directly. But the precedent is misleading for natural language where, as
we shall see, the only way to account for the proper relations between words, and
for inferences based upon them, is by giving a complete specification of their
meanings, including their relations to the world. What is deliberately missing in
the meaning postulate account is a definition of how "right" and "left" relate to
the world. The reason for this omission is obvious: the relations are so basic
that there is no way to define them in ordinary English. It is for this reason
that a complete theory of meaning must rely upon some more primitive notions.

Is it possible to save a propositional theory by sacrificing meaning postulates?
The answer depends, of course, on what processes are used to make inferences in
their stead. Any system that relies on rules that manipulate propositions will
have to introduce some machinery to handle transitive relations, and hence it will
be in imminent danger of falling into precisely the same difficulties. The only
escape route will be a method for handling the facts of transitivity without
relying on rules, postulates, or productions, for transitivity itself. This
prescription may seem to be impossible to fulfil; fortunately, there is at least
one way in which it can be met.

5. PROCEDURAL SEMANTICS AND A PROGRAM FOR SPATIAL INFERENCE

The definitions of spatial terms and the uncertainties of their transitivity can
be accommodated within a theory based on a "procedural semantics" (see Davies and
Isard, 1972; Johnson-Laird, 1977, 1983; Miller and Johnson-Laird, 1976; Woods,
1981). The theory can be illustrated by considering a computer program (written
in the list-processing language, POP-10) that I have devised in order to model a
theory of spatial inference. The purpose of the program is to evaluate premises
about the spatial relations between objects. It works by building up a model in
the form of a two-dimensional array that satisfies the premises given to it, and
indicates whether a premise is implied by, or is inconsistent with, what it has
already been told. It accordingly contains a number of general procedures for
constructing, recursively manipulating, and interrogating, sets of arrays. One
such procedure, for instance, given the location in an array of one item mentioned
in a premise, inserts the other item into the array at a place that is appropriate
according to the meaning of the premise. Another general procedure is used to
verify whether the relation specified to hold between two items, say, A and B,
obtains within an array. It works by locating B and then by scanning along a line
from B in order to determine whether or not A is somewhere on that line. If A is

found to lie on the line then the premise is true, otherwise it is false. The verification procedure contains two parameters, DI and DJ, whose values specify the direction in which to scan: they give the respective increments on the two axes of the array that define the locations to be examined. This use of parameters to specify directions is common to all the general procedures used by the program, including those for inserting new items into an array. This uniformity makes it possible to define the meanings of relational terms as procedures that work in a way that is utterly remote from meaning postulates and conventional decompositional theories (e.g. Norman and Rumelhart, 1975; Schank, 1975; Smith, Shoben and Rips 1974).

The meaning of "on the right of" consists of a single procedure: FUNCT(% 0, 1 %). This takes whatever general procedure is about to be executed, and which has been assigned as the value of the variable, FUNCT, and "freezes in" the value of 0 to its DI parameter and the value of 1 to its DJ parameter. The decorated parentheses are a standard device in POP-10 for freezing in the values of parameters, with the effect of converting a general procedure into a new more specific one. The effect of FUNCT(% 0, 1 %) on the verification procedure is accordingly to produce a more specific procedure that scans a sequence of locations lying in a particular orientation: the value of one axis is held constant (i.e. incremented by 0) while the value of the other axis is progressively incremented by 1. In other words, if you imagine the array laid out on a table in front of you, the procedure examines a sequence of locations lying progressively further to the right of B. It looks to see whether A is on the right of B. The same process of freezing in the values of parameters is used to convert the program's other general procedures into specific ones that depend on the relation specified in a premise.

The program's lexical entries define how words relate to its world; but they stipulate nothing about transitivity or intransitivity. However, a relation such as "on the right of" has the emergent property of transitivity, that is to say, whenever A is on the right of B and B is on the right of C, then as a matter of fact A will be on the right of C, whether the program is building, manipulating, or interpreting an array. The program can accordingly make transitive inferences even though it contains no rules, postulates, or productions, for transitivity itself. This facility depends on the use of spatial models and procedural definitions that relate directly to them. The definitions express meanings in terms of the primitive components of specific coordinate values that are only interpretable with respect to the spatial arrays. The meaning of a word is accordingly not a procedure that can do anything by itself; it is a procedure that applies to other procedures.

Several theorists have claimed that the apparatus of spatial arrays smuggles in the principle of transitivity by the back door. (Both Jerry Fodor and Zenon Pylyshyn have independently made this suggestion in conversation, though it would be wrong to saddle them with a strong commitment to it). Its plausibility rests on its confusability with a very different claim, namely, that it is possible to define transitive relations over spatial models. Obviously, this condition must hold if a transitive relation is to be represented in a spatial array. Spatial arrays, however, do not have transitivity built into them: if they did, they would be unable to represent intransitive relations, or relations that are transitive to varying degrees. Indeed, if the locus of the individuals in a reference situation is circular rather than rectilinear, then the same lexical entries used in relation to the frame of reference that each individual defines give rise to local transitivity, but sooner or later it breaks down as the individuals depart further and further from the required sequence of locations passing through the initial one in the series. Hence, with the introduction of procedures for representing an individual's frame of reference and the spatial arrangement, it will be possible to deal with the vagaries of transitivity without having to postulate an indefinitely large number of different meanings for a relational term. A single entry in the lexicon will suffice.

The use of meaning postulates to make spatial inferences places an unacceptable demand on the storage capacity of human memory: it becomes necessary to store a vast number of postulates just to cope with the meaning of a single relational term. Semantic primitives, however, do the job parsimoniously. The controversy over semantic primitives and meaning postulates is accordingly resolved: meaning postulates must be replaced by semantic primitives that relate words to mental models of the world. There is no need to suppose, however, that comprehension calls for a process of decomposition into semantic primitives: they play a direct role in the tacit construction of mental models.

6. MENTAL MODELS

The notion of a mental model, which was introduced in the previous section, is to be distinguished from the current conception of an image. It shares the crucial property that its structure represents information, but this structure need not necessarily possess any immediately 'pictorial' features. Of course, a mental model might combine both pictorial and non-pictorial information, such as a spatial array that represents the positions of chess pieces and, by a further convention, the tactical relations between them (cf. Simon and Barenfeld, 1969). But a mental model can also be entirely schematic in that only its topological properties are relevant to the processes that interpret it. This idea can be difficult to grasp, and it is best explained in terms of a recent theory of syllogistic inference and the interpretation of quantified sentences (Johnson-Laird, 1983; Johnson-Laird and Bara, 1983).

According to the theory, a statement about, say, a set of people in a room, such as:

> Some of the scientists are drivers

is mentally represented by a model in which an arbitrary number of elements stand for the relevant set of scientists, and a subset of them are linked to other elements standing for drivers:

$$s = d$$
$$s = d$$
$$(s) \quad (d)$$

Here, each <u>s</u> represents a scientist, each <u>d</u> represents a driver, and the arbitrary number of <u>parenthesized</u> elements indicate that there may be scientists who are not drivers and <u>vice versa</u>. The identity signs denote an identity between the entities that they link.

In order to make an inference, as opposed to evaluating a given conclusion, it is necessary to possess a heuristic, because logical principles alone can never determine which of the potentially infinite number of valid, though mainly trivial, conclusions should be drawn from a set of premises. Unfortunately, this point has often been overlooked in psychological theories of reasoning (e.g. Inhelder and Piaget, 1958, 1964) and in theories based on meaning postulates. The theory of mental models lends itself naturally to heuristics for drawing inform- ative conclusions (see Johnson-Laird, 1983). In the case of relational infer- ences, which include syllogisms, these heuristics reduce to a simple principle: try to form connections that link up end items by way of middle items. Thus, given the premises:

> Some of the scientists are drivers
>
> All the musicians are drivers

the heuristic yields the following combined model:

$$s = d = m$$
$$s = d = m$$
$$(s)\ (d)$$

where each $\underline{m}$ represents a musician. It will be easy to trace through the links to derive the $\overline{\text{conclusion}}$:

Some of the scientists are musicians

or its converse:

Some of the musicians are scientists

The heuristic has, of course, led one into error, though it is an error that many subjects make (Johnson-Laird and Steedman, 1978). In order to guarantee that a conclusion is valid, an attempt should be made to find an alternative model that falsifies it: only if there is no such model is the conclusion valid. In the case of the example, there is an alternative model that falsifies the conclusions:

$$s = d$$
$$s = d$$
$$(s)\quad d = m$$
$$d = m$$

Mental models of syllogisms are analogical in a crucial way: sets of entities are represented by sets of mental tokens, and relations between entities are represented by relations between the tokens in the model. Hence, a model unlike an image may contain no 'pictorial' information, though many models may take the form of images. The theory does indeed account for performance in syllogistic reasoning (see Johnson-Laird and Steedman, 1978; Johnson-Laird and Bara, 1983), and it does so, like the treatment of transitivity above, without postulating rules of inference. Hence, the theory answers two hitherto embarrassing questions: how children acquire rules of quantified inference, and why adults have no introspective access to them. The answers are simply that no rules of inference are learnt in childhood, and that there is no mental logic. These claims may seem paradoxical, but the paradox disappears once one realizes that the process of testing a conclusion by searching for counterexamples may well be carried out in a haphazard manner -- the process is radically different to the quasi-syntactic manipulation of propositional representations by rules of inference. Nevertheless, if the search for alternative models is carried out accurately, then any conclusions that survive unscathed are logically valid. The logicians who first formulated rules of inference may have relied in part on reflections about the invariant properties of their own mental manipulations of models.

7. MIMICKING THEORIES

Procedural definitions couched for the construction of mental models solve the problem of transitivity. But, how does this solution stand in relation to Anderson's (1976, 1978) proof that one representational theory can be mimicked by another provided that there is a one-to-one mapping between their respective representations? Could one not resolve the controversy about images and propositions by showing that mental models can be translated into a propositional theory? The two questions are intimately related, and in order to answer them we must consider Anderson's theorem in detail.

His argument is intended to establish that given a theory which embodies assumptions about mental representations and processes, it is possible, in principle, to construct other theories with different sorts of representations that nevertheless mimic the original theory by behaving in an equivalent manner. In fact, 'mimicry' is not the right word to describe Anderson's manoeuvre: rather the second theory invades the first and takes it over like a virus taking over an organism's machinery for producing DNA. Suppose, for instance, that one wishes to show that with suitable mental operations, a propositional theory can mimic an imaginal theory. The trick is to embed the whole of the imaginal theory within the operations carried out on the propositional representations. The imaginal theory assumes, say, that a stimulus is encoded as an image, which can be mentally rotated in order to determine whether it coincides with another stimulus. The propositional theory assumes only that a stimulus is encoded as a set of propositions. The imaginal theory is embedded within the propositional theory by the following sequence of operations applied to the propositional representation of the stimulus:

1.   Apply the inverse of the propositional encoding to the set of propositions in order to recover the original 'stimulus' (i.e. sensory image).

2.   Apply the imaginal encoding to the stimulus in order to obtain the corresponding image.

3.   Rotate the image.

4.   Apply the inverse of the imaginal encoding to the rotated image in order to obtain the corresponding stimulus.

5.   Apply the propositional encoding to the stimulus in order to obtain the set of propositions corresponding to the rotated image.

The decision about whether these propositions match the second stimulus can again, if necessary, rely on the imaginal theory:

6.   Apply the inverse of the propositional encoding in order to obtain the stimulus corresponding to the rotated image.
      (This stimulus is, of course, identical to the one obtained in step 4.).

7.   Apply the imaginal encoding to the stimulus to obtain the corresponding image. (This image is identical to the one obtained from step 3.).

8.   Compare the image to the one obtained from the second stimulus, and make the appropriate response.

Although this chain of operations can be postulated, its feasibility depends on two crucial conditions. First, the various functions must be computable. Second, it must be possible to apply the inverse of the propositional encoding to obtain the original stimulus, or, more plausibly, a sensory representation isomorphic to the original stimulus. However, since perception is likely to involve a many-one mapping, the inverse will not be a function since there will be many stimuli that it could produce. It is for this reason that Anderson imposes the condition that there must be a one-to-one mapping between the respective representations of the two theories. Granted this condition, the inverse of the propositional encoding can yield any of the stimuli that could have given rise to the original set of propositions, and it will not matter which stimulus is selected, because they will all be equivalent for the imaginal theory, too.

That a propositional theory can mimic an imaginal theory by importing wholesale the apparatus of images is plainly a trivial result. What is of interest is the possibility of a more direct method of mimicry that does not depend upon embedding one theory within another. Unfortunately, there is no guarantee that a direct method can always be found for two alternative representational theories. Anderson makes only the modest claim: "...it seems we can usually construct [the required operation] more simply than its formally guaranteed specification".

Moreover, if one theory encodes stimuli into classes that do not correspond one-to-one with the encodings of the other theory, then the whole system of mappings breaks down and the theorem ceases to hold.

Considerable care needs to be exercized in drawing conclusions on the basis of Anderson's theorem. He himself (Anderson, 1976, p.74) makes the following claim:

> Any behavior that can be computed from inspecting semantic primitives can be computed with the aid of 'meaning postulates' that interpret more complex semantic units. This follows from the theorem ... that any representation can mimic the behavior of any other, provided they impose the same equivalence class on their inputs.

The first assertion has, of course, proved to be false: meaning postulates cannot handle the vagaries of transitivity, but lexical entries based on procedural primitives can accommodate them. On the assumption that Anderson's theorem is sound, it follows that the two sorts of theory do not impose the same equivalence classes on their inputs. And this conclusion is clinched by considering sentences of the form: "A is in front of B, which is behind C". The sentence is unambiguous[2] and should accordingly receive a single propositional representation, but it is referentially indeterminate -- the relation between A and C is unspecified -- and can accordingly be represented by at least two different mental models. This distinction drives a wedge between sets of propositions and mental models that is not easily removed.

It might be supposed that the propositional representation could mimic the model representation, and yield two alternatives: one in which A is in front of C, and one in which C is in front of A. But, before such alternatives could be specified, it would be necessary to detect the indeterminacy in the first place. In general, a scheme for detection would have to be able to infer that the relation between certain items in a propositional representation was indeterminate. Unfortunately, this requirement leads straight back to the problems of transitivity: whether the relation between certain items is determinate or indeterminate may depend entirely on whether a transitive inference is valid or invalid. Since no finite system of rules based on a propositional representation can handle this problem, it follows that no such system can detect indeterminacies, or <u>a fortiori</u> set up alternative representations when they occur. Hence, a theory of propositional representation does not yield the same equivalence class of representations as the class yielded by the theory of mental models. The wedge remains securely in place.

Strangely enough, a major critic of imagery theories has made a related point. Pylyshyn (1973) wrote:

> It would be quite permissible ... to have a [propositional] mental representation of two objects with a relation between them such as 'besides'. Such a representation need not contain a more specific spatial relation such as 'to the left of' or 'to the right of'. It would seem an unreasonable use of the word 'image' to speak of an image of two objects side by side, without the relation between them being either 'to the left of' or 'to the right of'.

This point has empirical consquences. Mani and Johnson-Laird (1982) showed experimentally that spatial descriptions can be mentally represented either by models or by sets of propositions. When subjects formed a model of a description, they often reported that they had used imagery. Hence, the controversy is resolved: images and models can be distinguished both theoretically and empirically from propositional representations.

8. LEVELS OF DESCRIPTION

Is it really true that images are not equivalent to sets of propositions? That was the conclusion of the previous section, but doubtless it will be resisted by propositional theorists. There is one way in which they can sustain their objection, but only at the cost of trivializing the whole controversy. It all depends upon a source of much confusion in theoretical discussions, the level at which a particular theory is described. The issues can be illustrated by considering the problem of how to characterize the computer program that embodies the theory of spatial inference.

One approach is that since the program must ultimately be translated into the machine language of a computer before it can be run, we should concern ourselves with what the machine language instructions cause to happen in the machine -- the shifting of bits from one location in store to another, and so on. But this approach is misguided: the details of a specific implementation should not concern us. We should not worry about the particular computer and its machine code, since the program could be executed on some very different machines, and we do not want to make a separate characterization of the program for all these different sorts of computer. An alternative approach is provided by Scott and Strachey (1971), the pioneers of formal semantics for computing languages:

> Compilers of high-level languages are generally constructed to give the complete translation of the programs into machine language. As machines merely juggle bit patterns, the concepts of the original language may be lost or at least obscured during this passage. The purpose of mathematical semantics is to give a correct and meaningful correspondence between programs and mathematical entities in a way that is entirely independent of an implementation.

There is a very important analogy for psychologists here: psychology (the study of the algorithms) can be pursued independently from neurophysiology (the study of the machine and the machine code). The argument also provides a useful antidote to the excessive scepticism that can be induced by theorems demonstrating how one sort of representational theory can be mimicked by another. In order to try to substantiate this claim, and to clear up the confusion over levels of description, let us continue the characterization of the spatial inference program.

"It works by building up a two-dimensional array that satisfies the premises given to it." This description of the program is informal but at a high level, the level of psychological discourse. You may wonder how exactly an array is represented by the programming language. It is, in fact, a data structure of one or more dimensions in which the elements can be accessed and updated by giving appropriate coordinates. (An array is also a function in POP-10, which permits it to be represented by a rule rather than an explicit table). A programmer needs to know no more, since procedures for manipulating arrays can be written simply by thinking of them as n-dimensional spaces where each location is specified by an n-tuple of integers. A student of the 'psychology' of computers, however, may be curious about the invisible machinery that makes such an array possible. Its representation in the computer does not involve an actual physical array of locations in memory. That is quite unnecessary. Indeed, the physical embodiment of an array is irrelevant. What matters is that it should <u>function</u> as an array, that is, it has a set of addresses that are functionally equivalent to an array, its elements can be accessed as in an array, and its contents displayed or printed out in the form of an array. A psychological description should accordingly be a functional one.

Consider a program for spatial inference in which an assertion such as, "A is on the right of B" is represented by the following formulae: AT(A,1,6), AT(B,1,2) where the first integer in each pair gives the y-coordinate and the second integer gives the x-coordinate of the relevant item. The general procedure for verification works by looking for sequences of ordered pairs of integers as parts of such formulae. In order to verify the assertion, "C is on the right of B", it starts with B and its associated pair (1,2), and then looks for formulae corresponding to the sequence: (1,3), (1,4), (1,5) ... up to some arbitrary number. If the program finds C associated with a pair of integers in the series, then the assertion is true; otherwise, it is false. The series is defined by the procedure representing "on the right of", which freezes in the appropriate values for the incremental parameters of the verification procedure.

It should be clear that the whole of the original theory of spatial inference can be reconstructed in this way, even to the extent of coping with the problems of transitivity. Indeed, many adherents of propositional theories may wish to claim that a propositional theory of spatial inference has here been constructed that counters all the earlier criticisms. They would be wrong, but in a way that is most instructive. The construction of the new propositional theory of spatial inference is in reality simply a reconstruction of the original mental model theory at a lower level of description. The whole of the propositional apparatus, the ordered pairs of integers, the definition of "on the right of" in terms of incremental values of parameters, is parasitic upon the unacknowledged presence of a spatial array. Perhaps it is easiest to grasp this point by asking oneself how such a system could have been set up in the first place, how it could have been learnt, and where the definition of "on the right of" could have come from. The program functions as though it uses an array, and one seen from a particular viewpoint, too.

In general, a model is only a model at a certain level of description: that level at which it functions as one. A listing of the original spatial inference program in machine code is a level of description that obscures the program's use of models. The new 'propositional' theory is similarly a redescription of the old theory at a level that obscures its reliance on models; it is a description that could well pass as a slightly more detailed account of how to set up and manipulate arrays in a certain programming language.

There is, of course, nothing inconsistent about calling such a redescription a propositional theory. It would certainly resolve the controversy in favour of the propositional theorists, but it would do so in an entirely trivial way, for it would entail that any plausible theory of any psychological phenomenon is propositional. The conclusion follows from the fact that any theory which meets the reasonable criterion of being an 'effective procedure' can in turn be described by a set of propositions that determine, from moment to moment, precisely how the system should behave. The notion of proposition is here somewhat vague, and can be replaced by the much more precise notion of a Turing machine (see Minsky, 1967, p.106 et seq). To characterize a theory as propositional would accordingly be to say nothing of any empirical consequence: it would be equivalent to saying that a theory could be instantiated as a Turing machine. It is unclear whether those who advocate a propositional representation for images intend to make so trivial a point; certainly, they have not made a direct appeal to the notion of an effective procedure. What is noteworthy, however, is that they have freely introduced propositions expressing polar coordinates, vectors, and other spatial matters. Such concepts can obviously be expressed in the scientific meta-language, but there is no corresponding terminology for them in the object language -- the language of simple shapes that is under analysis. If the term "propositional" is to have any empirical content, then the following conclusion can be drawn: what a theorist constructs in such cases is, not a propositional theory, but a reconstruction of an imaginal theory at a lower level of description.

The term "propositional" has a perfectly good sense that we have already encountered, and one that makes a sensible contrast with the term, "model". This sense concerns theories of semantics. A characteristic feature of many semantic theories is that the terms of the vocabulary in which they encode propositions are closely related to the vocabulary of natural language. This feature, which may be

fortuitous, has been elevated into a theoretical principle by Fodor et al (1975).
They propose that "to each morpheme of the surface vocabulary of a natural
language there corresponds a primitive expression in the vocabulary of the
representational system", and that "meaning postulates mediate whatever entailment
relations between sentences turn upon their lexical content". Representations of
this sort are truly propositional, and they are distinct from representations
based on models, because the vocabulary of a propositional representation does not
now allow the use of procedures that depend upon semantic primitives for which
there are no readily available terms in the language under analysis. The contrast
between the two sorts of representation is important, and the present resolution
of the controversy about them establishes the need for both mental models and
propositional representations. Human beings have recourse to representations of
both sorts.

9. THE FORMS OF MENTAL REPRESENTATION

Three different sorts of representation have been discussed in this paper:
images, propositions, and models. Since the lines of demarcation between them may
seem to be vague, I want finally to try to draw some finer distinctions.

What is a propositional representation? The answer obviously depends on what a
proposition is. One view, which has much to recommend it, is a generalization of
the commonplace notion that to understand a proposition is to know what the world
would have to be like for it to be true. If we consider all the different ways in
which the world might be, as well as the way it actually is, that is, the set of
all 'possible worlds', then a proposition is, in principle, either true or else
false of each member of the set. Hence, we can treat a proposition as a function
from the set of possible worlds onto the set of truth values.[3] A logician might,
in turn, treat this function as a set of ordered pairs, each comprising a possible
world and a truth value (of the proposition in that world), but this conception is
highly abstract since the set of possible worlds is plainly infinite.

If a proposition is a function, then its representation is the representation of a
function. The way to represent a function is to express it in a language, and, as
Fodor et al (1975) have argued, it is useful to think of a propositional representation as an expression in a mental language. Although we may never delineate
the details of the mental language, we do know that it must have both a syntax and
a semantics (Fodor, 1976). It must be capable, for example, of representing
conjunction, and its mental syntax could take a variety of forms, e.g. "$(\alpha K \beta)$",
"$K(\alpha,\beta)$" or "$(\alpha,\beta)K$", where the Greek letters range over representations of
propositions, and "K" stands for some mental token representing conjunction. The
syntax is free to take any form provided it is associated with the appropriate
semantics.

The propositional description of a complicated object may well consist of a large
number of propositions. The question arises as to the nature of the structural
relations between them. In fact, one paradigm case of a propositional representation is simply an unordered set of expressions in some symbolic language such as
the predicate calculus. There are uniform proof procedures that will evaluate
inferences made in such a formalism; they rely in part on procedures that will
search the set for any particular atomic proposition, examining complex propositions to check whether it is a constituent of them. One might (just) imagine
that such a system could pass as a possible psychological theory with the addition
of a heuristic for making inferences. However, advocates of propositional
theories have almost invariably relied on some sort of semantic network (see
Anderson, 1976, 1978; Anderson and Bower, 1973; Baylor, 1971; Kintsch, 1974;
Moran, 1973; Norman and Rumelhart, 1975; Palmer, 1975). In a network, propositions about the same entity are gathered together and attached to the single
node for that entity. The structure facilitates the processes that encode or
retrieve information: it does not have an essential analogical role, since its
effect could as well be achieved in unstructured formulae by referential indices

that symbolize co-reference.

Mental models have a completely analogical structure. The way in which they contrast with propositional representations is clearest in relation to quantified assertions. Quantifiers, in fact, present a major problem for propositional representations. Even in the guise of semantic networks, propositional representations rely on the methods of formal logic (see Woods, 1975; Hendrix, 1979). One snag with all of them is that they do not readily account for the systematic biases and errors that occur in everyday reasoning. A further, more technical, difficulty is the possibility -- strongly urged by Hintikka (1974) -- that the semantics of natural language quantifiers is very much richer than is often supposed, and outstrips the strictly linear representations made available by standard quantification theory. Mental models solve both of these difficulties. They accommodate numerical and quasi-numerical quantifiers such as "most", "many", and "few". Likewise, they can represent discourse in general and account for the use and interpretation of anaphoric expressions (see Johnson-Laird, 1983).

The reason why mental models are so readily generalizable should be obvious: they assume, not an abstract propositional representation of statements, but one that mirrors the relevant aspects of a real state of affairs that would satisfy the statements. Thus, they use elements to stand for individuals, and links to stand for identities between them. But, they possess one other feature that distinguishes them from propositional representations. They represent a set of entities by introducing an _arbitrary_ number of elements that denote exemplary members of the set. Propositional representations of the sort proposed by Fodor _et al_ (1975) do not contain arbitrary features, whereas models ordinarily do so. Images share this property, too, which has often drawn comment from philosophers. You cannot form an image of _a triangle in general_, but only of a specific triangle. Hence, if you reason on the basis of a model or image, you must take pains to ensure that your conclusion goes beyond the specific instance you considered (see e.g. Hume 1896, vol. 1). The heuristic advantage of a model is balanced by the need for procedures that test the conclusions that can be derived from it -- a point that is borne out by the way in which the models for quantified assertions and spatial relations have to be manipulated in order to ensure validity. There must be recursive procedures that can revise models in order to correct assumptions that turn out to have been mistaken (see Johnson-Laird, 1983).

Of course models can have a richer analogical structure than those required for quantifiers. They may be two- or three-dimensional; they may be dynamic; they may take on an even higher number of dimensions in the case of certain gifted individuals. One advantage of their dimensional structure is that they can be scanned in any direction, regular or irregular, since the dimensional variables controlling the search can be determined from moment to moment by any mentally computable function. In the case of a propositional representation, as Simon (1972) points out, direct scanning can be performed only in those directions that have been encoded in the representation.

Models and propositions are interesting to compare on the criterion of economy. On the one hand, if a series of assertions are highly indeterminate, and one is not required to draw any profound inferences from them, it may be more economical to remember the propositions that were asserted rather than to interpret them in the form of a model. There is certainly a limit to the extent that human beings can manipulate models in order to ensure validity, and even certain syllogisms are taxing for this reason. The most plausible theory of comprehension accordingly calls for two stages: firstly, the utterance is translated into a propositional representation, which takes the form of a superficial linguistic representation that encodes _verbatim_ information; secondly, and optionally, the propositional representation is used as the input to a procedural semantics which uses it, together with inferences from general knowledge, to construct a mental model. At the heart of the theory lies the following idea: mental models represent the extensions of assertions, i.e. the situations they describe, and the superficial

linguistic representations, together with the recursive machinery for constructing
and revising models, represent the intensions of assertions, i.e. the sets of all
possible situations that they could describe. This theory and the evidence that
supports it is described in detail in Johnson-Laird (1983).

If the possession of arbitrary components and an analogical structure distinguishes models from propositions, then what is it that distinguishes models from
images? It seems likely that models are the basis of images, which simply
correspond to those features of them that are directly perceptible in the
equivalent real-world objects. An image may simply be a projection of a three-
dimensional mental model onto an internalized two-dimensional surface, thus giving
rise to a 'view' of the model from a particular standpoint. Conversely, models
may underlie thought processes without necessarily emerging into consciousness in
the form of images. Models are also likely to underlie the perception of objects
by providing prototypical information about them (see Roberts, 1965) in a form
that can be directly used in the interpretation of what Marr (1976) has referred
to as 'the primal sketch', the output of lower level visual processes.

10. CONCLUSIONS

To return to the two controversies with which I began, if the concept of a
proposition has any empirical force, then there are indeed distinctions to be
drawn between a set of propositions and a model or its perceptible counterpart, an
image:

1.   A model represents an object or a set of assertions analogically: its
     structure is constrained and is a crucial part of the representation. A
     propositional representation describes an object and corresponds to the
     linguistic structure of a set of assertions.

2.   A model based on a linguistic description embodies a number of arbitrary
     assumptions since language is inherently vague but models must be
     determinate. A propositional representation does not contain any arbitrary
     elements. The two sorts of representation accordingly do not have the same
     equivalence classes, and hence there is no guarantee that a theory based on
     one sort of representation can be made to mimic one based the other sort.

3.   A model represented in a dimensional space can be directly constructed,
     manipulated, or scanned, in any way that can be controlled by dimensional
     variables. A propositional representation lacks this flexibility and can be
     directly scanned only in those directions that have been laid down between
     the elements of the representation.

There are likewise distinctions to be drawn between semantic primitives and
meaning postulates:

1.   Semantic primitives are required by the semantic system that establishes a
     word's relation to the world, or strictly speaking to models of the world.
     Meaning postulates are neither intended to perform this function nor contain
     any machinery for defining truth conditions.

2.   The logical properties of a term need not be specified within the definitions
     of its truth conditions, rather they are emergent properties of that
     definition. Meaning postulates, however, are rules that explicitly specify
     the logical properties of terms, and the logical relations between them.

3.   Semantic primitives are ineffable in that there are no corresponding lexical
     items for them in the language under analysis. Meaning postulates in their
     psychological guise require a mental language that can be mapped virtually
     one-to-one onto the natural language.

What I have argued in this paper is that comprehension at its deepest level calls
for an initial propositional representation and the construction of a mental
model, which may take the form of an image of the state of affairs described in
the discourse. The process of constructing a mental model depends on a
representation of meaning that makes use of semantic primitives. Such a theory,
unlike one based solely on propositional representations and meaning postulates,
can cope with the logical vagaries of natural language. It can also account for
performance in a variety of inferential tasks. It does not follow that all
interpretations consist of mental models: no case has been presented against the
use of other forms of representation or rules of inference in other contexts.
However, if human beings habitually used only propositional representations and
meaning postulates, vagaries in the logical properties of language could never
have arisen in the first place.

REFERENCES

Anderson, J.R., Language, memory and thought. (Hillsdale, N.J., Erlbaum, 1976).
Anderson, J.R., Arguments concerning representations for mental imagery.
     Psychological Review, 85, (1978) 249-277.
Anderson, J.R., and Bower, G.H., Human associative memory. (New York, V.H.
     Winston & Sons, 1973).
Baylor, G.W., Programs and protocol analysis on a mental imagery task. First
     International Joint Conference on Artificial Intelligence, 1971.
Bower, G.H., Mental imagery and associative learning. In L. Gregg (ed.),
     Cognition in learning and memory. (New York, Wiley, 1972).
Brooks, L., The suppression of visualization by reading. Quarterly Journal of
     Experimental Psychology, 19, (1967) 280-299.
Bugelski, B.R., Words and things and images. American Psychologist, 25, (1970),
     1002-1012.
Byrne, B., Item concreteness vs. spatial organization. Memory and Cognition, 2,
     (1974), 53-59.
Carnap, R., Meaning and necessity: a study in semantics and modal logic. Second
     edition. (Chicago, University of Chicago Press, 1956).
Chase, W.G. and Clark, H.H., Mental operations in the comparison of sentences and
     pictures. In L.W.Gregg (ed.), Cognition in learning and memory. (New York,
     Wiley, 1972).
Clark, H.H. and Clark, E.V., Psychology and language: an introduction to psycho-
     linguistics. (New York, Harcourt Brace Jovanovich, 1977).
Collins, A.M. and Quillian, M.R., Experiments on semantic memory and language
     comprehension. In L.W. Gregg (ed.), Cognition in learning and memory. (New
     York, Wiley, 1972).
Cooper, L.A., Mental rotation of random two-dimensional shapes. Cognitive
     Psychology, 7, (1975), 20-43.
Davies, D.J.M. and Isard, S.D., Utterances as programs. In D. Michie (ed.),
     Machine Intelligence, 7. (Edinburgh, Edinburgh University Press, 1972).
Dennett, D.C., Content and consciousness. (New York, Humanities Press, 1969).
Fodor, J.A., The language of thought. (Hassocks, Sussex, Harvester Press, 1976).
Fodor, J.D., Semantics: theories of meaning in generative grammar. (Hassocks,
     Sussex, Harvester Press, 1977).
Fodor, J.D., Fodor, J.A., and Garrett, M.F., The psychological unreality of
     semantic representations. Linguistic Inquiry, 4, (1975), 515-531.
Funt, B.V., WHISPER: a problem-solving system utilizing diagrams. Fifth
     International Joint Conference on Artificial Intelligence, (1977), 459-464.
Galton, F., Inquiries into human faculty and its development. (London, Dent,
     1928, originally published 1880).
Gelernter, H., Realization of a geometry-theorem proving machine. In E.A.
     Feigenbaum and J. Feldman (ed.), Computers and thought. (New York, McGraw-
     Hill, 1963).
Hayes, J.R. On the function of visual imagery in elementary mathematics. In W.G.
     Chase (ed.), Visual information processing. New York: Academic Press, 1973.

Hendrix, G.G., Encoding knowledge in partitioned networks. In N.V. Findler (ed.)
    Associative networks: Representation and use of knowledge by computers.
    (New York, Holt, Rinehart, and Winston 1979).
Hintikka, J., Quantifiers vs. quantification theory. Linguistic Inquiry, 5,
    (1974), 153-177.
Holyoak, K.J., The form of analog size information in memory. Cognitive
    Psychology, 9, (1979), 31-51.
Hume, D., A treatise of human nature. Vol. I. Edited by L.A. Selby-Bigge.
    (Oxford, Clarendon, 1896).
Inhelder, B. and Piaget, J., The growth of logical thinking from childhood to
    adolescence: an essay on the construction of formal operational structure.
    (London: Routledge and Kegan Paul 1958).
Inhelder, B. and Piaget, J., The early growth of logic in the child: classifi-
    cation and seriation. (London, Routledge and Kegan Paul, 1964).
Johnson-Laird, P.N., Procedural semantics. Cognition, 5, (1977), 189-214.
Johnson-Laird, P.N., Mental Models: Towards a Cognitive Science of Language,
    Inference and Consciousness. (Cambridge, Cambridge University Press.
    Cambridge, Mass., Harvard University Press, 1983).
Johnson-Laird, P.N. and Bara, B., Syllogistic inference. Mimeo, MRC Applied
    Psychology Unit, 1983.
Johnson-Laird, P.N. and Steedman, M.J., The psychology of syllogisms. Cognitive
    Psychology, 10, (1978), 64-99.
Johnson-Laird, P.N., Gibbs, G. and de Mowbray, J. Meaning, amount of processing,
    and memory for words. Memory and Cognition, 6, (1978), 372-375.
Johnson-Laird, P.N., and Herrmann, D.J. Only connections: a critique of semantic
    networks. Mimeo, MRC Applied Psychology Unit, 1983.
Katz, J.J. and Fodor, J.A., The structure of a semantic theory. Language, 39,
    (1963), 170-210.
Katz, J.J. and Nagel, R., Meaning postulates and semantic theory. Foundations of
    Language, 2, (1974) 311-340.
Kieras, D., Beyond pictures and words: alternative information-processing models
    for imagery effects in verbal memory. Psychological Bulletin, 85, (1978),
    532-554.
Kintsch, W., The representation of meaning in memory. (Hillsdale, N.J., Erlbaum,
    1974).
Kosslyn, S.M., Information representation in visual images. Cognitive Psychology,
    7, (1975), 341-370.
Kosslyn, S.M., Images and Mind. (Cambridge, Mass., Harvard University Press,
    1980).
Kosslyn, S.M. and Pomerantz, J.R., Imagery, propositions, and the form of internal
    representations. Cognitive Psychology, 9, (1977), 52-76.
Lewis, D., General semantics. In D. Davidson, and G. Harman (eds.), Semantics of
    natural language. (Dordrecht, Reidel, 1972).
Lyons, J. Semantics, Vols. 1 and 2. (Cambridge, Cambridge University Press,
    1977).
Mani, K., and Johnson-Laird, The mental representation of spatial descriptions.
    Memory and Cognition, 10, (1982), 181-187.
Marr, D. Early processing of visual information. Philosophical Transactions of
    the Royal Society of London, Series B, 275, (1976), 483-519.
Miller, G.A. and Chomsky, N., Finitary models of language users. In Luce, R.D.,
    Bush, R.R. and Galanter, E. (eds.), Handbook of mathematical psychology, vol.
    II., (New York, Wiley, 1963).
Miller, G.A. and Johnson-Laird, P.N., Language and Perception. (Cambridge, Mass.,
    Harvard University Press; Cambrige, Cambridge University Press, 1976).
Minsky, M. Computation: finite and infinite machines. (Englewood Cliffs, N.J.,
    Prentice-Hall, 1967).
Moran, T.P., The symbolic nature of visual imagery. Third International Joint
    Conference on Artificial Intelligence, (1973), 472-477.
Moyer, R.S., Comparing objects in memory: evidence suggesting an internal psycho-
    physics. Perception and Psychophysics, 13, (1973), 180-184.

Norman, D.A. and Rumelhart, D.E., Memory and knowledge. In D.A. Norman, D.E.
     Rumelhart, and the LNR Research Group, Explorations in cognition. (San
     Francisco, Freeman, 1975).
Paivio, A., Imagery and verbal processes. (New York, Holt, Rinehart and Winston,
     1971).
Paivio, A., Perceptual comparisons through the mind's eye. Memory and Cognition,
     3, (1975), 635-647.
Paivio, A., Images, propositions, and knowledge. In J.M. Nicholas (ed.), Images,
     perception and knowledge. (Dordrecht, Holland, Reidel, 1977).
Palmer, S.E., Visual perception and world knowledge: notes on a model of sensory-
     cognitive interaction. In D.A. Norman, D.E. Rumelhart, and the LNR Research
     Group, Explorations in cognition. (San Francisco, Freeman, 1975).
Pylyshyn, Z.W., What the mind's eye tells the mind's brain: a critique of mental
     imagery. Psychological Bulletin, 80, (1973), 1-24.
Roberts, L.G., Machine perception of three-dimensional solids. In I.J.T. Tippett
     et al (eds.), Optical and electro-optical information processing.
     (Cambridge, Mass., M.I.T. Press, 1965.
Schank, R.C., Conceptual information processing. (Amsterdam, North-Holland,
     1975).
Scott, D. and Strachey, C., Toward a mathematical semantics for computer lang-
     uages. Proceedings of the Symposium on Computers and Automata, Polytechnic
     Institute of Brooklyn, April, 1971.
Shepard, R.N., Form, formation, and transformation of internal representations.
     In R. Solso (ed.), Information processing and cognition, The Loyola
     Symposium. Hillsdale, N.J., Erlbaum, 1975.
Shepard, R.N., The mental image. American Psychologist, 33, (1978), 125-137.
Simon, H.A., What is visual imagery? An information processing interpretation.
     In L.W. Gregg (ed.), Cognition in learning and memory. (New York, Wiley,
     1972).
Simon, H.A. and Barenfeld, M., Information-processing analysis of perceptual
     processes in problem solving. Psychological Review, 76, (1969), 473-483.
Sloman, A., Interactions between philosophy and artificial intelligence: the role
     of intuition and non-logical reasoning in intelligence. Artificial
     Intelligence, 2, (1971), 209-225.
Smith, E.E., Shoben, E.J. and Rips, L.J., Structure and process in semantic
     memory: a featural model for semantic decisions. Psychological Review, 81,
     (1974), 214-241.
Woods, W.A., What's in a link: foundations for semantic networks. In D.G. Bobrow
     and A. Collins (eds.), Representation and understanding: Studies in
     cognitive science. (New York, Academic Press, 1975).
Woods, W.A., Procedural semantics. In A.K. Joshi, I. Sag and B.L. Webber (eds.),
     Elements of Discourse Understanding. (Cambridge, Cambridge University Press,
     1981).

FOOTNOTES

1.   There is a danger of an infinite regress here. If an interlingua is needed
      to mediate between words and pictures, then perhaps a language is needed to
      mediate between words and the interlingua, or between the interlingua and
      pictures, and so on and on (see Anderson, 1978).

2.   Expressions such as "in front of", in fact, have two distinct spatial senses,
      a deictic sense that depends on the speaker's point of view, e.g. "Stand in
      front of the rock", and another sense that depends on the intrinsic parts of
      certain sorts of object, e.g. "The river was in front of the house" (see
      Fillmore, 1971; Miller and Johnson-Laird, 1976, Sec. 6.1.3). This compli-
      cation is not relevant to the present argument, and I have otherwise ignored
      it.

3.   Sentences in isolation rarely express single propositions. It is the
      sentence and its context that convey a proposition (see e.g. Lewis, 1972).

ACKNOWLEDGEMENTS

This paper is an extensively revised version of one that originally appeared in
Italian in <u>Ricerche di Psicologia</u> in a special issue on language, 1983, edited by
Bruno Bara. I am grateful to Bruno Bara, Kate Ehrlich, Alan Garnham, Steve Isard,
Christopher Longuet-Higgins, Stuart Sutherland, and Eric Wanner for helpful
criticisms of the earlier paper.

Computational Models of Natural Language Processing
B.G. Bara and G. Guida (eds.)
© Elsevier Science Publishers B.V. (North-Holland), 1984   247

NARRATIVE COMPLEXITY BASED ON SUMMARIZATION ALGORITHMS

Wendy G. Lehnert

Department of Computer and Information Science
University of Massachusetts
Amherst, MA, USA

Narrative structures can only be defined in terms of some
internal memory representation, but narrative complexity is
more properly characterized by information processing
requirements. Story grammars, plan and goal hierarchies, and
causal chain representation all provide a sense of structure
which is largely removed from the processes that produce or
access that memory representation. In this paper we introduce
the notion of algorithmic equivalence as a means of generating
more algorithmically-oriented taxonomies for memory
representations.

1. INTRODUCTION

A representational strategy for narrative text has been developed to account for
summarization behavior using relatively simplistic retrieval algorithms. When the
memory representation for a narrative is encoded in terms of plot units (Lehnert,
1980, 1981), it is possible to invoke retrieval algorithms that locate the central
most important concepts of the narrative by examining structural features of
cyclic graphs. Each node in the graph corresponds to a plot unit instantiation,
and two nodes are connected by an arc when they share a common internal component.

A plot unit is a fixed configuration of smaller components called affect states.
There are three affect state types designed to differentiate gross subjective
states within a single character: positive states, negative states, and neutral
mental states. These affect states emphasize emotional reactions to events and
states rather than goal-oriented planning behavior, and each character in a
narrative can be tracked in terms of an "affect state map" which chronologically
records the subjective mental states for that character.

Once an affect state map has been produced which tracks the major characters of a
narrative, we can look for instances of specific plot units within that
representation. A "top level" plot unit instantiation is one that is not subsumed
(fully contained) by any other plot unit instantiation. When all the top level
units are recognized, we create a plot unit graph in which the nodes of the graph
correspond to top level plot unit instantiations. Two nodes of the graph are then
connected by an arc whenever they share at least one common affect state. This
graph structure provides a level of memory representation that is especially
well-suited for text summarization (Lehnert, Black, and Reiser, 1981; Reiser,

This work is being supported in part by National Science Foundation grant
#IST-8217502 and in part by Office of Naval Research grant #N00014-83-K-0580.

Lehnert, and Black, 1981 ; Gee and Grosjean, 1982 ; Reiser, Black, and Lehnert,
 1982 ; Lehnert, Alker, and Schneider, 1983). Nodes which are structurally central
to this graph are expected to provide us with the conceptual content for a good
summary.

For example, suppose John asks Susan to marry him and she says no. This episode
would be represented by the denied request unit:

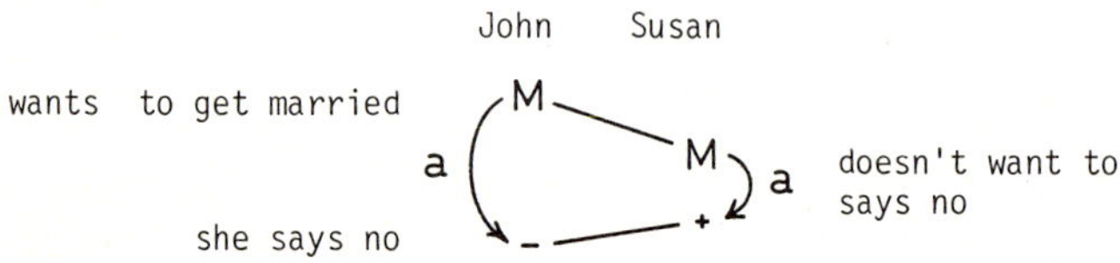

Now suppose John asks Karen to marry him and she says yes. This involves three
more top level units:

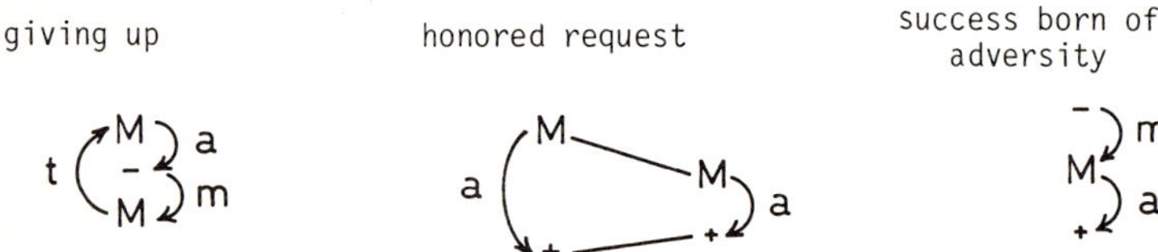

If we check for overlapping plot units, we find that our plot unit graph of four
units involves five arcs:

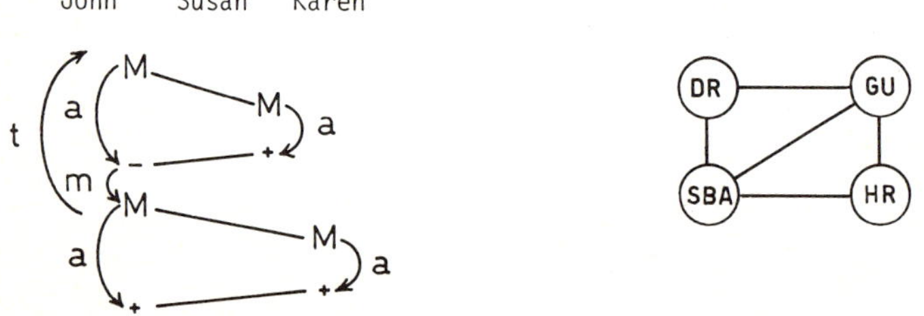

It is difficult to argue for the power of this representation when we are
summarizing a two sentence story, but plot unit graphs can involve hundreds of
units. For such complex narratives, we rely on structural features of the plot
unit graph to tell us which nodes contain the concepts that are most central and
critical to the story. For example, if a graph contains a unique node of maximal
degree, we want to examine the contents of that node in order to produce a summary
of the story. If a graph contains multiple nodes of maximal degree, we will have
to resort to a different retrieval algorithm. We can therefore pursue a notion of

narrative equivalence wherein two narratives are <u>algorithmically equivalent</u> (a-equivalent) if their plot unit graphs can be processed by the same summarization retrieval algorithm. It follows that narratives with isomorphic plot units graphs are a-equivalent, although narrative plot unit graphs can be a-equivalent without being structurally isomorphic. This notion of algorithmic equivalence creates a weaker partition than the more traditional relation of isomorphic equivalence.

2. NARRATIVE EQUIVALENCE CLASSES

Any partition of a-equivalent plot unit graphs determines a corresponding partition of narrative source texts. This in turn constitutes a taxonomy of narrative complexity. To identify such algorithmically-motivated equivalence classes, we must identify categories of graph structures that can be associated with specific retrieval algorithms. Any systematic development of such equivalence classes must be based on a large set of narrative representations that includes a wide variety of graph structures. This work is now in progress, but we have compiled enough narrative representations at the level of plot unit graphs to suggest some preliminary taxonomies. We are also developing a methodology for the identification of graph equivalencies which will allow us to proceed in a systematic manner.

The general strategy we are using to discover plot unit graph equivalencies is a combination of bottom-up exploratory work and top-down hypothesis testing. In the bottom-up phase we collect and analyze random narratives, to create a library of plot unit graph representations. We will later draw from this library for substantiating evidence and counterexamples, but the first phase of our research is simple compilation. We are using narratives that come from AI work in natural language processing, cognitive psychology research on text comprehension, and published short stories by popular authors. The source texts range in complexity from a single paragraph to about 50 pages. Our most complex narrative thus far is Arnold Toynbee's synopsis of the story of Jesus (Alker, Lehnert, and Schneider, 1984).

For each narrative we must hand-code a chronologically-ordered representation of affect state maps. We cannot automate this process with any generality because the text processing techniques involved are highly domain-dependent and would require extensive knowledge encoding for each narrative attempted - see Dyer (1983) for a good discussion of what would be involved . The graduate students who produce our hand-coded representations work together to assure uniformity in their encoding techniques, and we are developing encoding heuristics to aid others outside our immediate research group who would like to experiment with plot unit graphs.

Once a hand-coded affect state map has been produced, we process the representation with PUGG (the Plot Unit Graph Generator) (Lenhert and Loiselle (1984)). PUGG is designed to accept any set of plot units as our set of universal unit structures, and any affect state maps that are consistent with the structural conventions for legal affect state configurations. PUGG returns an adjacency matrix for all top-level units along with other useful information about disjoint subgraphs and immediate unit families.

One of the important parameters in this work is the specification of a universal set of top-level plot units. Graph structures will vary according to our selection of legal unit configurations, but we would ideally like to arrive at a taxonomy of graph structures that remains valid over a variety of universal sets. As a psychological theory of cognition and memory, we expect universal sets to vary across individuals. This variance could account for individual differences in summarization behavior as well as developmental differences between children and adults. It is therefore important to analyze each narrative with respect to more than one universal set, indexing each resulting graph with respect to its universal context.

To assure flexibility in this regard, we are analyzing each narrative with respect to three universal contexts. Context A is restricted to units involving no more than one or two characters. Context B is a subset of context A that contains only the simpler plot units of set A (most units in set B contain less than 10 affect states). Context C departs from set A and B insofar as it contains units that involve more than two characters. Context C consequently contains plot unit configurations that are more complicated than those found in context A. We do not require all three encodings for any given story to be a-equivalent according to our partition of graphs. It seems quite plausible that some stories will be easier to summarize under one universal set than another (this should be especially true if one set is relatively impoverished).

In the course of compiling this library of representations, we are seeing some patterns emerge:

(1) Most graphs are fully connected.

(2) If a graph contains a unique code of maximal degree, it is probably small (containing less than 15 units).

(3) Two distinct clusters that are strongly connected often describe the same events from different perspectives.

(4) If a graph can be partitioned into maximal clusters, boundary units between the clusters tend to be important.

With each new graph we generate, we must examine that graph to see where its critical nodes are located. Sometimes the critical nodes are structurally conspicuous. In these cases we can readily specify a plausible retrieval algorithm which appears to be appropriate for that graph. The same algorithm typically applies to a number of graphs, in which case we must identify necessary and sufficient conditions for the application of that algorithm. In other cases we may not be able to identify a simple algorithm, or a simple algorithm applies but does not produce a satisfactory summary. These apparent failures may force us to revise a previous summarization algorithm, or revise the necessary and sufficient conditions that signal the applicability of a particular algorithm.

The necessary and sufficient conditions that identify appropriate algorithms will define our graph equivalence classes. Hypothetical equivalence classes arise every time we propose a possible summarization algorithm, but we must be careful to maintain consistency throughout the system whenever a new class is proposed or an old class is altered. If we begin to amass a large number of equivalence classes, we will watch for hierarchical relationships among possible partitions. From a developmental perspective it seems quite likely that simple partitions might be refined into more complex partitions, and that such refinements would be associated with improvements in summarization behavior. With this in mind, we expect to find simplistic classifications that produce inferior summaries for some stories.

As our library grows, we will track error rates for each equivalence class as well as error rates for each set of universal plot units. In an ideal partition, the error rate across equivalence classes should be roughly uniform with respect to each universal context. On the other hand, the overall error rate across different universal contexts may vary considerably, in which case we will learn something about effective plot unit configurations. For example, if the error rate associated with Context C is significantly higher than the rates for Contexts A and B, we will have a strong argument against the inclusion of plot units involving more than two characters.

3. GRAPH TYPES AND SUMMARIZATION ALGORITHMS

Thus far, we have analyzed about 20 narratives with respect to universal Contexts A and B, and we have not yet formulated the units for Context C. (See Lehnert and Loiselle, 1984) for a complete list of Context A plot units, as well a micro-version of PUGG for those interested in running their own experiments.) We need to look at more narratives before we propose a set of equivalence classes, but on the basis of this initial library we have identified three core equivalence classes which appear to produce reasonable summaries for a majority of the narratives. We will summarize these categories briefly.

3.1 <u>Simple Graphs with Unique Pivots</u>

One class of graphs exhibit unique nodes of maximal degree. While this class seems to be restricted to smaller graphs, we can reliably look to such pivotal nodes for the concepts most central to the narrative as a whole. This was the first algorithm we identified, and is therefore discussed in some earlier publications (e.g. see Lehnert,1981). While our initial work suggests that it is very difficult for a long narrative to fall into this category, we may see a higher frequency of stories in this class as our universal set of plot units expands. For example, it should be easier to create graphs of this type within Context C than Context A.

To illustrate the occurrence of a unique pivot in a simple graph, consider the COMSYS story:

> John and Bill were competing for the same job promotion at
> IBM. John got the promotion and Bill decided to leave IBM to
> start his own consulting firm, COMSYS. Within three years
> COMSYS was flourishing. By that time John had become
> dissatisfied with IBM so he asked Bill for a job. Bill
> spitefully turned him down.

The affect state map for this story is short enough for us to show it in its
entirety. It involves only two characters, Bill and John:

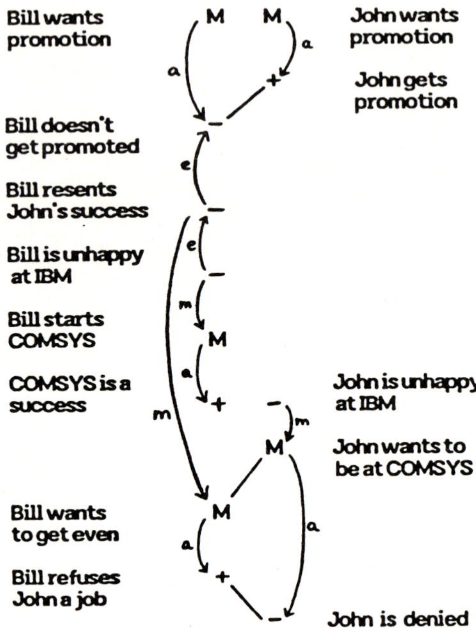

Figure 1: COMSYS affect state map

We derive five top-level plot units from this graph:

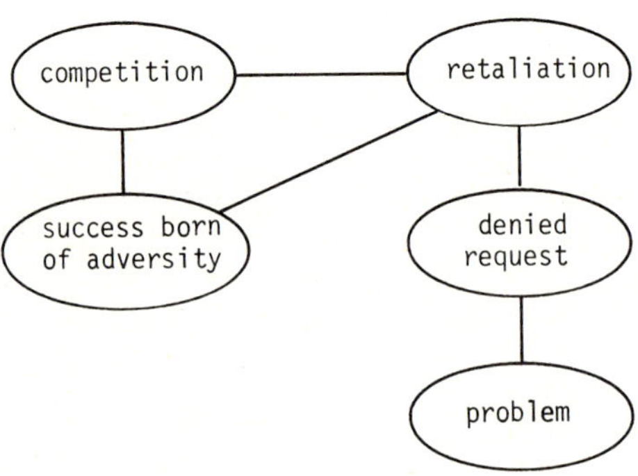

Figure 2: COMSYS plot unit graph

We see that there is only one unit of degree 3, so this unit (retaliation) is a unique pivot in our graph. Indeed, it is reasonable to summarize COMSYS by saying "John once beat Bill out of a promotion at IBM, so Bill refused to give John a job later". A separate program, PRECIS, has been designed to generate English summaries of this type from single plot units. For a more detailed discussion of the generation process involved in going from a plot unit graph to natural language, see Cook, Lehnert, and McDonald (1984).

3.2 Complex Graphs with Multiple Pivots

This group of graphs is quite large and must be divided into smaller subsets for effective categorization. In some cases we see two nodes of maximal degree whose immediate families partition the entire graph into two subgraphs. The maximal nodes on the boundary of this partition then serve to give us a one-sentence summary for the whole story. In other cases, we see graphs where the maximal nodes themselves provide critical concepts for summarization. This is especially common when the two maximal nodes are adjacent to one another, in which case they are frequently of equal importance.

As we investigate this class further, we may find it necessary to assign relative weights to nodes which vary with the surrounding environment. For example, suppose a node of degree 10 has 9 neighbors that all have degree 6 (this sort of dense connectivity is rarely encountered). We may want to assign a lesser salience to such a node, favoring instead a node of degree 9 whose neighbors all have a degree of 2. A particularly elegant solution for these larger graphs would be to simply locate the subgraph composed of nodes with minimal eccentricity, where the eccentricity of a node is defined to be the largest distance from that node to any other node of the graph (Proskurowski (1980)). There are many such possibilities, and our initial explorations have not adequately differentiated their strengths and weaknesses.

A simple example of a graph with multiple pivots can be seen by looking at an analysis of a BORIS narrative (Dyer (1983)). The BORIS divorce story contains five paragraphs:

> Richard hadn't heard from his college roomate Paul for years. Paul had loaned Richard money which was never paid back, but now he had no idea where to find his old friend. When a letter finally arrived from San Francisco, Richard was anxious to find out how Paul was.
>
> Unfortunately, the news was not goode. Paul's wife Sarah wanted a divorce. She also wanted the car, the house, the children, and alimony. Paul wanted the divorce, but he didn't want to see Sarah take everything he had. His salary from the state school system was very small. Not knowing who to turn to, he was hoping for a favor from the only lawyer he knew. Paul gave his home phone number in case Richard felt he could help.
>
> Richard eagerly picked up the phone and dialed. After a brief conversation, Paul agreed to have lunch with him the

next day. He sounded extremely relieved and grateful.

The next day, as Richard was driving to the restaurant, he barely avoided hitting an old man on the street. He felt extremely upset by the incident, and had three drinks at the restaurant. When Paul arrived, Richard was fairly drunk. After the food came, Richard spilled a cup of coffee on Paul. Paul seemed very annoyed by this so Richard offered to drive him home for a change of clothes.

When Paul walked into the bedroom and found Sarah with another man, he nearly had a heart attack. Then he realized what a blessing it was. With Richard there as a witness, Sarah's divorce case was shot. Richard congratulated Paul and suggested that they celebrate at dinner. Paul was eager to comply.

The affect state map for this story is too long to show here, but it produces a plot unit graph of 24 units. Two units (retaliation and competition) have maximal degree and act as multiple pivots within the same unit family (they both have the same set of unit relatives). (See Figure 3) This makes them very strong candidates for conceptual salience, and indeed, they seem to reside right at the heart of things. The competition is between Paul and Sarah for their shared possessions, and the retaliation unit described how Paul gets even with Sarah by finding her in bed with another man... thereby destroying her settlement claims.

The English generation for a story involving dual pivots is understandably more involved than that required by stories with unique pivotal units. We are working on text planning heuristics for these cases, but do not yet have a computer implementation operating at this level of sophistication.

3.3 Separable Graphs

This category contains large graphs (more than 50 nodes) composed of subgraphs that can be separated by deleting a single node. While it may seem that the nodes central to each potential component of the graph might be good candidates for conceptual salience, we have found that the best results are obtained by looking at the "deletion" nodes which keep the graph from separating. If there are multiple deletion nodes, we look for a path containing all the deletion nodes. The shortest path seems to be preferred, although maximal degree can enter in as a factor when more than one path is possible. These graphs tend to be associated with the longest and more complex narratives (see Lehnert, Alker, and Schneider (1983) for a detailed discussion of one such graph).

To see how topological salience works in larger graphs, we present the graph structure originally generated for Arnold Toynbee's synopsis of the New Testament. (See figure 4.)

This analysis yielded a graph of 100 top-level units, with three topologically critical nodes. These three nodes can stand alone to produce a reasonable summary of the new testament:

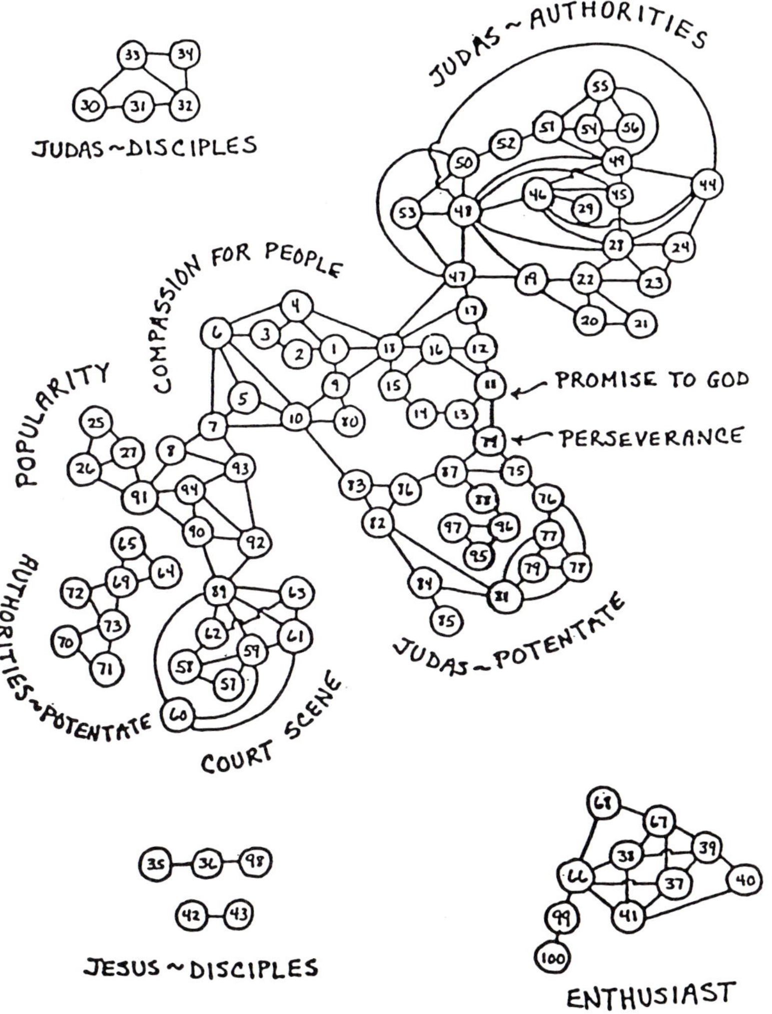

Figure 3: Christus Patients plot unit graph

The BORIS divorce story

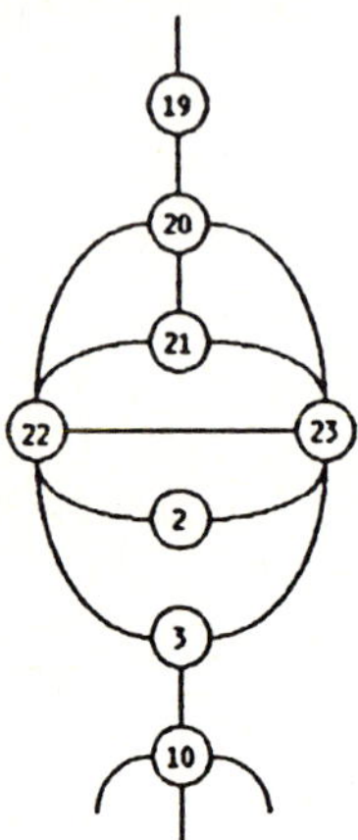

This is a partial graph from the BORIS
divorce story. (The full graph contains 24
units). This fragment contains the two units
of maximal degree, which act as the central
pivots for the whole story. More importantly,
the retaliation and competition units are
dual pivots for a common family.

Either one would suffice for a one-sentence
summary of the story. A more detailed summary
could be produced by expanding from each unit
in the common family (2,3,20,21,22, & 23) and
tying them together in a causally coherent
explanation of chronological events.

2. motivation (Sarah)

(wanting the divorce motivates
wanting the possessions)

3. motivation (Paul)

(wanting to preserve possessions
motivates wanting a lawyer)

10. motivated success (Paul)

(Richard promises to help Paul
when Paul asks for help)

19. motivated success (Paul)

(Paul goes home when he
decides to change clothes)

20. mixed blessing (Paul)

(Paul arrives at home and
finds Sarah with another man)

21. hidden-blessing (Paul)

(Paul finds Sarah with
another man and realizes
he's won the settlement)

22. retaliation (Paul, Sarah)

(When Sarah tries to take
everything from Paul, he
catches her in a compromising
position and ruins her case)

23. competition (Paul, Sarah)

(Paul foils Sarah's demands
in their divorce settlement)

Figure 4: Excerpts from a BORIS story

> "Jesus called on the people to support him. His popularity
> caused the authorities to arrest him. When Jesus refused to
> cooperate with the authorities, they crucified him".

If we establish a minimal path through these three critical nodes, we get a somewhat more detailed version of the story:

> "Jesus called on the people to support him. At the same time,
> the Roman government wanted to maintain its authority over the
> population. Jesus caused a scandal in the temple. Jesus was
> avenging God's will be taking the law into his own hands. His
> popularity caused the authorities to arrest him. When Jesus
> refused to cooperate with the authorities, they crucified him.
> Jesus' death (and resurrection) was a triumph for the people.
> The people worshipped Jesus."

While the nodes we can isolate from this graph provide us with conceptually
accurate information for a good summary, the generational mechanisms needed to
translate these nodes into a smooth summary are extremely ambitious. It will be
some time before we can hope to fully automate summaries of this sort.

Critical nodes (1)

 7 - motivation - Jesus calls on the people to support him.

47 - success-born-of-adversity - The authorities arrest Jesus.

89 - retaliation - The authorities crucify Jesus.

Minimal path

 7 - Jesus makes an appeal to the masses for support.

 9 - The government wants to maintain authority over the masses.

10 - Jesus causes a scandal.

18 - Jesus takes the law into his own hands to avenge God.

47 - The authorities arrest Jesus.

89 - Jesus is crucified.

92 - Jesus' death is a triumph.

93 - Jesus is worshipped.

---

(1) The removal of any of these nodes will disconnect at least 10% of the total
graph structure.

As we consider these three prelilminary a-equivalent classes, we see that processing complexity is determined to some extent by the size of the memory representation (or plot unit graph). This is hardly surprising, although the concept of a-equivalence suggests that there should be distinct plateaux of summarization competence, with severe drops in performance whenever a representation is incorrectly categorized. This provides us with a set of performance predictions which will be distinct from any models that predict strictly linear complexities based on the length of the input text or the size of an internal memory representation alone.

4. CONCLUSIONS

Our work to identify a-equivalent narratives continues on many fronts. We are expanding our library of affect state maps and the corresponding library of plot unit graphs. At this stage it seems appropriate to concentrate primarily on the taxonomy of necessary summarization algorithms, and secondarily on issues concerning universal sets of plot units. We hope to concentrate more fully on the question of universal sets after we have a firmer footing on the issue of algorithmic equivalence. It is too early to say anything about the status of algorithmic equivalence, as a concept of psychological import, but a plot unit approach to human text comprehension may dovetail very naturally with a developmental study of human summarization behavior. We might, for example, expect to see competent summarization behavior in some classes before others, in which case the notion of a-equivalence would provide a simple measure of narrative complexity in terms of human information processing capabilities.

On a more general level, we note that plot units are applicable to narrative text with human (or anthropomorphized characters) for whom an effect state analysis is possible. It is not obvious that an analogous system of memory representation can be applied to expository or purely instructional texts. At the very least, our approach suggests that the cognitive processes underlying summarization skills for narratives are very different from the processes of summarization required for other types of text. Narratives and expository texts may therefore reside within two basically disjoint a-equivalence classes, in which case competence in one area may not correlate very strongly with competence in the other. Such a situation would have immediate consequences for educators as well as other models of text comprehension.

REFERENCES

Alker H., Lehnert W., Schneider D. 1984. Two reinterpretations of Toynbee's Jesus: explorations in computational hermeneutics. In: Tonfoni G., ed., <u>Narrative summarization and analogical reasoning</u>. (In press).

Cook M., Lehnert W., MacDonald D. 1984. Text generation in narrative summarization using implicit content. Submitted to Tenth International Conference on Computational Linguistics, Stanford, Cal.

Dyer M. 1983. In-depth understanding: a computer model of integrated processing for narrative comprenhension. MIT Press, Cambridge, Mass.

Gee J.P., Grosjean F. 1982. Empirical evidence for narrative structure. Unpublished paper,Program in Applied Psycholinguistics, Boston University, Boston, Mass.

Lehnert W.G. 1980. Narrative text summarization. Proceedings of the First Annual National Conference on Artificial Intelligence. Palo Alto, Cal.

Lehnert W.G. 1981. Plot units and narrative summarization. Cognitive Science. Vol. 5, No. 4.

Lehnert W., Alker H., Schneider D. 1983. Affective plot structure of Toynbee's Christus Patiens. Proceedings of the Sixth International Conference on Computers and the Humanities. Washington, D.C.

Lehnert W., Black J., Reiser B. 1981. Summarizing narratives. Proceedings of the Seventh International Joint Conference on Artificial Intelligence. Vancouver, British Columbia.

Lehnert W., Loiselle C. 1983. Plot unit recognition for narratives. Department of Computer and Information Science, Technical Report #83-39, University of Massachusetts, Amherst, Mass.

Proskurowski A. 1980. Centers of maximal outerplanar graphs. Journal of Graph Theory. Vol. 4, pp.75-79.

Reiser B., Black J., Lehnert W. 1982. Thematic knowledge structures in the understanding and generation of narratives. Cognitive Science Technical Report #16. Cognitive Science Program, Yale University. New Haven,Conn.

Reiser B., Lehnert W., Black W. 1981. Recognizing thematic units in narratives.Proceedings of the Third Annual Cognitive Science Conference.Berkeley, Cal.

Computational Models of Natural Language Processing
B.G. Bara and G. Guida (eds.)
© Elsevier Science Publishers B.V. (North-Holland), 1984

USING FOCUS TO CONSTRAIN
LANGUAGE GENERATION

Kathleen R. McKeown

Department of Computer Science
Columbia University
New York, NY, USA

Computer generation of natural language requires the ability to make reasoned choices from a large number of possible things to say as well as from a large number of expressive possibilities. This paper examines in detail how one influence on a generated text, focus of attention, can be used to constrain the many possibilities that a generation system must consider. A computational treatment of focus of attention is presented that can be used to constrain what the system needs to consider when deciding what to say next. In this process, information is produced that provides constraints on which words and syntactic structures best express the system's intent, thus ensuring that its resulting text is coherent. This analysis has been used in the fully implemented TEXT system which generates paragraph length responses to questions about database structure.

1 INTRODUCTION

Computer generation of natural language requires the ability to make reasoned choices from a large number of possibilities and from a variety of knowledge sources. A system that communicates with its users must be able to decide *what* information to communicate, *when* to say what, and *which* words and syntactic structures among many possibilities best express its intent. Previous papers (e.g., McKeown 80, McKeown 82A, McKeown 82B) illustrate how the final text is influenced by a variety of factors, including commonly used rhetorical strategies, semantic information, focus of attention, and the discourse goal. This paper examines in detail how one of those sources, focus of attention, can be used to constrain the many possibilities that a generation system must consider. A computational treatment of focus of attention is presented that constrains what information to communicate and its order, and in the process produces information that constrains which words and syntactic structures best express its intent. Examples are given of how this analysis has been used in the fully implemented TEXT system, which generates paragraph length responses to questions about database structure.

Focus constraints are only part of the TEXT system's mechanism for responding to a question. TEXT also uses discourse plans and a mechanism for determining relevancy (McKeown 82A). To answer a question, TEXT first circumscribes a subset of the knowledge base containing information relevant to the given question. A discourse plan (called a schema (McKeown 82A)) is then used to guide the construction of an answer. The focusing mechanism aids in this process by constraining the selection of information to talk about next to that which ties in most appropriately with the previous discourse. Thus, focus information doesn't primarily determine the content of the response, but provides constraints on the many possibilities that must be considered and aids in shaping a coherent response. TEXT was

implemented using an ONR database containing information about military vehicles and weapons.
Examples are taken from this domain. In the following sections, various choices that a
generation system must make at different phases of processing are first described. How focus
information can be used to influence these decisions is then discussed.

2 CHOICES

One of the first steps in speaking or writing is the narrowing of attention to knowledge
relevant to the purpose at hand. Speakers and writers are capable of ignoring information in
their large body of knowledge about the world which is not specific to the current discourse
purpose. This process, called *global focusing* (Grosz 77) is modeled in TEXT by restricting
the information that needs to be considered when constructing an answer to a subset of the
knowledge base which contains information that could potentially be included as part of the
answer. Although this process is not discussed in detail here, the fact that it does occur is
critical for the success of later processes (see McKeown 82A for further details).

Once a system has determined what information is likely to be relevant to its current
discourse goal, it also must be able to determine what to say first, what next, and how to
close the discourse. Order of information can be crucial to a reader's understanding of a text.
Textual sequence alone can cause a reader to draw inferences about the relation between two
propositions, including temporal sequence, causality, and exemplification, among others. While
textual sequence need not always correspond to, for example, temporal sequence, the absence
of textual connectives specifying otherwise (e.g., "when", "after", "while") may indicate that it
does. It is important, therefore, that careful attention be given to how propositions are
ordered.

At the surface level, a generator must be able to make reasoned decisions about the
best lexical items to use, when to use pronominal reference, and about the syntactic
construction that should be used. Examples illustrating these choices are shown in 1-3 below.

1. Lexical choice (bought vs. sold)
   A) Jane bought $3.00 worth of
      bobby socks from Michael.
   B) Michael sold $3.00 worth of
      bobby socks to Jane.

2. Pronominal reference (Linda vs. she)
   A) Linda flew to Washington.
   B) She flew to Washington.

3. Syntactic structure
   (active vs. passive)
   A) John gave the book to Mary.
   B) Mary was given the book by John.

Textual order and surface choice are both influenced by a speaker's focus of attention.
In the following sections this influence is characterized in such a way that it can be used by a
language generator to resolve decisions in textual order and surface choice.

3 FOCUSING IN DISCOURSE

Focusing is a prevalent phenomenon in all types of naturally occurring discourse. Everyone, consciously or unconsciously, centers their attention on various concepts or objects throughout the process of reading or writing, speaking or listening. In all these modalities, the focusing phenomena occurs at many levels of discourse. For example, we expect a book to concern itself with a single theme or subject; chapters are given headings, indicating that the material included within is related to the given heading; paragraphs are organized around topics; and sentences are related in some way to preceding and succeeding sentences. In conversation, comments such a s "Stick to the subject ...", "Going back to what you were saying before ...", or "Let's change the subject ..." all indicate that people are aware that the conversation centers on specific ideas and that there are conventions for changing that focus of attention.

The use of focusing makes for ease of processing on the part of participants in a conversation. When interpreting utterances, knowledge that the discourse is about a particular topic eliminates certain possible interpretations from consideration. Grosz (77) discusses this in light of the interpretation of definite referring expressions. She notes that although a word may have multiple meanings, its use in an appropriate context will rarely bring to mind any meaning but the relevant one. Focusing also facilitates the interpretation of anaphoric, and in particular, pronominal, references (see Sidner 79). When the coherence provided by focusing is missing from discourse, readers and hearers may have difficulty in determining what a pronoun refers to. When speaking or writing, the process of focusing constrains the set of possibilities for what to say next. Having decided that he wants to talk about the weather, for example, a speaker need not consider what he could say about yesterday's movie. When a speaker or writer has not decided ahead of time on the specific themes he wants to convey, he will experience difficulty in proceeding. Incoherent text or conversation is often the result of such a situation.

Focusing also influences *how* something is said. Changing what is focused may involve marking the move for the hearer by using a different syntactic form. Continuing discussion of the same topic may require pronominalization. The use of marked syntactic structures can highlight new information about a previously mentioned item.

This use of focusing is what makes a sequence of sentences a whole. The fact that a sequence of sentences is *about* something, makes that sequence connected, coherent, and in some sense, a unit. Intuitively, then, a text is a connected, coherent sequence of sentences. In order to generate texts, some account of the use of focusing must be made.

4 USE OF FOCUSING FOR INTERPRETATION

Focusing has been used effectively as a computational tool in the interpretation of discourse by several researchers in artificial intelligence. Grosz (77) distinguished between two types of focus: *global* and *immediate*. Immediate focus refers to how a speaker's center of attention shifts or remains constant over two consecutive sentences. Both the ordering of sentence constituents and the interpretation of sentence fragments are affected by the immediate focus. Global focus, on the other hand, describes the effect of a speaker's center of attention throughout a set of discourse utterances on succeeding utterances.

In her work, Grosz defined the representation and use of global focus. She represented global focus by partitioning the entire knowledge base into a subset containing those items in focus at a given time in the discourse and the remaining knowledge base. Knowing which items are in focus makes further interpretation of discourse easier. For example, considering only a subset of the knowledge base at a given time limits the search for referents of definite noun phrases occurring in the discourse and makes it more likely that the correct referent will be found.

Sidner (79) extended Grosz's work with an extensive analysis of immediate focus. She used focus for the disambiguation of definite anaphora and thus, like Grosz, for aiding in the interpretation of discourse. She was able to explain types of anaphora which Grosz did not consider, particularly the use of pronouns. A major result of her work was the specification of detailed algorithms for maintaining and shifting immediate focus. She showed that a speaker has four basic options when moving from one sentence to the next:

1. continue talking about the same thing (immediate focus remains to same)

2. shift to talk about an item just introduced

3. return to a topic of previous discussion

4. talk about an item implicitly related to the current focus

5 FOCUSING AND GENERATION

Focus of attention can be used as a tool for the generation of discourse by providing constraints on the possibilities for what can be said next. Global focus constrains the entire knowledge base, producing a subset containing items which can be talked about. Immediate focus further constrains the subset since after any given utterance a smaller set of choices will be possible. Several problems arise in adapting work on focus of attention to generation. Since it considered *interpretation*, there was no need to discriminate between members of the set of legal foci; when more than one possibility for global or immediate focus existed after a given sentence, the next incoming sentence would determine which of the choices was taken. A generation system, however, must be able to decide which of the choices is better than the others in any given situation. The kinds of choices that must be made in generation, as well as the extensions which must be included in the focusing mechanism to accommodate these decisions, are described in the following sections.

5.1 Global focus and generation

In the TEXT system, a relevant knowledge pool, which contains information determined by the system to be potentially relevant to the input question, is constructed for each answer. It is equivalent to Grosz's concept of global focus. Since the relevant knowledge pool is constructed *on receiving an input question*, it limits what the system needs to consider when deciding what to say to a small subset of the entire knowledge base. For requests for definitions and information, a small area around the questioned object is circumscribed to delimit the global focus. For questions about the difference between objects, the conceptual difference between the objects in the generalization hierarchy is used to determine what information is included (see McKeown 82A). Note that the *final* content of the text is also influence by the schema, or discourse plan, used.

5.2 Immediate focus and generation

On producing a single utterance (controlled by a schema), TEXT narrows its focus of attention to a single object (or set of objects) in its pool of relevant information. Having made a decision about what to talk about first, it must support that decision in succeeding utterances if it wants its text to be easily understood. That is, having decided to focus on a particular object(s), its utterances constrain the set of possibilities for what can be said next if the system is to avoid jumping around from one topic to another. These are termed *immediate focus* constraints since they apply locally between utterances.

TEXT uses the constraints developed by Sidner (79) on how focus of attention can shift or be maintained from one sentence to the next. Sidner showed that a speaker can either maintain his/her current focus, shift to focus on an item just introduced, return to a previous focus, or focus on an item implicitly related to the current focus. The TEXT system uses these constraints to limit the number of possibilities it must consider when deciding what to say next. If its discourse plan allows for several next utterances, the system only considers propositions that have an element that can be focused in one of these ways.

While Sidner's constraints are sufficient for interpreting natural language, for generation a speaker may have to decide which of the constraints is better than any other at any point. In interpretation of discourse, this is not necessary because the choice is dictated by the incoming sentence. For generation, however, the speaker may have decide between any of the focusing alternatives.

An ordering on Sidner's constraints was developed for generation which dictates which of these is preferable (see Figure 1 below). A speaker may have to decide between continuing to talk about the same thing or starting to talk about something introduced in the last sentence. In this case, the preference ordering suggests that a speaker should shift to focus on an item just introduced into conversation if s/he has something to say about it. If the speaker chooses not to do so, that item will have to be re-introduced into conversation at a later point before the additional information can be conveyed. If, on the other hand, the speaker does shift to the item just mentioned, there will be no trouble in continuing with the old conversation. In that case, the speaker is returning to a topic of previous discussion, a legal focus move.

Several consecutive moves to items just introduced are not a problem. In fact, consecutive focus shifts over a sequence of sentences occurs frequently in written text. If this rule were applied indefinitely though, it would result in never-ending side-tracking onto different topics of conversation. However, the model of generation assumes that information is being presented in order to achieve a particular goal (e.g., answer a question). Only a limited amount of information is within the speaker's scope of attention because of its relevance to that goal (as defined by global focus). Hence only a limited amount of side-tracking can occur.

A speaker may also have to decide between continuing talking about the same thing or returning to a topic[1] of previous discussion. The second preference indicates that a speaker should continue talking about the same thing rather than returning to an earlier topic of conversation where possible. By returning to a previous discussion, a speaker closes the current topic. Therefore, having introduced a topic (which may entail the introduction of other topics), one should say all that needs to be said before returning to an earlier topic. The second preference guarantees that a speaker will avoid implying that s/he is finished talking about the current subject when in fact there is more to be said. If neither of the first two preferences apply then the speaker must return to an earlier topic of discussion (preference 3).

In cases where a speaker must choose between two propositions with the same focus, the preferences described so far proscribe no course of action. Rather than making an arbitrary choice, a speaker tends to group together in discourse those properties that are in some way related to each other. For example, in the following text, taken from the introduction to *Working* (Terkel 72), immediate focus remains unchanged until the last sentence (focus = "this book"), but an undercurrent of related themes occurs from one sentence to the next. Violence, physical violence, spiritual violence, and examples of violence are all related properties of the book that are described.

---

[1] Topic is used here loosely to refer to the subject or theme of a discourse. It does not refer to the linguistic notion of topic.

"This book, being about work, is, by its very nature, about violence – to the spirit as well as to the body. It is about ulcers as well as accidents, about shouting matches as well as kicking the dog around. It is, above all (or beneath all), about daily humiliations. To survive the day is triumph enough for the walking wounded among the great many of us."

Discussion of related properties results in a layering of foci that corresponds to the speaker's global focus. More than one thing is focused on at a time (global focus) and one of them is distinguished as immediate focus. In the generation process, this phenomenon is accounted for by choosing that proposition with the most mentions to previously mentioned items when the system has a choice between two propositions with the same focus (preference 4). This constraint ensures that the text will maintain the global focus of the text when possible.

This ordering doesn't dictate *absolute* constraints on the system. Just as a speaker may choose to suddenly switch topics, the system may choose to do so also. The ordered focus constraints are preferences which indicate the system's best move when faced with a choice. If the system's discourse plan indicates that no next choice meets these constraints, it will follow its plan making note of the abrupt switch in focus. This switch can then be syntactically marked to ease the transition for the user.

1. shift focus to item mentioned in previous proposition

2. maintain focus

3. return to topic of previous discussion

4. select proposition with greatest number of implicit links to previous proposition

FIGURE 1: Ordered Focus Constraints

6 FOCUS SETS

A discourse need not always focus on a single central concept. A speaker may decide to talk about several concepts at once and yet, the resulting discourse is still coherent. Sidner terms this type of phenomenon "co-present foci" and shows that it is a highly regulated phenomena. Introduction of a set into focus with subsequent discussion of one element of the set requires that the speaker eventually return to discussion of the other elements of the set. If the speaker chooses not to do so, the listener will wonder why the set was introduced in the first place.

Although Sidner describes the restrictions on how co-present foci can occur, she does not describe the reasons for its use or for the focus moves to elements of the focused set. For interpretation of discourse, the use of co-present foci is given by the incoming discourse, and there is no need to decide when its use is appropriate. Generation of discourse, however, requires that these kinds of decisions be made.

Decisions to use co-present foci rest in part on the rhetorical techniques used in discourse and thus, the discourse plan (e.g., the decision to define an object in terms of its sub-classes) and in part on the discourse goal (e.g., the decision to answer a question about the difference between two objects). In the first case, definition of a concept in terms of its sub-classes implies the use of a particular structure for discourse which requires focusing on the questioned object, followed by the introduction of its sub-classes and extended discussion of each of these in turn (see McKeown 82A for discussion of the *constituency schema* which encodes this type of discourse plan). In this case, the discourse plan forces the use of co-present foci and the changes in focus to set members.

As an example, consider the text shown below in (4) which the system generates in response to the question "What is a guided projectile?". In this text, the system introduces the set, *missiles and torpedoes* into focus, shifts to focus on each of these, and finally returns to focus on the *guided projectile* in the last sentence.

    4) (definition GUIDED)
    ;
    ; What is a guided projectile?
    ;

A guided projectile is a projectile that is self-propelled. There are 2 types of guided projectiles in the ONR database: torpedoes and missiles. The missile has a target location in the air or on the earth's surface. The torpedo has an underwater target location. The missile's target location is indicated by the DB attribute DESCRIPTION and the missile's flight capabilities are provided by the DB attribute ALTITUDE. The torpedo's underwater capabilities are provided by the DB attributes under DEPTH (for example, MAXIMUM OPERATING DEPTH). The guided projectile has DB attributes TIME TO TARGET & UNITS, HORZ RANGE & UNITS and NAME.

In the second case, the discourse goal is to provide a description of the differences between two objects. Associated with this discourse goal is a plan which calls for discussion of the similarities between the two objects, followed by a discussion of their differences (see McKeown 82A for discussion of the *compare and contrast schema*). Thus, the discourse will first center on the two objects and their common attributes; focus will then switch to the questioned objects in turn. Again, the discourse plan forces the use of co-present foci and the changes in focus to set members. An example illustrating this case is shown below in (5), with focus shifts indicated.

    5) (difference MISSILE TORPEDO)
    ;
    ; What is the difference between a missile
    ; and a torpedo?
    ;

Similarities: focus is on the set, the missile and torpedo

The torpedo and the missile are self-propelled guided projectiles. The guided projectile's propulsion capabilities are provided by the DB attributes under SPEED INDICES (for example, MAXIMUM SPEED) and FUSE TYPE. The guided projectile has DB attributes TIME TO TARGET & UNITS, HORZ RANGE & UNITS and NAME.

Focus shifts to the first element of the set, the missile

The missile has a target location in the air or on the earth's surface.   The missile's target location is indicated by the DB attribute DESCRIPTION and its flight capabilities are provided by the DB attribute ALTITUDE.   Other DB attributes of the missile include PROBABILITY OF KILL, SPEED, ALTITUDE, LETHAL RADIUS & UNITS and TIME TO TARGET & UNITS.   Missiles are carried by water-going vehicles and aircraft.

Focus shifts to the second element of the set, the torpedo

The torpedo has an underwater target location.   Its underwater capabilities are provided by the DB attributes under DEPTH (for example, MAXIMUM OPERATING DEPTH). Other DB attributes of the torpedo include FUSE TYPE, MAXIMUM DEPTH, ACCURACY & UNITS, HORZ RANGE & UNITS, and TIME TO TARGET & UNITS.   Torpedoes are carried by water-going vehicles.

Focus returns to the set

The torpedo and the missile, therefore, have the same travel means, although they have different target locations, reflected in the database by the torpedo's attribute DEPTH and the missile's attributes ALTITUDE and DESCRIPTION.

7 CHOOSING SURFACE EXPRESSIONS

There are many different ways in which a proposition can be expressed in English.   If the system makes an arbitrary decision about which to select in a given situation, an inappropriate decision could easily be made.   For example, if the propositions shown in 1-3 above are to be expressed as parts of discourse sequences, then one of the choices in each pair is clearly inappropriate (6-8 below).

6. Jane was in a hurry to finish her shopping. It was a
   chore she particularly despised. First,
   { Jane bought $3.00 worth of bobby
     socks from Michael.
     *Michael sold $3.00 worth of bobby
     socks to Jane.

7. We knew that Mary took the train to New York with Linda,
   but didn't realize that
   { Linda flew to Washington from
     there.
     *she flew to Washington from there.

8. John bought that great new book on data structures.
   He read the first three chapters and then
   { he gave the book to Mary.
     *Mary was given the book by John.

In these discourse sequences, the inappropriateness of the starred choice in each case can be explained by the speaker's focus over the discourse. A number of linguists (e.g.,

Halliday 67, Firbas 66) have discussed how thematic (or focus) information can affect the ordering of sentence constituents, suggesting that new (or unfocused) information usually occurs towards the end of a sentence. In order to place this information in its proper position in the sentence, structures other than the unmarked active sentence may be required (for example, the passive). Structures such as it-extraposition, there-insertion, topicalization, and left-dislocation can be used to introduce new information into discourse. Pronominalization is another linguistic device associated with focused information (Sidner 79); it is often used to signal the speaker's focus of attention.

In the example discourse sequences, focus accounts for the choices made in the following ways. In sequence (6), the focus is on Jane who is doing the action. The verb "bought" is selected over "sell" in order to allow Jane to be described as the focused participant in the action. In (7), Mary is the focused element of the factive "to know". If the second reference to Linda is pronominalized, we are likely to interpret the referent of the pronoun as the focused element, or Mary. In (8) the first sentence focuses on John. The active sentence is more appropriate since it places the focused information in surface subject position.

8 SURFACE CHOICE IN THE TEXT SYSTEM

Since focus information has been used to constrain the selection of propositions in the TEXT system, a record containing each proposition's focus and its potential focus list is available for the system to use when determining the specific syntactic structures that should be used in the answer. It can examine this information to determine how a proposition is related to previous discourse and therefore which of various surface-level choices should be made.

In TEXT, focus information is used in some limited situations to test whether pronominalization can be used. Part of the answer to the question "What is a ship?" where pronominalization was selected is shown in (9) below. In the first sentence of the answer, the ship is being focused on and reference to it in the following sentence can therefore be pronominalized.

9) (definition SHIP)

;

; What is a ship?

;

A ship is a water-going vehicle that travels on the surface.   *Its* surface-going capabilities are provided by the DB attributes DISPLACEMENT and DRAFT...

Focus information is also used to discriminate between use of the passive and active construction. The passive can be used to place the focused constituent in surface subject position when the logical subject of the sentence is not in focus. In TEXT, this construction may be necessary in describing binary relations in the ONR database. In the ONR database, weapons are associated through the relation "carry" with different vehicles. When answering a question about missiles, a weapon, the passive construction is used since the missile is in focus (see (10) below). When answering a question about the ECHO II, a type of submarine, the active construction is used in order to attribute information to the "ECHO II" (see (11) below)

    10) (difference MISSILE TORPEDO)
    ;
    ; What is the difference between a
    ; missile and a torpedo?
    ;

.... The missile's target location is indicated by the DB attribute DESCRIPTION and its flight capabilities are provided by the DB attribute ALTITUDE.   Other DB attributes of the missile include PROBABILITY OF KILL, SPEED, ALTITUDE, LETHAL RADIUS & UNITS and TIME TO TARGET & UNITS.   *Missiles are carried by water-going vehicles and aircraft...*

    11) (information ECHO–II–SUBMARINE)
    ;
    ; What do you know about Echo II's?
    ;

.... There are no sub-classes of echo II in the ONR database.   *Echo IIs carry 16 torpedoes, between 16 and 99 missiles and 0 guns....*

When the system decides to focus on a set of objects, with subsequent shifts in focus to each member of the set, there-insertion can be used to introduce the set as focus.   The use of there-insertion by the TEXT system is shown below in (12) in a portion of the answer generated to the question "What is a guided projectile?".   Use of there-insertion in this situation is one way to introduce the set of sub-classes of the guided projectile as focus into the discourse.

    12) (definition GUIDED)
    ;
    ; What is a guided projectile?
    ;

.... *There are 2 types of guided projectiles in the ONR database: torpedoes and missiles.* The missile has a target location in the air or on the earth's surface.   The torpedo has an underwater target location...

9 FOCUS CONSTRAINT IMPLEMENTATION

TEXT constructs an answer to a given question by repeatedly selecting[2] propositions to include in the answer, each of which is eventually translated to a sentence.   A proposition consists of a predicate and its arguments which are realized in the final English version as the verb of the sentence and its case roles.   TEXT uses its schema, or discourse plan, as a guide in determining what to include next and is constrained in its choice in the two ways discussed so far: 1) it is constrained in what it considers for inclusion by global focus and 2) the text constructed so far constrains what it can say next.   As a proposition is added to the answer, a focus record is filled out and added along with it.   The focus record associated with each proposition includes the focused argument and the potential focus list (other arguments which are candidates for a shift in focus).   This record is used both to constrain what proposition can follow as well as for the basis of surface choice.

---

[2] Actually by constructing the proposition since propositions don't exist as a whole in the knowledge base.

Immediate focus constraints (the preference ordering shown in Section 3.0) determine how the focus record is filled out. If any possible next proposition (of those that have been selected by the schema) has an argument that can be focused such that the first preference is met (i.e., the argument was a member of the previous proposition's potential focus list), that proposition is selected and its argument is recorded as the current focus of the proposition. All other arguments are included in the proposition's potential focus list as they are candidates for a shift in focus. If the first preference cannot be met, the same procedure is repeated for each of the remaining preferences until a proposition is selected.

Surface choice is made on the basis of the focus record associated with the proposition. It is used to select the sentence voice (active, passive, or there-insertion) and to determine whether pronominalization can be used. On selection of a verb for the sentence, sentence voice is also selected. When a verb is selected to translate a predicate, the predicate's arguments are mapped onto the case roles of the verb (e.g., protagonist, goal). If the protagonist is the focused argument, the active voice is selected; if the goal is focused, the passive voice is selected. The selection of voice there-insertion is slightly more complicated as it is based on the introduction of a set whose members are focused in succeeding utterances (see McKeown 82A for more details).

As an example, consider the proposition, consisting of a predicate, its arguments, and its focus record, shown in (13A) below. (13B) shows the proposition at an intermediate stage of generation. The verb "to carry" has been selected to translate the analogy-relation ON and the arguments of the relation have been mapped onto the case roles of the verb: the carrier has been mapped to the protagonist and the weapon to the goal. Since the goal is in focus, the passive voice is selected and the final sentence shown in (13C) is generated.

```
13A) predicate = analogy-relation
     relation  = ON
     carrier = (AIR-VEHICLE
               WATER-VEHICLE)
     weapon  =  MISSILE
     current focus = MISSILE
     potential focus list =
         ((AIR-VEHICLE WATER-VEHICLE)
          ON
          analogy-relation)


 B) verb === carry
    protagonist =
        conj === and
        head1 === aircraft
        head2 === water-going vehicle
    goal === missile
    voice = passive


 C) Missiles are carried by
    water-going vehicles and aircraft.
```

Pronominalization is determined on selecting a lexical item to translate a predicate argument. When choosing pronominalization, the focus record of the last proposition is checked. If the argument was in focus, pronominalization is selected in place of the full reference for the argument.

10 LIMITATIONS AND EXTENSIONS

The current formulation and implementation clearly show how focus information can be successfully used as the basis for surface choice. Further improvements can be made, however, by encoding the tests for surface choice as part of the grammar. The grammar used in TEXT is based on Kay's functional grammar formalism (Kay 79) and in fact allows for the explicit encoding of focus information. Enough information is available at that time to make the tests for an entire category (e.g., verb or noun phrase) instead of a lexical item, thus allowing for more generality in determination of choice.

The implementation can also be extended by including tests for additional types of surface choice which are signaled through focus information. When determining how to express an underlying message, a language generator must be able to decide when to use a sequence of simple sentences and when to use a single complex sentence. In very recent work (Derr and McKeown 83), we have shown how focus of attention can be used as the basis for this decision.

As an example, suppose that a system must choose between generating the two simple sentences shown in (14) below and the single complex sentence shown in (15) to express the same two propositions. If the system plans to focus on *John* first, shift to *Mary*, but return to *John* to supply additional information, the surface generator can signal that the shift to *Mary* is only temporary by combining the two propositions using subordination as in sentence (15). A textual sequence illustrating this possibility is shown in (16) below. On the other hand, if the system intends to continue focusing on *Mary* after the initial shift, then it is more appropriate to generate two separate sentences as in (14). It may even be possible to combine the second and third sentences which both focus on *Mary*, using conjunction as in the textual sequence shown in (17).

14) John gave Mary a book.
Mary needed the book.

15) John gave Mary a book that she needed.

16) John gave Mary a book that she needed.
He had seen it in the Columbia bookstore.

17) John gave Mary a book.
Mary needed the book and had been planning on
buying it herself.

This work was implemented by Derr as part of a surface language generator which uses functional information (such as focus of attention) within the Prolog Definite Clause Grammar (DCG) formalism (Pereira and Warren 80). The generator uses tests on functional information to determine the exact surface structure of the sentence to be generated and thus, allows for simplification of input as does the functional grammar used in TEXT. Tests on focus to choose between the active and passive construction as well as to choose between simple and complex sentences were encoded as part of the grammar, thus achieving generality in determination of choice. Furthermore, encoding a functional grammar as a DCG takes advantage of Prolog's efficient unification algorithm, resulting in an efficient surface generator.

The DCG generator was implemented as part of an explanation facility for a student advisor expert system currently being developed. Derr's system is capable of combining propositions using subordination when focus shifts temporarily (output from the system illustrating this case is shown in (18) below), of combining propositions using coordination on the basis of identity deletion (see (19) below), and of combining propositions using coordination when focus remains the same (see (20) below).

18) Assembly__language has a prerequisite that was taken.
Assembly__language does not conflict.

19) Analysis__of__algorithms requires Data__structures
and Discrete__math.

20) Introduction__to__computer__programming does not
have prerequisites and does not conflict.

We plan to investigate further criteria for text generation choices within this domain, which provides a rich testbed for experimentation. Some of the surface choices which require further investigation include the influence of focus on lexical choice (noted earlier, but not currently implemented in either system) and the use of textual connectives. The need for textual connectives may be signaled by underlying causal relationships between propositions, but it may also be signalled by a shift in focus. If focus shifts abruptly from one sentence to the next, a textual connective may be required to ease the transition for the reader. The implementation of these uses of focus information for surface-level choices remains a topic for future work.

11 CONCLUSIONS

The process of generating natural language has been shown to involve a system of choices across a wide spectrum of knowledge sources. A method has been presented that provides a theoretical basis which constrains generation decisions. Furthermore, it illustrates how information arising from decisions about what to say can be used to constrain choices in the surface level expression. While these choices can be arbitrarily determined, an inappropriate decision could easily be made. As systems become more sophisticated, it is imperative that they produce appropriate utterances in order that they communicate effectively with their users.

ACKNOWLEDGMENTS

This paper is an extended version of the paper "Focus Constraints on Language Generation" presented at the *Eighth International Joint Conference on Artificial Intelligence*.

I would like to thank Aravind K. Joshi, Bonnie Webber, Michael Lebowitz, and Kathy McCoy for their comments and suggestions on various drafts of this paper.

This work was partially supported by National Science Foundation grant #MCS81-07290, awarded to the Computer and Information Science Department of the University of Pennsylvania and by ONR contract N00014-82-K-0156 and ARPA contract N00039-82-C-0427 awarded to the Department of Computer Science, Columbia University.

REFERENCES

[1] (Derr and McKeown 83). Derr, M. and K. R. McKeown, Using focus to generate complex and simple sentences. Technical Report, Department of Computer Science, Columbia University, 1983.

[2] (Firbas 66). Firbas, J., "On defining the theme in functional sentence analysis." *Travaux Linguistiques de Prague* 1, Univ. of Alabama Press, 1966.

[3] (Grosz 77). Grosz, B.J., The representation and use of focus in dialogue understanding. Technical note 151, Stanford Research Institute, Menlo Park, Ca. (1977).

[4] (Halliday 67). Halliday, M. A. K., "Notes on transitivity and theme in English." *Journal of Linguistics* 3, 1967.

[5] (McKeown 80). McKeown, K.R., "Generating relevant explanations: natural language responses to questions about database structure." in *Proceedings of AAAI*, Stanford Univ., Stanford, Ca. (1980). pp. 306–9.

[6] (McKeown 82A). McKeown, K.R., Generating natural language text in response to questions about database structure. Technical Report MS-CIS-82-5, Univ. of Pennsylvania, Philadelphia, Pa. (1982).

[7] (McKeown 82B). McKeown, K.R., "The TEXT system for natural language generation: an overview." in *Proceedings of the 20th Annual Meeting of the ACL*, University of Toronto, Toronto, Canada (1982).

[8] (Sidner 79). Sidner, C.L., Towards a computation theory of definite anaphora comprehension in English discourse. Ph.D. Dissertation, MIT, Cambridge, Mass. (1979).

Computational Models of Natural Language Processing
B.G. Bara and G. Guida (eds.)
© Elsevier Science Publishers B.V. (North-Holland), 1984

TOWARDS AN INTEGRAL MODEL OF LANGUAGE COMPETENCE

Alexandre S. Narin'yani

Artificial Intelligence Laboratory-Computing Center
Siberian Division of the USSR Academy of Sciences
Novosibirsk, USSR

There is no satisfactory formal model of natural
language by now. The family of models which have
been proposed by machine translation research at
the beginning of seventies is not adequate for developing dialogue systems or coherent text parsers.
Under pressure of this crisis a new generation model has begun to take shape recently. In this paper we discuss a general outline of this future
model. It will consist of several closely interconnected submodels of the most important components of language competence. We consider here in
detail: (i) the model of speech interaction, (ii)
anaphora as a part of the model of coherent text,
and (iii) a fragment of the sentence model. We
discuss also the relationship of language competence with the world model and knowledge representation.
"... we will no longer be satisfied merely with
trying to describe the structure of language. What
we want to know is how people use language to communicate" (Yngve, 1969).

1. INTRODUCTION

The history of the efforts made by computational linguistics to ela-
borate a formal model of language oriented to coherent text processing has proved that the current ideas about this model are developing
very fast under the constant pressure of such different factors as:
- evolution of the formal tools which have developed toward a more
and more declarative, higher level, and problem-oriented structure;
- assimilation of deeper and deeper language levels, including semantics, pragmatics, and communication models;
- progress of the language theory, i.e. the linguistics itself;
- expansion of formally (more or less systematically) described
areas of language competence.

This development is so dynamic and the problem itself is so enormous
that many models became obsolete before their realization was over.
It seems that these premature deaths could be explained by the effect
of the inborn "ineffectiveness complex": the insolvable conflict between the naturalness and the power of the model on the one hand,
and the effectiveness of its realization on the other, has been systematically solved in favour of the latter. But, in the meantime, the
hardware and software progress had dismissed the causes which not so
far ago appeared to dictate with obvious necessity the fatal limitations that predetermined the final failure of several projects.

Experience proves that we have to separate the fundamental research
on formal models from the practical attempts of developing applied
systems aimed at obtaining limited results with limited resources.

The research projects of the last decade have demonstrated the obvious inadequacy of the natural language models restricted to the framework of an isolated sentence. It is quite clear by now that the problem of the analysis of coherent text (even if in restricted NL) requires a qualitatively new natural language model. So to say, a new
generation model has to be developed.

In this case it seems impossible to design the new model in an evolu-
tionary way, i.e. by improving and generalizing previous models, since
the structure and functions of the new model are radically different.
In contrast to the "yesterday" models which have been engaged in constructing a mapping between a text and some abstract representation
of it, the "tomorrow" model should focus on the communicative functions of language.

We are now observing a growing expansion of computational linguistics
towards such domains as text structure, speech interaction, communicative context, and pragmatic environment. The level of formalization
and integration of these works has not yet reached the threshold allowing us to formulate a new paradigm. But the totality of the results
obtained in the field has made possible to think of a rough draft of
the future model. It is our aim to discuss in this paper such an emerging proposal using as an illustration some results of the recent research carried out in our Laboratory.

2. PRELIMINARY REMARKS

We feel necessary to make several preliminary remarks useful to better
understand some general principles of our approach to the problem.

  (1) <u>The goal</u>. We prefer to formulate our goal as a natural language
competence model rather than a natural language model, as usual several years ago. This gives us the possibility to consider such domains
of research as linguistics, knowledge representation, inference, interpersonal communication, cognitive process, etc., as complementary
parts of the whole problem.
  (2) <u>Declarative character of the model</u>. We are basing on complete
separation of a "model" and a "mechanism" (Yngve, 1961), or, according to a more recent terminology, on a declarative character of the
model. The latter is considered as a system of interconnected structural descriptions rather than a process of analysis and/or synthesis.
  (3) <u>Formal tools</u>. This declarative character is supported by appropriate formal tools. The conflict of the two classical formal systems
of dependencies and of constituents played a positive role in the sixties, but most obviously has had no sense during the last decade.
The problem of generalization of these systems has been solved in
other domains long ago. The formal tools used in knowledge representation (embedded semantics, frames, etc.) are the obvious combination of these approaches. For example, the meaning of the sentence
"John tells Ann that he loves her" can be represented by a semantic
net of the type shown in Figure 1. Here a semantic net can be considered as a generalization of the dependencies and constituents approaches. In this example the nonterminal constituent A is a part of the
dependency configuration within the constituent B (arc 3) and , simultaneously, the constituents A and B are intersecting: the constituents <u>John</u>, <u>Ann</u>, and <u>t-interval j</u> belong to A as well as to B.

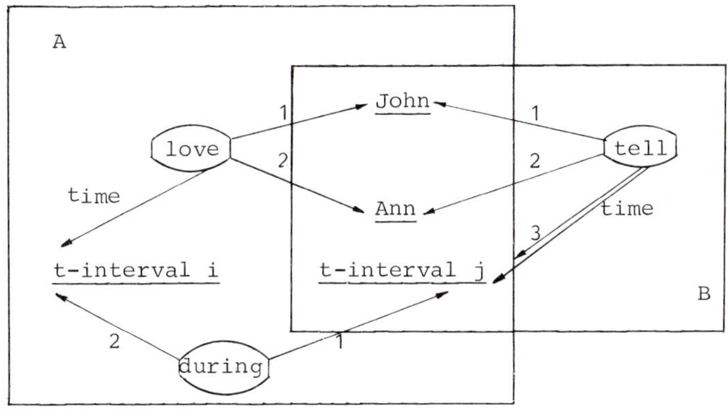

Figure 1
Semantic net representation of
"John tells Ann that he loves her".

The generalized structural unit which we are using for the description
of different language phenomena is the component introduced in
Narin'yani (1978). A non-elementary component has its description,
i.e. a set of attributes defining the constituents as a whole, and
its structure consisting of embedded components and their relations.
The nomenclature of component types, attributes, and relations is defined by the content of the described phenomena. A component can have
several facets and can simultaneously be included, as an embedded
unit, into different embedding components related to various projections of the natural language model.
  (4) Basic research. The model should not take into account specific
implementation problems or requirements of text processing. It is a
task of linguistic processor designers to find methods to effectively
use the linguistic information stored in the model which is necessary for developing actual systems.

The grammars for these processors are just projections of the natural
language model: they have to be oriented to the level, limitations,
and special requirements of the application, thus their construction
has no direct relation to linguistics in general and to our basic research in particular.
  (5) Multi-dimensional (vs. multi-level) model. It is widely accepted in contemporary linguistics that a natural language model has to
be multi-level, that means, in particular, that the text ⟶ meaning
mapping can be realized only with the help of intermediate supporting
constructions. The structure of the text and its semantic representation are considered to be so dissimilar that the relation between
them cannot be expressed as a direct mapping.

Most of existing approaches try to realize this correspondence through
a sequence of standard intermediate levels of representation (morphological, syntactic, etc.). These artifial levels are considered very
often to be real components of language. The number and the interpretation of these levels vary from model to model, but the main principle is always the same: any analysis or synthesis task has to be processed

through all the levels. This simple principle is rather disputable:
the fixed number of levels is generally too small for some types of
language constructs and obviously redundant for others. It seems to
us much more easy and adequate to describe natural language similarly
to any other complex subject domain, i.e. as a system of components,
each one reflecting a different projection (or subsystem) of the
language: prosody, word order, morphology, syntax, etc. up to the model of speech interaction. The relations which bind the components together within the subsystems and which specify the interconnections
between the subsystems are generally ambiguous. When generating or
analysing a text, the natural language model induces a process of refinement involving various subsystems which provide useful information for making the components more precise. The definition of some
points leads to a higher precision of the others, reducing at each
step the variety of possible forms of the text to be synthesized or
the possible meanings of the text being analysed. The tools which allow implementation of this kind of inference are being developed in our
Laboratory as a part of a knowledge representation system.

The method proposed makes it possible to implement a goal-directed
inference, which defines only the assigned components of the model
and advances the definition of the remaining components just as far
as necessary for the current task. This permits, in particular, the
organization of a semantics - oriented analysis procedure under which
the processor tries first of all to "reconstruct" the meaning of the
input text (by jumping to the content, ignoring syntactical and morphological information) and reconsider - as locally as possible - the
skipped "details" only to solve ambiguous points. Such an approach
(used by us in applied natural language processors) seems much more
natural than more traditional ones, and more practical for applied
systems with restricted subject domains. Moreover, it permits parsing
an "understandable" broken or uncorrect text because it makes possible
to disregard, to some extent, the syntactical norm, so poorly respect-
ed by end-users.

3. GENERAL STRUCTURE OF THE MODEL

In this section we sketch the research domain in general terms, i.e.
we define the models which are the main constituents of our integral
natural language competence model (NLC model) and we discuss their
interconnections within the overall schema (see Figure 2).

We begin by a model which is not a part of the NLC model but should
be considered as its environment and background. We mean the model
of interpersonal communication, which represents the forms, rules,
and laws of the interaction, including real world cultural, social,
and psychological components. Of course, each of the participants in
the communication has his own view on this information and uses it
to choose appropriate acts in the interaction process.

This model is closely related with the model of physical world, the
social environment, and the individual mind. The organization of this
model is similar to that of verbal interaction which is considered
in the section 4.

The model of verbal interaction is the main frame of the integral
NLC model. It covers only some part of the interpersonal communication model and can be considered as its projection realized by NL
means. In the verbal interaction model a dialogue is represented as an
interaction of two automata which define the linguistic competence

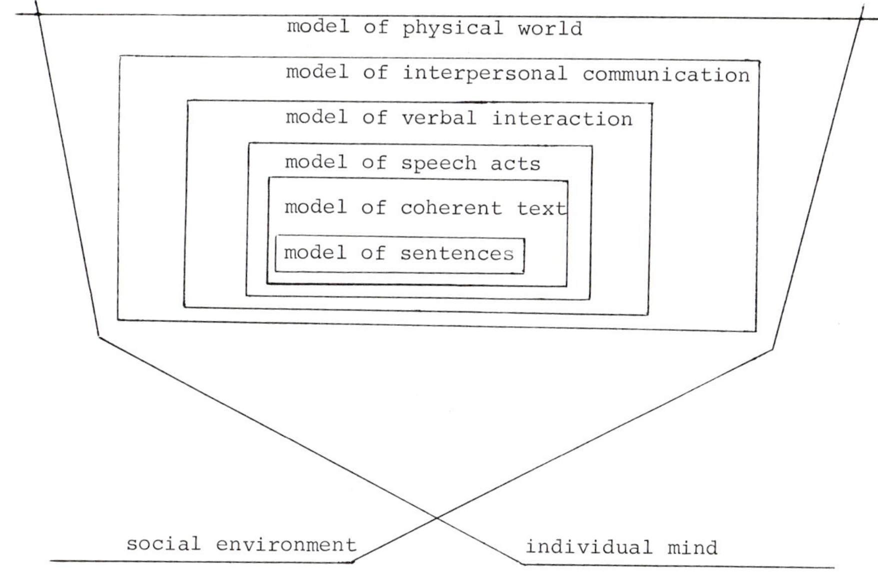

Figure 2

General schema of the integral NLC model
and its pragmatic context.

of the corresponding interlocutors. A state of a partner-automaton
is defined by the current state of its ideas about the reality, the
context of interaction, and the state of the interlocutor. The alphabet of the automaton is the nomenclature of the communicative functions of speech acts. When receiving a speech act the automaton
changes its state and generates, in turn, one of the possible speech
acts of the new state.

The information which is carried by a speech act transferred from one
of the partners to the other, includes, apart from the semantics of
the text of the given speech act (the dictum, according to Wierzbicka, 1980) also a specific communicative function. Very often this
latter represents the main content of a speech act and can even mask
its semantics as, for example, in the case of indirect speech acts.

The communicative functions of a speech act, together with its dictum define its inner structure, which belongs to the domain of the model of speech acts. This structure can be considered as a kernel for
the textual realization of the speech act. The model of speech acts
also includes a system of rules determining the choice of the form,
the style, the narrative line, and the disposition of the elements
of content by their importance.

The model of coherent text which is responsible for the realization
of the kernel provided by the model of speech acts, covers the laws

of lexicalization, the division of the content into sentences, the
organization of the connections between sentences (anaphora, old/new
information, focus, etc.). Its task is to form projects for individual sentences; the textual realization of the project belongs to the
domain of the last model we mention here, i.e. to the model of sentences.

Being a subsystem of the coherent text model, the <u>model of sentences</u>
can work only in close connection with the other models mentioned
above. For example, when participating in text synthesis it needs
not only the semantic representation of its dictum but also information about the structure of the surrounding text, its communicative
function, style, lexical structure, etc.

At the current stage of our work only some separate fragments of the
entire NLC model can be demonstrated in a more or less formal way.
In this paper we are able to present only a small part of this material. So we choose to discuss here three topics which can help to
form a general idea of the approach:
- a model of verbal interaction and speech acts, including dialogue:
  section 4.
- a fragment of the coherent text model, with particular attention
  to anaphora: section 5.
- a fragment of the sentence model, focusing on Russian parametric
  constructions: section 6.

4. A VERBAL INTERACTION AND SPEECH ACTS MODEL

As mentioned above, we consider verbal interaction as a system of
automata each representing the natural language competence of the corresponding partner of the interaction. Such an automaton R is defined
by the set Q of its states and by the alphabet V of the speech acts
it can process (understand or generate). The ability of R to comprehend speech acts is represented by a function $U:Q\times V\rightarrow Q$; being in a
state $q \in Q$ and receiving in input a speech act $v \in V$, the automaton R moves, after comprehension of v, into a new state $q'=U(q,v)$.
The ability of R to generate speech acts is represented by a function
$G:Q\rightarrow 2^V$ (where 2^V is the set of all subsets of V). The function G
defines for every current state $q \in Q$ a set $G(q) \subseteq V$ of speech acts
which can be generated in the given state q. Below we shall consider the interaction of two automata modeling the dialogue process.

In a general case the form and content of a speech act are defined
by the totality of information about the reality the producer of
the speech act has at his disposal. In this general model belonging
to a partner α (denoted as $M.\alpha$) we distinguish two components:
- $CC.\alpha$, which is the current state of the <u>communicative context</u>
of the interaction in the interpretation of α; this part of $M.\alpha$
represents the factors which are taken into account in the model in
explicit form;
- $M.\beta.\alpha$, which is α's interpretation of $M.\beta$, where β is the partner
of α in the dialogue; it is obvious that $M.\beta.\alpha$ includes α's idea of
$CC.\beta$ and $M.\alpha.\beta$.
This schema of dialogue is illustrated in Figure 3. Here, R_α and R_β

denote the automata representing the partners α and β, respectively.

We shall now consider in some detail the structure of the communication context and the main functions of a speech act, according to the
proposal of (Debrenne and Narin'yani, 1983).

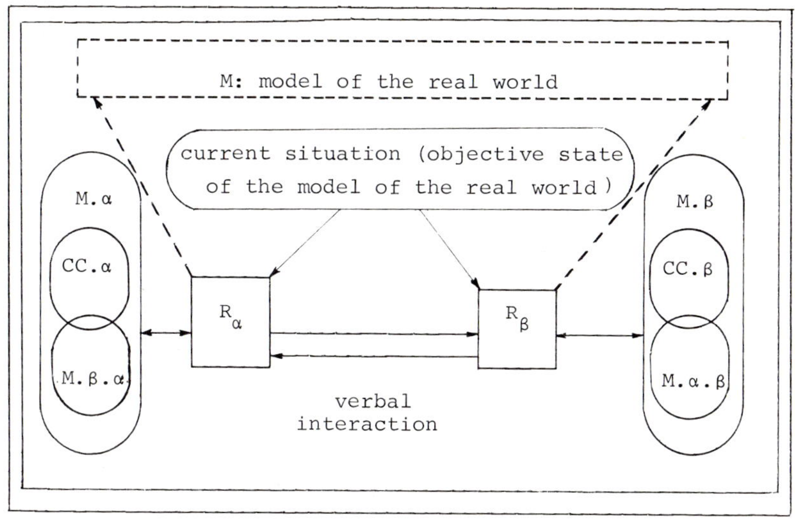

Figure 3

Schema of dialogue model

A speech act includes several functions in the verbal interaction model (The meaning of the terms "performative", "perlocutive", and "illocutive" is not the same as traditionally in the theory of speech acts (Searle, 1969 and 1975):

(a) the <u>performative</u> function,i.e.the function of the given speech act

beyond the model of verbal interaction; this function includes:

- the pragmatic component of performative communication (Austin,1962),

- the intended effect of the speech act on other people,

- the intended use of the form of the speech act (length, volume of sound, intonation, style, etc.) out of the verbal interaction;
(b) the <u>perlocutive</u> function which reflects the particular kind of performative effect directed to the mind of the partner (to scare, make glad, insult, calm, etc.);
(c) the <u>illocutive</u> function, connected with the choice of the conventional form of the speech act (command, question, assertion, etc.);
(d) the <u>reactive</u> function, which represents the interconnections between different speech acts within the structure of the verbal interaction model (answer, refuse, objection, confirmation, etc.);
(e) the <u>informative</u> function, which concerns the fact that every speech act from α to β can be considered as an information package containing, in explicit or implicit form, data of α's model of the world, including his view of the current communicative situation and of his partner. The content of the package is defined by the above functions (a)-(d).

Later in this section we shall consider an example of the illocutive
function and its informative content, but before that we have to discuss the structure of the communicative context in our model.

The sum of the factors included in the communicative context defines
the quality of the personal speech competence model represented by
the automaton R and, consequently, the quality of the entire model of
verbal interaction. We shall present below a simple variant of the
communicative context structure which includes the following components:
(a) The system of purposes of the partners. To produce any speech act
the partner α has to develop all functions considered above. The
particular content of each of the functions implies the corresponding
purpose of α; thus a speech act as a whole implies a set of purposes
connected with all functions of this speech act. A purpose is declared
at the moment of transmission of the speech act from α to β, and
kept in the communicative context until one of the partners closes
the communication (this closure may be successful or unsuccessful in
respect to the purpose of α). Therefore, at every given moment of the
dialogue the communicative context includes all the purposes of both
the partners which have been declared but have not been closed yet.
(b) The system of indices of the relation between the partners. We
select the following closely interconnected indices:
- dependency, which can vary from domination of one partner over the
other up to relative equality of the partners; in the simplest form
it can have the values ">", "=", "<";
- collaboration, which in the simplest case, assumes one of the three
values "cooperation", "neutrality", "conflict";
- trust, which specifies the level of trust between the partners.
(c) The system of the indices of interest of the partners in achieving the purpose of a speech act. It can be expressed with absolute
(α-INTER(X) = POSIT/NEG) or relative (α-INTER(X)/β-INTER(X)) values.
We suppose below that the interest of an actor in achieving the purpose of a speech act is always positive. Under cooperation
β-INTER$\neq$NEG and under conflict α-INTER$\geqslant\beta$-INTER. Development of a
more adequate system of indices should be the theme of a special investigation.

It is important to stress here the following:
- in the verbal interaction model the system of indices represent
a totality of social and psychological factors belonging to the general interaction model which is the background of the verbal interaction;
- on one hand, the notion of the current communicative context which
the producer of a speech act has, determines the choice of a particular content for every function of the speech act; on the other hand,
these functions contain by default some concrete information about
the notion of the communicative context.

We now discuss the informative content of the functions of a speech
act. It would be very long to analyse all the functions and all concrete forms of them. So we shall consider the illocutive function
as an example. The forms of the illocutive function of a speech act
are divided into three main classes:
        - inducing speech acts,
        - assertions,
        - questions.

In principle, every speech act includes components of inducement (α
induces β to perform an action D) and assertion (the informative

function of the speech act). But assertions and questions are distinguished as special part of the inducing speech act where action D has a special communicative character and belongs to the verbal interaction model itself: in the case of an assertion, the indicated action D is "a perception of the assertion by the partner β" and in the case of a question, D is "an answer to the question". Below we show the frame for an inducing speech act:

INDUCING SPEECH ACTS:

content: α induces β to perform D

[D is defined explicitly by the dictum of S]

purpose: P = (β performs D)

[The real purpose of α could be not D itself but some consequence D'; we consider such an application of S as a special case of the indirect speech act]

presupposition: (1) ((β performs D) is possible) and
                (2) ((β performs D) may not take place without S) and
                (3) (S can cause (β performs D))
[It is possible to introduce an index of confidence for each of these constituents of the presupposition, but we ignore these details here]

indication of success:
                (1) β has performed D
                (2) β has promised to perform D
[It could be necessary/possible to postpone performing D in case of sufficient level of trust of α to β]

i n d i c e s   o f   r e l a t i o n

dependency: (arbitrary)

collaboration: (arbitrary)

trust: sufficient level of trust of β to general intentions of α with respect to β

i n d i c e s   o f   i n t e r e s t

β-INTER (P): (arbitrary)
α-INTER(P)/β-INTER(P): (arbitrary)

Let us consider some more examples of special inducing speech acts:

(i) REQUEST is a more concrete type of the inducing speech act including the following information:

α-INTER(D) ≥ β-INTER(D)

dependency: α ≤ β

collaboration: sufficient level of cooperation.

(ii) An inducing speech act with an argument differs from a simple inducing speech act for the value of the slot

content: (α induces β to perform D using information I as an argument).

Information I should correct the indices of interest in the communicative context of β and this is based on the assumption that <u>trust</u> has a value corresponding to a sufficient level of trust of β to I.

As an example of a cooperative inducing speech act with an argument
we can use ADVICE, whose information I has the following structure:

I = (not to perform D is less advantageous for β than to perform D).
Information I may also contain additional data stressing that not to
perform D is disadvantageous and/or to perform D is advantageous for
β.

It is important to stress that the frame shown above specifies the
informative content of the illocutive function of an inducing speech
act: if some speech act is marked as an inducing speech act its illocutive function by default includes all the content of the frame.
The same is true for other variants of the illocutive function and,
in general, for all functions of a speech act: every variant of each
function of a speech act has its own purpose, presuppositions, etc.,
and the information of its frame is included in the information package of the speech act if the latter is marked in a proper way. The
means which α can use for marking the speech act to manifest its functions include combination of syntactic and lexical form, intonation,
style, correlation with communicative and pragmatic context, etc.

After having received the current speech act V of α the partner β
can react to different components of its information package. His reaction (taking some particular form of the reactive function of a new
speech act V' of β) can be directed   (i) at the content of the dictum, (ii) at its presuppositions, (iii) at the particular form of
some function of V, (iv) at the presupposition of V, (v) at the values of some index of CC.α, (vi) at the general presupposition of the
verbal interaction.

For example, consider the speech act of α:

Let's make a deal, Bob.

Possible reactions of β (in correspondence to the topics counted
above) are:
   (i) With pleasure.
   (ii) But we have no common business!
   (iii) Is it a request or an order?
   (iv) This is not in my power.
   (v) Drop your tricks, buddy.
   (vi) I don't even want to speak with you.
        I can hear not a single word of you.
        I cannot understand what do you mean by this.

In a general case the dictum of the speech act V' can be simultaneously a reaction to several components of the information package of the
opponent speech act V. And the information package of V' by default
contains reactions (confirmations or/and disagreements) to several
components of V. So this leads us to the conclusion that a substan-
tial part of information exchange between the partners is done through
the marks indicating by default the functions of the speech acts.

5. ORGANIZATION OF COHERENT TEXT: ANAPHORA

   In this section we shall introduce the model of coherent text and
discuss anaphora which is one of the basic mechanisms of this model
(Narin'yani, 1982 and 1983). For this purpose we shall simplify our
schema of a step of a dialogue:
A speech act in the form of the text T is directed from the sender α

to the receiver β, under the assumption that α and β have a common
model M of the world, i.e. M.α = M.β . M is in the state M.o between the previous and current speech acts.

Let the content of the dictum of the current speech act be a sequence
of components carrying new information to be added to M. Every component is coded by a corresponding text fragment t.i which will be called
a T-constituent.

We accept here that the process of comprehension of a text is sequential. Thus, when coming to the next T-constituent t.i+1, the receiver
has already understood the previous part of T (i.e., t.1,..., t.i)
which we denote as T.i. The information S.i extracted by ß from T.i
is added to M.o thus producing a new state of M which is denoted
as M.i (see Figure 4).

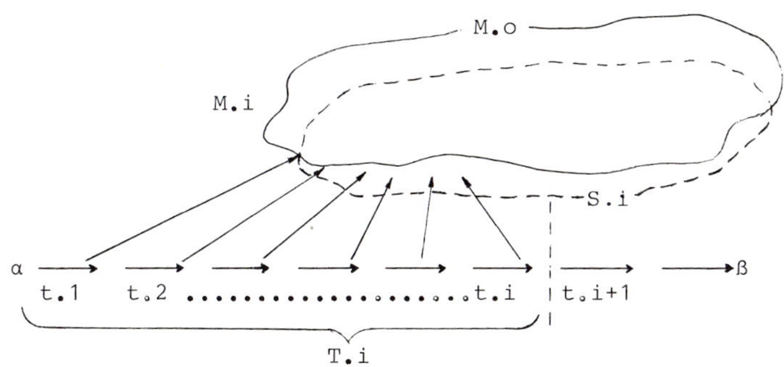

<u>Figure 4</u>

Transmission of the current
speech act from α to ß.

Each of the elements included in S.i can be associated with the element of the text T.i, which was the source of the corresponding addition to current M.i. The content of s.i+1 of the T-constituent
t.i+1, as well as the content of the previous T-constituents, is presented in the same form as the model of the world M. The content extracted by ß from t.i+1 has to be attached to M.i. This attachment
is realized by superposing those elements in M.i and s.i+1 which
have common pragmatic originals, i.e. which represent the same entity.

To define the correspondence between the vertices to be attached,the
elements of s.i+1 which have to be superposed to the elements of
M.i, are labelled and a special address is introduced for each of
them in the text t.i+1 allowing detection of the correct referent
(Hirst, 1981).

Clearly, the components of the addresses in s.i+1 don't carry any
new information: they are the old (known) part of the content of
t.i+1.

We consider two methods of addressing (below we suppose for the sake
of simplicity that s.i+1 includes only one element X to be attached):

(A) <u>Direct</u>: s.i+1 includes a pattern, i.e. an associative description of the referent of X (denoted by X!) which guarantees a reliable
recognition in M.i. Thus the content of t.i+1 can be split into
two parts, namely s.i+1 and the pattern t.i+1(X!). We put the index i+1 to the pattern since it is formed under the state M.i. A
pattern of the same referent under previous or consequent states of
M would be either simpler or more complex depending on the presence
of other elements in M similar to X! by their context in M. Let
us consider an example:
t.i: Flat number 15 was occupied by two girls, one of them was from
     Kiev and the other from Moscow.
t.i+1: The name of <u>the Moscow girl</u> was Masha.
t.i+2: <u>Masha's</u> friend living next door was from Moscow too and had
     the same name.
t.i+3: <u>Masha from flat 15</u> was fond of dance and pop music.

The underlined patterns in t.i+1, t.i+2 and t.i+3 have the same
referent but their complexity is different because the context of
the referent in M is changing.

If the method (A) were the only possible one, text understanding
would be a very difficult task since every new t-constituent would
require a pattern which in complex cases should be represented by a
text consisting of other t-constituents, and so on.

(B) <u>Indirect</u>: the constituent t.i+1 includes a pointer to the previous element of the text representing the referent X!. Let us consider
two examples:
    (1) t.i: It cost her a lot of trouble to find the second, third,
             and seventh volume.
        t.i+1: <u>The first two</u> were in the neighbour room and the <u>last</u>
             <u>one</u> was in the kitchen behind the refrigerator.
    (2) t.i: They came to look at his yacht.
        t.i+1: <u>It</u> was really beautiful.

We can note that the address in these examples does not include an
explicit pattern as in (A). The use of pure forms of addressing like
(A) and (B) is rather exception than rule. In a general case the address to X! is composite. It consists of a pattern for the text (T-
pattern) and a pattern for M (S-pattern). The first one points to a
limited subdomain of M.i through the text which X! belongs to, or
to X! itself; the second one is a pattern of type (A) but much simpler than in a pure case since the range of pattern-matching is restricted by the limits defined by the T-pattern.

Such a mechanism allowing a referent to be recognized through the corresponding text element by means of a T-pattern added to a S-pattern
will be referred here as <u>anaphora</u>.

In a general case none of the two patterns (T- and S-patterns) forming an anaphoric address is sufficient individually to find the referent. This can be achieved only by means of a combination of the
two. The rule of application of the double pattern is stated as follows:

The referent of the anaphoric address of the constituent t.i+1 is
the element of M.i which matches the S-pattern of the address and
which belongs to the subdomain of M.i induced by the text element
Ant (named antecedent) which is the nearest to t.i+1 of all the
text elements matching the T-pattern.

According to this rule, the referent may not only coincide with the image of Ant, but also be in other relations to it. Let us consider two examples:
    (1) Last year he was living in Moscow. <u>That building</u> does not exist now...
    (2) Mary met her future husband at a history lecture. <u>At that time</u> she was interested in...

It is well known that the relation between the content of the text $T.i$ and the context which the referent belongs to can also be very complex, as in the following example:
    Andy slapped him in the face in public. The tragic end of <u>the duel</u>...

But this case involves mechanisms for the reconstruction of text consistency by default, which are more general than those we are discussing here.

The information of an S-pattern is not limited to the content directly extracted from the text fragment representing the pattern but it is substantially augmented by the context of X in $s.i+1$. For example:
    he is reading: he = a male human;
    she has two decks and three masts: she = a sailing-ship.

A lexical implementation of T- and S-patterns may be either separate or superposed.

    Separate: <u>this</u> [T] hat [S]
          at <u>that</u> [T] time [S]
  Superposed: It is <u>that</u> [T'+S'] <u>he</u> [T"+S"] cannot see ···
          (two different pairs of superposed patterns)
          <u>Then</u> [T+S] Peter was absent.

Combinations of these cases are possible too, for example:
    Yesterday Mary bought a new hat. <u>Her purchase</u> was a great success.

Here the indicator "purchase" is an S-pattern including as a separate component an anaphoric indicator "her", which is a superposed one.

On the basis of the model presented it is possible to develop a classification of the anaphoric addresses. Let us consider several types of T-patterns:

    (i) <u>A simple T-pattern</u> is a functional unit which does not have own meaning but is provided with a set of selective syntactic attributes for identification of the antecedent. This unit is realized only in superposed form in combination with some lexem of the S-pattern (usually, personal and possessive pronouns, anaphoric conjunctive words, etc.). For example, in Russian the following attributes are used as selective ones:

    gender + singular number: который, он, ее <книга>, etc.;
    plural number: которые, <для> них, etc.;
    animation: слон, которого ему подарили vs.шар, который ему подарили; человек, чью книгу мы нашли, etc.

    (ii) <u>An anaphoric marker</u> is a degenerative case of T-pattern possessing no selective attributes. It is realized both in separate (some cases of definite article as well as demonstrative pronouns) or in superposed (special marked lexems, like then, there, thus, etc.) form. Its function is to differ those S-patterns which should be

treated by the anaphora mechanism (i.e. the referent should be looked
for through the textual component nearest to the marker) from the
non-anaphoric S-pattern which should be looked for in all domain M.i.

The T-patterns of the types (i) and (ii) may be omitted in those frequent cases when they can be easily reconstructed by default on the
basis cf the context and the communicative structure. For example:

   Маша жила в крайнем доме. (Этот) дом был старый, с узкими окнами.

   There remains only half an hour before the dinner.(So) he began
   to hurry up.

   (iii) A large special class of anaphoric addresses is formed by
structural textual T-patterns. This T-pattern individuates the antecedent by defining its place in the text structure of T.i, rather
than by means of an associative description as a direct pattern does.
T-patterns of this type are realized in the following ways:

   - by direct reference to a particular text fragment provided with
an identificator; for example:
   theorem T.11,
   on pages 24 and 25, etc.

   - by reference to a text unit through definition of its place in
the general structure of the text or its position with respect to
other units; for example:
   in the third sentence,
   mentioned at the beginning of the paper, etc.

   - by reference defining the position of the antecedent with respect to the position of the indicator itself, for example:
   in the previous paragraph,
   this last one,
   everything being said up to the moment, etc.

   - by reference to components of the structure of the narration
(to the meta-text), for example:
   the main hero of Peter's thoughts,
   the culmination of our story,
   this comment, etc.

   - by a combination of references of the types considered above,
for example:
   the first of these (considered above) alternatives,
   in the middle of the previous chapter (chapter 3),
   the events mentioned in the discussion prior to the appearance of
our hero, etc.

We can see from these examples that in some cases a combined structural T-pattern is built as a complex system of embedded more elementary T-patterns.

In the discussion above we have considered text as a sequence of
T-constituents. It is obvious that text structure is much more complex. We suppose that it is a superposition of interacting hierarchies
of components of different levels. Accordingly, all the lexical, syntactic and other kind of features involved in anaphora (i.e. participating in the realization of T-patterns) are related to some
specific level of locality:

   - within a phrase (his <bag>, herself, etc.);

   - within a complex sentence: anaphoric conjunctive words

(whom, which, etc.);

- immediately after the antecedent (within a distance of one or two sentences);

- with unrestricted gap.

6. A FRAGMENT OF THE SENTENCE MODEL: PARAMETRIC CONSTRUCTIONS

Up to the moment we have investigated several large fragments of Russian syntax, including adverbial groups (Gaft et al., 1979a), quantitative constructions (Kononenko et al., 1980), adjective constructions (Gaft et al., 1979b), and some other constructs.So we have enough information on the syntactic aspect of the sentence model. Other parts, such as lexicalization, communicative structure, denotative status of substantive groups, etc., are demanding further investigation.

These gaps, however, seem not crucial for our discussion, since we are concerned here with the global structure of the integral NLC model, rather than with the classic problem of the sentence model. We think that the fragment of formal description of Russian parametric constructions taken from (Kononenko and Pershina, 1982 and 1983), which is shown below as an example, can help the reader to form an idea of the role and functions of the sentence model within the general schema.

We introduce three types of components: semantic, lexical, and syntactic. The latter ones can be terminal and non-terminal. Every terminal syntactic component is simultaneously a lexical one, and vice versa.

Most lexical and all non-terminal syntactic components represent some semantic component, which, in turn, can be elementary or non-elementary. The model of Russian parametric constructions includes the following five elementary semantic components (in parentheses the concrete interpretation in our example is given both in English and in Russian):

$$K_o = \text{OBJECT} \quad (= \text{building, здание})$$

$$K_p = \text{PARAMETER} \quad (= \text{height, высота})$$

$$K_f = \text{FUNCTION} \quad (= \text{more, больше})$$

$$K_n = \text{NUMBER} \quad (= \text{hundred, сто})$$

$$K_u = \text{UNIT} \quad (= \text{meter, метр})$$

Choosing concrete lexical units we can assemble several semantic components into one lexical component up to compressing the whole construction into one lexem (for example, the adjective "four kilogram" includes three elementary semantic components = {PARAMETER, NUMBER, UNIT}, and the noun "fiver" includes all the five components = "a banknote with its value equal to five dollars").

The lexicalization and formation of the non-terminal syntactic components induce non-elementary semantic components. Possible forms of syntactic relations for pairs of semantic components are described by syntagms. A syntagm specifies the syntactic shape of both the components and the type of connection between them. Two types of the connections are simple, they are labelled 'actant' and 'attribute', others may be complex, like in syntagm 2b in the example discussed below, where two components are connected through the copulative verb. Syntagms can be comleted with semantic, lexical, and/or syntactic conditions.

Let the initial set of lexicalized components be K_o, K_{pf}, K_n, K_u. The chosen components are related with the following syntagms:

1) $(K_o\ K_n)$ - only with K_f= 'equal'

2) $(K_o\ K_{pf})$

3) $(K_o\ K_u)$ - only with K_f= 'equal'

4) $(K_o\ Qnt,unit)$ - only with K_f= 'equal'

5) $(K_n\ K_u)$

6) $(K_{pf}\ Qnt,unit)$

7) $(K_{pf}\ K_n)$

(K_{pf} denotes here the non-elementary semantic component made up of the union of K_p and K_f; in our example, = higher, выше). The syntagms (1),(3), and (4) are excluded since the particular values of the components K_p and K_f in their conditions do not coincide with the chosen ones. Therefore we have:

syntagm (2)

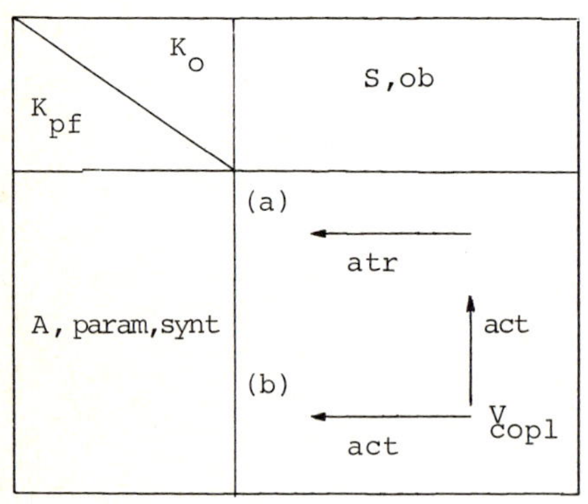

(a) здание выше
    (building higher)

(b) здание - выше
    (the building is higher)

syntagm (5)

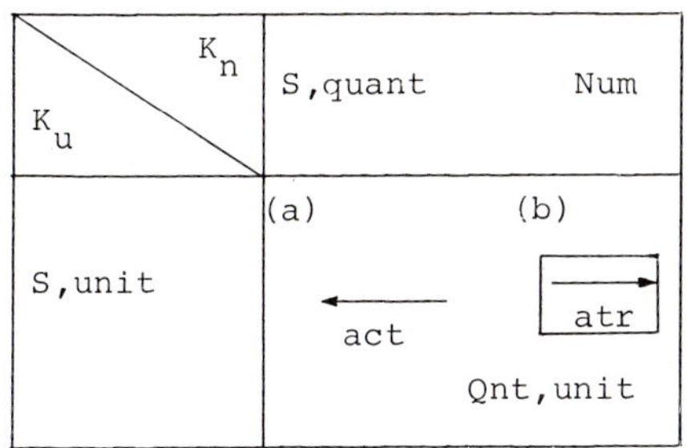

(a) сотня метров
   (one hundred of meters)

(b) сто метров

   (hundred meters)

in variant (b) non-terminal component Qnt,unit is formed being non-
-elementary semantic component K_{nu}.

syntagm (6)

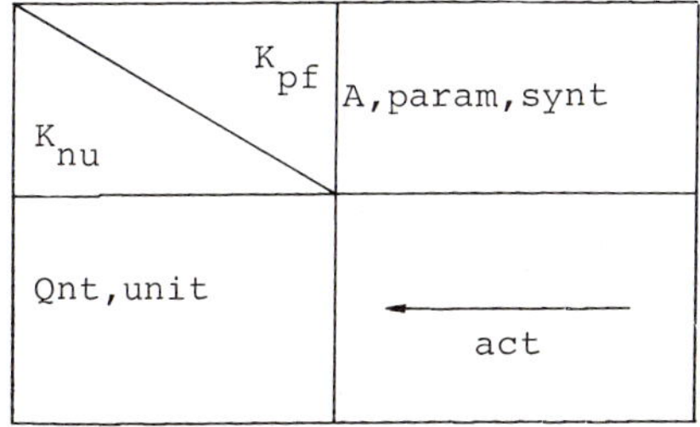

выше ста метров

(higher than one hundred meters)

syntagm (7)

выше сотни

(higher than one hundred (of))

Let us consider a couple of examples of the construction mechanism.
A. The realization of the component K_n by a numerative (сто, hundred)
eliminates syntagm (7) and, through variant (5b), generates the structure:

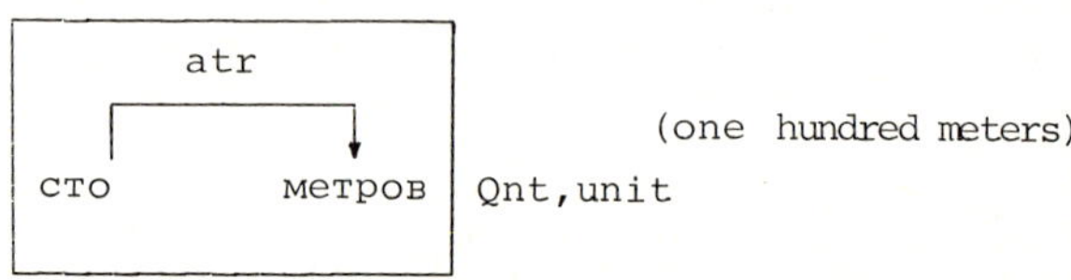

(one hundred meters)

This leaves the only possibility of using syntagm (6), which generates:

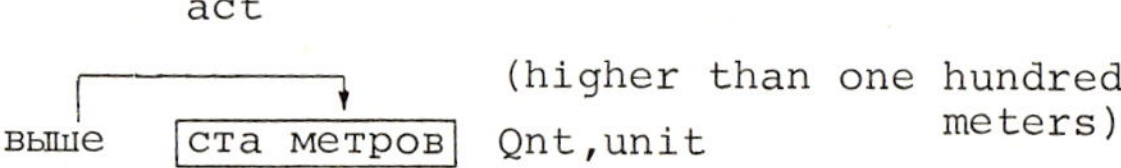

(higher than one hundred meters)

Syntagm (2) could be applied before (5b), between (5b) and (6), as
well as after (6), producing as a result:

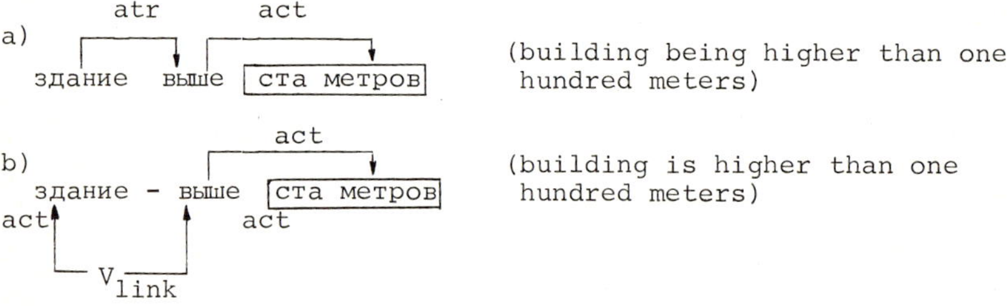

a) (building being higher than one hundred meters)

b) (building is higher than one hundred meters)

B. Starting from syntagm (7) we get:

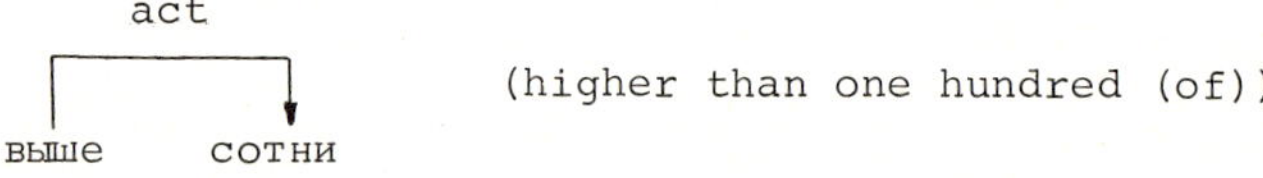

(higher than one hundred (of))

This eliminates (5b) and, consequently, (6). In next step both (5a)
and (2), which are independent of (7), are possible. As a result we
get two variants:

after (2a): здание выше сотни метров (building being higher than one
                                      hundred of meters - a noun
                                      phrase)
after (2b): здание - выше сотни метров (the building is higher than
                                      one hundred of meters - a
                                      sentence)

To make the illustration as easy as possible, we have chosen a very simple, almost trivial case of synthesis and we have excluded from our discussion operators involving morphologic attributes of syntactic components.

The complete model of Russian parametric constructions includes now 139 syntagms describing more than 90 possible textual realizations. It can work for analysis as well as for synthesis.

7. CONCLUSION

We have discussed above the outlines of a next generation natural language model which should constitute an integral model of natural language competence. Decomposing the integral model into a system of specific interacting submodels is the only possible way of investigating the enormously complex and multi-dimensional problem of natural language competence.

This method allows us to develop in parallel several autonomous submodels covering some chosen components of the entire research domain. Each submodel allows a researcher to investigate the correspondent component from a very specific and abstract point of view, to reach a higher specialization, and to get better results. Such submodel can be helpful even by itself in several related projects. For example, we are using our speech interaction model not only as a basis for further linguistic research, but also for developing adaptive high-level dialogue tools for applied systems. The same is true for the anaphora model. As for the parametric constructions model, we plan to use it, and possibly other fragments of the sentence model, in the applied ZAPSIB linguistic processors designed for natural language interaction with limited subject domains (Narin'yani, 1979a, 1979b and 1980). These processors are based on a semantics-oriented analysis procedure, and, in the simplest version, they do not use any syntactic information.

We have stressed the crucial role the model of the real world plays in the integral NLC model. There is no space here to discuss the structure of the real world model, we can only mention some of its fundamental constituents which include: time, space, cause-effect and part-whole relations, quantitative and qualitative estimations, etc. Regretfully, up to the recent time investigations in this field have been limited to specific experiments mostly directed at developing representation formalisms (for example, time logics). We mention (Kandrashina, 1983a, 1983b, and 1983c) as the most advanced and complete model of time and (Narin'yani and Kandrashina, 1982) as a preliminary study of the space model. It should also be noted that existing formal tools for knowledge representation and processing are still very far from being satisfactory (consider, for example, the crucial task of dealing with incomplete and imprecise knowledge – our laboratory has recently made some progress in this direction through the theory of sub-definite data types (Narin'yani, 1982 and 1983).

ACKNOWLEDGMENTS

I would like to thank several colleagues and especially the Editors of this volume for their suggestions concerning the structure of the paper, as well as Natalia Cheremnykh for her help in editing the English version.

REFERENCES

Austin, J.L.   How to do things with words. London: Oxford University
          Press, 1962.
Debrenne, M., Narin'yani, A.S.   Speech act as an element of dialogue
          interaction. Tartu, University Press. (In Russian).
Gaft, R.I., Gryaznova, G.M., Dinenberg, F.G., Kononenko,I.S., Pershi-
          na,E.L.   Structural description of adverbial groups. (Pre-
          print 140). Novosibirsk: Siberian Division of Academy of
          Sciences of the USSR, Computing Center,1979.(In Russian).
Gaft, R.I., Gryaznova,G.M., Dinenberg,F.G., Nesgovorova,G.P.   On the
          structure of Russian language adjective constructions. In
          A.S.Narin'yani, (Ed.), Syntactic and semantic components of
          lingware. Novosibirsk: Siberian Division of Academy of Scien-
          ces of the USSR, Computing Center, 1979. (In Russian).
Kandrashina, E.Yu.   Time in knowledge representation: Relations be-
          tween isolated events. (Preprint 438). Novosibirsk: Siberian
          Division of the Academy of Sciences of the USSR, Computing
          Center, 1983. (a) (In Russian).
Kandrashina, E.Yu.   Time in knowledge representation: Relations be-
          tween sequences of events. (Preprint 463). Novosibirsk: Si-
          berian Division of Academy of Sciences of the USSR, Computing
          Center, 1983. (b) (In Russian).
Kandrashina, E.Yu.   Representation of temporal knowledge. Paper pre-
          sented at the meeting of the International Joint Conference
          on Artificial Intelligence, Karlsruhe, 1983.(c).
Kononenko, I.S., Krasnova, V.A., Pershina, E.L.   The structure of the
          Russian quantitative constructions. (Preprint 237). Novosi-
          birsk: Siberian Division of Academy of Sciences of the USSR,
          Computing Center, 1980. (In Russian).
Kononenko, I.S., Pershina, E.L.   A model generating syntactic struc-
          tures of some Russian parametric constructions. In A.S.Na-
          rin'yani, (Ed.), Formal representation of linguistic infor-
          mation. Novosibirsk: Siberian Division of Academy of Scien-
          ces of the USSR, Computing Center, 1982. (In Russian).
Narin'yani, A.S.   Formal model: The outlines and choice of adequate
          means. (Preprint 107). Novosibirsk: Siberian Division of Aca-
          demy of Sciences of the USSR, Computing Center, 1978. (In
          Russian).
Narin'yani, A.S.   Linguistic processors ZAPSIB. Part I: Aims of the
          project. (Preprint 199). Novosibirsk: Siberian Division of
          Academy of Sciences of the USSR, Computing Center, 1979.(a)
          (In Russian).
Narin'yani, A.S.   Linguistic processors ZAPSIB. Part II: General scheme
          and the main models. (Preprint 202). Novosibirsk: Siberian
          Division of Academy of Sciences of the USSR, Computing Cen-
          ter, 1979. (b) (In Russian).
Narin'yani, A.S.   Interaction with a limited object domain: ZAPSIB
          Project. Paper presented at the meeting of the International
          Conference on Computational Linguistics, Tokyo, 1980.
Narin'yani, A.S.   A simplified anaphora model within the framework of
          an NL understanding system. Paper presented at the meeting
          of the International Conference on Computational Linguistics,
          Prague, 1982.(a) (A separate issue).
Narin'yani, A.S.   Subdefinite models and operations on subdefinite
          values. (Preprint 400). Novosibirsk: Siberian Division of
          Academy of Sciences of the USSR, Computing Center, 1982.(b)
          (In Russian).
Narin'yani, A.S., Kandrashina, E.Yu.   A sketch of a model of space in
          the system of knowledge about reality. (Preprint 368). Novo-

sibirsk: Siberian Division of Academy of Sciences of the
USSR, Computing Center, 1982. (In Russian).

Searle, J.R. Speech acts. London: Cambridge University Press,1969.

Searle, J.R. Indirect speech acts. In Syntax and semantics (Vol.III).
New York: Academic Press, 1975.

Wierzbicka, A. Lingua mentalis: The semantics of natural language.
Sydney: Academic Press, 1980.

Yngve, V.H. MT at Massachusetts Institute of Technology. Paper presented at the meeting of the National Symposium on Machine
Translation, Englewood Cliffs, 1961.

Yngve, V.H. On achieving agreement in linguistics. In R.Brinnick et
al. (Eds.), 1969.

Computational Models of Natural Language Processing
B.G. Bara and G. Guida (eds.)
© Elsevier Science Publishers B.V. (North-Holland), 1984

AN OBJECT-ORIENTED PARSER

Brian Phillips

Computer Research Laboratory
Tektronix Inc.
Beaverton, OR, USA

The parser works in a text understanding environment where structural
ambiguity is a major problem. It is designed to transmit sub-sentential
constituents to a semantic interpretation component. It uses a
left-corner parsing algorithm with a reachability matrix for further
rule filtering. As blind transmission could send spurious constituents, a delay mechanism is used to queue constituents until all
alternative analyses of a phrase have been completed. The delay
mechanism necessitates a breadth-first control structure. The system is
implemented using the "Flavor" system in ZLISP.

1. INTRODUCTION

The parser is a component in a textual knowledge retrieval environment. The
input phase, understanding the text, constructs a knowledge base that a user will
access via a question-answering system or use an index of key concepts to retrieve
whole documents. Information is retrieved for a purpose: creating a composite
report, confirming a hypothesis, comparison with competing views, checking its
accuracy, and more. From comments gathered from users of the system, it is
intended to develop facilities to support the management and organization of
retrieved data.

This paper describes the parser. Only a brief overview of the semantic component is given. The other portions of the project are at the design stage.

The structural ambiguity of many extended segments of English text makes it
desirable that these ambiguities be resolved quickly to prevent an explosive
growth of alternatives. This requires the parser be able to access general and
pragmatic knowledge at intermediate points in its analysis. An up-to-date source
of pragmatic knowledge can be maintained if the representation of content is built
in parallel with syntactic analysis. To assist in achieving these goals, the
parser transmits sub-sentential constituents to a conceptual translator with the
resulting translation being immediately added to the store of knowledge. When
structural ambiguity is present, knowledge will be used to eliminate some (ideally
all-but-one) of the competing syntactic constituents.

The data are patent abstracts; an example is shown in Figure 1. These
descriptions pose a realistic challenge to the state of the art in language understanding. Their syntax is relatively simple and the domain knowledge — micro-
electronic solid-state devices — is more tractable than, say, descriptions of
social activities or situations involving "common-sense" knowledge. Nevertheless,
they do exhibit a high degree of structural ambiguity that will test syntactic-
semantic interaction: in Figure 1, the "means for applying ..." phrase can be
attached either to "a modulator comprising ..." or to "two transistors each having
...". Also note that the initial "sentence" of the description has the form of a
noun phrase, not of a clause. We could allow the parser to accept matrix noun
phrases but this is not necessary because of the continuous content extraction.

A modulator comprising two transistors each having collector, emitter
and base electrodes, means for applying a direct voltage across said
emitter electrodes, a center-tapped source of alternating signals connected between said base electrodes, said collector electrodes being
connected together and to the center tap of said source. A load
impedance connected between said collector electrodes and said emitter
electrode of one of said transistors, and a variable resistor connected
between the base electrode and the emitter electrode of said one
transistor.

Figure 1: A patent abstract

2. DESIGN FEATURES

2.1 <u>Integrating</u> <u>syntax</u> <u>and</u> <u>semantics</u>

Semantic Grammars (Hendrix, 1977) merge semantics into the grammar to achieve
semantic filtering during syntactic analysis. However, system development will be
easier if each component has a formalism that is most appropriate to its own function rather than one constrained by the structure of other components. Further,
having domain knowledge separate from syntax makes it simpler to change domains.
In short, we prefer to achieve integration through the control structure rather
than through a data structure.

When trying to understand structurally complex texts, syntax cannot be
ignored: knowing the phrasal grouping of words is vital. Thus semantically driven
systems (Schank, 1975) are less likely to perform well.

Cascaded ATNs (Woods, 1981; Christaller & Metzing, 1982; see also Bobrow,
1978) pass intermediate syntactic constituents to later (semantic) processes in
the analysis. We would like to allow a bidirectional flow of information.
Halliday and Hasan (1975) claim that the density of cohesive links is greater
within paragraphs than across them. A system could draw upon this variation to be
more predictive when within a paragraph and be more bottom-up just after paragraph
boundaries. It might appear that only conceptual prediction is possible: "the
number of ... forms which could realize any given speech act seems to be large and
unlimited" (Linde & Labov, 1975, p. 934). However, Linde & Labov (1975) found
that in subjects' descriptions of apartments, the syntactic form of the realization could be correlated with knowledge of the apartments, for example

(a) Major rooms [kitchen, living room, dining room, and bedroom] may be
introduced with definite articles, minor rooms [study, den, laundry
closet, etc.] are not.

(b) Major rooms may be introduced as subject noun phrases, minor rooms
only in complements. (p. 935).

They also determined that sentence boundaries display regularity. Thus we do not
want to preclude the possibility of complex interactions between the components of
the system.

When knowledge sources can be used in parallel by communicating processes,
there is the possibility of greatly reducing the overall search; Kornfeld (1982)
calls this a "combinatorial implosion." The PARNAX natural language database
query system (Comino et al., 1983) has such a parallel architecture. A hypothesis
in either process is filtered out if there is not a construct in the other process
matching the same concepts. They found that PARNAX could perform both syntactic
and semantic analysis in less time than syntactic analysis took in isolation.
PARNAX uses a dependency grammar and production rule semantics and covers some

aspects of language that differ from those that appear in patent descriptions but it exemplifies the behavior we are seeking.

2.2 Forming constituents

A parser cannot simply transmit any constituent it forms, as category and phrase structure ambiguity in English cause the appearance of spurious constituents. For example, in a sentence made from the first part of the example of Figure 1:

> A modulator comprises two transistors each having
> collector, emitter and base electrodes.   (1)

there are false constituents "two", "a modulator comprises two transistors", "emitter and base electrodes" and others. In fact, there are nine correct constituents but crude transmission would send 19 for interpretation; see the Appendix for more details. The specious phrases have to be controlled or their effects will be as devastating as those due to structural ambiguity.

Look-ahead can eliminate erroneous constituents but a single word would not suffice: garden path sentences (e.g., "The horse raced past the barn fell.") exemplify its inadequacy; inspection based on structure is needed. Parsifal (Marcus, 1978) is a design for a deterministic parser that uses a more general scheme to avoid constructing any fallacious components. The problems of conjunction and categorical ambiguity that we find in the patents are not yet covered in Parsifal.

The present parser controls the flow of constituents by counting the number of on-going alternative analyses and retains intermediates until the alternatives have terminated, either successfully or by failure. For example, in the analysis of (2), only when "is" is encountered will the last of the possible NP's have been completed.

> The left front tire is flat.   (2)

Transmittability depends on the constituent being on a still-viable parse-path. For example, after "the left" is taken as a NP in (2), "front" will not be successfully analyzed as a verb (number agreement fails), hence the NP is not valid.

2.3 Depth- or breadth-first?

The analyser has to know the state of alternative parses that start from any word position. Does such a mechanism require a depth- or breadth-first system?

If the system were depth-first the current parse path cannot know if yet-to-be-tried paths will contain another analysis. Only when all paths have been examined would such information be available. By waiting, the normal flow of depth-first parsing will rule out spurious constituents, but it also prevents any interaction with knowledge to resolve genuine cases of structural ambiguity. On the other hand, a breadth-first system can be aware of all concurrent alternatives: a (pseudo-)parallel control structure is thus appropriate.

Chester (1980) allows a phrase to be extended, either by right extension, say adding a relative clause to a noun phrase, or by right recursion, say with prepositional phrases. More microscopic issues, of noun-noun modification for example, are not considered. His control mechanism is depth first, and thus it could not know if other analyses of a segment might appear and so it could not safely transmit segments to another component.

3. THE PARSER

3.1 The grammar and dictionary

The grammar has the form of an augmented phrase structure system, based on
Local Grammar (Saenz, 1982). The context-free phrase structure component is augmented with Blocking Rules and Percolation Rules; Figure 2 shows a typical rule.
Each rule-segment of the phrase structure may contain any number of alternative
terminal and non-terminal categories, each of which may be optional (marked by the
affix +) or repeated any number of times (affix *).

```
NP -> (DET+) (ADJ*) (NMOD+) (N)             PHRASE STRUCTURE

   (WHEN (EQUAL (DTYPE 1) ARTICLE)
         (NOT-BOTH (GAP 3) (GAP 4))
   (WHEN (EQUAL (NUMBER 4) SING)            BLOCKING
         (EXIST 1)))

   (NUMBER (NUMBER 4))                      PERCOLATION
   (GAP (GAP 4))
```

Figure 2: A Local Grammar rule

Blocking rules give the constraints within a constituent. The grammar only
permits constraints that are local to a phrase. The rule language contains logical predicates and linguistic ones such as AGREE, EMBEDDED, EXIST. The feature
attributes cover tense, number, gapping, etc. and have associated functions to
retrieve their value from a constituent.

Percolation rules show features to be extracted from particular constituents
of phrases and the features of parents that should be given these values. In the
rule in Figure 2, the NP will receive GAP and NUMBER features from the N.

The rule format as implemented does not permit a sequence of categories to be
jointly optional or repeatable; a single category has to be placed in the grammar
and expanded in a separate rule, as in:

```
NP         -> (NP) (COMMA-NP*) (CONJ) (NP)
COMMA-NP -> (COMMA) (NP)
```

Null realizations for noun phrases are allowed: NP -> Ø. The phrase-structure
rules:

```
CLAUSE -> (COMP+) (NP) (VERB_GROUP)
PP       -> (PREP) (VERB_GROUP)
```

do not explicitly include the syntactic object segments of the VERB_GROUP. These
are determined during analysis. The dictionary entry for a verb form, e.g.,
"bought" in Figure 3, gives its type: trans(itive), ditrans(itive), etc. This
feature is percolated to the VERB_GROUP. The blocking rules for a phrase containing a VERB_GROUP include a function SPLICE that uses the feature to add the
appropriate objects to the rule.

In the spirit of Lexical-Function Theory (Bresnan & Kaplan, 1982), dictionary
entries contain information for semantic interpretation. These are the "si"
features in Figure 3. For verbs, the translation includes a case-frame. The
cases are listed in the order of appearance of the corresponding syntactic

```
bought     v      affix      tense
                  vtype      trans
                  number     all
                  person     all
                  si         *buy* agt obj

           v      affix      tense
                  vtype      ditrans
                  number     all
                  person     all
                  si         *buy* agt obj exp
                             *buy* agt obj instr
```

Figure 3: A dictionary entry

fillers: e.g., in a sentence with a transitive verb: "John bought the book" the
concept "john" will fill the ag(en)t case, and "book" the obj(ective). Percolation of the verb type feature ensures that the various objects have the correct
syntactic form, noun phrase, prepositional phrase, etc.

The system requires that the dictionary contains syntactic category and
appropriate features for each inflected form (Lapointe, 1977). Morphological
rules are not used while processing a sentence; they should be used to create the
dictionary but at the moment it is hand-coded.

3.2 The parsing algorithm

The parser follows the Left-Corner algorithm (Griffiths & Petrick, 1965),
modified to a pseudo-parallel format for the reason mentioned earlier. This algorithm builds phrases bottom-up from the left-corner, i.e., rules are selected by
the first symbol of their right-hand-sides. For example, for a category c, a rule
of the form X -> c ... will be chosen. The remaining rule segments of the
right-hand side are predictions about the structure of the remainder of the sentence and are processed left-to-right. Subsequent inputs will directly match successive rule segments if the latter are terminal symbols of the grammar. When a
non-terminal symbol is encountered, a subparse is initiated. The subparse is also
constructed bottom-up from the left-corner, following the rule selection just
described. When an embedded rule is completed, the phrase formed may have the
structure of the non-terminal category that originated the subparse and so complete the subparse. If there is no match, it will become the left-corner of a
phrase that will eventually match the originating category. The bottom-up approach
avoids the problems that top-down systems have with left-recursive rules.

With recursive rules, both the above-mentioned actions take place. Figure 4
illustrates this. The originating category is an NP and NP-1 has just been completed. Now NP-1 can fill the goal slot, but because of the rule:

    NP -> (NP) (CLAUSE)

it can also become part of NP-2, with NP-2 being a later filler of the goal slot.

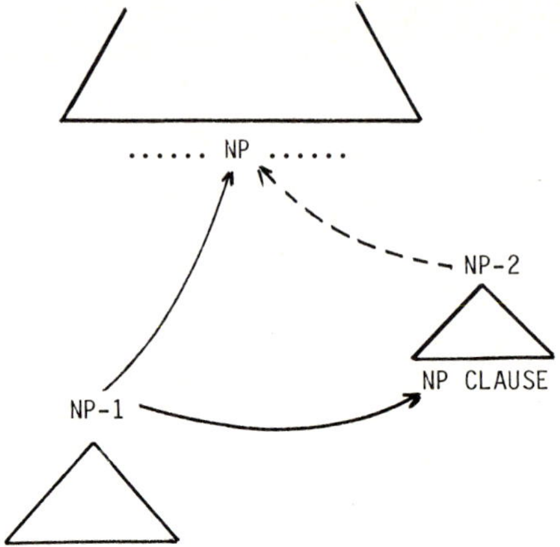

Figure 4: The effect of recursive rules

The parser includes a Reachability Matrix (Griffiths & Petrick, 1965) to provide top-down filtering of rule selection. The matrix indicates when a node A can dominate a node B, with node B being on the left-most branch. The entry for NP, for example, shows it can dominate: NP NPMOD NMOD NPCONJMOD DET ADJ N PRON PROPN. The matrix is static and can be derived from the grammar in advance of any parsing. It is computable as the transitive closure of the boolean matrices giving the immediate domination in the left branch of all terminal and non-terminal categories in the grammar. It is used as a further constraint on rule selection. For example, when the goal is to construct a sentence and the category of the first word of input is c, then rule selection, giving X -> c ..., will also be constrained to have the property S -*-> X ... The filtering is applicable whenever a rule is selected: during subparses the constraint is to reach the category originating the subparse. In the example patent, when the parser encounters "means" it has created a subparse for an NP (see Figures 14 and 15) and, although "means" has both verb and noun dictionary entries, no rule starting with the former can be selected.

The parser also uses early constituent testing (Slocum, 1982) so that blocking rules are used as soon as possible; their use does not await completion of the entire phrase.

For the long sentences found in the patents, it is believed that left-corner parsing with top-down filtering is an efficient combination. (Slocum, 1982).

3.2.1 Implementation

The system is implemented using the Flavor system in ZLISP (Weinreb & Moon, 1981). This object-oriented approach simplifies implementing pseudo-parallelism and bidirectional communication.

Only Noun Phrases, Verb Groups, and Clauses are transmitted by the parser. The first build entity concepts in knowledge, the second retrieve the case structures of verb concepts, and the last are equivalents of completed case frames.

A "constituent" flavor creates an object that is associated with a rule of the grammar. Figure 5 shows an object that is part way through processing the rule (as it appears in the grammar):

```
PP -> (PREP) (VERB_GROUP)
      (SPLICE (VTYPE 2))
      (EQUAL (AFFIX 2) GERUND)
```

The percolation of the verb type feature "ditrans" from the verb has enabled the SPLICE function to add the (NP)(PP) sequence and the existence requirement on the NP to the rule. The "si" feature has also been percolated from the verb. Once satisfied, blocking rules are deleted.

```
NAME:                   CONST-36

CATEGORY:               PP
GOALS-LIST:             ((PP . CONST-27))
PART-PARSE:             ((1 FOR ((PREP)))
                         (2 CONST-35 ((VERB_GROUP
                                       (NUMBER . NIL)
                                       (AFFIX GERUND)
                                       (VTYPE DITRANS)
                                       (SI (*BUY* AGT OBJ EXP)
                                           (*BUY* AGT OBJ INSTR))))))
RULE-TAIL:              ((NP) (PP))
BLOCKERS:               ((EXIST 3))
PERCOLATERS:            NIL
SEGMENT-COUNTER:        3

INPUT-WORD:             A
DICT-ENTRY:             ((DET (DTYPE ARTICLE)))

ALTERNATE:              NIL
CONTINUE:               NIL
ACTIVE:                 (CONST-38 CONST-37)
COUNT:                  2
QUEUE:                  NIL
LEVELLERS:              (CONST-38 CONST-37)
```

Figure 5: A constituent object with its grammar rule

In Figure 5, the first group of variables describe the rule-state. The GOALS-LIST variable is used by the reachability matrix, it shows the categories in which the constituent must eventually become embedded. The second group of variables is the current word and its dictionary entry. The other variables are used to monitor specious constituents and will be explained later.

A book-keeper maintains a queue of active constituents and a list of constituents that have failed. A scheduler takes in a word of input and delivers it to active constituents.

A constituent object tries to advance its state by matching the current input against the first rule-segment on RULE-TAIL using the methods of the flavor. The principal processes in the methods are:

FAIL — the rule fails; input may not match the current rule-segment or a blocking rule may fail. The object is moved to the failed list in the book-keeper.

SKIPPABLE — the current segment can be skipped: it has either optional or nullable elements. The existing object skips the rule-segment and another object is set up to investigate the full form of the rule. The

ALTERNATE variable in a constituent (see Figure 5) points to a constituent that has been split off in this manner. Both versions of the rule
are then served by the scheduler.

TERMINAL MATCHES — the object can itself directly match the input
against a terminal category from the present rule-segment. It advances
to the next rule-segment and awaits the next word of input.

NON-TERMINAL MATCHES — the object sets up subparses for non-terminal
elements in its rule-segment. The parent "sleeps", awaiting the results
of the subparses. Whenever a subparse is about to be set up, a test is
made to see if another constituent has already set up such a subparse;
if so the paths are merged. This is equivalent to having a well-formed
sub-string table, and results in multiple goal categories on GOALS-LIST.

END OF RULE — the object has instantiated its rule. It will then
become part of higher constituents and be removed from the list of
active constituents. If a subparse has been completed, control passes to
the parent constituent. The parent makes a copy of itself to be used in
the continuing analysis: a pristine parent has to be left to capture
other subparses that may finish later. The subparse constituent and its
context are recorded in QUEUE (Figure 5) of the original parent, which
also retains pointers to its copies in its CONTINUE variable. When the
categories do not match, the completed constituent will become the left
corner of a structure that will eventually complete the subparse.

END OF SENTENCE — this tries to force END OF RULE for constituents that
have unexamined segments (RULE-TAIL, Figure 5) that can be skipped; see
SKIPPABLE, above.

As a rule-segment can have several categories in it, more than one of these
events may occur for any one object.

The ALTERNATE AND CONTINUE variables exist to maintain an explicit linking of
objects on a parse path. They enable parse paths spawned from any constituent to
be followed to see if they are currently viable.

3.2.2 The counting scheme

ACTIVE (Figure 5) keeps a list of the subparse constituents and COUNT counts
them. COUNT is measure of the number of structures that could fill the slot in
the parent. This number will grow when constituents split off to follow alternative aspects of a rule. It can also grow as intermediate structures appear on the
way to creating a subparse.

The count will diminish when a subparse fails or is completed.

As was mentioned earlier, when a subparse is completed and recursive rules
exist, intermediate structure can also be created. Figure 4 illustrates this.
Recursive rules complicate the counting scheme. We do not want to wait until a
recursive structure is completed before examing embedded components. In Figure 4,
examination of NP-1 should not be dependent on the completion of NP-2. However,
control of transmission should apply separately to the various levels of recursion: NP-2 and its alternatives have to be monitored to control their transmission.

Thus we introduce the notion of levels. The first level contains constituents set up from the non-terminal category in the grammar rule of the parent
object. The initial COUNT keeps track of these objects only. ACTIVE and LEVELL-
ERS (Figure 5) are initialized with these objects. When, at completion of a

subparse, recursive rules are selected, COUNT is diminished because of the placement of the constituent in the intermediate structure, the now-attached constituent is removed from the ACTIVE list, and the new object is added to the ACTIVE
list, but not to LEVELLERS. Thus all subparses are recorded in ACTIVE, but COUNT
only records those active on the current level. QUEUE records completed subparses.

When COUNT becomes 0, the objects still on the ACTIVE list are used to reset
LEVELLERS and COUNT. The parameters are then in a state to monitor the next level
in the subparse.

The level mechanism as described here may not be completely adequate. An
explicit tagging of constituents with level may be needed. We have assumed synchrony of levels (i.e., while counting on Level I, only Level I+1 constituents
appear), which may not always be the case. The present feeling is that syntax
provides sufficient constraints to prevent overly convoluted structures from arising.

COUNT is only responsive to structures that will fill the non-terminal slot
in the parent. However, within those structures, transmittable constituents may
appear. These must also be monitored to ensure correct transmission. For example, in Figure 6, a CLAUSE segment in the parent and a DET input category set up
an NP. The progress of this NP needs to be monitored, but the parent is only
tracking structures that will grow to the CLAUSE, of which the NP's are a subset.
For such items, ephemeral parents having the required counting capabilities are
used.

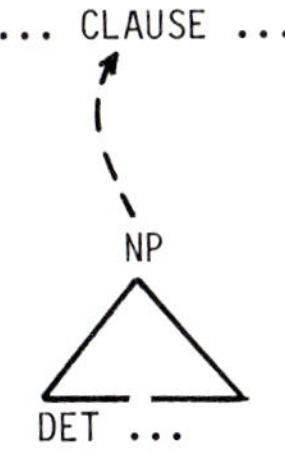

Figure 6: The role of ephemeral parents

At the end of the processing of a word, any constituents that are deemed
ready for transmission (i.e., were placed on a global queue from constituents'
QUEUEs when COUNTs became 0) are examined and only those that belong to still
valid parse paths are transmitted.

4. AN EXAMPLE

In Figures 7-13 the categories "COMMA-NPMOD" and "COMMA-NMOD" have been
replaced by ", NPMOD" and ", NMOD" to simplify their appearance. The use of
parentheses has also been modified to the same end.

Suppose we are at a point in an analysis where the remaining input string is
"on the hill with ...." and the preposition has caused the rule:

```
PP -> (PREP) (NP)
     (EXIST 2)
```

to be selected for Object 1 (Figure 7).

On the next word-cycle the scheduler passes control to Object 1 with the word "the". A null realization of "NP" is followed by Object 1 and Object 2 is spawned without this null realization. Object 1 is eliminated by its blocking rule.

Now it is the turn of Object 2. The rule-category encountered is non-terminal "NP" causing subparses to be set up. Rule selection chooses the two rules:

```
        NPMOD -> (DET) (ADJ*) (NMOD+) (N)              [object 3]
                 (EXIST 4)
                 (EQUAL (NUMBER 4) SING)

        NP    -> (DET) (ADJ*) (NMOD+) (N)              [object 4]
                 (WHEN (EQUAL (DTYPE 1) ARTICLE)
                       (NOT-BOTH (GAP 3) (GAP 4)))
                 (WHEN (EQUAL (NUMBER 4) SING)
                       (EXIST 1)))
```

Object 2 then has the counting information shown in Figure 7.

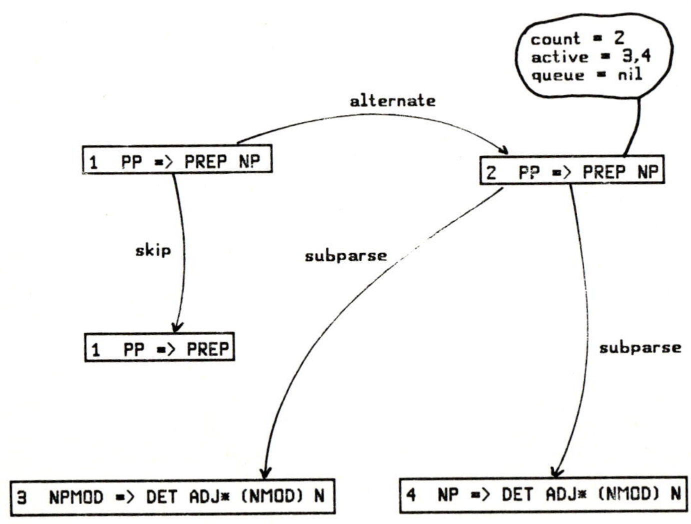

Figure 7:   A subparse

A new word-cycle starts with "hill". When Object 3 is activated, the current input does not match "ADJ", but the "ADJ" is skippable. The rule form is then:

$$\text{NPMOD} \rightarrow (\text{DET})\ (\text{NMOD+})\ (\text{N})$$

Object 3 skips the optional "NMOD" but spins off Object 5 to consider the "NMOD". Similarly Object 4 sets up Object 6. The existence of the new objects is reflected in the changes in the count in Object 2. Figure 8.

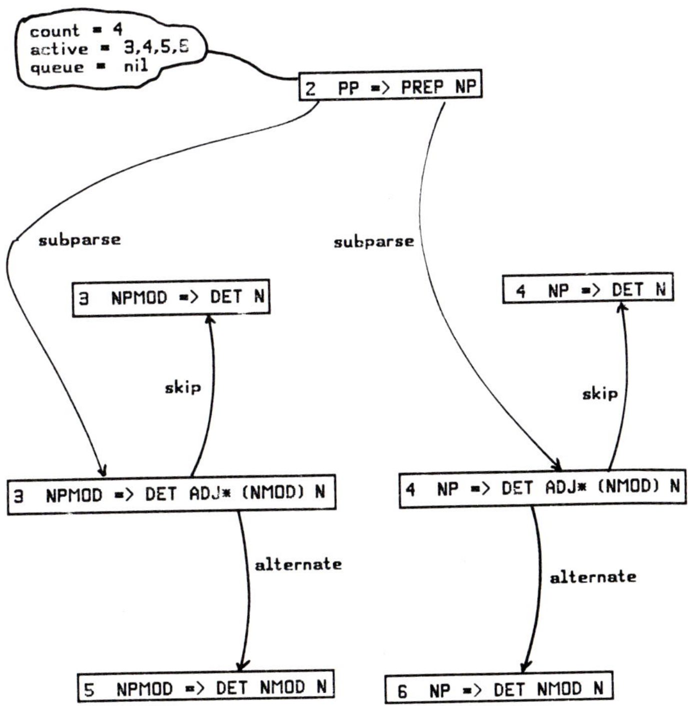

Figure 8: Optional segments

On activating Object 5, a subparse for the "NMOD" is initiated, Object 7.
The counting information for this subparse is set up in Object 5.　Object 6 is
also looking for an "NMOD" and so merges with Object 7, Figure 9.

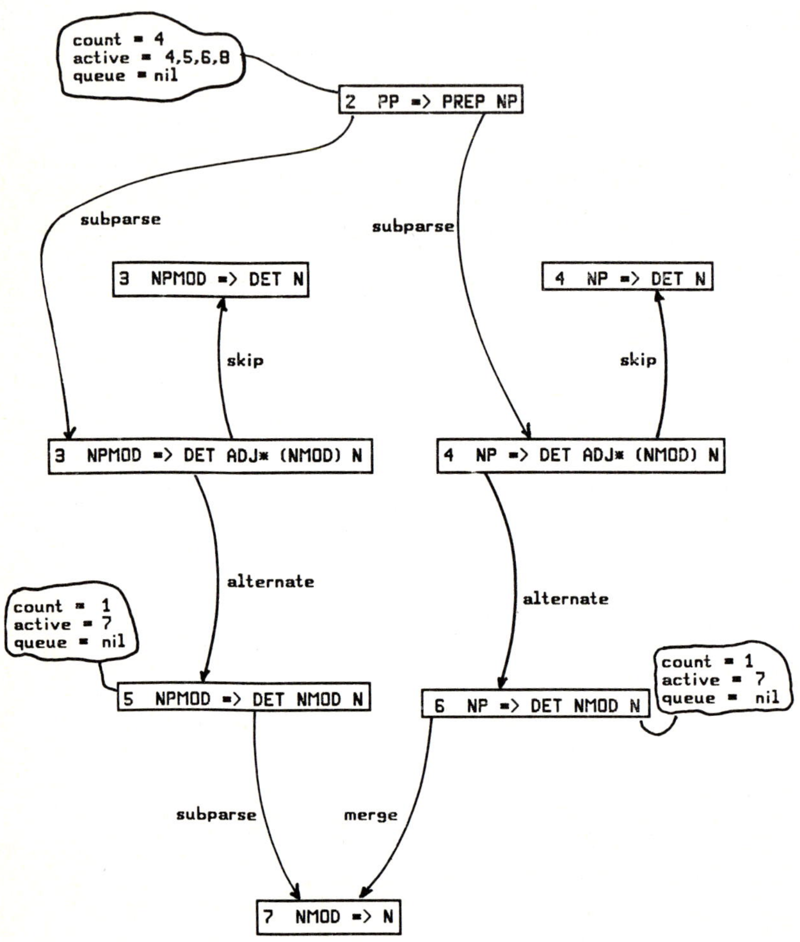

Figure 9:　A merge

The next word is "with". In Figure 10, Object 3 reaches the end of its rule.
It is not an instantiation of an "NP" and so cannot fit into the "NP" slot in
Object 2. Further intermediate structure must be created. The only appropriate
rule is:

        NPCONJMOD -> (NPMOD) (COMMA-NPMOD*) (CONJ) (NPMOD)

and Object 8 is formed, Figure 10.

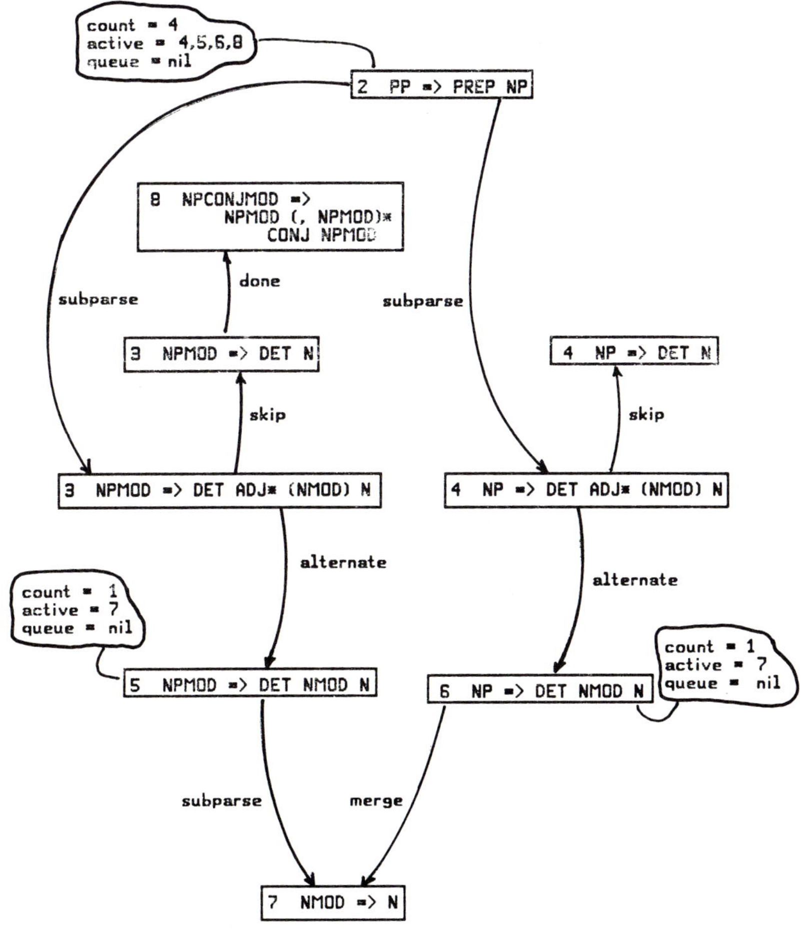

Figure 10: Completion of a rule

Object 7 was completed by the noun "hill" on the previous word cycle. Now it is found that it can fit into the slots in Objects 5 and 6 that initiated the sub-parse and also, as there are the rules:

```
NMOD -> (NMOD) (COMMA-NMOD*) (CONJ) (NMOD)
NMOD -> (NMOD) (N)
```

intermediate structure can be formed, Objects 9 and 10 in Figure 11.

Objects 5 and 6 create copies of themselves, Objects 11 and 12 respectively, with Object 7 filling the "NMOD" slots. Objects 5 and 6 retain their original state to be ready to capture other subparses that may still be active. Objects 9 and 10 are the still-active subparses that are counted in Objects 5 and 6. In queue of Object 5 is the record of the attachments of Object 7; in this case in the contexts of Objects 9, 10, and 11. Object 6's queue shows Object 7 attached in the contexts of Objects 9, 10, and 12.

The counts in Object 2 are incremented to reflect the creation of Objects 11 and 12.

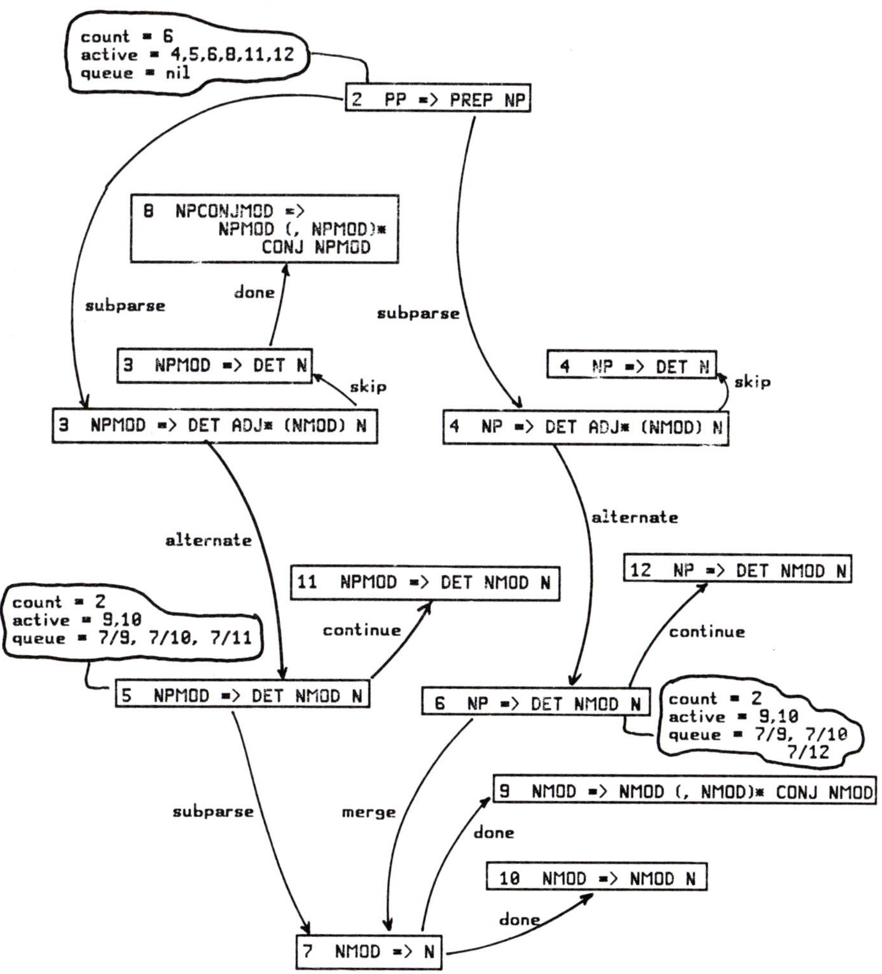

Figure 11:   Recursive rules

Finally, in Figure 12 we have Object 4 reaching the end of its rule. As there are the rules:

```
NP -> (NP) (CLAUSE)
NP -> (NP) (PP)
NP -> (NP) (COMMA-NP*) (CONJ) (NP)
```

intermediate Objects 13, 14, and 15 are created. Object 4 can fit into the slot in Object 2, so the continuance of Object 2, Object 16 is formed. The count in Object 2 changes to reflect this situation. Now Objects 13, 14, and 15 are on the next level and so are distinguished from Objects 5, 6, 8, 11, and 12 which are attempting to form an "NP" on the first level. Thus the count of the prevailing level is 5, not 8. Objects 13, 14, and 15 will only enter into the count when the first level is complete. Object 4 has been attached in the context of Objects 13, 14, 15, and 16 and this is the information in QUEUE.

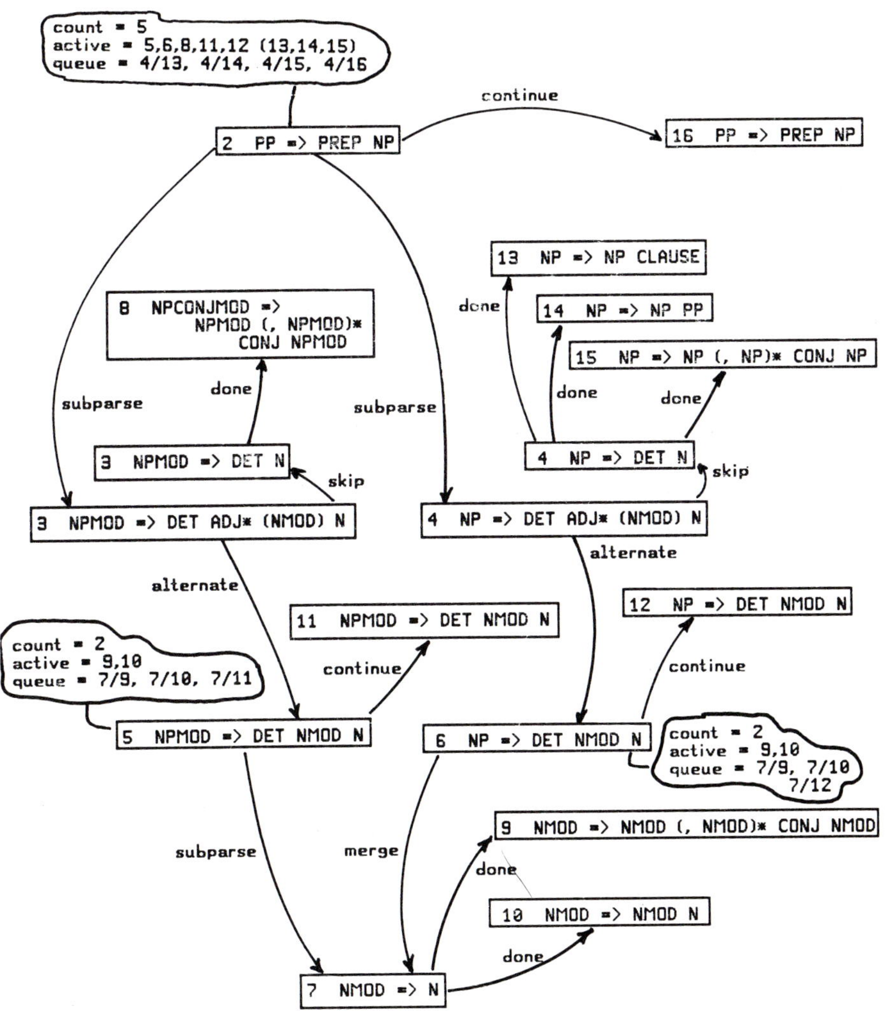

Figure 12:   Completing a NP

Later Objects 5, 6, 8, 11, and 12 will finish and the count will go to zero.
Now the objects and their contexts will be examined to see which is on a viable
parse path. For example, Object 15 will have been eliminated from consideration
if the next input symbol was not a comma or a conjunction. The counting information in Object 2 will be reset to track the progress of Objects 13, 14, and 15.

Object 16 contains the analysis of "on the hill" as a complete PP; if a subsequent PP, the one that will start with the "with", should be taken as modifying
the NP "the hill", then Object 14 is poised to follow this path.

Figure 13 correlates the appearance of the Objects with the input words.

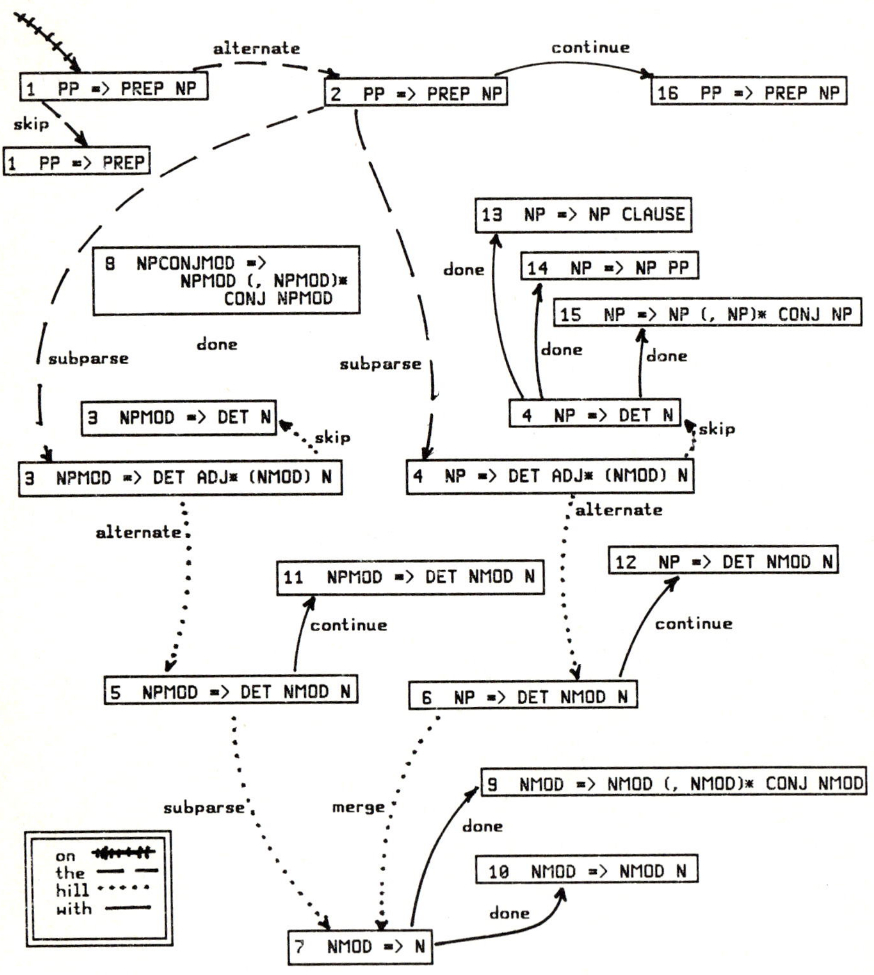

Figure 13: Correlating events and input

5. THE BEHAVIOR OF THE SYSTEM

In the Appendix the constituents formed during the analysis of "A modulator comprises two transistors each having collector, emitter and base electrodes." are shown. Inspection of the time of delivery of the constituents shows that the system does not complete most higher level constituents until the sentence terminator is encountered. It is the case that any constituent will not be transmitted until all possible continuations of it have terminated. For noun phrases and prepositional phrases there are many in which they can be extended. In the example, it was the sentence terminator that closed them off; in other sentence positions it could be encountering a verb phrase. Structural ambiguities do not jell into attached structures and can be transmitted until their components are completed.

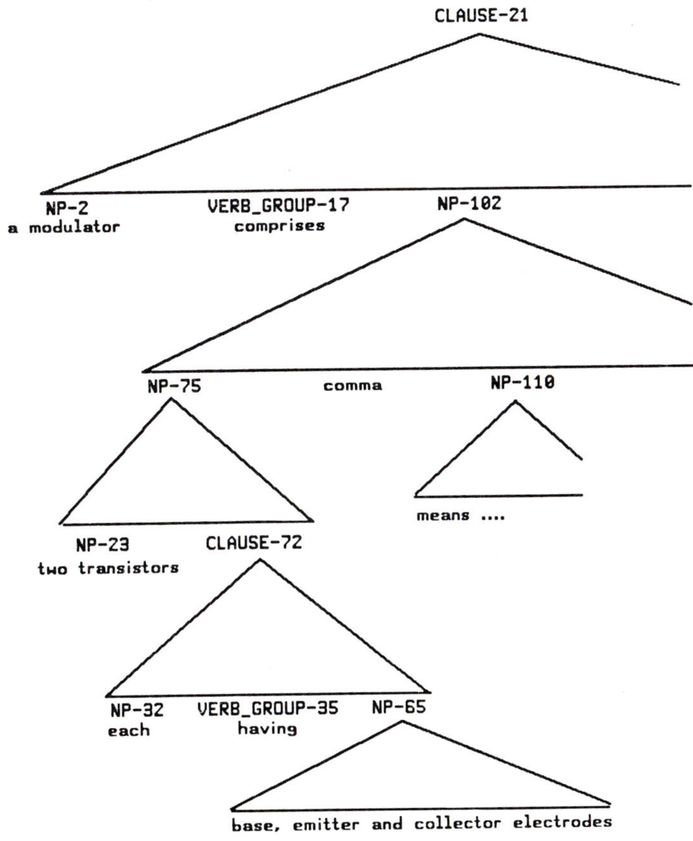

Figure 14: Tree for structural ambiguity I

In the ambiguity of the attachment of the "means ..." phrase of Figure 1, the parser has only delivered the constituents NP-2, VERB_GROUP-17, NP-23, NP-32, VERB GROUP-35, and NP-65 (Figures 14 and 15) at the time the phrase is encountered. To build the conceptual representation, the translation process has to probe ongoing parse structures. Examination of the two active parses shows that these are either "modulator comprises ... means ...", Figure 14, or "each

[transistor] having ... means ... ", Figure 15, and the translator invokes general
knowledge to eliminate the latter.

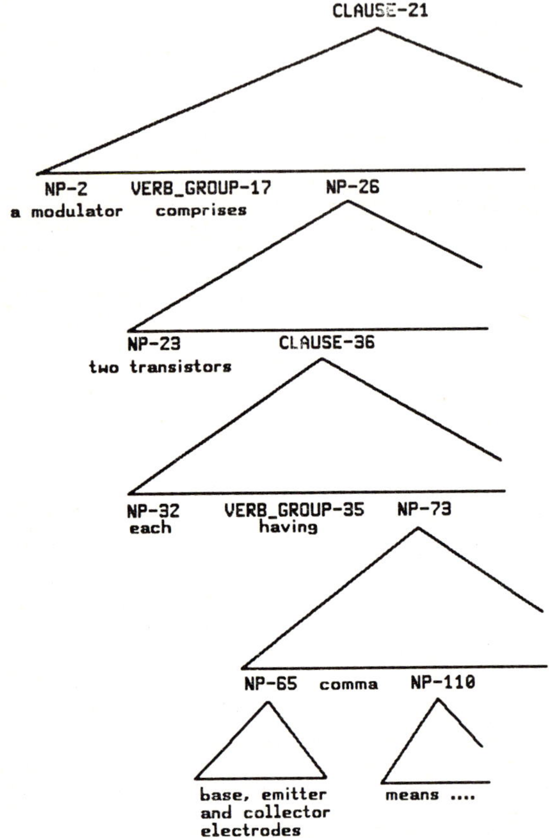

Figure 15: Tree for structural ambiguity II

6. THE SEMANTIC COMPONENT

The knowledge base is a semantic network (Phillips, 1978) but implemented
using objects. Nodes in the network correspond to objects and arcs now designate
neighboring objects and the kinds of message they can be sent. An early statement
of the implementation, communication between syntax and semantics, and translating
syntactic structure to semantic form is given in Phillips & Hendler (1982). The
notion of concepts as active processes is also to be found in Small & Rieger
(1981) where sense discrimination is achieved through the interaction of modular
"word experts."

The patents extensively group components and quantify over these groups. The
conceptual knowledge structure is presently being extended to accommodate these
needs.

Representations of patents and of general knowledges are recorded in the same knowledge base. Patent descriptions become instantiations of general concepts. The same processes that refer to general knowledge can thus access any newly-added fragments of a patent description.

The semantic component is presented with sentential fragments and has word-to-concept translations from the dictionary. The incremental composition of the meaning of sentential fragments can be guided by logic-based approaches to language analysis (e.g., Montague, 1974; Warren, 1983).

7. CONCLUSION

The efficiency of complex language analysers cannot yet be definitively established theoretically. The worth of the features of the parser that should allow it to perform efficiently in a text understanding environment must be evaluated experimentally. Slocum (1982) compared a variety of parsing algorithms on a broad sample of sentences. Drawing on his findings we chose the left-corner algorithm. The studies on the PARNAX system (Comino et al., 1983) show that parallel processing can reduce the analysis time. This is the evidence that supports our design, but extensive testing of the present system is still needed to ensure that our processing overhead does not counterbalance the advantages.

Several hundred patent abstracts are available; the grammar to cover all of these has not yet been written. The general knowledge base is still rudimentary and requires much effort before we can have a complete system to test the ease of integration offered by the design.

There are complex knowledge representation issues in the patents but we do not have to solve all of the problems to create a usable system: the nature of the use precludes questions, say, about complex geometrical arrangements of components in a device. For example, we do not have to have a deep understanding of "across" to build an adequate representation of "means for applying a direct voltage across ... said emitter electrodes." This is not the kind of detail that a patent attorney would seek. We can treat many such complex concepts as primitives.

Allowing null realizations of the noun phrase category is apparently necessary for the analysis of ellipsis. If the full range of ellipsis were incorporated into the grammar, for example to allow the parsing of "(She loves him.) And he her", then the grammar may be so unconstrained to approach worthlessness. This is obviously undesirable and indicates an area where prediction could be useful in guiding a less permissive grammar. The parser might only be expected to find low-level constituents and not necessarily larger aggregations. The translation process would then use the structure of previous sentences and knowledge to establish the correct semantic association for the fragments. Our parser has the potential to allow us to explore this view.

The flexibility offered by the message-passing methodology leads us to hope, at an even more distant point in the future, that it will be a useful tool in exploring the analysis of ungrammatical texts.

8. REFERENCES

[1]   Bobrow, R.J., The RUS system, Report 3878, Bolt Beranek & Newman Inc., Cambridge, MA. (July 1978).
[2]   Bresnan, J., and Kaplan, R., Introduction: Grammars as mental representations of language, in: Bresnan, J. (ed.), The Mental Representation of Grammatical Relations (MIT Press, Cambridge, MA, 1982).
[3]   Chester, D., A parsing algorithm that extends phrases, American Journal of Computational Linguistics 6 (1980) 87-96.
[4]   Christaller, T., and Metzing, D., Parsing interactions and a multi-level parser formalism based on cascaded ATNs, Unpublished paper, University of Hamburg (1982).
[5]   Comino, R., Gemello, R., Guida, G., Rullent, C., Sisto, L., and Somalvico, M., Understanding natural language through parallel processing of syntactic and semantic knowledge: An application to data-base query, in: Proceedings of the International Joint Conference on Artificial Intelligence, Karlsruhe, W. Germany, 1983, 663-667.
[6]   Griffiths, T.V., and Petrick, S.R., On the relative efficiencies of context-free grammar recognizers, Comm. ACM 5 (1965) 289-300.
[7]   Hendrix, G.G., Human engineering for applied natural language processing, in: Proceedings of the 5th International Joint Conference on Artificial Intelligence, Cambridge (1977).
[8]   Halliday, M., and Hasan, R., Cohesion in English (Longmans, London, 1975).
[9]   Kornfeld, W.A., Combinatorially implosive algorithms, Comm. ACM 10 (1982) 734-738.
[10] Lapointe, S., A lexical reanalysis of the English auxiliary system, Unpublished paper, Dept. of Linguistics, University of Massachusetts (1977).
[11] Linde, C., and Labov, W., Spatial networks as a site for the study of language and thought, Language 51 (1975) 924-939.
[12] Marcus, M.P., A Theory of Syntactic Recognition (MIT Press, Cambridge, MA, 1979).
[13] Montague R., The proper treatment of quantification in ordinary English, in: R.H. Thomason (ed.), Formal Philosophy: Selected Papers of Richard Montague (Yale U.P., New Haven, 1974).
[14] Phillips, B., A model for knowledge and its application to discourse analysis, American Journal of Computational Linguistics Microfiche 82 (1978).
[15] Phillips, B., and Hendler, J.A., A message-passing control structure for text understanding, in: Proceedings of the International Conference on Computational Linguistics (Mouton, The Hague, 1982).
[16] Saenz, R., Local grammar, Unpublished paper, Dept. of Linguistics, University of Massachusetts (June 1982).
[17] Schank, R.C., Conceptual Information Processing, (American Elsevier, New York, 1975).
[18] Slocum, J., A practical comparison of parsing strategies for machine translation and other natural language purposes, Technical report NL-41, Dept. of Computer Science, University of Texas (August 1981).
[19] Small, S., and Rieger, C., Parsing and comprehending with Word Experts (A theory and its realization), Technical report 1039, Computer Science Dept., University of Maryland (April 1981).
[20] Warren D.S., Using lambda-calculus to represent meanings in logic grammars, Technical report 83/044, Computer Science Dept., State University of New York at Stony Brook (January 1983).
[21] Weinreb, D., and Moon, D., Lisp Machine Manual, (MIT AI Laboratory, Cambridge, 1981).
[22] Woods, W.A., Cascaded ATN grammars, American Journal of Computational Linguistics 6 (1980) 1-12.

APPENDIX: Constituents formed and delivered

This shows the constituents found in "A modulator comprises two transistors each having collector, emitter and base electrodes."

Of the seventeen found, only NP-1, VERB_GROUP-2, NP-4, NP-5, VERB_GROUP-6, NP-10, CLAUSE-13, NP-16, and CLAUSE-17 are valid and are transmitted. False parses could be formed from CLAUSE-13 and NP-14 but they are trivially eliminated from knowing that the end of sentence has not been reached.

The constituents are readied for transmission at the end of the word-cycle after the termination of the longest alternative under consideration.

<u>A</u>

<u>MODULATOR</u>

<u>COMPRISES</u>

```
                NP-1
              /  \
            /      \
          /__________\
        DET           N
         a          modulator
```

<u>TWO</u>

```
              VERB_GROUP-2
                   |
                   V
               comprises
```

<u>TRANSISTORS</u>

<u>EACH</u>

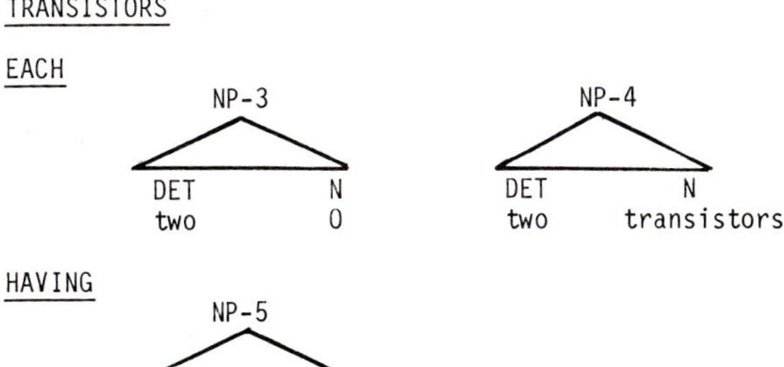

```
          NP-3                        NP-4
        /  \                        /  \
      /      \                    /      \
    /__________\                /__________\
   DET          N              DET          N
   two          0              two      transistors
```

<u>HAVING</u>

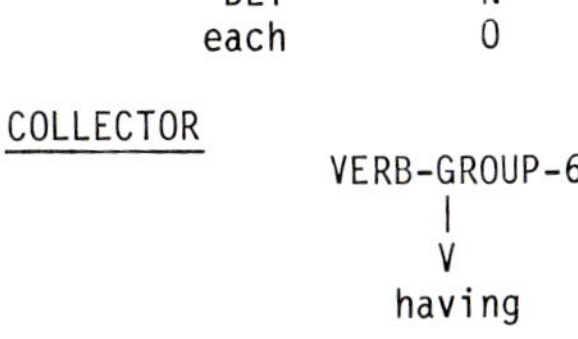

```
          NP-5
        /  \
      /      \
    /__________\
   DET          N
   each          0
```

<u>COLLECTOR</u>

```
            VERB-GROUP-6
                 |
                 V
              having
```

COMMA

EMITTER

AND

BASE

ELECTRODES

PERIOD

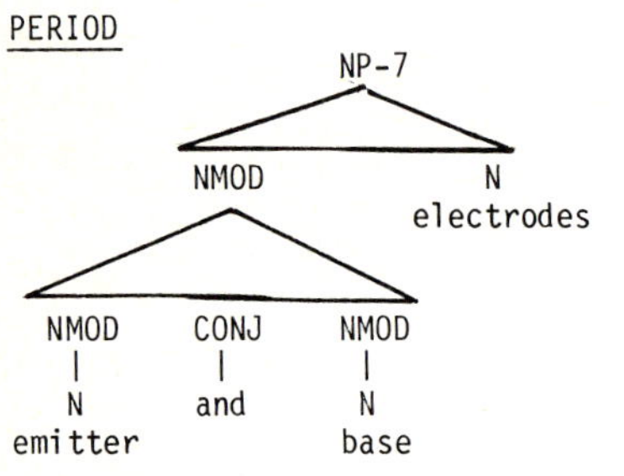

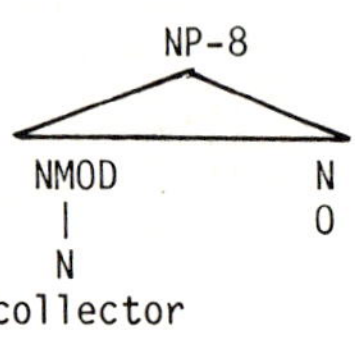

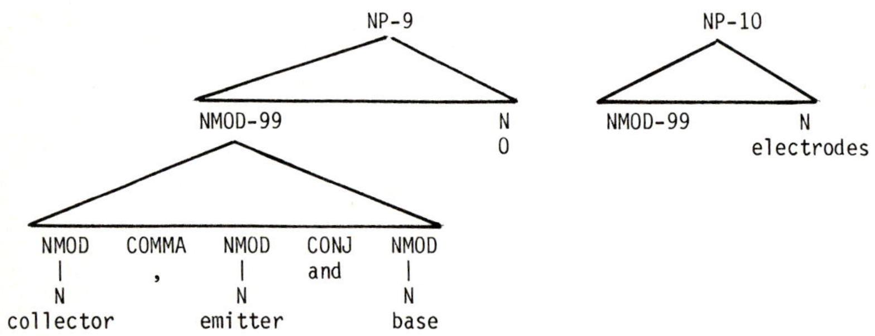

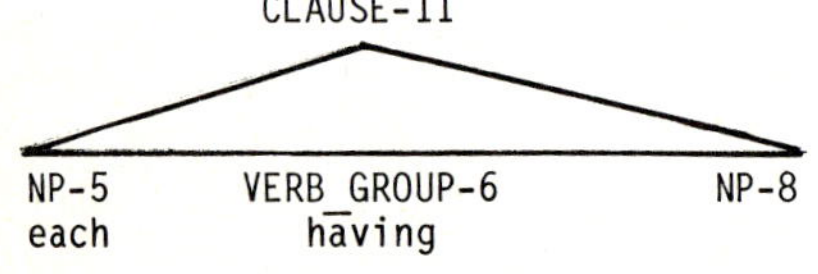

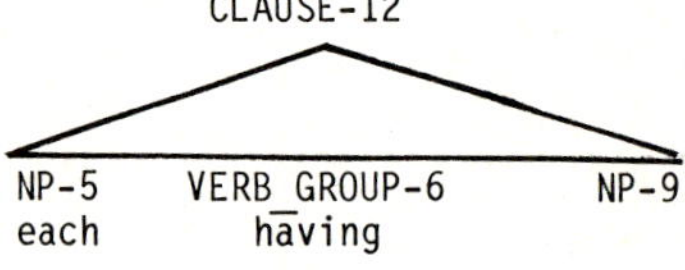

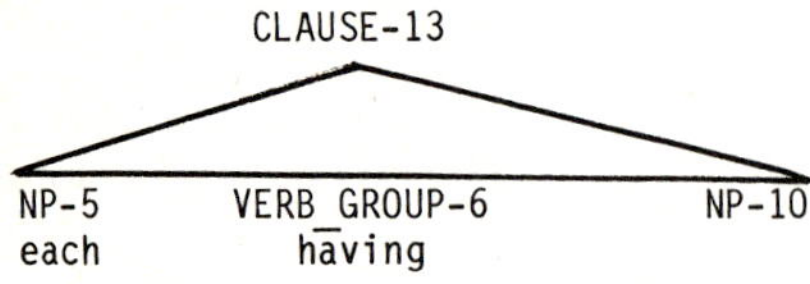

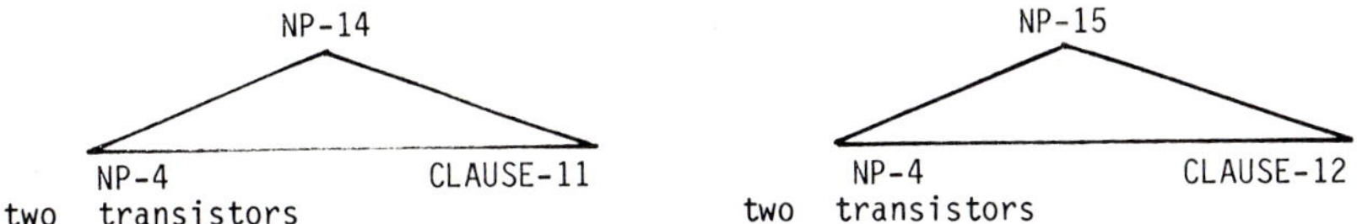

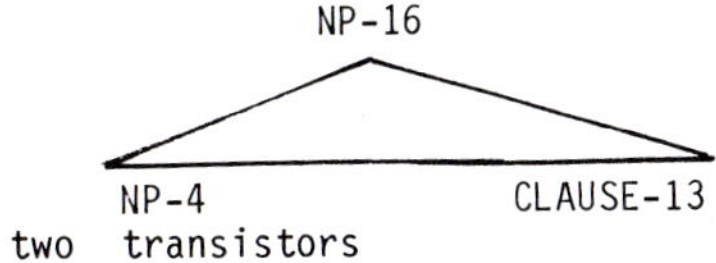

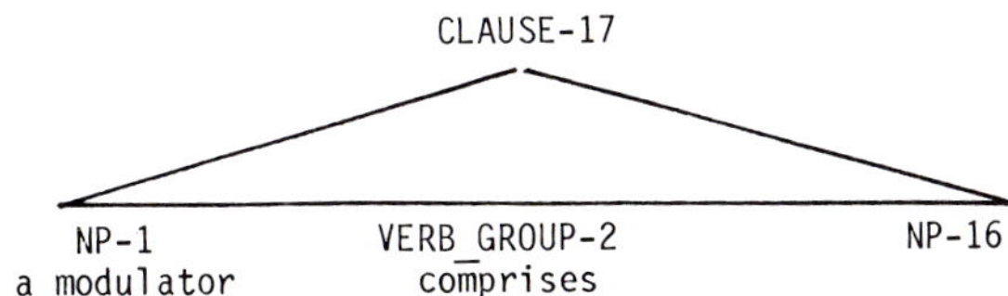

Acknowledgement

This work was carried out at Texas Instruments Inc., Dallas, Texas. The author gratefully acknowledges TI's permission to publish the paper.

AUTHOR INDEX

LIST OF CONTRIBUTORS

Airenti G.

Unità di ricerca di intelligenza artificiale
Università di Milano
via F. Sforza, 23
20122 Milano, Italy

Bara B.G.

Unità di ricerca di intelligenza artificiale
Università di Milano
via F. Sforza, 23
20122 Milano, Italy

Cappelli A.

Istituto di Linguistica Computazionale del CNR
via della Faggiola,32
56100 Pisa, Italy

Castelfranchi C.

Istituto di Psicologia del CNR
via dei Monti Tiburtini, 509
00157 Roma, Italy

Chen Y.

Shenyang Institute of Automation
Academia Sinica
P.O. Box 210
Shenyang, Liaoning, China

Colombetti M.

Progetto di Intelligenza Artificiale
Dipartimento di Elettronica
Politecnico di Milano
piazza Leonardo da Vinci, 32
20133 Milano, Italy

Cottrell G.W.

Department of Computer Science
The University of Rochester
Rochester, NY 14627, USA

Ferrari G.

Istituto di Linguistica Computazionale del CNR
via della Faggiola, 32
56100 Pisa, Italy

Fum D.

Laboratorio di Psicologia E.E.
Università di Trieste
via Tigor, 22
34124 Trieste, Italy

Guida G.

Progetto di Intelligenza Artificiale
Dipartimento di Elettronica
Politecnico di Milano
piazza Leonardo da Vinci, 32
20133 Milano, Italy

Hajičová E.   Faculty of Mathematics and Physics
                           Charles University
                           Malostranské, 25
                           118 00 Praha 1, Czechoslovakia

Hovy E.H.   Computer Science Department
                           Yale University
                           2158 Yale Station
                           New Haven, CT 06520, USA

Jiang X.   Shenyang Institute of Automation
                           Academia Sinica
                           P.O. Box 210
                           Shenyang, Liaoning, China

Johnson-Laird P.N.   MRC Applied Psychology Unit
                           15 Chaucer Road,
                           Cambridge CB2 2EF, United Kingdom

Lehnert W.G.   Department of Computer and Information Science
                           University of Massachusetts
                           Amherst, MA 01003, USA

Li Y.   Shenyang Institute of Automation
                           Academia Sinica
                           P.O. Box 210
                           Shenyang, Liaoning, China

McKeown K.R.   Department of Computer Science
                           Columbia University
                           New York, NY 10027, USA

Moretti L.   Istituto di Linguistica Computazionale del CNR
                           via della Faggiola, 32
                           56100 Pisa, Italy

Narin'yani A.S.   Computing Center
                           USSR Academy of Sciences - Siberian Branch
                           Prospekt Nauki, 6
                           6300 90 Novosibirsk 90, USSR

Parisi D.   Istituto di Psicologia del CNR
                           via dei Monti Tiburtini, 509
                           00157 Roma, Italy

Phillips B.   Computer Research Laboratory
                           Tektronix, Inc.
                           P.O. Box 500, D/S 50-662
                           Beaverton, OR 97077, USA

Prodanof I.

Istituto di Linguistica Computazionale del CNR
via della Faggiola, 32
56100 Pisa, Italy

Schank R.C.

Computer Science Department
Yale University
2158 Yale Station
New Haven, CT 06520, USA

Sgall P.

Faculty of Mathematics and Physics
Charles University
Malostranké, 25
118 00 Praha 1, Czechoslovakia

Small S.L.

Departments of Computer Science and Psychology
The University of Rochester
Rochester, NY 14627, USA

Stock O.

Istituto di Psicologia del CNR
via dei Monti Tiburtini, 509
00157 Roma, Italy

Tasso C.

Istituto di Matematica, Informatica e Sistemistica
Università di Udine
via Antonini, 8
33100 Udine, Italy